HANDBOOK ON SMALL NATIONS IN THE GLOBAL ECONOMY

Handbook on Small Nations in the Global Economy

The Contribution of Multinational Enterprises
to National Economic Success

Edited by

Daniel Van Den Bulcke

*Emeritus Professor of International Management and Development,
University of Antwerp, Belgium and Chairman, European International
Business Academy (EIBA)*

Alain Verbeke

*McCaig Chaired Professor in Management, Haskayne School of Business,
University of Calgary, Canada, Associate Fellow, Centre for International
Business and Management, Judge Business School, University of
Cambridge, UK and Solvay Business School, University of Brussels
(VUB), Belgium*

Wenlong Yuan

*Assistant Professor of International Business, Faculty of Management,
University of Lethbridge, Canada*

Edward Elgar
Cheltenham, UK • Northampton, MA, USA

Published by
Edward Elgar Publishing Limited
The Lypiatts
15 Lansdown Road
Cheltenham
Glos GL50 2JA
UK

Edward Elgar Publishing, Inc.
William Pratt House
9 Dewey Court
Northampton
Massachusetts 01060
USA

A catalogue record for this book
is available from the British Library

Library of Congress Control Number: 2009933359

Mixed Sources
Product group from well-managed
forests and other controlled sources
www.fsc.org Cert no. SA-COC-1565
© 1996 Forest Stewardship Council

ISBN 978 1 84376 592 9

Printed and bound by MPG Books Group, UK

Contents

Contributors

Frank Barry, Professor of International Business and Development, Trinity College Dublin, Ireland

Gabriel Robertstad G. Benito, Professor, Department of Strategy and Logistics, BI Norwegian School of Management, Oslo, Norway

John Cantwell, Professor of International Business, Rutgers University, USA

John Cassidy, School of Business, University College Dublin, Ireland

Ludo Cuyvers, Professor of International Economics, Faculty of Applied Economics, and Director of Centre for ASEAN Studies (CAS), University of Antwerp, Belgium and Professor Extraordinary, Faculty of Economics and Management Sciences, North-West University, Potchefstroom Campus, South Africa

Filip De Beule, Assistant Professor, Lessius University College, Antwerp and LICOS Centre for Institutions and Economic Performance, Catholic University of Leuven (KU Leuven), Belgium

Peter Enderwick, Professor of International Business, Auckland University of Technology, Auckland, New Zealand

Robert Grosse, Director, Global Leadership Development and Learning, Standard Bank of South Africa Limited, South Africa, and Professor of International Business at Thunderbird School of International Management, USA

John Hagedoorn, Professor of Strategy and International Business, Maastricht University, the Netherlands

Annelies Hogenbirk, Adjunct Chief Economist, Department of Knowledge and Economic Research, Rabobank Nederland, the Netherlands

Andreja Jaklič, Assistant Professor, Faculty of Social Sciences, Centre of International Relations, University of Ljubljana, Slovenia

Jorma Larimo, Professor, Department of Marketing, University of Vaasa, Finland

Rajneesh Narula, Professor of International Business Regulation, University of Reading, UK

Torben Pedersen, Professor, Center for Strategic Management and Globalization, Copenhagen Business School, Copenhagen, Denmark

Jahan Ara Peerally, Assistant Professor, Department of International Business, HEC Montréal, Canada

Matija Rojec, Associate Professor, Faculty of Social Sciences, Centre of International Relations, University of Ljubljana, Slovenia

Joanna Scott-Kennel, Senior Lecturer in International Business, School of Marketing and International Business, Victoria University of Wellington, Wellington, New Zealand and Visiting Scholar, Helsinki School of Economics, Finland

Reth Soeng, Post-Doctoral Fellow, Flemish Centre for International Policy and Research Fellow, Centre for ASEAN Studies and Department of International Economics, International Management and Diplomacy, University of Antwerp, Belgium

Marjan Svetličič, Professor, Faculty of Social Sciences, Centre of International Relations, University of Ljubljana, Slovenia

Ilke Van Beveren, Assistant Professor, Lessius University College, Antwerp and LICOS Centre for Institutions and Economic Performance, Catholic University of Leuven (KU Leuven), Belgium

Daniel Van Den Bulcke, Emeritus Professor of International Management and Development, Institute of Development Policy and Development (IOB), University of Antwerp, Belgium and Chairman, European International Business Academy (EIBA)

Chris van Egeraat, Research Fellow, National Institute for Regional and Spatial Analysis, Department of Geography, National University of Ireland, Maynooth, Ireland

Hans van Kranenburg, Professor of Corporate Strategy, Nijmegen School of Management, Radboud University Nijmegen, the Netherlands

Alain Verbeke, McCaig Chaired Professor in Management, Haskayne School of Business, University of Calgary, Canada, Associate Fellow, Centre for International Business and Management, Judge Business School, University of Cambridge, UK and Solvay Business School, University of Brussels (VUB), Belgium

Wenlong Yuan, Assistant Professor of International Business, Faculty of Management, University of Lethbridge, Canada

Acknowledgements

The publishers wish to thank the following who have kindly given permission for the use of copyright material.

M.E. Sharpe, Inc. for Gabriel R.G. Benito, Jorma Larimo, Rajneesh Narula and Torben Pedersen (2002), 'Multinational enterprises from small economies: internationalization patterns of large corporations from Denmark, Finland, and Norway', *International Studies of Management & Organization*, **32** (1), Spring, 57–78.

Every effort has been made to trace all the copyright holders but if any have been inadvertently overlooked the publishers will be pleased to make the necessary arrangements at the first opportunity.

1 Small nations in the global economy: an overview
Daniel Van Den Bulcke, Alain Verbeke and Wenlong Yuan

Professor Michael Porter (Harvard Business School) published *The Competitive Advantage of Nations* in 1990. This path-breaking book conveyed the message that the success (and international competitiveness) of specific industries in a nation critically depends on the configuration of – and interplay among – four sets of parameters: factor conditions; demand conditions; related and supporting industries; and strategy, structure and rivalry. The outcome of a favourable configuration and interplay, according to Porter, then leads to a strong national 'diamond' and, therefore, to an internationally competitive industry, as measured by exports or outward foreign direct investment (FDI). In Porter's work, success in international markets follows prior domestic success in terms of innovation, productivity improvements, clustering etc.

However, in the case of small open economies, favourable diamond conditions are unlikely to exist for each of the four sets of parameters simultaneously if only domestic elements are taken into account. Here, linkages with other nations, whether on the sourcing side or the demand side, are often critical from the outset to create strong industries. More specifically, both inward and outward FDI may be important tools to gain access to external resources that can complement national diamond determinants, and lead to high, sustainable domestic production and employment per capita *vis-à-vis* other nations (sustainability implies the absence of government shelter as a critical factor explaining observed success). FDI should therefore be viewed not simply as an outcome of domestic economic success, but as critical inputs to achieve such success. For example, inward FDI by multinational enterprises may imply an infusion of technological and managerial knowledge, and therefore productivity improvements in the domestic economy. In contrast, outward FDI may provide access to raw materials (resource-seeking investments), to foreign demand (market-seeking investments), to strategic assets (strategic-asset-seeking investments) or to production efficiencies not achievable in a domestic context (efficiency-seeking investments), in each case raising the living standards in the domestic economy, as compared to the situation without multinational activity.

The main thesis advanced in this book is that small nations increasingly need to rely heavily on both home-grown and foreign multinational enterprises to achieve domestic economic success in industries characterized by international competition, as these firms augment the domestic diamond determinants with foreign components, thereby permitting sustainable high production and employment per capita as compared with other nations.

The book consists of 11 chapters. This chapter synthesizes the findings of the following country-based chapters: the Netherlands, Belgium, Ireland, Slovenia, Canada, Chile, Mauritius, New Zealand and Cambodia, and highlights common features as well as differences in the success stories. Three Nordic countries, Denmark, Finland and Norway, are discussed in a separate chapter. This enables us to derive a number of implications

Table 1.1   *Competitiveness of the selected countries (WEF* World Competitiveness Index *and IMD* Global Competitiveness Index 2007–08*)*

	WEF 2008	WEF 2007	IMD 2008	IMD 2007
Denmark	3	3	6	5
Finland	6	6	15	17
Netherlands	8	10	10	8
Canada	10	13	8	10
Norway	15	16	11	13
Belgium	19	20	24	25
Ireland	22	22	12	14
New Zealand	24	24	18	19
Chile	28	26	26	26
Slovenia	42	39	32	40
Mauritius	57	60	n.a.	n.a.

for managers and public policy makers that should help to increase the contribution of multinational enterprise activity in general, and inward and outward FDI flows specifically, to domestic economic success in small open economies. As noted above, two domestic success indicators, namely sustainable high production and employment per capita *vis-à-vis* other nations, in specific industries, constitute the rationale for the selection of the case studies. These provide wide geographical coverage, including North America (Canada), South America (Chile), Africa (Mauritius), Western Europe (Belgium, Ireland, the Netherlands and Nordic countries), Eastern Europe (Slovenia), Asia (Cambodia) and Oceania (New Zealand). This selection also covers a diversity of national circumstances, with low-, middle- and high-income countries represented, as well as economies that are developing, in transition from socialism, and highly industrialized. The countries also vary widely in terms of size, whether measured by area, population or GDP.

The countries studied in this book represent a number of successful economies from across the world. According to the World Economic Forum (WEF) *Global Competitiveness Index 2007–2008* and the IMD *World Competitive Index 2007–2008*, Denmark, Finland, the Netherlands and Canada can be classified in the top ten; Norway, Belgium, Ireland and New Zealand are postioned between the tenth and 25th place; and Chile, Slovenia and Mauritius are positioned between 25th and 60th place (see Table 1.1). Only Cambodia is missing.

According to UNCTAD's *World Investment Report* 2007 (UNCTAD, 2007), five of the ten developed countries with the highest Transnationality Index (TNI) are included in this volume. The TNI 2004 is calculated as the average of four criteria or shares, i.e. FDI inflows as a percentage of gross capital formation for three years (2002–04); FDI inward stocks as a percentage of GDP in 2004; value added of foreign affiliates as a percentage of GDP in 2004; and employment of foreign affiliates as a percentage of total employment in 2004. This measure of so-called transnationalization puts Belgium in first position with an index of 70.1 per cent, ahead of Ireland and New Zealand as third and seventh with respectively 46.3 and 31.6 per cent in this classification. The Netherlands ranks ninth with 31.4 per cent, just above Denmark, which occupies the tenth spot. With a percentage score between 15 and 20 per cent, Finland, Norway, Slovenia and Canada are found in 17th, 20th, 21st and 23rd position respectively on this UNCTAD (2007) list. UNCTAD also positions countries in a matrix in which the 'inward performance index' and 'inward potential index' are combined (for details about these indexes, see UNCTAD, 2007). Countries with a high inward FDI performance and high FDI potential index are classified as 'front runners'. Three of the countries included in this volume are placed in this category, namely Belgium, Chile and the Netherlands. Countries discussed in this volume and considered to have a high FDI potential but facing a low FDI performance are labelled as 'below potential' and include, in alphabetical order, Canada, Denmark, Finland, Ireland, New Zealand, Norway and Slovenia. Because of lack of data, Cambodia and Mauritius could not be ranked.

For the most part, the various country-based chapters discuss the foundations of domestic economic success of each nation selected using essentially the same template so as to increase the reader friendliness, intellectual rigour and conceptual integrity of the book. The template begins with a short description of the strengths of the national economy in terms of Porter's diamond determinants, with a focus on the most successful international industries, as measured by sustainable domestic production (whether by home-grown firms or subsidiaries of foreign multinational enterprises), and employment per capita *vis-à-vis* other nations.

This is followed by a description of the role of inward and outward FDI and multinational enterprise activity in the successful industries considered, including the historical evolution of overall inward and outward investment flows. Building upon this background, for each of the industries, both inward and outward investments are analysed, focusing on the specific reasons why inward investment was attracted into the nation studied: to what extent did internalization arbitrage occur, i.e. the combination of the firm-specific advantages of foreign multinational enterprises from specific foreign nations with domestic location advantages?

The geographic concentration (associated with clustering benefits) of domestic production and employment in the successful industries is then studied, including discussion of the role of multinational activity in domestic cluster functioning. The last section of each case assesses the impact of government policy (or the lack thereof) on the success of the industries studied to establish whether specific types and processes of government intervention were particularly effective in facilitating 'internalization arbitrage' through linking (a) inward FDI with domestic location advantages, and (b) outward FDI with both domestic and foreign location advantages, thereby creating internationally competitive value chains. The key question is whether some types of government policy might be viewed as best practices that merit replication by other nations, or whether they were effective primarily in a specific institutional context, a particular path-dependent trajectory of events or an idiosyncratic cultural environment.

The first country chapter, Chapter 2, considers the case of the Netherlands, a small, rich country with a very long history of far-flung international activities dating back to the days of its colonial empire, centuries ago. Hogenbirk, Hagedoorn and van Kranenburg identify its greatest natural resources as its fertile soil (recently augmented by natural gas that allows more intensive exploitation through the use of greenhouses) and the strategic location of its main seaport on river transportation routes leading into the European heartland. These natural gifts have been augmented by heavy investment in transportation infrastructure and human resources. As a result, the country has captured a key role in the flows of goods and services into and out of Europe, a role that has grown in importance as the increasing economic integration of the European Union (EU) has eased the passage of goods and people across European borders. Dutch outward investment has been concentrated in sectors related to trade and transportation (trading, banking, insurance etc.) and in those that benefit from inexpensive bulk transportation (such as petroleum). A similar pattern prevails in inward investment. The key sectors analysed are food and health, machinery and modular construction (e.g. dredging equipment, a necessity in a country that relies on ports, rivers and canals), and chemicals and fuels. Both national and supranational levels of government have played a key role in propelling the Netherlands into its current position as the 'Gateway to Europe'. Economic and political integration under the EU has made it possible for investors to locate in the most efficient place from a logistical standpoint, which, through the good fortune of geography, often happens to be in the Netherlands, while Dutch national policy has made it attractive to do so by providing strong infrastructure and a well-educated, productive, disciplined workforce. This is the first example of a pattern that is repeated frequently: governments must act to make sure that the infrastructure provided matches the needs of the business community, thereby improving its overall growth and profitability potential.

The Netherlands' neighbour, Belgium, is the subject of Chapter 3. De Beule and Van Beveren identify its strategic location for transportation into and out of Europe as Belgium's key location advantage as well. As in the Netherlands, this advantage has been consolidated by heavy investment in infrastructure, *inter alia* in the Port of Antwerp and in a pipeline network. This port and pipeline network have facilitated the development of the chemical industry, which then evolved to include the other two related sectors they examine, pharmaceuticals and biotechnology. The close integration of infrastructure has led to high levels of goods traffic and services flows into and out of neighbouring countries, so that they have become Belgium's principal trading and investment partners. The close attention devoted to preserving the high levels of economic and political integration that make such a multi-country industrial region possible are reflected in the location of the headquarters of multinational organizations such as the EU and NATO in the Belgian capital of Brussels.

Cassidy, Barry and van Egeraat profile Ireland in Chapter 4. Long economically stagnant and perhaps better known as a source of emigrants than of exports, in the 1990s a revitalized Ireland was dubbed the 'Celtic Tiger'. The ICT hardware and software sectors and the pharmaceutical industry, attracted by a new low corporate tax rate and a low-cost, English-speaking labour force with the diverse skill levels required, drove this transformation by making Ireland their base for supplying the EU and other markets beyond as well. The authors show that the multinational enterprise (MNE) subsidiaries in these sectors are generally tightly integrated into their parents' networks and enjoy little autonomy apart from day-to-day operational issues. They have tended to enjoy little interaction with the domestic economy apart from hiring workers and buying packaging, although substantial government efforts to ensure a ready supply of technically proficient workers and to encourage R&D activity have paid some dividends. Now that Irish cost advantages have largely disappeared with the rise in the standard of living, and the EU transfer payments that helped support the Irish transformation have diminished, the challenges facing industrial development authorities will be greater than ever. Their hope must be that if the business environment can be kept favourable, inertia will keep firms there until the emerging ties that bind them to Ireland can fully mature.

Slovenia is the subject of Chapter 5, by Jaklič, Rojec and Svetličič. Although Slovenia is one of the richest and most trade-dependent of the new members of the EU, it has seen relatively little inward or outward FDI. The authors attribute this to the country's relatively high costs, gradualist approach to transition (made possible by its relatively strong initial position), and its early policies towards both inward and outward FDI, neither of which were notably activist or favourable. Inward FDI has nevertheless made some contribution to the upgrading and restructuring of the economy. Interestingly, outward FDI, primarily market seeking, has been concentrated in the less economically advanced areas of the former Yugoslavia, as the country's larger and more successful firms in effect attempt to recreate their previous national diamond. Whether this will prove a successful strategy in the longer term remains to be seen.

In Chapter 6, Benito, Larimo, Narula and Pedersen examine the internationalization of the ten largest non-financial, private sector firms in each of three Nordic countries, Norway, Denmark and Finland. Their focus is on the balance between centrifugal forces encouraging the international expansion of firms from small, open economies ('SMOPECs') and the centripetal forces encouraging them to stay rooted in their home countries, at least for some activities. They find that the largest firms from all three economies share certain features: most are resource based, became more internationalized during the 1990s, and are only middling in size in a world of MNE giants. The principal difference was that over the period studied Norwegian firms internationalized more rapidly (from a lower base) and were also somewhat more prone to internationalize not only production, but the 'strategic' activities that are at the heart of MNE competitiveness, such as R&D. Interestingly, the authors suggest that one of the factors that may have led to Norway's idiosyncratic patterns was its semi-outsider status as a non-member (though close collaborator) of the EU. They conclude that country-level differences do indeed affect the internationalization patterns of MNEs from SMOPECs.

Yuan and Verbeke focus on Canada in Chapter 7. Canada is by far the largest of the countries studied in this book, with twice the population of the next-largest subjects (Chile and the Netherlands) and over 25 times that of the smallest (Mauritius), not to mention a huge geographical land mass. It also has a long history of close economic cooperation with its neighbour to the south, the USA, with whom it shares a border thousands of kilometres long, as well as membership in a continent-wide trade agreement, NAFTA (North American Free Trade Agreement). The results of their survey of US and EU MNEs operating in Canada, as well as MNEs headquartered in Canada, suggest that most manufacturing MNEs entered to secure access to the Canadian market, while energy firms entered to secure access to the country's raw materials. Most of the subsidiaries were considered to have relatively low capabilities, and the market itself was mostly considered of low strategic importance. However, a subset of exceptions, mostly US rather than EU based, offered some hope for a more proactive Canadian role in MNE networks. US subsidiaries were also more likely than EU subsidiaries to be ranked as equal to or better than their parent's best subsidiary. Benefits from NAFTA-based regional integration were found to be concentrated in back-end activities such as logistics, innovation and production, with Canadian-based MNEs more positive about

NAFTA's benefits than American subsidiaries, and EU-based subsidiaries least enthusiastic of all. One interpretation of these results is that US firms, with their much longer
experience in the Canadian environment, a guarantee of secure market and resource
access under NAFTA, and easier access to their parent's home operations (often just a
few hundred kilometres away), have been better positioned to exploit Canada's location
advantages. The border has simply become much less of an obstacle to them than to their
European counterparts.

In Chapter 8, Grosse tackles Chile, which since the early 1970s has tended to buck
the Latin American tendency towards statism and fear of foreign influence and has been
rewarded with one of the region's highest standards of living. The industries examined
are copper mining, fish (salmon and trout) farming and wine production. Copper mining
went from initial foreign domination to nationalization in the 1970s to a mixture of
foreign and domestic public and private ownership today. While it is a major contributor
to exports and employment, it remains something of an enclave, with few supply linkages and little value-added processing. The wine industry has existed for centuries, but
only evolved beyond small-scale, low-quality production for the local market when the
industry, along with the rest of the economy, was opened up to foreign investment, which
brought significant improvements in quality and market access, and allowed Chilean
wines to reach their full potential. Salmon farming was introduced by Japanese partners
and, after a period of fragmented local ownership, achieved top position in the world
under a mixture of local and (mostly) foreign ownership. The wine and salmon industries
are particularly interesting, since Chile's potential in these areas lay dormant until the
economy was opened up and government actively promoted their development.

Peerally and Cantwell document the story of Mauritius in Chapter 9. A seemingly
unlikely candidate for prosperity as a tiny state of little over a million people far from
any continental land mass, let alone major markets, Mauritius was once written off as
little more than a 'barracoon' (temporary enclosure for slaves or convicts) and a likely
location for Malthusian economics to play out. Instead, it has become an African success
story. The economy was initially based on sugar plantations, but recognizing that these
were uneconomic and unlikely to survive if preferential access agreements with former
colonial powers ever ended, the government moved actively to exploit the preferential
access it received for garment exports to develop a successful export zone based on the
garment and textile industries, then moved on to up-market tourism, and has future
plans for offshore finance and duty-free shopping. What is remarkable here is that many
countries received the same duty-free access to rich country markets that Mauritius did,
but it has been considerably more successful than most in exploiting this windfall. Not
only did it attract inbound investment, but indigenous firms have also emerged, and
some backward integration has occurred. Moreover, the recognition that preferential
garment access could one day end (the Multifibre Agreement, for example, has already
been phased out) meant that the government did not rest on its laurels, but instead
continued to develop strategies to remain one step ahead. Foreign firms have played an
important, but not exclusive, role in the development of the sectors that have emerged to
replace the declining sugar industry.

Chapter 10, by Enderwick and Scott-Kennel, considers another small island state,
New Zealand. Once a model of prosperity, it later slipped far behind the major nations
it viewed as its peer group. A severe financial crisis in the mid-1980s led to widespread

restructuring and a much more open economy. Although there is a considerable stock of inward FDI, inflows have been declining and outflows are modest, with many New Zealand MNEs actually divesting and shrinking back to their home base. International linkages are primarily through trade rather than investment. The authors focus on forestry, export education and information and communications technology (ICT). Forestry benefits from vast tracts of fast-growing radiata pine, but is handicapped by infrastructure problems and does little value-added processing. Forest ownership has been privatized and separated from the processing industry, and is now largely in the hands of foreign investors. Export education has major regulatory barriers to inward investment. Some outward investment has occurred, but ironically the sector seems slow to learn the lessons needed to keep up with more aggressive competitors. ICT shows low levels of outward investment, with most of what there is being motivated by market access. Foreign investors, however, have been active in buying up any promising local firms. They have tended not to locate production in New Zealand, but rather have placed some skill-based activities such as R&D there in response to the lower cost of specialized labour and strong government encouragement.

In the final chapter, Cuyvers, Soeng and Van Den Bulcke consider the case of Cambodia. Ravaged by decades of external and internal conflict, in the mid-1990s Cambodia implemented an open market policy that has seen FDI flow into the garment/textile and tourism/transportation sectors. The latter is largely based on the drawing power of the ancient Angkor Wat complex. The garment and textile influx has been mostly from its Southeast Asian neighbours and China. While China's access to lucrative markets in Europe and North America was blocked by quotas, as a least developed country Cambodia benefited from preferential trading arrangements and investing there offered a way of circumventing these barriers by 'quota jumping'. However, although the garment industry creates significant and much-needed employment, most raw materials are imported and there are few backward or forward linkages. The industry is handicapped by poor infrastructure, rampant corruption, a low-quality labour force and persistent political instability. While the sites that draw tourists are immobile and likely to remain attractive for centuries (assuming enough political stability to allow safe access), the future of Cambodia's export platform is less certain if these problems are not addressed.

What more is known about the research thesis after examining these case studies?
Are there best practices policies of general applicability, or do governments need to base their strategies on their specific institutional context, particular path-dependent trajectory of events or idiosyncratic cultural environment?

We can gain some insight into these questions by comparing various groups and pairs of the subject nations. Fate has dealt every country a different hand. Some, like the Netherlands and Belgium, benefit from their location *per se* (e.g. at the mouths of navigable rivers, giving easy transport access to vast hinterlands), some have desirable natural resource endowments (e.g. Canadian energy, Chilean copper), and others have artificial advantages thrust on them (such as the preferential market access treaties upon which the Mauritian and Cambodian garment industries were based). However, what matters for lasting prosperity is what use the nation, through its government, makes of whatever it has been dealt. Belgium and the Netherlands built on their fortunate locations by investing heavily in transportation infrastructure and their workforces, and thereby built a basis for lasting prosperity, as not only these industries, but others that depend on good transportation (such as bulk petroleum and chemicals), found it profitable to locate there. Mauritius's intrinsic location, hundreds of miles out into the Indian Ocean and thousands of miles from any rich country market, could hardly be less auspicious. Yet when it received a man-made windfall in the form of preferential market access for locally made garments (i.e. trade diversion), through purposeful government action it was able to build a successful industry where dozens of other countries with similar preferential access failed, even though they were closer to the markets, had larger economies, and generally seemed better primed for success. Similarly, both Ireland and Slovenia have preferential access to the European market as members of the EU, yet Ireland aggressively promoted itself and has boomed on the basis of an influx of firms in the hardware, software and pharmaceutical industries, while Slovenia, overcome by fear of selling off assets too cheaply, largely missed the FDI boom in Eastern Europe and now muddles along trying to re-establish past glories in the former Yugoslavia. Chile has built world-class wine and salmon industries based on little more than a favourable climate, while New Zealand, having planted vast tracts of radiata pine, wonders what to do with the 'wall of wood' as the trees mature.

What distinguishes the more successful cases?
While governments were activist in the sense of ensuring that companies had access to good information, low taxes and minimal bureaucratic obstacles, they were realistic in their targets. Mauritius did not try to build a steel mill, nor Chile an auto-assembly industry. Mauritius knew it had the solution to a problem faced by many quota-constrained garment exporters: easy access to rich-country markets. It therefore marketed this solution to its problems. Chile knew it could produce wine, it just needed to upgrade it. Ireland might seem like an exception, given that it had no specific resources that were essential to software or pharmaceutical firms. But closer inspection shows that it had two desirable assets: a stable English-speaking environment that made it easy for (especially US) firms to move in, and the ability and willingness to cut taxes in a trading bloc where very high taxes were the norm. Thus, while the industries it attracted were in some sense 'footloose', it made them an offer they couldn't refuse, and then set to work making them less footloose by, for example, tailoring its educational system to churn out exactly the types of graduates they needed.

   This example brings up the broader question: once you get the foreign investors in, how do you keep them? How do you keep the momentum and provide a reason for investors to stay when they no longer have to (e.g. because trade liberalization has wiped out a preferential arrangement, or rising labour costs mean it is time for Akamatsu's (1961) flying geese to migrate to the next low-wage, low-tax location)? This is a question that Cambodia, for example, faces acutely. Without preferential market access, a benefit that basically dropped out of the sky through no effort of its own, it would have few other attractions for the garment industry. It has a large supply of low-wage unskilled labour, but so do probably 100 or more other countries. Labour force upgrading is one part of the answer, as shown in Ireland (science graduates) and Mauritius (with its hotel and tourism school). Social stability is obviously a prerequisite. More generally, beneficiaries of such good fortune (Porterian 'chance'[1]) need to reinvest today's benefits in generally accessible, location-bound complementary capabilities and hope the beneficial circumstances last long enough for these to develop to the extent that they provide a reason for firms to stay. (An alternative strategy has been adopted by Norway, which received a windfall in the form of oil and gas revenues far too large to invest in the local economy without risking 'Dutch disease'. It locks the vast majority of this windfall into long-term investment funds, which also helps to preserve the other industries that will again have to become the basis of the economy when the oil reserves run out.)

In short, a successful country strategy consists of three elements. First, the border must be made as permeable as possible to international trade and investment flows. This means making it easy for foreign investors to bring in capital, raw materials, intermediate goods, personnel, or whatever else they need, through reducing the perceived difference in comfort level for these firms between a domestic investment and one in the desired location. It also means ensuring that access to the likely market for the products of the investment is as smooth as possible, particularly where the target market is not the location of production. This requires constant vigilance, as there seems to be an innate tendency for borders to 'thicken' if active efforts to thwart this are not made (for example, the USA–Canada border has 'thickened' considerably as enhanced security measures have lengthened border crossing times to the point of putting just-in-time delivery at risk).

Second, the sectors targeted for priority development must be those where there is at least a latent location advantage that can be 'unlocked'. This could be strategic location, favourable climate, or underutilized resources (such as a pool of cheap labour or unused trade quota). The first and second factors go hand in hand: location advantages often lie dormant for extended periods of time if access to them is not made easy, as was the case with Chile's potential for wine and salmon production. A country's diamond can be like a real-life gem locked in a vault, and of no use to anyone unless (and until) it is made easy for investors to access it. In other words, international success requires 'unlocking' latent location advantages, i.e. improving access to these advantages for 'qualified' economic actors, both domestic and foreign.

Third, once the investment process begins and some early positive outcomes are achieved, including higher government income, this must be reinvested in developing location advantages at the macro and sectoral levels. These new location advantages must be crafted in such a way that they complement and augment the firm-specific advantages of foreign companies especially, so as to bind these firms more strongly to their new host environment. Most often such advantages are either human resources (Ireland's science grads or Mauritius's tourism diploma holders) or infrastructure (the ports, railways, airports and pipelines of the Netherlands and Belgium). These location advantages build a certain level of inertia and geographic mobility barriers, helpful to making future MNE location decisions somewhat less responsive to unexpected changes in economic circumstances, especially if these are likely to be temporary (e.g. exchange rate fluctuations).

None of this is easy. Making markets accessible often means stepping on the powerful toes of vested interests. Identifying and unlocking true latent location advantages at the macro and sectoral levels, and differentiating these from the hopes, dreams and often self-delusions

		Government policies to increase resource linkages across borders					
		Improving permeability of borders		Unlocking latent location advantages		Crafting new location advantages	
		weak	strong	weak	strong	weak	strong
Porter's single diamond	Factor conditions						
	Demand conditions						
	Related and supporting industries						
	Strategy, structure and rivalry						

Figure 1.1   Augmenting the single diamond in small open economies

of decision makers, is tricky. Building complementary location advantages takes time, and though generally accessible in principle, may be perceived as undue favouritism benefiting foreign investors. Nothing worthwhile is easy. However, the success stories outlined in this book suggest that the effort is worth making, and that with an appropriate policy regime FDI can, indeed, add both new facets and sparkle to the diamonds of small open economies.

From a conceptual perspective, the country cases confirm that Porter's single-diamond components (domestic factor conditions, domestic demand conditions, domestic related and supporting industries, domestic strategy, structure and rivalry) reflect merely a set of initial conditions that can be improved upon through both inward and outward investment, thereby creating resource linkages between the home and host environments of the MNEs involved, a point also made elsewhere, see Rugman et al. (1995), Van Den Bulcke and Verbeke (2001), and Rugman and Verbeke (2008, 2009). Figure 1.1 illustrates this important point. On the vertical axis, we have positioned Porter's single-diamond determinants. On the horizontal axis, we find the three main sources of resource linkages between the domestic economy and foreign economies that could potentially augment Porter's single-diamond determinants: the improved permeability of borders, the unlocking of latent location advantages, and the crafting of new location advantages. Porter's perspective is that the potential impact and value of these international resource linkages is weak (left columns for each parameter in Figure 1.1). Several country studies in this book paint a very different picture, however, as shown by the shaded right columns for each policy approach. From a strategy perspective, the key question for policy makers is which of the 12 cells in the shaded right columns of Figure 1.1 should be activated, and in which order, to improve their small open economy's single-diamond conditions. Irrespective of the specific answers given, the right-hand-side shaded columns of Figure 1.1 reflect the essence of the country-level international competitiveness for small open economies: cross-border resource linkages are critical and therefore a double-diamond or multiple-diamond perspective should prevail.

In other words, optimal government policy in small open economies to improve international competitiveness requires overcoming both the 'liability of domestic diamond isolation', affecting domestic economic actors, and the 'liability of outsidership', affecting foreign MNEs. This approach is diametrically opposed to attempting to strengthen the domestic, single-diamond components from the inside, as advocated by Porter (though a partial self-correction can be found in his later work on clusters). Here, the three broad lines of attack as described in Figure 1.1 should allow multinational enterprises, both domestic and foreign, to act as 'diamond connectors', but always keeping in mind that in the long run positive societal spillover effects from multinational activity are not guaranteed. Such spillovers fundamentally depend on the recipient country's absorptive capacity, i.e. the substantive learning and subsequent further recombination/deployment of the elements learned from foreign MNEs (especially best-practice routines in innovation, production, marketing, and firm-level governance) by domestic economic actors.

Note

1. Porter's 'chance' factor is perhaps one of the least-studied aspects of his model.

References

Akamatsu, K. (1961), 'A theory of unbalanced growth in the world economy', *Weltwirtschaftliches Archiv* **86**: 196–215.

Porter, M.E. (1990), *The Competitive Advantage of Nations*, New York: The Free Press.

Rugman A.M. and A. Verbeke (2008), 'Location, competitiveness and the multinational enterprise', in Alan M. Rugman (ed.), *Oxford Handbook of International Business*, 2nd edn, Oxford: Oxford University Press, ch. 6.

Rugman A.M. and A. Verbeke (2009), *Global Corporate Strategy and Trade Policy*, 2nd edn, London and New York: Routledge.

Rugman A.M., J. Van den Broeck and A. Verbeke (1995), *Global Strategic Management Beyond the Diamond*, Greenwich, CT: JAI Press.

Van Den Bulcke D. and A. Verbeke (2001), *Globalisation and the Small Open Economy*, Cheltenham, UK and Northampton, MA, USA: Edward Elgar.

UNCTAD (2007), World Investment Report 2007, *Transnational Corporations, Extractive Industries and Development*, New York: United Nations.

2 Globalization in the Netherlands

Annelies Hogenbirk, John Hagedoorn and Hans van Kranenburg

The Netherlands has an exceptionally long history when it comes to international activities. As early as 1602 the Dutch East India Company was established to carry out colonial activities in Asia. During the seventeenth and eighteenth centuries, Dutch companies built up a worldwide presence through trading settlements in many countries. Efficient transportation due to innovations in shipbuilding compensated for the lack of raw materials in the home base. Dutch economic development heavily relied on resources imported from abroad (in particular bulk goods – such as iron ore, grain, furs and wood – from the countries bordering the Baltic Sea, and more luxurious merchandise – such as spices, salt, gold, silver and porcelain from Asia, Africa and America). In what is now known as 'Holland's Golden Age', the Netherlands became one of the most prosperous countries in the world (Goey, 1999).

But even after the colonial era ended, the Netherlands continued to be a significant player in the world economy, unlike other historical trading nations such as Spain and Portugal. For instance, significant investments were made in the Russian railway and shipping industries in the nineteenth century. Furthermore, at the end of the nineteenth century and during the early years of the twentieth century, many Dutch companies were established that are still known as large multinationals today, such as Unilever, AKZO, Rabobank, Philips, Shell and Wolters Kluwer. All of them benefited from business opportunities abroad that helped them to grow quickly, whether through shareholdings, takeovers, licences or direct investments (van Zanden, 1997). As a result, nowadays Dutch business overseas is no longer restricted to trading as in earlier days, but is also carried out through foreign direct investment (FDI) and more recently through strategic alliances and networks (see, e.g., van Kranenburg et al., 2001). Currently, the Netherlands is the fifth-largest outward investor in the world (UNCTAD, 2006), an extraordinary position for a small country. Although always a net outward investor, the Netherlands also quickly recognized that incoming FDI could contribute to the economic well-being of the country, since FDI not only involves financial flows, but also transfers of materials, components, finished products and intangible assets, e.g. in the form of knowledge about production processes, markets, distribution channels, and management and entrepreneurship (Andersson et al., 1996). Furthermore, foreign firms can act as growth accelerators for the Dutch economy as they are generally active in sectors that create a lot of indirect employment, resulting in additional growth (Berenschot, 2007). Worldwide, the Netherlands is the sixth-largest recipient of FDI (UNCTAD, 2006). This is an exceptional position for such a small economy as well. More than 7000 foreign affiliates were operating in the Netherlands during the last decade (Hogenbirk, 2002; Hogenbirk and van Kranenburg, 2006).

This chapter analyses the characteristics of the Dutch economy that have allowed this

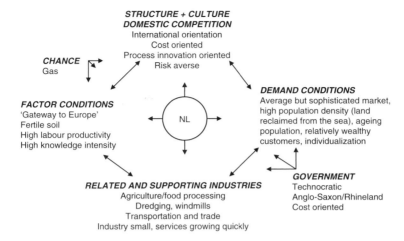

STRUCTURE + CULTURE
DOMESTIC COMPETITION
International orientation
Cost oriented
Process innovation oriented
Risk averse

CHANCE
Gas

FACTOR CONDITIONS
'Gateway to Europe'
Fertile soil
High labour productivity
High knowledge intensity

NL

DEMAND CONDITIONS
Average but sophisticated market,
high population density (land
reclaimed from the sea), ageing
population, relatively wealthy
customers, individualization

RELATED AND SUPPORTING INDUSTRIES
Agriculture/food processing
Dredging, windmills
Transportation and trade
Industry small, services growing quickly

GOVERNMENT
Technocratic
Anglo-Saxon/Rhineland
Cost oriented

Source: Adapted and extended from Jacobs and de Jong (1992) and Jacobs and Lankhuizen (2005).

Figure 2.1   Porter's diamond applied to the Netherlands

unique FDI position to develop and persist to this day. First the strengths of the Dutch economy are considered using Porter's 'diamond'. This is followed by a description of the Dutch FDI position in recent decades. A general overview of both the size and destination of FDI stocks and flows is followed by a thorough discussion of the outward FDI position of Dutch firms. The discussion of FDI inflows into the Netherlands will then cover both historical and recent patterns, concentrating on the period from the mid-1980s onwards. Encouraged by a generally favourable economic climate and the progressive liberalization of international capital movements, from this period onwards global direct investment accelerated sharply, with an accompanying major shift of emphasis in host and home countries, modes and activities. The penultimate section will discuss clustering patterns in Dutch inward FDI and we conclude with remarks on the uniqueness of the Dutch investment position and the role of the government.

The strengths of the Dutch economy
In 1990, Michael Porter introduced the diamond and four interrelated sets of factors that determine the competitive strength of a nation. Besides these four elements, Porter identified two sets of additional factors that have to be taken into account when assessing a country's competitiveness: chance and the role of the government. Dunning (1997) extended the diamond model. He introduced an additional factor, multinational business activities, into Porter's scheme. He noted that multinational firms that operate within a particular country influence the diamond, as do the foreign activities of the country's domestic firms. Porter's diamond can be used to identify which sectors in a country are competitive internationally and which are not.

Jacobs et al. (1990), Jacobs and de Jong (1992), Jacobs (1995) and Jacobs and Lankhuizen (2005) have applied Porter's ideas to the Netherlands.[1] Figure 2.1 presents specifics on the four influences making up the diamond for the Netherlands.

Factor conditions
Factor conditions in Porter's methodology include both the quantity and cost of resources (such as natural resources, human resources etc.). Furthermore, infrastructure in all its aspects is included in this category as well. The Netherlands has significantly benefited from its favourable coastal location on the North Sea at the estuaries of great rivers, such as the Rhine and the Meuse. Significant investments in infrastructure (Amsterdam Schiphol Airport, Rotterdam Harbour, fast railway connections, extensive highways) built on this natural asset to make it more sustainable and useful for business purposes. This geographical advantage helped the Dutch to become the strongest economic power in the world in the seventeenth century. Nowadays, this favourable location facilitates access to the rest of the EU and the Netherlands is frequently characterized as the 'Gateway to Europe'.

Fertile soil and the discovery of natural gas have contributed to the agricultural/ greenhouse success of the Netherlands (Dutch flowers are famous worldwide). Furthermore, the Dutch labour force is characterized by high labour productivity and high education levels. Most workers are multilingual, facilitating the international ambitions and activities of both national and foreign firms. The workforce is increasing due to government policies aimed at stimulating women to enter the workforce and the elderly to stay in the workforce for a longer period. However, Dutch female employees have a strong preference for part-time employment and pressures exist on the labour market in several sectors, such as construction and business services.

Demand conditions
Porter argues that demand conditions may affect the competitiveness of firms in the domestic and international market by providing an impetus for domestic firms to produce high-quality, well-designed, reliable and differentiated goods, relative to those supplied by their foreign competitors. The demand conditions in a country also influence the extent to which foreign firms are willing to invest in the country, and hence their contribution to other parts of the diamond. Although the Netherlands is small in size, the population density is high, with almost 400 people per km^2 in 2005. Therefore over 16 million (potential) consumers inhabit the country. To accommodate all inhabitants, the Dutch have reclaimed almost one-fifth of the entire land area from the sea. Over 60 per cent of the total population lives below sea level (on 25 per cent of the Dutch land area), protected by an extensive system of dykes.[2] GDP per capita income is high, over \$30 000 per annum on a PPP (purchasing power parity) basis, making Dutch customers relatively wealthy. The Dutch home market is characterized by sophisticated buyers who demand quality and service, with older generations being considered particularly thrifty. Dutch consumers make their purchasing decisions individually based on the available information. Shopping on the Internet is becoming more usual. The population is ageing, but in the European perspective, the country is relatively well prepared for the resulting increases in social security and health care costs. The financial position of the elderly is taken care of through a sophisticated welfare and pension system.

Related and supporting industries
Porter emphasizes the importance of advanced supplier industries for economic success. Information flows and technical exchange between these industries and their customers

will result in more competitive activities in the home country. The Dutch have a long tradition in agriculture and food processing. Even today the primary sector contributes 3.3 per cent to GDP, which is more than double the contribution made by this sector in other developed markets such as Belgium, Germany, the UK and the USA (OECD, 2005). Furthermore, sophisticated transportation facilities and trade have always supported business activities. An advanced dredging industry and windmill production have developed due to the geographic location and the need for protection against the sea. Nowadays, as in most advanced countries, the share of the industrial sector in the country's value added (27 per cent) and employment (22 per cent) is declining rapidly. The service sector – in particular business services and the financial sector – on the other hand has grown quickly. Services are now the most important contributor to GDP in the Netherlands.

The structure and culture of domestic competition
The fourth broad determinant of a nation's competitive advantage is the context in which firms are created, organized and managed. It includes, for instance, the orientation of firms towards competing globally. The modern Dutch economic structure is characterized by its international competitiveness and its strong international orientation. Even though it is quite common for any small country to be more dependent on foreign trade than its larger counterparts, the ratios of exports and imports to GDP are exceptionally large in the Netherlands. The country was the sixth-largest exporter in the world in 2005, following Germany, the USA, China, Japan and France, all significantly larger countries (WTO, 2006). Total exports amounted to US$402 billion (3.9 per cent of world trade) in 2005. Imports amounted to US$350 billion (3.3 per cent of the world total), making the Netherlands the eighth-largest importer worldwide. Having to compete internationally forces Dutch companies to be cost oriented. They invest heavily in process innovations to help reduce costs and keep competitiveness high.

Most (92 per cent) of the 740 000 enterprises in the Netherlands are small or medium sized, employing up to ten people. Less than 1 per cent of all Dutch firms employ over 100 people (CBS, 2006). Compared to other European countries, the Dutch are relatively uninterested in self-employment and entrepreneurship (European Committee, 2004). The majority of the Dutch labour force would rather be employed by a company than take up the challenge, responsibility and risks of being self-employed.

For the Netherlands the factor of chance relates in particular to the discovery of natural gas in Slochteren in 1959. This source meets over half of Dutch energy needs. In addition, it provides the Dutch government with an important financial injection that is expected to continue at least until 2030, when production is expected to end. As far as the role of the government is concerned, the Netherlands is characterized by a relatively stable political environment. Most politicians have a technocratic background and are highly skilled. The government plays a significant role in the economy through permit requirements and regulations pertaining to almost every aspect of economic activity. It combines a rigorous and stable macroeconomic policy with wide-ranging structural and regulatory reforms. The role of the government in the economy has been gradually reduced since the 1980s. Privatization and deregulation continue unabated, motivated by cost reduction. The economy now has characteristics of both the Rhineland model (a regulated market economy with a large social security system) and the Anglo-Saxon model (shareholder capitalism aimed at maximizing profits), although the Rhineland model still dominates.

FDI position

The overall characteristics of the Netherlands discussed above proved a good breeding ground for multinational enterprises (MNEs) and also attracted many foreign firms to the country. The Netherlands occupies a special position among small[3] developed countries when FDI is considered. It is among the most internationally oriented countries in the world. Van Nieuwkerk and Sparling (1985) attribute the international orientation of Dutch firms to the small size of the Netherlands and the openness of its economy. Opportunities for expansion are soon exhausted due to saturation of the relatively small domestic market. In addition, there have been few hindrances to the flow of capital, labour and raw materials, facilitating international expansion.

Figure 2.2 gives an overview of both inward and outward FDI stocks and flows from 1984 to 2005.[4] Total outward FDI amounted to €533 billion in 2005. Inward FDI stock amounted to €379 billion. The graph shows a particularly strong increase in both inward and outward Dutch FDI activity from the mid-1990s onwards. In general, the Netherlands has always been a net outward foreign investor. At only one point in time, i.e. in 2001, have inward FDI flows actually exceeded outward flows.[5]

The USA has always been the most important destination for Dutch FDI (Figure 2.3). Dutch interests in the USA have grown particularly strongly since the mid-1970s. Key reasons have been declining growth and earnings prospects in the Netherlands itself, and better opportunities in that respect in the large US market, with its substantial purchasing power. The relatively cheap dollar was a further reason, as it made it attractive for Dutch firms to buy their way into the US market.

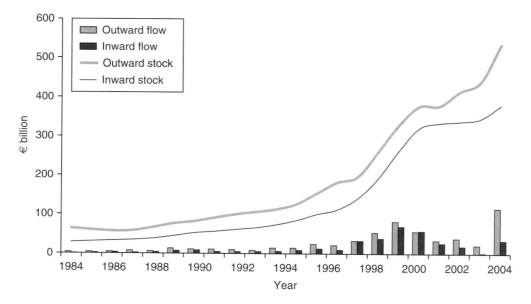

Figure 2.2   Stocks and flows of FDI in and from the Netherlands, 1984–2005

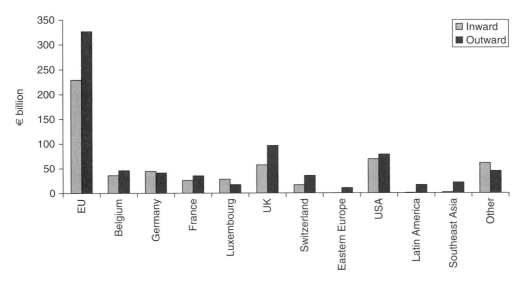

Figure 2.3   FDI stock in the Netherlands by country of origin and destination, 2005

The low stock market valuation of many US companies contributed as well to such acquisitions.

Since the 1990s the EU as a group has become much more important for Dutch FDI as a destination area. In the run-up to the Single Market, mutual investment among the EU countries expanded strongly. Among the target countries for Dutch foreign investment in the EU, the Belgium–Luxembourg Economic Union (BLEU), Germany, and the UK saw the strongest growth. In the BLEU, it was interests in the banking and insurance industry and in trade that expanded particularly strongly. In the UK, there was more than proportionate growth in the interests in the transport, storage and communications (especially telecom) sectors, in banking and insurance, and other financial services (Sparling, 2002).

Although still small, Dutch investments in Southeast Asia are increasing due to strong economic expansion and privatization in these markets, combined with increasing prosperity and low production costs. The Dutch investments occur primarily in the industrial sector, with the emphasis on metals and electrical engineering (South Korea, Taiwan) and oil and chemicals (Singapore). In the services sector, these latter investments are concentrated in trade and the banking and insurance industry (Sparling, 2002).

A similar regional pattern holds for incoming investments as well (Figure 2.3). Although most investments originate in the EU (60 per cent of the total stock in 2005), the USA is the most important individual investment partner (18 per cent of the total stock in 2005). During the second half of the 1980s and the beginning of the 1990s, investors from outside the EU hastened to secure a place in the highly promising future Single Market. The combined population and GDP of the EU market are almost equal to those of the USA. But intra-EU investments also grew strongly in anticipation of the creation of the Single Market. The main investment partners were BLEU, the UK and Germany. Together they accounted for 72 per cent of total EU investment in the Netherlands in 2005.

Outward FDI

Although it can be argued that large countries offer a better base for the emergence of multinationals, the Netherlands has been presented as an unusually fertile soil for the growth of large multinationals. As early as the 1980s Dutch MNEs were among the most internationalized firms (Van Den Bulcke, 1983). This was still true in 2005. A large share of Dutch value-added activities is conducted with the explicit purpose of serving foreign markets. Large firms listed on the Amsterdam Stock Exchange on average make 88 per cent of their sales outside the Netherlands (van der Schoot, 2005). The Netherlands is therefore home to some of the largest multinational companies in the world (van Hoesel and Narula, 1999). In 2006, the Global Fortune 500 list included 14 Dutch companies: Royal Dutch Shell (no. 3), ING Group (no. 13), ABN AMRO Holding (no. 82), Royal Ahold (no. 83), EADS (no. 130), Royal Philips Electronics (no. 145), Aegon (no. 149), Rabobank (no. 183), Mittal Steel (no. 208), SHV Holding (no. 341), Gasunie Trade and Supply (no. 353), TNT (no. 387), Akzo Nobel (no. 418) and Royal KPN (no. 457). Two other companies based in both the Netherlands and another country are listed. Fortis, a Belgian–Dutch financial conglomerate, ranked 18th, while Unilever (UK–Dutch) held the 108th position in the 2006 ranking.

However, not only large MNEs operate internationally. Since the 1970s medium-sized companies have started to internationalize as well. Apart from the need not to get left behind in the technology race, the shortage of opportunities for expansion in the small Dutch home market was an important reason for extending operations beyond the nation's borders. Medium-sized Dutch companies are generally motivated primarily by cost cutting through economies of scale and spreading risk by taking advantage of international variations in the economic cycle (Sparling, 2002).

There are several reasons for the extraordinary outward FDI position of the Netherlands. Industrial innovations in the nineteenth and early twentieth centuries in margarine, oil refining and lighting provided the necessary intangible firm-specific assets needed for Dutch firms to invest abroad (van Zanden, 1997). Furthermore, large MNEs were stimulated by favourable government policies, such as plans for industrialization, the 'guided wage policies' of 1945–63, and the lack of intellectual property protection up to 1912 (van Tulder, 1999). It should also be noted that the Netherlands has been well endowed with both financial and human capital. MNE investments were also stimulated by the knowledge of foreign markets due to extensive trading (particularly with Germany) resulting from the Netherlands' favourable location on the North Sea.

Worldwide, FDI attained substantial proportions in the twentieth century. From the 1960s onwards, FDI grew rapidly due to improved transportation facilities, financial innovations and trends in protectionism. The majority (three-quarters) of Dutch overseas investments during this period occurred through acquisitions by the ten biggest Dutch multinationals[6] (van Nieuwkerk and Sparling, 1985). The peak of the Dutch presence in the world was recorded in 1980, when 8.1 per cent of the world's outward FDI stock originated in the Netherlands, making it the fourth-largest investor in the world. Since then, the importance of industrial multinationals has decreased, as a consequence of both the decreasing significance of the industrial sector and the growth of the services sector, including banks, insurance institutions and consultancy firms. New multinationals in the services sector gained importance quickly.[7] By 2005, Dutch investors still occupied fifth position worldwide, but their share in total investments had declined to 6.0 per cent due to the emergence of large investors from Asia (Japan, Hong Kong, Singapore) and other European countries (UNCTAD, 2006).

The sectoral composition of Dutch outward FDI confirms the spectacular worldwide increase in the services sector (Table 2.1). Its share in total investment grew from 31 per cent in 1984 to 58 per cent in 2005 (DNB, 2006). Other services made up 37 per cent of the total outward investment stock in 2005. Included in this category are activities relating to non-banking business services and treasury activities, including those of financial subsidiaries of Dutch enterprises and leasing companies, as well as investment in foreign real estate, both direct purchases and investment in real-estate companies. Trade activities and banking and insurance each make up 8 per cent of total outward FDI stock. The internationalization of banking and insurance activities was dictated largely by the saturation of the home market and the need to spread risks and 'scale up' (Boot, 1999). This latter point was particularly important in order to compete in the large US market and the EU Single Market. Cross-border investment was made easier by the financial liberalization and deregulation that took effect in the second half of the 1980s. Within the industrial sectors (whose overall share in investment declined from 69 per cent in 1984 to 41 per cent in 2005), mining, oil and chemicals account for one quarter of all outward FDI by Dutch firms. Within this broad category, most investments should be attributed to the chemical industry.

Inward FDI

Although the outward FDI position of the Netherlands has always attracted a lot of attention (van Hoesel and Narula, 1999), much less is known about inward FDI in the Netherlands. Like outward FDI, inward FDI grew rapidly during recent decades, particularly during the period surrounding European economic integration. Industrial FDI dominated the overall inward FDI position in the Netherlands for many years. Within the industrial sector, most investments occurred in oil, mining and chemicals (similar to the outward investment position). Investments took place in the metals and engineering sector and the food, drink and tobacco sector as well, although these were substantially smaller in size (Table 2.2).

The share of services in total inward FDI in the Netherlands (65 per cent) has outgrown industrial FDI. In the case of services investment, the main sector is other services, and within that sector, non-banking financial services in particular. The attractiveness of the Netherlands as a distribution centre is reflected in the extensive foreign interests in trade. In banking and insurance the BLEU was the largest individual investor in 2000 with interests of over €4 billion, due to the strong expansion of Belgian interests in this sector in 1998 as a result of the new organizational structure of Fortis activities in the Netherlands and Belgium. Until recently, foreign interests in the transport, storage and communications sector were not significant. However, after 1996, and particularly in 2000, they expanded rapidly as a result of investments in telecommunications. Important investments in these sectors included Deutsche Post's acquisition of Nedlloyd's land-based activities, British Telecom's acquisition of the Dutch Railways share in Telfort, the interests acquired by France Télécom in Casema and Dutchtone, and the Japanese firm Docomo's stake in KPN Mobile (Sparling, 2002).

Nowadays most new foreign investments occur through mergers and acquisitions. Table 2.3 shows an overview of the largest acquisitions involving Dutch firms in 2005.

Table 2.1   Outward FDI stock from the Netherlands by sector (€ million), 2005

	EU	Switzerland	USA	Latin America	Japan	Southeast Asia	Other countries	Total
Agriculture and fishing	120	0	10	118	0	0	41	289
Mining, oil and chemicals	85605	8398	9235	6096	787	6216	3037	137429
Metal & electronics	23155	1807	6522	896	332	8404	2958	42190
Food, drink and tobacco	13281	3864	6541	3923	−476	828	69	31993
Other industry	5854	242	4096	37	17	249	35	10841
Total industry	127896	14312	26392	10951	660	15696	3457	222452
Construction	1746	21	489	486	0	86	155	2972
Trade	32583	6936	1102	956	−182	1013	2896	44650
Transportation, storage and communication	22584	918	−1270	347	29	279	200	23836
Banking and insurance	21072	460	9390	5994	307	1767	547	42791
Other services	120809	12637	42357	5562	272	2581	17551	196993
Total services	197047	20951	51579	12859	426	5641	21190	308270
Total FDI	326820	35283	78470	24413	1086	21424	24805	533984

Source: DNB (2006).

Table 2.2 *Stock of inward FDI in the Netherlands by sector (€ million), 2005*

	EU	Switzerland	USA	Latin America	Japan	Southeast Asia	Other countries	Total
Agriculture and fishing	145	0	20	2	0	0	0	167
Mining, oil and chemicals	36894	1053	7127	17016	374	59	3037	65560
Metal & Electronics	16166	360	2254	475	2165	121	2958	24499
Food, drink and tobacco	4994	3578	13342	57	225	204	69	22469
Other industry	16133	332	1531	188	182	18	35	18419
Total industry	76829	5323	24255	17737	2946	401	3457	130948
Construction	367	9	24	137	1	0	155	693
Trade	27929	1507	6187	2968	5927	636	2896	48050
Transportation, storage and communication	12439	636	1535	711	40	128	200	15689
Banking and insurance	12060	423	1929	143	428	172	547	15702
Other services	99635	8757	35190	5520	340	771	17551	167764
Total services	152065	11323	44841	9342	6735	1708	21190	247204
Total FDI	229404	16655	69140	27217	9682	2109	24805	379012

Source: DNB (2006).

Table 2.3   Top ten acquisitions by multinationals from the Netherlands, 2005

Foreign company bought	Dutch buyer	Payment (€ billions)	Dutch company bought	Foreign buyer	Payment (€ billions)
Banco Antonveneta (Italy)	ABN Amro	6.27	Nedlloyd	Maersk (DK)	2.58
EAC Nutrition (Singapore)	Numico	1.20	NIB Capital Bank	J.C. Flowers (VS)	2.10
Lumileds Lighting (VS)	Philips	0.80	Versatel	Tele2 (Sweden)	1.01
Solvus (Creyff's) (Belgium)	United Services Group	0.78	CSM Zoetwaren	CVC Capital (NL) Nordic Capital (Sweden)	0.85
Ivan Taranov Brewereis (Russia)	Heineken	0.45	Petroplus	Carlyle (UK)	0.63
Mellin (Italy)	Numico	0.40	Multikabel	Warburg Pincus (VS)	0.52
Berna Biotech (Switzerland)	Crucell	0.33	AM Development	Morgan Stanley (VS)	0.48
Central Coast Bancorp (VS)	Rabobank	0.31	Wehkamp	Industri Kapital (Sweden)	0.39
NDC Health Information Services (VS)	Wolters Kluwer	0.31	Verdugt	Kemira (Finland)	0.15
Novartis Dieetvoeding (France)	ABN Amro Capital	0.22	Deli XL	The Bidvest Group (South Africa)	0.14

Source: KPMG Corporate Finance (2006).

For some firms, buying a competitor, supplier or customer is considered to be the best strategy to secure and advance their international competitive advantages. Generally, the purpose of strategic asset seeking is to acquire core competences from the host-country market. These assets may take a variety of forms, from innovative capability and organizational architecture to access to marketing distribution channels and a better understanding of local consumers' tastes (Dunning, 1994). With these investments foreign investors access knowledge-intensive assets in the host country and learn from the experience of the targeted firm (Dunning, 1998) and the business environment in the host country.

The factors that make the Netherlands an attractive host for FDI largely match the characteristics of the Dutch Porter diamond discussed above. Foreign entrepreneurs have always favoured the Netherlands for their investments in Europe because of several specific factors (Hogenbirk, 2002; van Nieuwkerk and Sparling, 1985; Sparling, 2002), such as its strategic location in relation to the hinterland with good infrastructural facilities (large rivers and good road links). Many chemical companies such as DuPont, Hoechst, Dow Chemical, ICI, Exxon, Texaco/BP and Kuwait Petroleum chose the Netherlands for this reason (Minne, 1997). In addition, for many years economic growth in the Netherlands has been high in comparison with that in other West European countries. Most inward FDI in the Netherlands is therefore market seeking in nature. The market, however, should not be interpreted as just the Netherlands and its 16 million inhabitants, but the entire EU, which can easily be reached from the Netherlands. Many electronics firms – Canon, Digital, Apple, Texas Instruments, Compaq, Sun Microsystems, Toshiba, Sony, IBM – have a European distribution centre in the Netherlands that is used to supply the entire European hinterland.

Other factors making the Netherlands an attractive host are the high educational standards and the language skills of the Dutch workforce. The government has reformed the labour market significantly to introduce more flexibility. Compared to other EU countries, the trade unions have a moderate attitude, and strikes and loss of working days are rare. Although the country has few natural resources, with the exception of natural gas and fertile soil, high-quality labour attracts resource-seeking investments to the Netherlands.

Furthermore, traditionally favourable tax provisions for foreign firms have made the Netherlands an attractive host country.[8] Efficiency-seeking firms tried to benefit from these favourable policies. In addition, economic integration in Europe allowed efficiency-seeking investors to restructure their activities, establish in one location and exploit economies of scale and scope on a European level.

Besides these asset-exploiting foreign activities that take advantage of locally existing resources and capabilities, a fourth type of inward FDI exists in the Netherlands. Strategic-asset-seeking investments are conducted by firms that engage in FDI mainly to acquire assets that will strengthen their long-term global innovatory or production competitiveness.[9] These firms are encouraged to locate in close proximity to large Dutch MNEs to benefit from technology spillovers.

Globalization has changed the way affiliates are positioned in host countries. As competition in many industries has become increasingly global, import-substituting affiliates – focusing on the supply of national markets – have become less viable. Instead, in most industrial sectors, especially in electronics and pharmaceuticals, marketing and sales activities are now located in one particular host country to serve a broader market, for instance the European market (Calliano and Carpano, 2000). MNEs that want to stay competitive in regionalizing or globalizing markets (such as the EU) have to make the most effective use of their worldwide assets. Consequently, ownership advantages are no longer solely developed at the corporate headquarters and leveraged abroad to a network of affiliates (Birkinshaw and Hood, 2000; Taggart, 1998a). Instead, as these foreign affiliates grow in size and develop their own unique resources or tap into the local resource base of their host country, they themselves become important sources of competitive advantage for the MNE (Bartlett and Ghoshal, 1986). Consequently, the role of the affiliates in host markets has frequently shifted from import substitution towards an export-oriented strategic position in the MNE group's global network (Birkinshaw and Hood, 1998; Papanastassiou and Pearce, 1994).

Due to globalization, regional integration and technological developments, foreign affiliates are now taking on an increasing variety of roles (Jarillo and Martinez, 1990;

Taggart, 1998b). Whereas foreign affiliates used to begin as 'market access' operations for selling the MNE's products in the host country, most of them now also perform a geographically dispersed set of value-adding activities (Birkinshaw et al., 2000). Instead of supplying products only to a host market, MNEs increasingly have the option of allowing individual affiliates to make positive use of their potential for export orientation to supply a much wider regional or global market (Pearce and Papanastassiou, 1997; Yip, 1994). These affiliates develop a competitive strategy across two dimensions – the value-added scope of activities and market scope.

Building on these studies, Hogenbirk and van Kranenburg (2006) have analysed the role of foreign affiliates in the electronics and electrical applications sector that are partly attracted to the Netherlands by the presence of Philips Electronics. They found that one in four firms in their sample could be classified as a regional-product-mandated hub that supplies both the local and foreign (particularly EU) markets, with a large number of activities (including manufacturing, R&D and logistics) conducted from the Dutch location. Another quarter of all firms use their Dutch affiliate as an export platform, with few value-adding activities but a broad sales focus. For half the sample firms the Dutch market itself clearly is too small, but the favourable location in Europe and the easy access to this much larger market encouraged the firm to enter the Netherlands. Over 40 per cent of foreign affiliates focus strictly on local sales in the Netherlands. Most of this latter group of firms have been in the Netherlands for a long time and have not changed their strategy under the influence of globalization. Furthermore, they are frequently owned by a European parent, making sales to the rest of Europe from the Netherlands less necessary. Least likely to occur are so-called 'miniature replicas'. To exploit economies of scale and scope the Dutch market generally is too small and does not warrant a full production and distribution base.

Geographic concentration/clustering
Foreign firms in the Netherlands carefully choose their location and appear to cluster together in three Dutch provinces: Noord Holland, Zuid Holland and Noord Brabant (Hogenbirk, 2002). More than two-thirds of all foreign affiliates are located in these provinces, compared to a little over half of all Dutch firms. In general, new foreign entries in host markets tend to cluster geographically around other foreign establishments in an attempt to benefit from agglomeration economies resulting, for instance, from a pool of specialized labour and inputs and technical and knowledge spillovers among firms (Hogenbirk, 2002; Shaver, 1998).

Historically, industrial clustering patterns were quite common in the Netherlands. Several regionally based industrial clusters existed, such as textiles in the region of Twente, and leather and shoes in the province of North Brabant. This traditional pattern dissolved during the postwar period as manufacturing became more integrated on both a national and even an international level (Jacobs and de Jong, 1992). However, new clusters have emerged. Jacobs and de Jong (1992) identified three main industries[10] in which the Netherlands are competitive internationally in terms of the Porter diamond, in particular food and beverages, petroleum and chemicals, and transportation/services. In these sectors the Dutch export share in total world exports exceeds the overall position of the Netherlands. Building and extending on this study, Jacobs and Lankhuizen (2005) identified 100 products out of 886 OECD categories in which the Netherlands stands out.[11] Surprisingly, not much has changed during the last 15 years. The same sectors are still the most competitive ones.[12]

At the top of the present list are fresh flowers. The Dutch share in world exports is 84 per cent, and this sector's worldwide sales from the Netherlands were over US$2.8 billion in 2003. The sector therefore also makes a significant contribution to overall Dutch GDP. Many more agricultural and food products are on the list, including flower bulbs, mace, coconut oil, cashew nuts, brussels sprouts, tomatoes, chicory, butter, nutmeg, sole, herring and mussels. The food and flower cluster therefore remains most important to the Dutch economy when Porter's methodology is used. Some of these products are niches in the Dutch economy, while others also make a large contribution to Dutch GDP.[13] Not surprisingly, therefore, 'food and flowers' is also one of the four sectors identified by the Dutch government as innovation target themes or key regions (so-called *sleutelgebieden*).[14] A considerable effort is made to sustain this unique position into the future. The food and flowers sector benefits from the fertile soil and the relative abundance of greenhouses that use the natural gas extracted in Slochteren. Sophisticated auctions have developed to support the trade in over 16,000 flower and plant types in the Netherlands. Dutch infrastructure (in particular Schiphol Airport) facilitates quick transportation of food products and flowers to the final destination countries. Both Dutch and foreign firms benefit from the favourable Dutch circumstances and many well-known firms have a Dutch base or presence: Unilever, Heineken, Numico, Nestlé, Danone, Sara Lee, McCain and Mars.

Jacobs and Lankhuizen (2005) mention several high-tech products on their list as well. The wafer steppers produced by ASML rank highly (eighth position), as over 60 per cent of world exports of this product originate in the Netherlands, with a total sales value equalling €1.6 billion in 2003. In addition, almost one-third of the world's dredging machinery is exported from the Netherlands. In fact, the machinery and modular construction sector is the most dynamic and vital Dutch economic cluster. It represents export sales of over €80 billion, value added of €14 billion and over 270 000 employees. The sector benefits strongly from the high knowledge intensity in the Netherlands. Given the relatively limited size of Dutch demand, these firms – such as Philips Medical Systems, Océ, ASML, Grasso and Vanderlande – naturally operate in international markets. Like food and flowers, the high-tech systems cluster is also an innovation target theme.

Besides food and health and machinery and modular construction, chemicals and fuels, representing export sales of over €77 billion, value added of over €20 billion and over 280 000 employees, is the third key cluster in the Dutch economy. Several (petro-)chemical products can be found on the list established by Jacobs and Lankhuizen (2005), such as ethylene, phosphoric acids and hydrogen. Polaroid film, photographic paper and film, and materials for photographic laboratories also largely originate in the Netherlands. Many well-known large Dutch multinationals operate in the chemicals and fuels sector, such as Shell, Akzo Nobel, and DSM. Their economic success has also attracted many foreign firms to the Netherlands, in particular in the area of Rotterdam Harbour (with foreign establishments of Exxon, Fina, Kuwait Petroleum, Dow Chemicals, DuPont de Nemours, and Solvay, *inter alia*). These firms use the extensive Dutch infrastructure to reach their customers worldwide. They tap into a pool of highly skilled, multilingual workers.

As shown in Table 2.3, successful Dutch firms (including those in key clusters) are interesting acquisition targets. CSM Zoetwaren in the food cluster was acquired by a Dutch–Swedish consortium in 2005. In 2002 DSM's petrochemical activities in Geleen were acquired by Sabic (Saudi Arabia). Nedlloyd and KLM used to be important flagships of the Dutch transportation sector, but have recently been acquired by foreign firms. Maersk from Denmark bought Nedlloyd in 2005. AirFrance and KLM merged in 2004. In general, it is more common nowadays for foreign firms to buy or merge with a local competitor or supplier than to start a new branch themselves. The Netherlands is no exception to this rule.

Uniqueness of the Netherlands
The Dutch FDI investment position is unusual. The large outward investment position was built by just a few big multinationals that have been successful for more than a century and that make significant contributions to domestic employment, R&D and exports. These Dutch MNEs have undoubtedly been responsible for pushing the Netherlands up the rankings of technologically sophisticated nations and underlie its strong trade orientation (van Tulder, 1999). The presence of these large, successful Dutch MNEs has posed particular policy-making problems to consecutive Dutch governments. In general, policy freedom in small and open economies is more limited than in large, closed nations. Dutch governments therefore have had to be creative in reconciling their limited policy latitude and the private interests of these large, internationally oriented firms (van Tulder, 1999). During recent decades, policy formulation and implementation in the Netherlands has therefore been conducted in close cooperation with a number of large Dutch MNEs and trade unions (van Tulder, 1999). The pragmatic manner in which these groups cooperated has been dubbed 'corporatism' (Visser and Hemerijck, 1997)[15] or the 'Polder model' (consensus model). Initially, in the 1980s, the employers, trade unions and the government began negotiating policies that could facilitate an economic recovery. The three parties agreed to strive for wage moderation in exchange for shorter working hours (the Wassenaar agreement), an overhaul of the social security system, and policies to strengthen the public finances. The constructive dialogue between the three parties also led to other results.

Philips's former CEO Wisse Dekker launched a plan called 'Europe 1990: An agenda for action' (van Tulder, 1999). This initiative helped to overcome the 'eurosclerosis' that had threatened new initiatives in the economic integration of Europe. The Dutch had much to gain from further economic integration in Europe. Opening up the European market would increase the attractiveness of the Netherlands as a transportation hub and 'Gateway to Europe'. The government and firms worked together to rejuvenate the European integration trajectory and many of Wisse Dekker's ideas from the 1985 White Paper were adopted. The opening up of the entire European market further increased the attraction of the Netherlands as a location for foreign affiliates by increasing the benefits of one of its most attractive features, its strategic geographic location, where several rivers empty into the North Sea.

Given the natural attraction of a favourable geographic location, the Dutch government's foremost aim was and should always be to maintain or improve the investment climate (Ministerie van Economische Zaken, 2006). Both local and foreign firms benefit from investments in infrastructure and education, and the reduction of administrative burdens. A favourable economic environment will encourage more multinationals to choose and to stay in the Netherlands.

Notes

1. Other studies identifying Dutch cluster patterns include Kusters and Minne (1992) and Nooteboom (1993). Jacobs is preferred, because of the recent update and the fact that he and his co-authors have tried hardest to follow Porter's original methodology.
2. The area in the Netherlands known as the Randstad (broadly covering the provinces of Noord Holland, Zuid Holland and Utrecht) is located on the North Sea. It is the most densely populated area. Therefore, even though only 25 per cent of the land is below sea level, over 8 million people are in danger of flooding.
3. When considering population size, the Netherlands is considered small on Walsh's (1988) definition. With 16.4 million inhabitants, the Netherlands is considerably smaller than other European countries (Germany, France, the UK, Italy and Spain have respectively 82, 61, 61, 58 and 40 million inhabitants).
4. The data reported by the Dutch Central Bank (DNB) on Dutch and FDI are taken from the conclusions of a compulsory annual report by Dutch industry on cross-border participation in capital and reserves. The data from this report are supplemented with information obtained via the balance-of-payments recording system on intra-group lending, internal current account relationships, and investment other than via equities. Acquisitions of real estate by individuals are also reported. The report was produced for the first time in 1973, and has continued on an annual basis since.
5. That year FDI outflows slowed for several reasons. First, there was a marked fall-off in new purchases in comparison to 2000, when there was a temporary peak in cross-border mergers and acquisitions. Second, amortizations of foreign holdings (including the telecom sector) slowed outward FDI growth as they were only partially offset by the positive effect of the higher dollar exchange rate that year. Inward FDI also came under pressure from amortizations but these were considerably smaller than in the case of Dutch direct investment abroad.
6. Including: Royal Dutch Shell, Unilever, Philips, AKZO, Heineken, Van Leer and Océ van der Grinten.
7. Including: Hollandse Beton, Volker-Stevin, Ballast-Nedam, ABN Amro Bank, Aegon, ING Group, Ahold, Vendex, KPMG.
8. However, many other countries, such as Belgium, France and Ireland, have also introduced favourable tax regimes.
9. This happens when an investment opens up new markets, creates R&D synergies, production economies, or results in increased market power, lower transaction costs, or a better spreading of risk.
10. Porter's analyses rely heavily on international export statistics. These are scarcely available for services. Considering the increasing importance of services for many industrialized countries, this is a serious limitation. Creating these statistics is difficult. Some services can easily be exported (such as consultancy, transportation, dredging), others much less so (teaching, hairdressing, construction, retail shops). Jacobs and Lankhuizen (2005) used the OECD export statistics covering 5500 product groups.
11. Jacobs and Lankhuizen (2005) also identified several services sectors in which the Dutch are competitive internationally. The most important ones are business services (a very broad category covering employment agencies, translators, cleaning and real estate for businesses, but also the distribution of electricity, water, gas and other oil products), construction services (which includes not only house construction but also infrastructure and dredging), and postal services. Transportation by sea and air of both passengers and freight also ranks highly, which is to be attributed to success of both Rotterdam Harbour and Amsterdam Schiphol Airport.
12. Some new sectors have been added, because the new data provide more detail.
13. Overall, food and health is considered the third most important cluster in the Netherlands, with export sales amounting to €30 billion, overall value added of €13 billion, and 150 000 employees.
14. The Dutch Innovation Platform was started to help the Dutch government reach the EU's Lisbon targets. It has distilled four promising innovation themes from information provided by the business community and knowledge institutions: water, flowers and food, creative industry, and high-tech systems and materials. In these areas the Dutch can excel, now and in the future.
15. Van Tulder (1999) discusses other Dutch policies that contributed to past success, such as the Dutch refusal to comply with international patenting laws that contributed favourably to the growth of some large MNEs (Philips, Unilever).

References

Andersson, T., T. Fredriksson and R. Svensson (1996), *Multinational Restructuring, Internationalization and Small Economies. The Swedish Case*, London: Routledge.

CBS (2006), Business Statistics on Statline, www.cbs.nl.
Bartlett, C.A. and S. Ghoshal (1986), 'Tap your subsidiaries for global reach', *Harvard Business Review*, **64** (6), 87–94.
Berenschot (2007), *Buitenlandse investeerders zijn groeiversnellers voor de Nederlandse economie!*, Utrecht.
Birkinshaw, J. and N. Hood (1998), 'Multinational subsidiary evolution: capability and charter change in foreign-owned subsidiary companies', *Academy of Management Review*, **23**(4), 773–95.
Birkinshaw, J. and N. Hood (2000), 'Characteristics of foreign subsidiaries in industry clusters', *Journal of International Business Studies*, **31**(1), 141–54.
Birkinshaw, J., U. Holm, P. Thilenius and N. Arvidsson (2000), 'Consequences of perception gaps in the headquarters–subsidiary relationship', *International Business Review*, **9**, 321–344.
Boot, A.W.A. (1999), 'European lessons on consolidation in banking', *Journal of Banking and Finance*, **23** (2–4), 609–13.
Calliano, R. and C. Carpano (2000), 'National systems of technological innovation, FDI, and economic growth: the case of Ireland', *Multinational Business Review*, **8** (2), 16–25.
DNB (Dutch Central Bank) (2006), www.dnb.nl.
Dunning, J.H. (1994), *Multinational Enterprises and the Global Economy,* Reading, MA: Addison-Wesley.
Dunning, J.H. (1997), 'The competitive advantage of countries and MNE activities', in H. Vernon-Wortzel and L.H. Wortzel (eds), *Strategic Management in the Global Economy*, New York: John Wiley & Sons, pp. 186–204.
Dunning, J. H. (1998), 'Location and the multinational enterprise: a neglected factor?', *Journal of International Business Studies*, **29** (1), 45–66.
European Committee (2004), Flash Eurobarometer 160 'Entrepreneurship'.
Goey, F. de (1999), 'Dutch overseas investments in the very long run' in R. van Hoesel and R. Narula (eds), *Multinational Enterprises from the Netherlands*, London: Routledge, pp. 32–60.
Hogenbirk, A.E. (2002), *Determinants of Inward Foreign Direct Investment: The Case of the Netherlands*, Maastricht: Datawyse.
Hogenbirk, A.E. and H.L. van Kranenburg (2006), 'The roles of foreign owned subsidiaries in a small economy', *International Business Review*, **15** (1), 53–76.
Jacobs, Dany (1995), 'Alle clusters groot en klein', in D. Dany Jacobs and A.-P. de Man (eds), *Clusters en concurrentiekracht*, Alphen a/d Rijn: Samsom.
Jacobs, D. and M.W. de Jong (1992), 'Industrial Clusters and the Competitiveness of the Netherlands', *De Economist*, **140** (2), 233–52.
Jacobs, D. and M. Lankhuizen (2005), *De sterke Nederlandse clusters volgens de Porter-methodiek anno 2003*, Rijksuniversiteit Groningen.
Jacobs, D., P. Boekholt and W. Zegveld (1990), *De economische kracht van Nederland. Een toepassing van Porters benadering van de concurrentiekracht van landen*, Den Haag: Stichting Maatschappij en Onderneming.
Jarillo, J.C. and J.J. Martinez (1990), 'Different roles for subsidiaries: the case of multinational corporations', *Strategic Management Journal*, **11**, 501–12.
Kusters, A. and B. Minne (1992), *Technologie, marktstructuur en internationalisatie: de ontwikkeling van de industrie,* CPB, Den Haag (onderzoeksmemorandum no. 99).
Ministerie van Economische Zaken (2006), *In actie voor acquisitie. Hoe Nederland profiteert van buitenlandse investeringen*, Den Haag.
Minne, B. (1997), *International Battle of the Giants. The Role of Investment in Research and Fixed Assets*, Den Haag: CPB.
Nooteboom, B. (1993), 'Een aanzet tot industriebeleid (I)/(II)', *Economisch Statistische Berichten*, **17** (3), 240–49.
OECD (2005), *Economic Surveys*, various issues, Paris: OECD.
Papanastassiou, M. and R. Pearce (1994), 'Host-country determinants of the market strategies of US companies' overseas subsidiaries', *Journal of the Economics of Business*, **1** (2), 199–217.
Pearce, R. and M. Papanastassiou (1997), 'European markets and the strategic roles of multinational enterprise subsidiaries in the UK', *Journal of Common Market Studies*, **35** (2), 243–65.
Porter, M.E. (1990), *The Competitive Advantage of Nations*, New York: The Free Press.
Shaver, J.M. (1998), 'Do foreign-owned and US-owned establishments exhibit the same location pattern in US manufacturing industries?', *Journal of International Business Studies*, **29** (3), 469–92.
Sparling, R.P. (2002), *Het externe vermogen van Nederland*, Amsterdam: De Nederlandsche Bank.
Taggart, J.H. (1998a), 'Configuration and coordination at subsidiary level: foreign manufacturing affiliates in the UK', *British Journal of Management*, **9**, 327–39.
Taggart, J.H. (1998b), 'Strategy shifts in MNC Subsidiaries', *Strategic Management Journal*, **19**, 663–81.
UNCTAD (2006), *World Investment Report 2006, FDI from Developing and Transition Economies: Implications for Development*, New York.

Van Den Bulcke, D. (1983), 'Multinationale ondernemingen in de Europese Gemeenschap', *Maandschrift Economie*, **47**, 304–26.

van Hoesel, R. and R. Narula (eds) (1999), *Multinational Enterprises from the Netherlands*, London: Routledge.

van Kranenburg, H. van, M. Cloodt and J. Hagedoorn (2001), 'An exploratory study of recent trends in the diversification of Dutch publishing companies in the multimedia and information industries', *International Studies of Management and Organization*, **31** (1), 64–86.

van Nieuwkerk, M. and R. Sparling (1985), *The Netherlands International Direct Investment Position*, Dordrecht: Nijhoff.

van der Schoot, W. (2005), 'Overheid, koester grote bedrijven', *Het Financieele Dagblad*, **6** (7).

van Tulder, R. (1999), 'Small, smart and sustainable? Policy challenges to the Dutch model of governance (together) with multinationals', in R. van Hoesel and R. Narula (eds), *Multinational Enterprises from the Netherlands*, London: Routledge, pp. 282–301.

van Zanden, J.L. (1997), *Een klein land in de 20e eeuw*, Utrecht: Het Spectrum.

Visser, J. and A. Hemerijck (1997), '*A Dutch Miracle', Job Growth, Welfare Reform and Corporatism in the Netherlands*, Amsterdam: Amsterdam University Press.

Walsh, V. (1988), 'Technology and competitiveness of small countries: a review', in C. Freeman and B.-A. Lundvall (eds), *Small Countries Facing the Technological Revolution,* London: Pinter Publishers, pp. 37–66.

WTO (World Trade Organization) (2006), World Trade Statistics online.

Yip, G.S. (1994), 'Industry drivers of global strategy and organization', *International Executive*, **36** (5), 529–56.

3   Belgium's competitiveness: a comparison of foreign and domestic enterprises
Filip De Beule and Ilke Van Beveren

This chapter analyses Belgium's diamond of competitiveness, including the importance and role of multinational enterprises (MNEs). As MNEs follow, to some extent, the path of least resistance, and as policies, attitudes and environments of individual countries – also known as location specific advantages – differ, so do levels of multinational activity. Relevant factors that may attract and possibly deter foreign direct investment (FDI) specifically include the political and economic situation, the government's policy towards foreign-owned enterprises, the size of the market, as well as the availability of good infrastructure, skilled labour, supporting industries, favourable tax system, efficient capital market, competitive environment or the lack thereof.

These features are the different facets of Porter's diamond, which not only foster domestic firms but also attract foreign firms and which can either sharpen the competitiveness of existing goods and services in the host-country supply system through responsive market-seeking behaviour, or widen the product range and technological scope through knowledge-seeking activity. These characteristics also embed domestic and foreign firms in a mutually dependent and sustainable fashion in the local evolutionary processes.

The following section analyses Belgium's status as a small open economy, using data on FDI and international trade. The next section looks more specifically at the importance of foreign and domestic multinational firms in a sector analysis, while the next one analyses in more detail the chemical, pharmaceutical and biotechnology sector. The chapter ends by drawing some, we hope interesting, conclusions from the analysis.

Small open economy
Belgium is the quintessential example of the small open economy. With an area the size of the state of Brandenburg (Germany), Catalonia (Spain) or Maryland (USA) and a population of about 10 million people, similar to mere cities like Chicago, Paris or Guangzhou; Belgium is nevertheless a significant player in the world economy. Belgium ranks 139th in the list of countries in terms of geographical area, and 77th in terms of population, with 0.16 per cent of world population. Yet its GDP in 2005 was $370 billion, making Belgium the 17th economy in the world, ahead of countries such as Turkey, Poland, Indonesia and South Africa. GDP per capita ($35 712) was estimated to be the 15th highest in the world in 2005 (IMF, 2006).

Historically, coal mining and heavy industry enabled Belgium to become one of the most industrialized countries in Europe. However, these sectors lost their dominant status in the second half of the twentieth century. Mining was no longer viable in the face of foreign competition via cheaper imports of coal and iron ore. The steel sector also declined sharply during the same period as a result of the restructuring of the global steel industry. In Wallonia – the French-speaking southern part of Belgium – which was the base of Belgium's initial industrial development, large areas are still struggling with economic restructuring. The Walloon government recently launched a large-scale 'Marshall Plan' to boost the region's economy.

During the same period and especially after the Second World War, Dutch-speaking Flanders was moving up in the world. It owed this mainly to its favourable location and the port of Antwerp. The supply of oil and the investments from large foreign, e.g., German, companies led to the expansion of the largest concentration of petrochemical activity in the world after Houston. The automobile industry also attracted a great deal of investment. US companies, such as Ford and General Motors, played an important role. After the war they started looking for market opportunities, and with the launch of the European Economic Community (EEC), they wanted to take advantage of the additional predicted growth. In Flanders, they found reliable workers who were considerably cheaper than the Walloons and much less prone to striking. Flanders also focused on light industry, such as textiles instead of heavy industry, for its economic success. Flanders was therefore able to catch up with Wallonia in industrial terms.

Currently, Flanders is substantially more prosperous than Wallonia. Productivity levels are about 20 per cent higher in Flanders than they are in Wallonia, while unemployment is significantly higher in Wallonia than in Flanders. The WEF's *Global Competitiveness Report 2007-2008* ranked Belgium 20th. If the index for Flanders had been calculated separately, it would have ranked fifth after Switzerland, Finland, Sweden and Denmark, but before Singapore, the USA and Japan (Bowen et al., 2007).

Belgium lies at the heart of one of the largest concentrations of wealth in the world. Within a radius of 500 km, 140 million EU consumers can be reached, representing 60 per cent of Europe's purchasing power. To take advantage of its central location, it has developed an extensive transport infrastructure. It has one of the highest-density road and rail networks in the world, and one of the largest seaports in Europe – Antwerp. With an annual turnover of about 170 million tonnes of international seaborne cargo, it is Europe's second-largest seaport and ranks among the world's top ten (POA, 2007).

Strangely enough, costs remain relatively low compared to those in the neighbouring countries. Belgium offers one of the lowest real-estate costs in Europe. In the world ranking of most expensive office locations, Brussels occupies the 35th spot whereas London, Paris, Frankfurt, Dublin and Luxembourg are all in the top ten (DTZ, 2006). In the 2006 ranking of 144 cities by Mercer Human Resources Consulting, Brussels occupied the 71st spot for cost of living, while London (fifth), Geneva (seventh), Milan (13th), Paris (15th), Amsterdam (41st), Luxemburg (56th) and Frankfurt (61st) were all more expensive. The Brussels agglomeration is unsurprisingly a preferred location for national, regional or corporate headquarters and coordination centres.[1]

Politically, Brussels is also the host of EU and NATO headquarters, and hundreds of other international organizations and international NGOs. Belgium is right at the heart of the political and economic decision-making centres in Europe. The *European Public Affairs Directory* for 2006 lists some 800 European trade and professional associations, 450 interest groups, 300 corporations with European public affairs offices, 85 European think-tanks, over 100 international organizations and law firms, and over 140 consulting bureaux, all located in or around Brussels.

Belgium is also consistently ranked among the most productive nations (output per worker) in the world. The *World Competitiveness Yearbook* published by the Institute for Management and Development (IMD) (Lausanne) ranks Belgium's workforce sixth in the world for productivity per hour. Because of Belgium's location and history, its educational system is, for instance, highly oriented towards the instruction of foreign languages. In 2006, Belgium was ranked in the top ten worldwide for the quality of its educational system and the skills of its labour force (IMD, 2006).

Labour costs are relatively high, especially because of labour taxation. However, Belgium has one of the lowest effective tax rates on capital as from 1 January 2006. The Belgian effective tax rate on capital declined from 23.5 per cent in 2005 to –4.4 per cent in 2006, resulting from the introduction of a so-called 'notional interest deduction' for equity financing.[2] Due to the gradual disappearance of the special tax regime for Belgian coordination centres, Belgian supposedly lost a major part of its attractiveness to foreign investors. The notional interest deduction has to make up for that loss. Moreover, this measure is EU-proof because it is available to all companies. Foreign companies with subsidiaries in Belgium can also enjoy notional interest deductions without having to compensate for these abroad (Mintz, 2006).

Belgium's neighbours all have effective tax rates around 20 per cent (Netherlands, Luxembourg), or around 30 per cent (the UK, France). Among industrial and leading developing nations, China has the highest effective tax rate (47 per cent), largely driven by its non-refundable 17 per cent value-added tax applied to purchases of machinery.[3] China is followed by Brazil, Germany, the USA and Russia, all with rates near 40 per cent.

According to the World Trade Organization (WTO), more than 85 per cent of Belgian GDP was exported in 2005, making Belgium the tenth-largest exporter of goods, and the thirteenth-largest exporter of services globally in absolute terms, ahead of countries such as Russia, Brazil and Korea. The main Belgian export products in 2005 were chemicals and pharmaceutical products (23.1 per cent), transport equipment (12.7 per cent), machinery and appliances (12.7 per cent), metals (8.7 per cent), and plastics and rubber (8.1 per cent). Likewise, Belgium imports more than 80 per cent of its GDP, making Belgium the tenth-largest importer of goods and the fourteenth-largest importer of commercial services globally.

When Belgium exported and imported an average of almost 85 per cent of its GDP by 2005, this was up from an average around 60 per cent in 1995. Belgium has comparatively one of the highest ratios of trade openness in the world, similar to countries like Singapore and Hong Kong (see Figure 3.1). In comparison, Europe as a whole exports and imports just over a third of its GDP.

In terms of investment flows, Belgium is also substantially more open than most other (European) countries. Its average value of inward and outward FDI flows as a percentage of GDP is likewise substantially higher than the European average, fluctuating between 6 and 12 per cent of GDP; whereas the European average fluctuates, together with global trends of FDI flows, between 1 and 4 per cent of its GDP (Eurostat, 2006).

According to the United Nations Conference on Trade and Development (UNCTAD) Belgium was also the ninth-largest recipient of FDI flows in the world in 2005, and is the sixth-largest host country of FDI stock on a historical basis (UNCTAD, 2006) with over $492 billion, ahead of countries such as Brazil, Mexico and even China. Outward stock

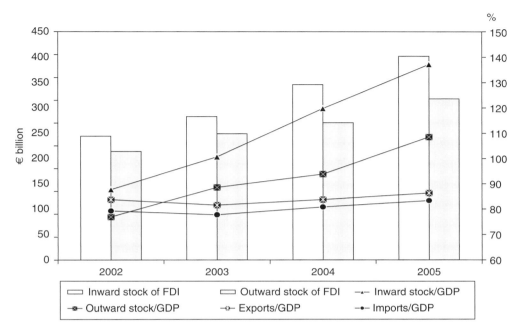

%

Source: Authors' calculations based on UNCTAD, IMF and WTO.

Figure 3.1 Degree of trade and investment openness of Belgium, 2002–05

of FDI has likewise increased, although not to the same extent as inward FDI. Inward FDI stock as a percentage of GDP has increased 50 per cent from 87 per cent to 137 per cent, while outward FDI stock has increased from 76 to 108 per cent of GDP between 2002 and 2005, respectively.[4]

Given its relatively small economic size at less than 3 per cent of EU GDP, Belgium has a comparatively strong FDI position in the EU. The cumulative outward FDI of Belgium accounted for almost 5 per cent of the EU's total outward FDI stock in 2005, ranking fifth in the EU list of outward investors. The country is also one of the most important host countries (fourth position) for inward FDI in the EU, after the UK, France and Germany, accounting for almost 7 per cent of cumulative EU inward FDI.

However, the highly 'globalized' Belgian economy is characterized by its 'regionalized' concentration, in terms both of investment and trade. The most important host countries for Belgian FDI, for instance, are its immediate neighbouring countries. The regional concentration of inward and outward FDI activities of Belgium with its neighbouring countries/regions is related to Belgium's central location and its role in the distribution of goods and services across the European continent. This concentration is also linked to the high intra-firm and inter-firm trade linkages that often result from the hosting of and/or the participation in industrial clusters in Europe.

This leads to a substantially positive trade balance within the EU, as Belgium is used as a conduit to other European countries, but to a negative trade balance with countries outside the EU. Although, on the whole, Belgium has a positive trade balance at around

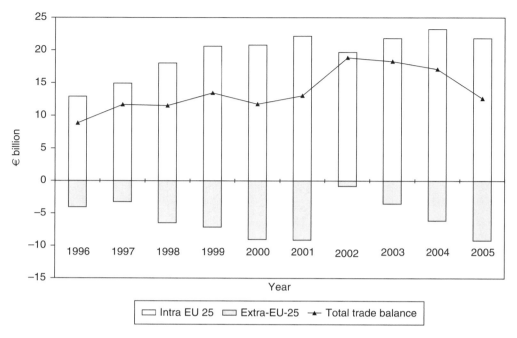

Source: Authors' calculations based on Eurostat (2006).

Figure 3.2   *The regionalized trade balance of the Belgian economy, 1996–2005*

€10 billion (see Figure 3.2), this is entirely due to intra-EU trade. For instance, Belgium has a substantial positive trade balance with most European countries except for the Netherlands and Ireland. It also has a negative trade balance with countries such as the USA, Japan and China, yet a substantial positive trade balance with India, mainly due to the diamond trade through Antwerp. On the whole, Belgium's most important trading partners are Germany, France, the Netherlands, the UK, the USA, Italy and Spain.

Data on FDI indicates that the lion's share of inward FDI in Belgium also comes from the EU. The most important host countries for Belgian FDI are its immediate neighbouring countries: Germany with 53 per cent, France with 14 per cent, the Netherlands with 7 per cent and the UK with 5 per cent. Belgian inward FDI is also strongly linked with these countries; France with 25 per cent, Germany with 20 per cent, the Netherlands with 19 per cent and the UK with 4 per cent. US firms are one of the largest non-European sources of FDI in Belgium. In 2006 Belgium ranked as the sixth-most-popular destination for US direct investment within the EU-15 and while it was ranked as only the fifteenth-most-attractive country worldwide for US direct investment, it was the fifth-most-popular destination for FDI (AMCHAM, 2008).

US investments in Belgium are increasingly being made in the service sector rather than in the manufacturing sector, even though the latter sector is still larger in terms of jobs, employing 72 106 people as compared to the 55 596 people employed in the services sectors (AMCHAM, 2008). A similar trend is noticeable in a more general sectoral analysis of FDI flows and stocks in Belgium, which clearly indicates an emphatic dominance of investment flows in the service sector.

Analysis of 'Belgian' companies

While the focus in the literature is often on the contribution or differing performance of foreign multinationals in the host country,[5] the focus in this analysis will be on the different performance of both foreign and domestic multinationals, compared to uninational firms. Van Den Bulcke (1981) showed that multinational corporations differed significantly from Belgian firms in terms of output per worker, which could be explained by the larger capital intensity of these foreign firms. Castellani and Zanfei (2006) provide evidence that domestic multinationals in Italy are different in terms of productivity and innovation performance, not only from their national competitors, but also from their foreign counterparts.

Data

The dataset used in this chapter is constructed from the *Belfirst Database* (November 2006 edition), which groups annual account data from the National Bank of Belgium.[6] The database is commercialized by Bureau Van Dijk (2006). Firms in the database are uniquely defined by their company number and data on employment, net value added, wages etc., is available for 1996–2005. The sector classification used is the NACE–Bel nomenclature, i.e. a five-digit extension of the NACE classification commonly used for European statistics. The database also contains information on the ownership structure of firms, in terms of both subsidiaries and shareholders, either domestic or foreign. Information on the legal status of companies (e.g. subject to a merger or bankruptcy) and type of account filed (consolidated or not) is also available.

While the database includes virtually the entire population of firms active in Belgium, firms that reported no employment have not been included in the analysis as they would necessarily have to be excluded from most of the statistics and analyses presented below because, for example, no meaningful measure of labour productivity or capital per worker can be calculated. Between 1996 and 2005, 321 566 companies reported positive net value added in at least one year, while only 165 106 of these firms provided employment figures during the same period. Despite the exclusion of about half the number of firms from the database, it should be noted that companies with positive employment over the sample period account for more than 93 per cent of the total value added generated between 1996 and 2005.

A firm is considered a foreign multinational in the dataset if it has some foreign ownership. Likewise, a firm is identified as a domestic multinational if it has subsidiaries in countries other than Belgium and it is not foreign-owned. Although, ideally, the identification of multinational firms on the basis of some minimum direct share of ownership (typically 10 per cent) is preferred, this information is unfortunately missing for the majority of cases. Another drawback of the ownership measure is that it is time-invariant: it refers to the latest year available. However, the legal status variable allows us to identify firms that have been subject to an ownership change. Therefore all firms that were involved in a merger, takeover or break-up between 1996 and 2005 are omitted from the sample (1927 firms). Furthermore, in order to avoid double counting, all companies with consolidated accounts are omitted from the analysis (785 firms). Finally, to

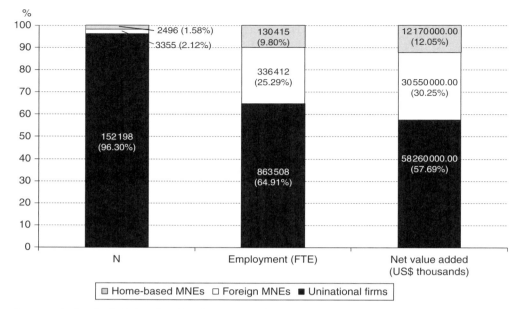

Source: Authors' calculations based on Bureau van Dijk (2006).

Figure 3.3   Impact of multinational firms on the Belgian economy: employment and value added (1996–2005)

ensure internal consistency, all observations with missing data on any of the relevant variables for analysis (e.g. missing wages with recorded employment) are also omitted.

The above-mentioned adjustments result in an unbalanced sample of 158 049 firms and 917 513 observations over the years 1996–2005. The sample is unbalanced in the sense that it allows for the dynamics of entry and exit; firms established in 2000, for instance, will have data only for the last five years, while firms exiting the market in 2000 are observed only during the first five years. In what follows, these data will be analysed in somewhat more detail.

Ownership characteristics of Belgian companies
Figure 3.3 shows the distribution of firms by type of ownership, in terms of number of firms, employment and net value added,[7] and presents annual averages for the period 1996–2005, with the corresponding shares indicated in parentheses. The figure indicates that more than 96 per cent of all companies with positive employment between 1996 and 2005 are so-called uninational firms (152 198 companies). Yet, although multinational firms account for less than 4 per cent of the total number of firms, their share of the total employment amounts to 35 per cent, while they generate on average 42 per cent of annual total net value added. About 72 per cent of total employment and value added generated by multinational firms is accounted for by foreign-owned companies, i.e. respectively 25 and 30 per cent of the sample total. Domestic multinationals employ about 10 per cent of the workforce in the sample and generate 12 per cent of total value added; hence their share within the group of multinationals amounts to about 28 per cent.

Table 3.1   Summary statistics of nationality of ownership in Belgium, 1996–2005

Variable	Uninational firms	Foreign MNEs	Domestic MNEs
Number of observations	873 001	25 867	18 645
(% of total)	(95.15)	(2.82)	(2.03)
Age	15.07	21.43	20.36
(years)	(12.05)	(18.32)	(16.03)
Size	9.89	130.05	69.95
(Number of employees, fte)	(71.41)	(574.44)	(414.51)
Wage per employee	38.37	67.35	53.61
(US$ thousands)	(29.94)	(158.39)	(35.02)
Labour productivity[a]	80.72	129.75	142.83
(US$ thousands)	(664.78)	(473.20)	(864.38)
Wage/value added	0.72	1.02	0.78
	(3.23)	(8.47)	(2.68)
Capital per employee	166.45	730.46	1022.96
(US$ thousands)	(2 889.30)	(14 417.45)	(16 277.26)

Notes:
Reported values (apart from the number of observations) represent sample means over the period 1996–2005. Standard deviations are given in parentheses.
[a] Labour productivity is measured as value added (VA) per employee. For a detailed description of the variables introduced here see Appendix A.

Source: Authors' calculation based on Bureau Van Dijk (2006).

Table 3.1 reports summary statistics for the pooled sample, distinguished by ownership type. The number of observations is identical for all reported measures and is given in the first row of the table. All reported measures (apart from the number of observations) represent averages over the sample period; the standard deviations are reported in parentheses. The table shows that multinational firms are on average, older, larger, pay higher wages and achieve higher labour productivity than uninational firms. The average multinational is about five years older than a purely domestic company and employs seven (for domestic MNEs) to 13 (for foreign MNEs) people for each person employed by a uninational company. Within the group of multinationals, foreign firms tend to pay higher wages than domestic MNEs, while domestic multinationals have higher labour productivity than foreign firms (on average).

If value added is considered a proxy for total output,[8] the ratio of the total wage bill over value added can be interpreted as a measure of competitiveness at the firm level, since it measures to what extent workers earn back their pay in terms of labour productivity (Konings, 2005). The figures given in Table 3.1 suggest that foreign firms are, on average, less competitive than their domestic counterparts, either uni- or multinational; the average foreign firm pays about 1 euro in wages for each euro of value added generated, compared to 72 cents for uninational firms and 78 cents for the average domestic MNE. The last row in Table 3.1 shows that multinationals tend to be more capital-intensive than uninational firms. Compared to uninational firms, the ratio of total fixed

Table 3.2   OLS regression of firm characteristics on ownership status in Belgium (pooled sample), 1996–2005

Dependent variable	ln(Emp_{it})	For_i	Dom_i	R^2 (adj.)
ln(Emp_{it})	–	1.83[a]	1.33[a]	0.2173
		(0.007)	(0.008)	
ln($Wage_{it}/Emp_{it}$)	0.04[a]	0.37[a]	0.20[a]	0.2370
	(0.000)	(0.003)	(0.004)	
ln(VA_{it}/Emp_{it})	−0.09[a]	0.40[a]	0.37[a]	0.2132
	(0.001)	(0.004)	(0.005)	
ln(TFA_{it}/Emp_{it})	−0.27[a]	0.28[a]	1.08[a]	0.1816
	(0.001)	(0.01)	(0.01)	

Notes:
[a]   Significant at 1 per cent level.
[b]   Significant at 5 per cent level.
[c]   Significant at 10 per cent level.
   All regressions include industry (3-digit NACE) and year dummies as well as the log of employment to control for size effects (except when employment is the dependent variable). The number of observations for all regressions is 917 513. Reported values are coefficients; standard errors are given in parentheses.

Source: Authors' calculations based on Bureau Van Dijk (2006).

assets (TFA) over the total number of employees is four times higher for the average foreign multinational and six times higher for the domestic MNEs.

Since the simple summary measures presented in Table 3.1 do not take the heterogeneity across sectors and time into account, Table 3.2 reports the results of an OLS (ordinary least squares) regression of a number of firm characteristics on ownership status.[9] All regressions reported in the table are controlled for industry (at 3-digit NACE level) and time effects. Following Bernard and Jensen (1995), all regressions (except for total employment) are controlled for firm size, proxied by employment, in order to account for the likely differences in production structure across plants of different sizes. All continuous variables are in logarithms; hence the coefficients on the dummy variables indicating multinational ownership represent the percentage differences compared to the baseline category (uninational firms).

All coefficients reported in Table 3.2 for the multinationality dummies are positive and significant at the highest level. These results suggest that multinationals tend to be larger, more productive and pay higher wages, even after controlling for industry and time effects. Apart from the regression where capital intensity, as measured by ln(TFA_{it}/Emp_{it}), is used as dependent variable, the coefficients for foreign multinationals (For_i) are larger than for domestic multinationals (Dom_i). While these results suggest that the overall contribution of multinational firms to the Belgian economy is positive (i.e. they generate an important share of employment and value added, are larger, more productive and pay higher wages), two countervailing facts are worth noting here.

First, a number of recent papers have found support for the popular notion that multinational firms are more 'footloose' than purely domestic firms due to their ability to respond more swiftly to adverse shocks. Van Den Bulcke et al. (1979) found that multinational corporations in Europe were significantly more inclined to divest than local firms. Both Bernard and Sjöholm (2003) and Görg and Strobl (2003) provide evidence that foreign multinationals, in Indonesia and Ireland respectively, are more likely to exit the market compared to domestic firms, after controlling for various industry and firm characteristics. Bernard and Jensen (2007) provide similar evidence for US multinationals in their home market. Specifically for Belgium, Van Beveren (2007) finds that, after controlling for industry and firm characteristics, both foreign and domestic multinationals are more likely to shut down operations than uninational firms in the manufacturing sector; in the services sector, only foreign firms are found to exhibit significantly higher exit rates (*ceteris paribus*). Second, Vandenbussche and Tan (2005) find, in a comparative study of effective corporate tax rates at the firm level, that there is considerable tax discrimination in Belgium in favour of foreign companies. Unfortunately, however, they do not distinguish between domestic firms with and without access to a global network.

The results presented in this section are in line with findings in the literature. Lipsey (2002) reviews the evidence on host-country effects of FDI and concludes that foreign firms (in general) tend to pay higher wages and are more productive than domestic firms. Van Den Bulcke (1981) showed this for Belgium. Castellani and Zanfei (2006) present similar results for a sample of Italian firms. The next section provides a general overview of the sector distribution of firms by type of ownership.

Sector analysis

Figure 3.4 displays the sector distribution of the firms in the sample. The primary sector, which includes both agricultural and mining activities (NACE sectors 1–14), is clearly the smallest sector, accounting for about 2 per cent of the number of firms and even less in terms of total employment and value added creation. Almost 12 per cent of all firms in the sample are active in manufacturing (NACE sectors 15–37), accounting for 31 per cent of total employment generation and 35 per cent for value added. This implies that more than 80 per cent of all firms are active in services (including construction, NACE sectors 40–99), representing more than 60 per cent of employment and value added created during 1996–2005.

In order to streamline the discussion, it was decided to rely on the sector classification for manufacturing and services as established by Eurostat (2006). For manufacturing, this classification is based on the Eurostat/OECD system, which uses the ratio of R&D to value added and production to rank (3-digit) industries according to their technology intensity (Eurostat, 2006). On the basis of this ranking, manufacturing industries are classified into four groups: low-technology (LTM), medium-low-technology (MLTM), medium-high-technology (MHTM) and high-technology (HTM). For services, a primary distinction is made between knowledge-intensive (KIS) and less-knowledge-intensive services (LKIS); and within the first group a further distinction is made between high-technology (HTKIS), market (MKIS) and financial (FKIS) knowledge-intensive services (Eurostat, 2006). Table 3.3 provides a breakdown of both classifications, in terms of the NACE sectors included in each category.

The primary task in this section is to identify sectors in which multinational firms (either foreign or domestic) are concentrated. Industrial concentration can be calculated using either employment or net value added data,[10] and measures whether firms from a specific group (either uninational, domestic MNE or foreign MNE) generate a higher

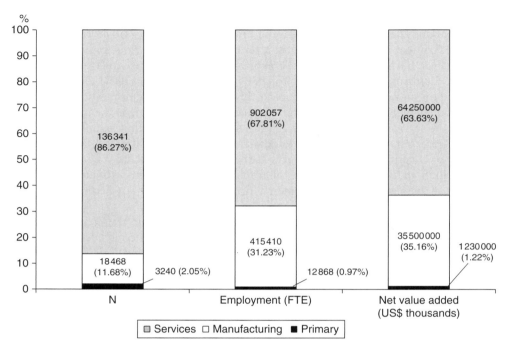

Source: Authors' calculations based on Bureau Van Dijk (2006).

Figure 3.4   Sector distribution of firms in Belgium (1996–2005)

share of employment or value added in that specific industry, compared to the industry's overall share in employment or value added (Zhang and Van Den Bulcke, 2000). Specifically, the industrial concentration ratio is calculated as follows:

$$ICR_{jt,Own} = \frac{\dfrac{\sum\limits_{i \in j} X_{it,Own}}{\sum\limits_{\forall i} X_{it,Own}}}{\dfrac{\sum\limits_{i \in j} X_{it}}{\sum\limits_{\forall i} X_{it}}}$$

where i represents firm, t years, j sectors, *Own* refers to ownership status, and X can be employment or net value added. A specific ownership group is overrepresented in a particular sector if its industrial concentration ratio exceeds 1 and underrepresented if the ratio is smaller than 1.

The sector distribution of firms for manufacturing and services respectively is given in Figures 3.5 and 3.6. As discussed above, sectors are classified according to their technology and knowledge intensity. The values in the figures represent percentages of the total

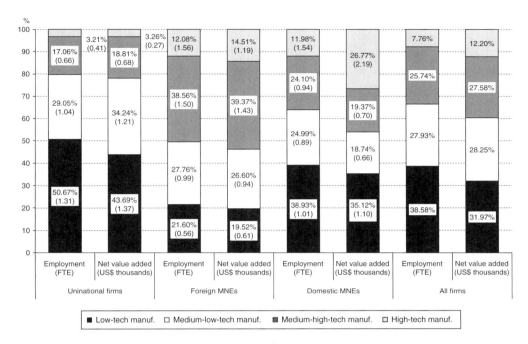

Source: Authors' calculations based on Bureau Van Dijk (2006).

Figure 3.5 *Distribution of Belgian manufacturing firms, by ownership and level of technology: employment and net value added (2005)*

employment or value added generated by each ownership group (uninational, domestic or foreign MNE). The industrial concentration ratio is given in parentheses.[11]

For manufacturing, Figure 3.5 indicates that uninational firms tend to be strongly concentrated in sectors with a medium-low to low technology intensity (e.g. food, textiles, paper, plastics etc.), while foreign MNEs are overrepresented in medium-high to high-technology-intensive sectors, such as chemicals and computers. Domestic MNEs are concentrated in high-technology manufacturing, and particularly so in terms of value added creation. Overall, more than half of manufacturing activities in Belgium are concentrated in the medium-low to low-technology-intensive segment, in terms of both value added and employment generation.

For services, Figure 3.6 shows that the bulk of all service activities in Belgium are concentrated in the less-knowledge-intensive sectors, such as transport activities, hotels and restaurants, and wholesale and retail trade. Foreign MNEs tend to be concentrated in market- or high-tech knowledge-intensive sectors (KIS), such as air and water transport, real estate and computer services. Domestic MNEs are overrepresented in financial KIS and high-tech KIS.

Belgian clusters of competitiveness
The Institute for Strategy and Competitiveness has put forward 38 clusters, including apparel, automotive, business services, chemicals, biopharmaceuticals, plastics and

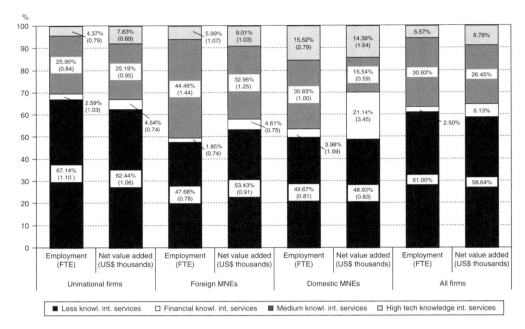

Source: Authors' calculations based on Bureau Van Dijk (2006).

Figure 3.6   *Distribution of Belgian service firms, by ownership and level of knowledge: employment and net value added (2005)*

textiles.[12] An analysis of the size, specialization and dominance of these clusters in Belgium lists some of the following sectors: textiles (carpets and other woven-textile floor coverings, tufted carpets, vegetable textile fibres), chemicals (especially organic chemicals), automotive (passenger transport vehicles), biopharmaceuticals (glycosides, hormones, antiserum, vaccines and similar products; miscellaneous medicaments), jewellery (diamonds), and plastics (polymers). These sectors demonstrate a leading position both by world export share and by world export value. The life sciences have become an important and booming sector in Belgium. Both chemical products and biopharmaceuticals (biotechnological and pharmaceutical products) are clearly some of the most dominant and growing sectors, and will form the focus of analysis in the next section.

Life sciences
Belgium has a long tradition in what is now called the life sciences.[13] The chemical industry, for instance, is an example of an indigenous industry that was first set up in Belgium by now world-renowned companies – such as Solvay, Union Chimique Belge (UCB) and Agfa Gevaert – that have globalized over time (OECD, 1992). The research activities of Janssen Pharmaceutica were launched by the late Dr Paul Janssen in 1953. In 1961, Janssen joined Johnson & Johnson, and in Belgium alone Janssen Pharmaceutica employs some 4500 people. In the biopharma and biotechnology sector, Belgium has seen a major growth of companies over recent years. Home companies with an international

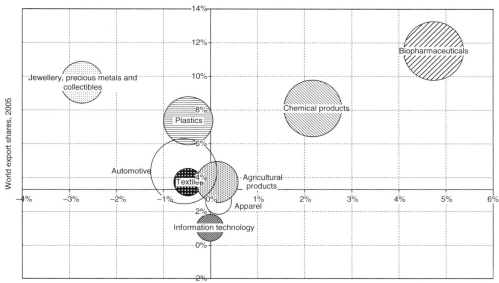

Change in Belgium's share of world exports, 1999–2005

Sources: Authors' calculations based on UN Commodity Trade Statistics Database; IMF Balance of Payments Statistics; Institute for Strategy and Competitiveness (2007).

Figure 3.7 Belgian clusters of competitiveness

reputation include Innogenetics, Tibotec and Virco, while overseas firms have also formed bases in the region, such as Genzyme and International Brachytherapy.

The chemical industry is the second-largest manufacturing sector in Belgium. The chemical sector generates over one-fifth of the turnover of the Belgian industrial sector and the total Belgian exports. In terms of turnover within the European chemical industry, Belgium ranks fifth after Germany, France, Italy and the UK but ahead of the Netherlands and Spain. In terms of turnover per capita, only Ireland precedes Belgium, which scores about twice as high as the Netherlands and nearly three times higher than Germany, France, Japan and the USA (Fedichem, 2006).

The yearly average turnover growth of the chemical industry reached almost 5 per cent between 1995 and 2005. Belgium's immediate neighbours, Ireland and the USA are the major trading partners in chemicals. The geographic breakdown shows that the EU accounts for about 72 per cent of total Belgian chemical exports. Within the EU, Germany, France and the Netherlands remain the major trade partners, which, combined, account for more than 60 per cent of Belgium's intra-European exports in chemicals. Worldwide, the USA is the third-largest export market, with a share of about 12 per cent. The EU accounts for more than 80 per cent of the total imports of chemicals in Belgium. The neighbouring countries (France, Germany and the Netherlands), traditionally Belgium's main trading partners, accounted for 44 per cent of the total imports of chemical products in 2005. Since 2002, France and the Netherlands have been outranked by Ireland as a key supplier, a consequence of the expansion of a major distribution centre of pharmaceutical products, importing from Ireland and distributing all over the world.

The number of jobs in the chemical sector is estimated to have reached 93 800 in 2005, while the employment share of the chemical industry in the manufacturing industry in general has grown to 16 per cent in 2005 compared to 14 per cent in 1995. Apart from direct employment inside the sector, the chemical industry generates, through its activities, indirect employment in other sectors of the economy such as transportation, accountancy, ICT and wholesale. On average, each direct job in chemicals generates 1.5 indirect jobs in the Belgian economy. Moreover, the chemical industry in Belgium is characterized by an important layer of small and medium-sized enterprises. It is interesting to note that about 75 per cent of the chemical companies employ fewer than 100 people. According to the latest figures from Fedichem, the chemical employers' federation, about 25 000 people work for chemical-related wholesale activities. If those wholesale activities are included, the chemical sector directly generates more than 120 000 jobs in the Belgian economy (Fedichem, 2006).

One of the chemical sector's main characteristics is its high degree of internationalization. More than 75 per cent of the total investment value in the chemical industry in Belgium originates from foreign-based parent companies. Expenditure on R&D within the chemical industry in Belgium amounted to €2.15 billion in 2005, an increase of 7.5 per cent compared to 2004. The share of 'life sciences', i.e. including pharmaceuticals and biotechnology, increased steadily during the last few years. In 2005, this share was about 70 per cent. Moreover, the chemical industry is responsible for nearly half of the total R&D expenditures in the private sector in Belgium.

A large number of chemical companies have plants in the different regions of Belgium. These factories complement each other and are part of the local cluster and European network created by these companies. With a turnover of over €34 billion, the chemical industry in the Flemish region represents 73 per cent of the total turnover of the chemical sector in Belgium. The port of Antwerp is located in the centre of the world's largest and most diversified petrochemical cluster, the Antwerp–Rotterdam area.

The growth of Antwerp as a chemical cluster stretches back half a century. From the mid-1950s until 1970, the port experienced a boom in petrochemical investments and production. Another build-up of facilities developed during the 1980s in organic chemistry. The investments continue in what is now a third wave of expansion, this time in fine and speciality chemicals. Companies gain from the cluster effect. They are able to integrate their operations with those of other companies, particularly suppliers, in a stable business and production environment. In terms of infrastructure, the presence of a large cluster means that energy, utility and transport facilities are available and that specialized logistics service providers and equipment are close at hand. The port of Antwerp is the major hub of the Western European pipeline system and, in addition, Antwerp's own pipelines are the main transport mode for product exchanges between companies within the port. Some firms have even decided to co-site on the same plant to take cooperation even further (such as Bayer, Ineos and Monsanto).

The chemical sector in the Walloon region represented 19 per cent of total turnover of the Belgian chemical sector in 2005. Base chemical manufacturing activities are mainly concentrated in the province of Hainaut. In addition, Wallonia has an important biotechnological pole and high-tech pharmaceutical industry in the province of Walloon Brabant and the North Hainaut area. Wallonia-based companies account for 28 per cent of total R&D expenditures of the chemical sector in Belgium.

Despite a comparatively modest contribution to the sector's turnover (8 per cent), the Region of Brussels-Capital remains an essential link in the chain of activities of the chemical sector in Belgium. While only a few chemical production facilities are located in this region, it is home to various head offices and coordination centres (see above). The proximity of several international organizations and institutions adds another incentive for information and consultation.

Conclusions

This chapter has analysed the contribution of multinational enterprises to Belgium's economic success within the framework of Porter's diamond. Several salient conclusions emerge from this analysis.

First, Belgium is the quintessential example of the small open economy. Its prime location in the heart of political and economic Europe has enabled it to grow into a highly internationally oriented economy. Locational advantages, such as relatively low real-estate costs, favourable taxation measures and economic advantages, such as high labour productivity, form the basis of this success. Furthermore, Belgium's economy is substantially more open than that of most of its European neighbours, with the ratio of exports to GDP amounting to 85 per cent and the ratio of inward FDI stocks to GDP reaching 137 per cent in 2005. This high degree of openness is characterized by regional concentration, with the majority of trade and investment taking place with other EU countries.

Second, this open-economy nature of Belgium is also reflected in the presence and contribution of multinational firms. Although multinational firms, either foreign or domestic, represent less than 5 per cent of the total number of active firms in Belgium, they account for more than 30 per cent of employment and 40 per cent of value added generated between 1996 and 2005. Multinationals also tend to be larger, more productive and capital-intensive, and pay higher wages than national firms. Furthermore, multinational firms tend to be relatively more represented in medium-high to high-technology-intensive sectors, such as chemicals and computers, compared to uninational domestic companies.

The trends outlined above were illustrated for the chemical industry in Belgium. This sector is a particularly interesting case, given Belgium's long tradition in the life sciences and its high degree of internationalization. More than 75 per cent of total investment in the Belgium chemical industry originates from foreign-based companies. Moreover, the chemical industry accounts for more than half of total private R&D expenditures in Belgium.

Notes

1. Coordination centres, sometimes known as shared services centres, are used by multinational groups to centralize tasks, such as financing and R&D, and provide them to other parts of a group. From 1983, after discussions with the European Commission, the Belgian authorities applied a favourable tax regime, including lower corporation tax, capital duty, property tax and withholding tax, to these establishments. In 2003, the European Commission declared that the reliefs amounted to state aid and did not comply with the EC Treaty. Coordination centres whose ten-year period of approval was under way were allowed to avail themselves of the benefits of the scheme until the end of that period until 31 December 2010 at the latest. The Commission banned Belgium from renewing approvals when they expired after the end of 2005.
2. The central idea behind this incentive is to let companies that use their own equity for investments deduct a fictitious or 'notional' interest from their tax base. In this way the differences in the tax treatment between risk capital and debt capital will be eliminated.

3. China has enacted a new indirect tax law as from 1 January 2009. It changed from a production-based to a consumption-based system, thereby eliminating the value-added tax on equipment. Together with the new company income tax law from 2008 this will substantially reduce the effective tax rate in China, although most tax incentives for foreign invested enterprises have been revoked.
4. FDI statistics for Belgium and Luxembourg used to be incorporated in the Belgium–Luxembourg Economic Union (BLEU), and only reported on an aggregated level for both countries together. FDI data have only been separated since 2002. Older data are not comparable as they include data for Luxembourg, and are mentioned only as a point of reference.
5. For a review of the literature dealing with home- and host-country effects of FDI, see Lipsey (2002).
6. Limited-liability firms have to file their annual accounts and/or consolidated accounts with the National Bank of Belgium. The database therefore consists of the complete population of limited-liability firms in Belgium.
7. Appendix A provides a definition of the variables used.
8. Companies reporting their annual accounts to the National Bank are required only to report data on turnover (and a number of other variables) once a certain threshold is reached in terms of number of employees, turnover and/or total assets. This implies that data on turnover are missing for the majority of firms in the sample; hence value added is used as a proxy for total sales.
9. Bernard and Jensen (1995) perform a similar exercise for exporters versus non-exporters in the US manufacturing sector. Castellani and Zanfei (2006) similarly compare innovative and productive performances of firms exhibiting different degrees of internationalization (domestic uninational firms versus exporters versus different types of multinational firms).
10. Industrial concentration can also be calculated on the basis of total assets, number of firms, etc.
11. The industrial concentration ratio can be calculated by taking the ratio of the share of a particular sector for a particular ownership group and the corresponding share for all firms (displayed in the last two stacked columns in the figure). For instance, for uninational firms that are active in high-tech manufacturing, the corresponding ratio amounts to 3.21/7.76 or 0.41, as indicated in parentheses in Figure 3.5.
12. Porter initially put forward 41 clusters, which were formed by firms from various industrial sectors working together. The translation of the 879 SIC codes into the European NACE codes meant that three clusters literally got 'lost in translation'.
13. The term 'life sciences' is used as a comprehensive term for the chemical, pharmaceutical and biotechnological sectors, although it sometimes refers to a more restrictive definition of biotechnology firms. The pharmaceutical manufacturing industry (NACE 244) is part of the larger chemical industry (24), while the biotechnological sector (research and experimental development on natural sciences and engineering, NACE 731) is quite separate.

References

AMCHAM (2008), *US Direct Investment in Belgium 2008 Report*, Brussels: American Chamber of Commerce.
Bernard, A.B. and J.B. Jensen (1995), 'Exporters, jobs and wages in US manufacturing 1976–1987', *Brookings Papers on Economic Activity: Microeconomics*, 67–119.
Bernard, A.B., and J.B. Jensen (2007), 'Firm structure, multinationals and manufacturing plant deaths', *The Review of Economics and Statistics*, **89** (2), 193–204.
Bernard, A.B. and F. Sjöholm (2003), 'Foreign owners and plant survival', *NBER Working Paper 10039*, Cambridge, MA.
Bowen, H., J.G. Chavez, K. De Witte and W. Moesen (2007), 'The position of Flanders in the World Economic Forum Competitiveness Ranking', Steunpunt Ondernemen en Internationaal Ondernemen, http://www.ondernemen.be.
Bureau Van Dijk (2006), *Belfirst Database* (DVD-ROM, November).
Castellani, D. and A. Zanfei (2006), *Multinational Firms, Innovation and Productivity*, Cheltenham, UK and Northampton, MA, USA: Edward Elgar.
DTZ (2006) *Global Office Occupancy Costs Survey*, http://www.dtz.com.
Eurostat (2006), *High-technology Manufacturing and Knowledge-intensive Services Sectors*, Luxembourg: Statistical office of the European Communities.
Fedichem (2006), 'Chemical industries in Belgium', http://www.fedichem.be.
Görg, H. and E. Strobl (2003), '"Footloose" multinationals?', *The Manchester School*, **71** (1), 1–19.
IMD (2006), *IMD World Competitiveness Yearbook 2006*, Lausanne: Institute for Management Development.
IMF (2006), *World Economic Outlook Database*, Washington, DC: IMF.
Institute for Strategy and Competitiveness (2007), 'International Cluster Competitiveness Project', Harvard Business School, http://data.isc.hbs.edu/iccp.

Konings, J. (2005), 'Wage costs and industry (re)location in the enlarged European Union', *Swedish Economic Policy Review*, **12**, 57–81.

Lipsey, R.E. (2002), 'Home and host country effects of FDI', NBER Working Paper Series 9293.

Mintz, J.M. (2006), 'The 2006 Tax Competitiveness Report: proposals for pro-growth tax reforms', C.D. Howe Institute Commentary 239, C.D. Howe Institute, Ottowa, Canada.

OECD (1992), *International Direct Investment: Policies and Trends in the 1980s*, Paris: OECD.

POA (2007) *Annual Report 2006*, Antwerp: Port of Antwerp.

UNCTAD (2006), *World Investment Report 2006*, Geneva: United Nations.

Van Beveren, I. (2007), 'Footloose multinationals in Belgium?', *Review of World Economics*, **143** (3), 483–507.

Van Den Bulcke, D. (1981), *De buitenlandse ondernemingen in de Belgische industrie*, Gent: SERUG.

Van Den Bulcke, D., J.J. Boddewyn, B. Martens and P. Klemmer (1979), *Investment and Divestment Policies of Multinational Corporations in Europe*, Farnborough, UK: Saxon House.

Vandenbussche, H. and C. Tan (2005), 'The taxation of multinationals: Firm level evidence for Belgium', LICOS Discussion Paper 160/2005, Licos Centre for Transition Economics, KU Leuven, Belgium.

Zhang, H. and D. Van Den Bulcke (2000), 'The ownership structure of Belgian companies: evidence about a small open economy in the globalisation process', Discussion Paper No. 2000/E/42, Centre for International Management and Development Antwerp, http://www.ua.ac.be/cimda.

Appendix A

Definition variables:

Age_{it}	Difference between year t and the official year of incorporation
Emp_{it}	Average number of employees (full-time equivalents, fte) in year *t*
$Wage_{it}$	'Remunerations, social security costs and pensions' per employee (fte), measured in thousands of US$
VA_{it}	Net value added, measured in thousands of US$
TFA_{it}	Total fixed assets, measured in thousands of US$. Used as proxy for capital
For_i	Foreign multinational ownership variable. A firm is considered to be foreign owned if it has some foreign ownership
Dom_i	Domestic multinational ownership variable. A firm is identified as a domestic MNE if it has subsidiaries in countries other than Belgium and is not foreign owned

Data source: Belfirst database (Bureau Van Dijk, 2006).

Table 3A.1   Sector classification according to technology and knowledge intensity

Manufacturing			Services		
Sector	NACE code	Description	Sector	NACE code	Description
Low-technology manufacturing (LTM)	15–22	Food, beverages, tobacco, textiles, clothing, leather, wood, paper, publishing	Less-knowledge-intensive services (LKIS)	50–52	Retail & wholesale trade
				55	Hotels & restaurants
				60	Land transport
				63	Supporting transport activities
	36–37	Recycling & manufacturing n.e.c.		75	Public administration/defence
				90–99	Other service activities
Medium-low-technology manufacturing (MLTM)	23	Coke & petroleum products	Financial knowledge-intensive services (FKIS)	65–67	Financial intermediation
	25–28	Rubber, plastic, metals, non-metallic mineral products			
	351	Building/repairing of ships			
Medium-high-technology manufacturing (MHTM)	24	Chemicals (excluding 244)	Market-knowledge-intensive services (MIKS)	61	Water transport
	29	Machinery, equipment		62	Air transport
	31	Electrical machinery		70	Real-estate activities
	34	Motor vehicles		71	Renting activities
	35	Other transport equipment (excluding 351 & 353)		74	Other business activities
High-technology manufacturing (HTM)	244	Pharmaceuticals	High-tech knowledge-intensive services (HTKIS)	64	Post & telecommunications
	30	Office machinery/computers		72	Computer & related

Source: Eurostat (2006).

4 Porter's diamond and small nations in the global economy: Ireland as a case study

John Cassidy, Frank Barry and Chris van Egeraat

The Irish economy has boomed in recent years and become a model economy, particularly for EU accession countries. This chapter sets out to provide a deeper understanding of Ireland's success in the context of Porter's 'diamond' model of national competitiveness. A number of analyses have been done in Ireland on the relevance of Porter's diamond theory to national competitiveness. O'Connell et al. adopted a Porter diamond analysis in examining clusters in the Irish dairy industry (1997); O'Gorman et al. (1997) examined national competitive advantage through clusters in the Irish software sector; and Clancy et al. (2001) similarly examined industry clusters in Ireland in relation to the software industry, the dairy industry and the popular music industry. These aforementioned papers summarize the determinants of national competitive advantage and provide critiques of Porter's diamond theory in the context of Ireland, notably in regard to the important role of FDI (foreign direct investment) in the Irish economy.

Criticisms of Porter's model point to its lack of precision, its determinacy, its strong predictive ability and its irrefutability (Beije and Nuys, 1995; Davies et al., 1995; Grant, 1991; Rugman and D'Cruz, 1993). What unifies these analyses is the perception that Porter's model does not explain the success of small open economies such as Canada, Finland, New Zealand and Ireland, where favourable domestic demand conditions are unlikely to prevail simultaneously and rivalry between domestic companies may not be significant (Bellak and Weiss, 1993; O'Donnell, 1997; O'Donnellan, 1994; Rugman and D'Cruz, 1993; Rugman and Verbeke, 2003). Porter (1990) sees the role of MNEs (multinational enterprises) as potentially acting as a catalyst to the emergence of a cluster in the form of sophisticated customers or related industries. He does not perceive them as a driving force of competitiveness. A whole body of literature has emerged in recent years supporting the economic multiplier effect to be had from MNE location.

Porter's diamond (1990, 1998) identifies four determinants of national competitiveness: factor conditions, demand conditions, related and supporting industries, and firm strategy, structure and rivalry. Both the role of government and that of chance are seen as additional variables that influence the four determinants. He argues that the process of clustering is critical to the success of this system.

This chapter is an analysis of three of the most successful international industries in Ireland through the prism of Porter's diamond determinants. The industries highlighted are: the ICT hardware sector, the ICT software sector and the pharmaceuticals sector. The first section profiles Ireland based on the Porter diamond perspective and the international sectors chosen, while the second examines inward and outward FDI in Ireland with reference to these sectors. The third section examines the type of inward investments in Ireland and why they were attracted to Ireland as a location. The relative level of embeddedness of subsidiaries is also analysed based on Taggart's (1998) classification

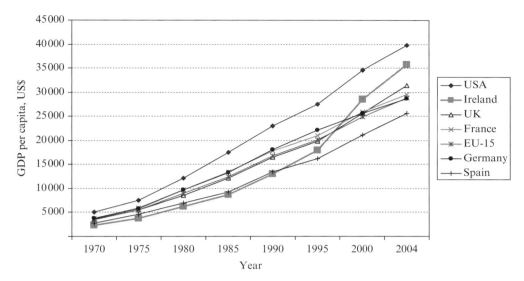

Note: ^a GNP is often preferred to GDP, given the distorting effect of MNEs through transfer pricing. In 2006, Ireland's Central Statistics Office reported GDP per capita of €40,648 and GNP per capita of €34,848 – a differential of 16.6 per cent. Interestingly, in 2003, 2005 and 2006 GNP growth rates have superseded those of GDP due to strong domestic performance.

Source: www.oecd.org.

Figure 4.1 GDP per capita of selected countries at current prices, PPP basis^a (US$), 1970–2004

of decision making and integration of activities. Next outward direct investment from the aforementioned sectors is addressed, together with the reasons for their chosen destinations as well as the clustering effect and cluster formation in regard to the successful industries. An analysis of the role of government policy, which has been a crucial catalyst in the story of Irish economic success, concludes the chapter.

Ireland, Porter's diamond and the ICT hardware, ICT software and pharmaceutical sectors

Background
In recent years, the Irish economy has been characterized by high growth rates, low inflation, balance-of-payments surpluses, sound public finances and low unemployment, and has emerged as one of Europe's fastest-growing economies. Figure 4.1 shows GDP per capita across selected countries, 1970–2004. From 1994 to 2001, GDP at PPP (purchasing power parity) grew at an annual rate of 9.7 per cent. The EU average for the corresponding period was 4.4 per cent. This was a marked contrast with Ireland in the latter part of the 1980s, when high unemployment, balance-of-payment deficits and emigration were the order of the day and the economic future looked bleak.

What caused this turnaround? In an age of globalization, judicious government policies in the realm of education, a young, highly skilled and relatively low-cost workforce, the attraction of FDI, and sound macroeconomic management provided the platform for an Irish economic resurrection. Partnership programmes between the government, trade unions and employers on the broad direction of economic and social policy were crucial. Whereas, in the past, emigration was the only choice for the young, in its stead, immigration, notably from EU accession countries, has provided an added boost to Ireland's strong economic growth. Asymmetric shocks notwithstanding, Ireland's strong performance is expected to continue in the short to medium term.

The role of FDI in Ireland's economic about-face cannot be overstated and the low corporate tax of 12.5 per cent provided fertile ground for MNE subsidiaries to flourish in the Irish ecosystem. Globalization through membership in the EU and WTO (World Trade Organization), grant incentives, EU transfers, an educated workforce, competitive wage costs, an English speaking population and the responsiveness of government policy to MNE skills requirements have made Ireland an attractive location, particularly for US companies. Irish culture, characterized by (Hofstede's) high uncertainty avoidance, as well as flexibility and creativity, has also been seen as vital.

The ICT hardware, ICT software and pharmaceutical sectors proved to be of particular economic importance in the provision of skilled jobs (still a fundamental political and strategic policy issue, recent low unemployment levels notwithstanding), export earnings, and engagement in the virtuous circles of globally competitive networks. The success of the MNE sector contrasts with the traditional indigenous sectors, which have lost competitiveness, particularly in manufacturing. In recent years, the domestic sectors that have shown strong growth have been software, dairy, medical devices and the popular-music industry. Importantly, in 2006 growth in exports from the indigenous sectors was higher than in the multinational sector for the first time, reflecting the increasing dynamism of indigenous companies but also the competitiveness challenges facing MNEs located in Ireland due to increased operating costs, particularly in the ICT hardware sector.

Ireland's low corporate tax rate at 12.5 per cent is often cited as the main reason for MNEs locating in Ireland. Figure 4.2 shows corporate tax rates across selected countries in 2005. There was a downward trend in corporate tax rates from 2004 to 2005, with Germany down from 38.29 per cent to 26.38 per cent, France down from 34.33 per cent to 33.33 per cent, Finland down from 29 per cent to 26 per cent, Italy down from 37.25 per cent to 33 per cent, and the USA down from 40 per cent to 35 per cent.

Ireland, an island country, has limited natural resources apart from reasonably fertile land. By virtue of being an island off the northwestern Eurasian landmass, Ireland has access to a continental shelf and its fishery resources. The southern part of the island has particularly fertile land. The agricultural sector, however, is circumscribed by EU membership and the Common Agricultural Policy (CAP). Politically, the agriculture lobby is strong in Ireland, as it is in France and Japan, and WTO demands for CAP reform are problematic. Nevertheless, a globally competitive dairy industry has emerged, and its cluster provides an interesting comparison to that of New Zealand. Counterintuitively, although Ireland is an island country, its fisheries sector has not developed, as it was assigned a low priority on entry into the Common Market in 1973 in favour of agriculture, with its greater political importance.

Much of Ireland's economic success in recent years has been attributed to the prescience of the Lemass government in the 1960s with respect to education policy and its free

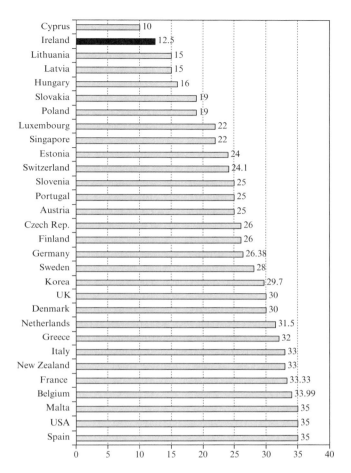

Cyprus	10
Ireland	12.5
Lithuania	15
Latvia	15
Hungary	16
Slovakia	19
Poland	19
Luxembourg	22
Singapore	22
Estonia	24
Switzerland	24.1
Slovenia	25
Portugal	25
Austria	25
Czech Rep.	26
Finland	26
Germany	26.38
Sweden	28
Korea	29.7
UK	30
Denmark	30
Netherlands	31.5
Greece	32
Italy	33
New Zealand	33
France	33.33
Belgium	33.99
Malta	35
USA	35
Spain	35

Note: New Zealand and Switzerland data based on KPMG (2004).

Source: Deloitte and Touche (2005).

Figure 4.2   Corporate tax rates for selected countries (%), 2005

market philosophy. Indeed, Ireland was one of the first European countries to grasp the economic importance of education for economic success (OECD, 2006). The historic achievements of ending mass unemployment and mass emigration could not have been realized without the dramatic increase in participation at secondary and tertiary levels of education. High birth rates particularly in the 1970s and 1980s led to a high dependency ratio, which, while a short-term economic burden, would later translate into a pool of relatively low-cost, educated and skilled employees.

Porter's diamond – the ICT hardware, ICT software and pharmaceutical sectors
Given Ireland's low corporate tax regime, transfer-pricing issues have arisen in recent years. Thus, to measure sustainable production, employment rather than production or

exports is generally considered to represent a more accurate measure of a sector's presence in the economy.

In examining the competitiveness of the selected sectors *vis-à-vis* Porter's diamond, Table 4.1 summarizes the key points. In this section the ICT hardware, ICT software and pharmaceutical sectors will be examined. The hardware sector is predominantly multinational; the software sector is multinational with a dynamic domestic sector. As shown in Table 4.1, the ICT sector in Ireland is vital for employment (see also Box 4.1). It commands global and European market leadership, including the leading global companies. It accounts for a disproportionate percentage of Irish exports and is dynamic in terms of local employment generation creation. It is beginning to develop R&D capacities rather than purely manufacturing, taking advantage of Ireland's higher proportion of science graduates than other EU countries. It also contributes strongly to the value-added component of Irish GDP.

Box 4.2 demonstrates the economic significance of the pharmaceutical and chemical industries to the Irish economy. It provides highly skilled jobs, is the main sector for exports, accounting for 45 per cent of total exports in 2004, and the levels of R&D activity are increasing.

The ICT hardware sector   In Ireland, the ICT hardware industry benefits from the availability of skilled and relatively low-cost labour, though recent wage increases are creating a competitive challenge. High-level skills are of more relevance in the manufacture of Intel microprocessors than in the assembly of Dell computers. Both companies have locations in Ireland and their taxes and export earnings contribute disproportionately to the exchequer. Given the small population of Ireland (an estimated 4.3 million in 2006), domestic demand is limited. Ireland buys only 2 per cent of the ICT hardware it produces. In the context of domestic demand, the Irish state is an important customer, accounting for as much as 50 per cent of domestic demand for Dell products annually.

ICT hardware companies are located in Ireland as a platform for access to the EU market. They locate in Ireland to take advantage of low corporate tax rates[1] and access to low-cost skilled and unskilled labour. ICT hardware companies in Ireland view their Irish operation as the parent operation for the EMEA region (Europe, Middle East and Africa), with Asia sometimes included (EMEAA). Sourcing from domestic companies is limited (see the section below on clustering). Logistics in the form of trucking companies are well developed. The targeting and pursuit of these ICT MNEs by the IDA (Industrial Development Association Ireland) coincided with their globalizing strategies. It has been argued that Ireland's strength in manufacturing and logistics goes back to its colonial infrastructure. The UK is still a major export market and conduit for exports to other markets. In 2006, Intel exported goods to the value of €3 billion to/through the UK and on to other markets.

In terms of firms' strategy, structure and rivalry, no subsidiaries compete with one another. Subsidiaries are nodes in a global network. Dell imports finished Intel chips from the UK. English is the spoken language. Culturally, the Irish understand the US psychology and have mutual trust. Ireland ranks higher than the UK and the USA in uncertainty avoidance. Irish national culture is seen as an important determinant of competitiveness – it has flexibility and creativity. Florida (2002) ranked Ireland number one on his global index of creativity.

Table 4.1   *Porter's diamond – the Irish ICT hardware, software and pharmaceutical sectors*

Porter's diamond	Hardware sector	Software sector	Pharmaceutical sector
Factor conditions	Availability of low-skilled and high-skilled low-cost labour. Good telecommunications and physical infrastructure and logistics. Low corporate taxes. Also entitled to financial/other government supports	High-skilled relatively low-cost labour; high percentage of tertiary-level graduates. Low corporate taxes. MNE and indigenous companies entitled to financial/other government supports. Software education and research. Internet infrastructure, formerly competitive, now low broadband penetration. Winmax certification supported by Intel 2006	Initially: low corporate tax and ample supply of both low-cost unskilled and suitably qualified labour (chemical engineers). Since the 1990s, low corporation tax, qualified and increasingly specialized labour; fiscal and financial incentives for R&D activities through Science Foundation Ireland and an upgrading of the institutional research infrastructure through the Programme for Research in Third-Level Institutions, launched in 1998, and the Science Foundation Ireland, launched in 2000
Demand conditions	Global – domestic market very small (2%). Global integration through EU and WTO means that market is EMEA (Europe, Middle East and Africa) region followed by USA and Asia.	Indigenous companies: strong domestic demand but primarily international. Domestic customers in banking & financial services and process flow industries. MNEs: many of them trade with each other, many never sell to other MNEs in Ireland. Sophisticated demand: prevalence of MNEs – exacting standards; strong export competitiveness of indigenous sector	Insignificant strategic importance of the Irish market has no impact on competitiveness of the Irish companies and means that Ireland is at a disadvantage compared to some of the larger markets in attracting FDI
Related & supporting industries	Limited local vertical manufacturing linkages. Strong logistics. Strong manufacturing culture	Software development has linkages into the Irish ecosystem – Microsoft gets graduates from universities/ITs,	Pharmaceutical plants in Ireland have very few local raw material supply linkages. Attraction of FDI is facilitated by a substantial number

Table 4.1   (continued)

Porter's diamond	Hardware sector	Software sector	Pharmaceutical sector
		involved with Science Foundation Ireland for R&D grants. Links to MNE ICT hardware, the MNE telecom sector as well as other MNEs, and indigenous companies with large ICT depts. Most indigenous Irish IT software entrepreneurs have work experience in other indigenous software companies or MNEs	of multinational process engineering and construction management companies, increasingly specialized in pharmaceutical projects. (The competitive dairy processing and brewing sectors may be regarded as related industries)
Firms' strategy structure and rivalry	Globalization strategies; access to EU market; competitors are in Ireland. Access to low tax base. Access to low-cost skilled labour. Sector stagnating. No subsidiary–subsidiary rivalry in MNE sector	Indigenous companies, small or medium sized: have niche product specialization, very export market focussed. Small Irish market, influence of the state development agencies directing their export strategy. Technical competence is high but marketing expertise is perceived as low. No subsidiary–subsidiary rivalry in MNE sector – but strong among indigenous firms	Strategy and structure influenced by developments in main markets and new technologies. Much M&A activity on global level. Strategy determined at global HQ. Strategy of tax avoidance, supported by complex corporate structures and facilitated by Irish taxation policies, increases attractiveness of Ireland as location for manufacturing as well as R&D and other value-added activities. Very little evidence of subsidiary–subsidiary rivalry playing any role in driving the efficiency/competitiveness of the sector in Ireland
Role of government	Critical. IDA (Industrial Development Association) targeting of top MNEs. Government policy on ICT sector created relevant	Critical. Provision of grants at start-up, equity involvement by state agencies, employment grants. Provision of skilled employees through responsiveness of	Critical. Low corporate tax rate. Since the 2000s, growing fiscal and financial incentives supporting R&D projects. Quality of the IDA actions and its strategy of targeting the

Table 4.1   (continued)

Porter's diamond	Hardware sector	Software sector	Pharmaceutical sector
	advanced factors in terms of skills and infrastructure. Proactive and reactive to IT skill needs. Created a facilitative environment not least in regard to the low corporate tax base	education system. Focused indigenous companies towards export market. Low corporate tax rate. Quality of IDA strategy. Upgrading of factor conditions and development of factor-creating mechanisms (tertiary-level education and, recently R&D infrastructure)	pharmaceutical sector since the 1970s. Upgrading of factor conditions and development of factor-creating mechanisms (tertiary-level education and, recently, R&D infrastructure)
Role of chance	Low due to proactive government policy in providing qualified personnel and good business environment, not least low tax	Low due to proactive government policy in providing qualified personnel and good business environment, not least low tax	Low. The low corporation tax rates and factor-creating mechanisms were generally put in place specifically to attract the pharmaceutical companies

The Irish government has been critical in terms of creating the fertile ground – 'the ecosystem' – for MNEs to flourish. The low corporate tax rate was, of course, key. But the Irish government also makes itself available and responds to the needs of MNEs. Realistically, the EU today is the major decision maker. The Irish government lobbies on behalf of MNEs, particularly US MNEs, at the EU level. The low corporate tax rate of 12.5 per cent is in place until 2015. Despite threats, it is unlikely that the EU will bring it down as Ireland has proved itself an example of what the EU can achieve. In 2007 Ireland became a net contributor to the EU.

The computer hardware sector consists of the data categories NACE 3002 (computer equipment) and NACE 3210 (electronic components). In the year 2000, these subsectors accounted for 0.6 per cent and 1 per cent of EU manufacturing employment. The data in Table 4.2 report the importance of these subsectors in the various EU-15 countries, relative to their overall importance in the EU.[2] Employment in both hardware segments is seen to be particularly important in two peripheral EU economies: Ireland and Scotland.[3] Table 4.3 shows the shares of individual countries in world exports of the two segments of the hardware industry in the equivalent SITC categories.[4]

The ICT software sector   As mentioned above, in recent years Ireland has become one of Europe's top locations for software development. In 2003, Ireland was the largest exporter of software in the world (IMD, 2003). In attracting multinational investment in this sector to Ireland, IDA Ireland, the agency or one-stop shop responsible for

---

BOX 4.1   KEY FACTS ABOUT THE ICT SECTOR IN IRELAND

- Employment of 90 700 people in over 1300 companies, up from 19 000 in 1990 (ICT Ireland, 2007)
- Over 300 overseas companies with a presence in Ireland, directly employing approximately 61 000 (Goodbody Stockbrokers)
- Ireland is the largest exporter of software in the world (*IMD World Competitiveness Yearbook 2003*)
- Seven of the world's top ten leading ICT companies have a substantial base in Ireland (IDA Ireland)
- One-third of all PCs sold in Europe are manufactured in Ireland (Eurostat)
- Turnover in the ICT sector was over €51 billion in 2001, with three of Ireland's top exporters (Dell, Microsoft and Intel) accounting for 18 per cent of total exports between them (Forfás)
- The top ten ICT companies in Ireland employ more people than they did at the beginning of 2000 (IDA Ireland)
- In 2002, 32 IDA-backed ICT companies undertook to invest €120 million in R&D (IDA Ireland)
- Ireland has a higher proportion of science graduates than any other EU member state (Eurostat)
- Value added in the ICT sector accounted for 11.6 per cent of Ireland's GDP in 2000, compared with an EU average of 5.1 per cent (Economic Intelligence Unit Business Environment Rankings)

Source: ICT Ireland (2007), based on data from Forfás (2007), Central Statistics Office, IDA Ireland.

FDI, focused on US companies. Some examples of such companies that have set up their European operations centres in the Dublin region since the 1980s are Microsoft, Symantec and Oracle. Ireland has become the main European location for software localization. The indigenous software industry is dynamic in nature, characterized by small firms and aided by public and private equity. The multinational branch of the Irish software sector is primarily packaged software or product companies. The indigenous companies in contrast are characterized by strong niche products with small volumes and an export orientation. The following section is drawn from extant research on the ICT software sector in Ireland by O'Gorman et al. (1997).

In terms of factor conditions, the quality of the labour force is very important, with a very high percentage of tertiary-level graduates. Low corporate taxes create the potential for greater access to profits depending on the financial structure of the company and the parent–subsidiary relationship. Indigenous companies are entitled to a range of financial and other supports from various government agencies, from start-up costs to employee pay. Infrastructure for software education and research is available at most of the universities, and notably the Tyndall Research Centre, University College Cork. In terms of competitive threats, broadband roll-out in Ireland is among the lowest in the EU.

BOX 4.2 KEY FACTS ABOUT THE PHARMACHEMICALS INDUSTRY IN IRELAND

- Employment during the last ten years has increased by over 56 per cent. The industry employs over 24 000 people, with over half of them tertiary graduates
- In 2004, exported products reached a value of €7.5 billion, accounting for some 44.7 per cent of national exports, and imported €50 billion (14 per cent of national imports)
- Ireland remains a location of choice for the manufacture of pharmaceutical and chemical products: 16 of the top 20 pharmaceutical companies in the world have established facilities in Ireland
- Wyeth Biopharma is constructing the largest biomanufacturing plant in the world in Ireland
- Bristol-Myers Squibb is constructing a brand new chemical synthesis plant at Cruizerath in Dublin
- The Japanese company Takeda announced the construction of a pharmaceuticals ingredient plant in Dublin, adding to the pharmaceutical finished products plant that it currently operates in Bray, County Wicklow
- Pfizer Pharmaceuticals are nearing completion on a series of major investment projects in Cork, where they have expanded their synthesis capacity and constructed a drug products facility

Source: Pharmachemical Ireland.

Irish indigenous companies sell to a wide range of customers in Ireland, notably banking and financial services, and process flow industries such as pharmaceuticals, chemicals, drinks, dairy products and other foods (O'Gorman et al., 1997). In regard to the multinational sector, on the one hand many of them trade with each other, particularly in the initial stages after set-up. On the other hand, there are many who never sell to other MNEs in Ireland. The responses to Taggart's questionnaire later in this chapter suggest that the latter is definitely the more common pattern in 2007. The ICT software sector in Ireland could be characterized as having sophisticated demand given the prevalence of MNEs and their accordingly exacting standards, as well as the export competitiveness of the indigenous sector. There is some local demand but companies are generally oriented towards the European market for localization. With respect to the indigenous software companies, it should be noted that most firms, while dynamic, are still at the developmental stage and expect to be taken over. They may exhibit promise but they are not profitable. Indigenous software companies that are more geared towards services provision tend to grow and become more profitable, while pure software companies get taken over quickly.

Regarding the existence of related and supporting industries, software development has linkages into the Irish ecosystem. Microsoft hires graduates from universities and institutes of technology. The MNEs and indigenous companies are involved with Science

Table 4.2   The relative importance of ICT hardware employment in EU countries

	Computer equipment	Electronic components
	NACE 3002	NACE 3210
Belgium	0.21	0.79
Denmark	0.55	0.65
Germany	0.82	0.90
Spain	0.48	0.44
France	1.48	1.80
Ireland	10.42	3.77
Italy	0.48	0.69
Austria	0.15	1.75
Portugal	0.06	0.71
Finland	0.31	1.07
Sweden	0.46	0.79
UK	1.79	1.10
Of which: Scotland	7.90	3.05
Netherlands	1.54	0.54

Note: Data not available for Luxembourg and Greece.

Source: Eurostat New Cronos.

Table 4.3   EU country shares (%) in world ICT hardware exports, 1992 and 2000

	SITC 752		SITC 75997	
	2000	1992	2000	1992
France	0.04	0.05	0.02	0.04
Germany	0.05	0.07	0.04	0.05
Ireland	0.05	0.02	0.06	0.05
Italy	0.01	0.03	0.01	0.03
Netherlands	0.08	0.04	0.05	0.05
UK	0.08	0.09	0.04	0.07

Source: UN trade statistics.

Foundation Ireland. The policy of Forfás[5] is to create fertile ground for the creation and growth of a cluster. In 1996, the MNE ICT hardware, the MNE telecommunications sector as well as other MNEs, and indigenous companies with large ICT departments, constituted the related and supporting industries element of Porter's model (O'Gorman et al., 1997). In terms of work experience, most indigenous Irish IT software entrepreneurs worked with other indigenous software companies before starting up on their own, with around one-third having worked with MNE software companies.

With respect to strategy, structure and rivalry, indigenous companies are small or medium sized, have a niche product specialization, and are highly export market focused. The limiting size of the Irish market and the influence of the state development

Table 4.4   The relative importance of computer software employment in EU countries, 2003

Country	Relative share
Belgium	0.89
Denmark	1.25
Germany	0.61
Spain	0.62
France	1.05
Ireland	1.32
Italy	1.04
Netherlands	1.25
Austria	0.78
Portugal	0.27
Finland	1.25
Sweden	1.95
UK	1.47

Source: Barry and Curran (2004).

agencies in directing their export strategy are regarded as important (O'Gorman et al., 1997). Technical competence is high but marketing expertise is perceived as low. Most indigenous companies say that they encounter strong competition from other Irish subsidiaries of MNEs and they see this factor as contributing to Ireland's global competitiveness (O'Gorman et al., 1997). While there is strong competition, there is also strong cooperation. One critical perspective is that Ireland in general is good at manufacturing but indigenous companies in particular lack marketing skills and therefore indigenous software companies have problems bringing their products to market.

Table 4.4 reports the importance of computer software employment in EU countries, again measured relative to the EU average (this time taken relative to total employment in manufacturing and market services). Software employment records its highest proportionate shares in Sweden, the UK and Ireland. According to the OECD (2002), however, Ireland was the largest global exporter of software, driven by the substantial presence of foreign software giants, *inter alia* Microsoft, Lotus and Oracle.

The pharmaceutical sector   This section examines the pharmaceutical industry. Since its arrival in the 1950s the pharmaceutical sector has been characterized by virtually continuous growth. By 2004, the pharmaceutical industry had developed into one of the main industrial sectors in Ireland, employing nearly 24 000 people in 95 operations, and Ireland had become an important global location for the pharmaceutical industry (van Egeraat, 2006; van Egeraat and Breathnach, 2007). The sector was the largest contributor of corporation tax in 2001, and by 2003 had become the largest export category in Ireland, accounting for 42 per cent of all manufactured goods exported (ICSTI, 2003). The main subsectors in Ireland are the production of active pharmaceutical ingredients (API) and the formulation of drug products.

The industry is dominated by foreign companies. In 2003, they accounted for 93 per cent of total employment in the sector, and virtually all employment in the API subsector. The indigenous companies are mainly active in the formulation of human and veterinary pharmaceuticals and, to a lesser extent, diagnostics products. Most indigenous operations have remained relatively small. In 2006, 13 of the top 15 global pharmaceutical companies had large-scale operations in Ireland (IDA Ireland, 2006). Six out of ten and 12 out of 25 of the world's top-selling drugs are produced in Ireland. The products are often manufactured for global markets. Since the 1990s a substantial number of foreign subsidiaries have been supplementing their initial manufacturing activities with process R&D and other higher-value-added activities. The discussion of competitiveness in the pharmaceutical industry below will focus on the foreign-owned segment, ignoring the recent development of a small number of internationally competitive indigenous companies.

The primary factor in the rapid expansion of the foreign-owned pharmaceutical sector has been the low rate of corporate tax. In addition, the main positive factor conditions included, initially, an ample reservoir of low-cost unskilled labour and a sufficient supply of suitably qualified labour (chemical engineers). Experience in the foreign-owned companies steadily increased the skill levels in the local labour force. In addition, in response to the needs of the sector, new and expanded tertiary educational institution programmes increased the output of qualified and increasingly specialized staff. This labour has now become the main factor condition influencing the competitiveness of the Irish pharmaceutical industry. In 2006, a reduction in the number of students pursuing science-related courses became a cause for concern at the policy level.

In relation to R&D, arguably more than in other sectors, the location of internationally mobile pharmaceutical R&D projects is strongly influenced by the country's technological system (Bartlett and Ghoshal, 1989). Ireland's technological system in the area of pharmaceuticals has been, and still is, of limited strategic importance for multinational companies. The Irish government has started to address this disadvantage by upgrading the institutional research infrastructure, notably through the Programme for Research in Third-Level Institutions, launched in 1998, and projects arising from these programmes are starting to play a role in attracting internationally mobile R&D projects, notably in the area of process R&D.

In relation to market conditions, national policies of governments in strategic markets (*inter alia* the USA, the UK, France and Japan) on pharmaceutical pricing, reimbursement and health insurance can influence the location of manufacturing and R&D facilities of multinational pharmaceutical companies on an international scale (Gambardella et al., 2000; Lance and Probert, 2004). The insignificant strategic importance of the Irish market means that Ireland is at a disadvantage compared to some of the larger markets with appropriate policies. In addition, there is nothing to suggest that Irish customers are particularly demanding or sophisticated.

Pharmaceutical plants in Ireland have very few local raw material supply linkages that could have a positive impact on the competitiveness of the industry. The growth of the pharmaceutical industry did help to attract a substantial number of international process engineering and construction management companies to Ireland in the 1980s and 1990s (see also Kearny, 2003). Although it is questionable whether these engineering companies positively influenced the competitiveness of the pharmaceutical companies, they did support the IDA in its efforts to attract pharmaceutical plants to Ireland.

Table 4.5   *An index of the relative significance of EU countries' NACE 244 employment (2000)*

EU-15	Relative index of NACE 244 employment
Belgium	1.52
Denmark	1.41
Germany	0.88
Greece	–
Spain	0.84
France	1.44
Ireland	1.98
Italy	0.87
Luxembourg	–
Netherlands	0.98
Austria	0.99
Portugal	0.45
Finland	0.80
Sweden	1.38
UK	0.94

Source: Eurostat New Cronos.

Strategies and structures are determined at global headquarters and mainly influenced by developments in main markets and the emergence of new technologies. The Irish subsidiaries have typically very little influence on the development of such global strategies. Ireland did, however, benefit strongly from the global strategies of the pharmaceutical companies. Their strategy of tax avoidance, supported by complex corporate structures and facilitated by Irish taxation policies, made Ireland very attractive as a location for manufacturing as well as R&D and other value-added activities (Smyth, 2006). There is no evidence to suggest the existence of local subsidiary–subsidiary rivalry, nor the idea that it plays any role in driving the efficiency/competitiveness of the sector in Ireland.

Clearly the Irish government has been instrumental in the development of the large grouping of pharmaceutical companies in Ireland in a number of ways. Companies have been primarily attracted by the low rate of corporation tax. In addition, the government has worked towards the upgrading of factor conditions and development of factor-creating mechanisms, notably tertiary ('third-level') education and, recently, R&D infrastructure. In the last few years (2000–06), the government has introduced new fiscal and financial incentives for establishing corporate R&D functions – schemes that have been taken up by several companies. Finally, Ireland's success in attracting foreign investment projects since the early 1970s has in no small degree been supported by the excellence of the IDA, widely acclaimed as one of the most sophisticated industrial development agencies in the world.

Table 4.5 reports the index for relative employment across the EU in the pharmaceuticals sector. As before, an index of 1.0 indicates that pharmaceutical employment as a share of manufacturing was at the EU-15 average. Ireland's index of 1.98 is the highest of any EU-15 country and illustrates that the sector is almost twice as important in Ireland (in employment terms) as in the Western EU as a whole.

Table 4.6   Ireland's inward and outward FDI stock (US\$ millions, current prices)
(1980–2005)

Year	Inward stock	Outward stock
1980	31 281	n.a.
1990	33 826	17 204
2000	136 921	27 925
2005	211 190	117 909

Source: UNCTAD (1998, 2004, 2005, 2006).

As in the case of the other sectors discussed above, Ireland's ranking in the export stakes is even stronger. In 2002, for example, it accounted for some 13 per cent of total EU-15 pharmaceutical exports.

The role of inward and outward FDI in the ICT hardware, ICT software and pharmaceutical sectors

Inward and outward FDI
This section is limited by a dearth of data broken down by sector. Ireland is the most FDI-intensive economy in the EU with around half its manufacturing workforce and a higher-than-average share of services workers employed by foreign-owned firms. Its FDI inflows have become increasingly high-tech in nature. Only 12 per cent of employment in foreign manufacturing firms in Ireland in 1974 was in sectors classified as high-tech by the OECD. The current figure comes to almost 60 per cent. The sectors that account for the bulk of foreign-firm employment in Ireland are ICT hardware, pharmachemicals, medical devices and internationally traded services such as shared services and call centres.

Table 4.6 shows the picture of Irish inward and outward FDI stocks. FDI inward stock in Ireland in 1990 was \$34 billion. By 2000 it was \$137 billion and in 2005 it reached \$211 billion. Irish FDI outward stock was \$17 billion in 1990, \$28 billion in 2000 and \$118 billion in 2005 (UNCTAD, 2006). FDI inward stock in 2005 represented an increase of 35 per cent on 2000. In contrast, FDI outward stock in 2005 represented an increase of more than 322 per cent over the 2000 level.

As Figure 4.3 shows, in terms of flows, inward FDI flows peaked in 2000 at \$26 billion. FDI outflows reached their highest level at \$16 billion in 2004. The peak/trough cycle of inward FDI flows points to some underlying dynamics. Inward flows are disaggregated by the Central Statistics Office in Ireland into equity investments, reinvested earnings and other capital (repayment of loans, payout of dividends, and tax repayment). Major outflows in the 'other capital' category of €13 billion in 2004 and €31.1 billion in 2005 accounted for the overall reduction in inward FDI flows into Ireland.

In 2005, Ireland's inward FDI stock as a percentage of GDP was the second highest in the EU after Belgium/Luxembourg (UNCTAD, 2006). In regard to outward FDI stock as a percentage of GDP, Ireland moved from being the third lowest in the EU in the late 1990s after Greece, Portugal and Austria (Barry et al., 2003), to being the second highest.

Much inward FDI into Ireland comes via holding companies established in the Netherlands. However, Figure 4.4 shows 2001–03 inward investment flows based on the

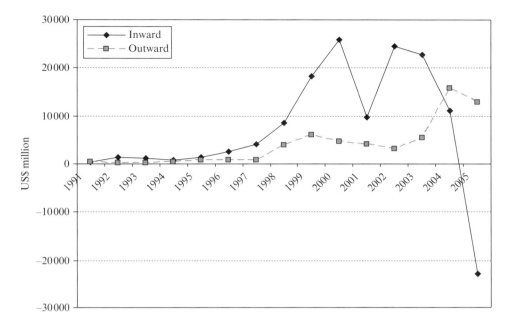

Note: The 1991 figure for inflows and outflows is generated from an average for the years 1986–91 inclusive.

Source: UNCTAD (1998, 2004, 2005, 2006).

Figure 4.3 Ireland's FDI inflows and outflows (US$ millions, current prices, 1986–2005)

ultimate ownership of FDI rather than proximate FDI flows. The USA accounts for 53 per cent, the UK 23 per cent, and the Euro area 11 per cent (Lane and Ruane, 2006).

Moreover, Barry et al. (2003) note the importance of distinguishing inflows to the International Financial Services Centre (IFSC) Dublin and other sectors. The transfer of capital by foreign companies to their financial subsidiaries in the IFSC is counted as inward direct investment. Most of these flows are reinvested in overseas assets and exit as portfolio outflows.[6]

The USA and the UK are the main destinations for Irish outward investment, with the US appearing to be more important. Central Statistics Office data show that 70 per cent went to non-EU countries, predominantly the USA.

Though frequently at variance with each other, both UNCTAD and OECD data agree that Ireland's outward FDI stock relative to GDP is now above the EU-15 average. In 2004, for the first time, the flow of outward direct investment (ODI) from Ireland exceeded the gross FDI inflow. To take the analysis further requires information on both the geographic and sectoral destination of outflows. The geographic destination is considered first. The pre-eminence of the USA and the UK as host locations is clear from Table 4.7, which is derived from a database on overseas acquisitions by Irish companies. Over 70 per cent of overseas acquisitions annually were made in the UK and the USA at the end of the 1990s. Acquisitions in turn are thought to be the main vehicle by which Irish companies invest overseas (Forfás, 2001). Data for 2005 show that Irish companies

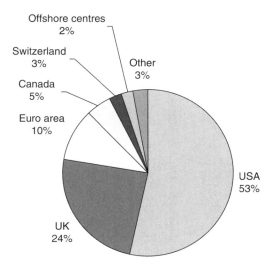

Source: Lane and Ruane (2006).

Figure 4.4   *Origin of inward investment into Ireland (in %), 2001–03*

Table 4.7   *Overseas acquisitions by Irish companies (£000 and %) (1995–98)*

Region	1995		1996		1997		1998	
	£000	%	£000	%	£000	%	£000	%
UK	453 350	67	979 140	42	484 190	24	1 028 000	39
USA	64 550	10	999 300	43	1 300 060	66	891 000	33
ROW	157 650	23	371 100	15	197 996	10	743 000	28

Source: CFM Capital (various years).

spent €4.55 billion acquiring overseas assets. Irish companies spent 130 per cent more on foreign acquisitions than was used by overseas interests in acquiring Irish firms. Irish companies are increasingly looking internationally for opportunities. The international construction group CRH plc was particularly acquisitive, primarily in the USA. The UK in value terms was the most popular destination, but more deals were done in the USA (CFM Capital, 2005).

Growth in the stock of Irish FDI in the UK is confirmed by UK Office of National Statistics data, which report numbers employed in foreign-owned firms in the UK manufacturing sector. In the first year these data were reported, 1981, Irish-owned firms employed 8900 workers in the UK. By 1996 this had climbed to over 23,000, though it dropped to 19,000 in 1997. The USA appears to be even more important than the UK as a destination for Irish outward FDI. For the few years for which Irish Central Statistics Office data are available, around 70 per cent of FDI outflows from Ireland went to non-EU countries, and primarily, it is thought, to the USA. Given the scarcity of Irish source data on outward flows and given that the USA is the most important source of

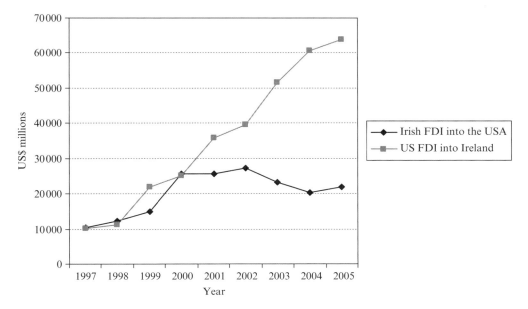

Source: US Bureau of Economic Analysis (2006).

Figure 4.5   Bilateral inward FDI stock: Ireland and the USA compared (US$ millions at current prices), 1997–2005

FDI flows into Ireland, the bilateral Ireland–USA FDI relationship is worth studying based on the US Department of Commerce data on foreign-owned assets.

During the 1980s and 1990s, Irish FDI in the USA grew even more rapidly than US FDI in Ireland. By 1997, the stock levels were similar. This result is quite surprising, given the focus of academics and policy makers on Ireland as a host country for inward investment rather than as a base for outward investment. However as Figure 4.5 shows, US inward FDI stock went up considerably from 2000 to 2005.

Table 4.8 compares the sectoral distribution of overseas acquisitions by Irish companies and EU firms during the period 1993–99. Given the importance of the USA as a location for Irish acquisitions, the sectoral distribution of acquisitions by overseas companies within the USA is also shown. The latter is seen to conform fairly closely to the distribution for all overseas acquisitions by EU companies. The sectoral distribution of Irish acquisitions differs substantially from both other series, however. Irish investment is notable in construction and property; financial services; food, drink and agriculture; and print, paper and publishing.

Contribution of ICT hardware, ICT software and pharmaceutical sectors in Porterian terms to Irish economy
Tables 4.2, 4.4 and 4.5 report employment data across the ICT hardware, ICT software and pharmaceutical sectors respectively. The key points articulated there were as follows. Employment in both hardware subsectors is particularly important in two peripheral EU economies: Ireland and Scotland. Software employment records its

*Table 4.8   Cross-border M&A activity by sector (average annual shares):
(i) by EU firms, (ii) within the USA and (iii) by Irish firms, 1993–99*

Sector	Cross-border M&A purchases by EU firms	Cross-border M&A sales within the USA	Cross-border M&A purchases by Irish firms
Food, drink and agribusiness	5.9	5.7	17.5
Print, paper and publishing	2.8	4.5	16.2
IT, telecommunications and electronics	5.1	7.8	4.0
Chemicals and pharmaceuticals	14.4	17.0	9.5
Other manufacturing	24.2	20.5	5.8
Construction, property	1.0	1.8	22.2
Financial services	32.4	22.5	22.5
Services (consulting, retail, wholesale etc.)	14.3	20.2	2.3

highest proportionate shares in Sweden, the UK and Ireland, with Ireland as the largest global exporter of software, driven by the substantial presence of foreign software giants, *inter alia* Microsoft, Lotus and Oracle. The pharmaceuticals sector is almost twice as important in Ireland (in employment terms) as in the western EU as a whole.

How has this investment contributed to building competitiveness viewed through Porter's diamond? Would the competitive elements of Porter's model be there without this investment? From the perspective of resource-based strategic thinking, Ireland has built up a stock of resources through receipt of a stock of inward investment across the three sectors chosen. It has built up skills. Employees of MNE subsidiaries have gained experience in globally competitive sectors. The indigenous medical devices industry has emerged and the indigenous software industry has also developed. Is there a connection between the development of these two indigenous sectors and the multinational sectors?

Subsidiary decision making and integration of activities
As already mentioned, the key determinant of Ireland's success in attracting FDI has been the low corporate tax rate of 12.5 per cent, which stimulated MNEs to take advantage of the country's other location advantages. EU membership allowed Ireland to become an export platform for MNE subsidiaries. Ireland, like the UK, is English speaking with strong cultural links with the USA, and both jurisdictions have become favoured locations for US FDI (Barry, 1999). The availability of the appropriate skills, the quality of the workforce, the quality of public infrastructure, the efficiency of public administration and the expertise of the Industrial Development Agency (IDA) are also cited by MNE executives as important advantages of Ireland as a location for FDI. One may sum up by saying that inward direct investment into Ireland has been efficiency seeking given that the low corporate tax rates generate more profit.

Decision making and integration of activities of subsidiaries
This section reports the results of field research in representative MNE subsidiaries in Ireland using Taggart's questionnaire (Taggart, 1998, pp. 680–81) as a template to

ascertain the subsidiaries' decision-making capacities and relative level of integration. It has to be admitted that Taggart's questionnaire is less relevant for many Irish MNE subsidiaries than it is for the UK, which was the focus of his research. Indeed, where in the UK there is a large home market with multiple subsidiaries, and where most subsidiaries have a sales and marketing department, this is not often the case in Ireland. Several of the questions in the decision-making section of Taggart's questionnaire delve into activities that are generally absent from MNE subsidiaries in Ireland. There are very few marketing activities at Irish subsidiaries: their main activity is production, not sales. MNEs that have located in Ireland and are supported by the IDA have very little to do with market area, product range or advertising, which are generally parent functions. The IDA describes the Irish companies as being involved in value chain activity rather than fully integrated business.

Porter defines a subsidiary as a displaced activity. The role of the parent is to configure and coordinate these activities. The Irish subsidiary has to be viewed in this context. The subsidiary as such does not sell, but rather its output is part of its role as a node in a network. The subsidiary is not autonomous, but exercises some systemic influence as part of this network. A subsidiary may serve three markets: internal, local and/or global. In general, Irish MNE subsidiaries serve the internal, parent, market, not the local or global end market, some exceptions notwithstanding. Taggart's decision-making questions are of greatest relevance to fully integrated subsidiaries such as Guinness (a subsidiary of Diageo), which does have manufacturing and sales and marketing in one subsidiary, but such companies are the exception in Ireland.

There are also some conceptual problems in the 'integration of activities' section of Taggart's questionnaire: the explanatory comments on the left and right sides of the response scale do not always represent opposite ends of a true continuum, and the questions themselves do not always fully reflect the underlying complexity of subsidiary–parent relationships.

These issues will be addressed more fully as they arise in the discussion below.

The ICT hardware sector based on the Taggart classification Table 4.9 reflects the responses from the field research regarding the division of decision-making responsibility between the parent and subsidiary.[7] Briefly, a score of 1 indicates the parent decides the matter without consulting the subsidiary; 2 indicates that the parent decides after consulting the subsidiary; 3 indicates that the subsidiary decides after consulting the parent; and 4 indicates that the subsidiary decides without consulting the parent. Thus higher scores indicate greater subsidiary autonomy in the area in question. In Table 4.9, the pattern is clearly one of low subsidiary autonomy, with subsidiaries having at best some consultative role, and little change evident over the past five years.

While government officials and employees of ICT hardware MNE subsidiaries based in Ireland would like to believe that the MNEs are embedded in Ireland, if rising operating costs threaten global competitiveness, these results suggest that decisions about the plant's future are made by the parent, not the subsidiary, irrespective of its level of embeddedness in the local economy.

Table 4.10 reports the responses from the field research in the area of integration into MNE networks in the hardware sector. In each case, responses can range from 1 (a high level of integration) to 5 (a low level of integration). Question (a) deals with market

Table 4.9   Taggart's decision-making classification applied to the Irish ICT hardware sector

	5 years ago	Today
Market area	2	2
Product range	2	2
Advertising	2	3
R&D	1	1
Product capacity	1	2
Manufacturing technology	1	1

Table 4.10   Taggart's integration classification and the Irish ICT hardware sector

	a	b	c	d	e	f
5 years ago	1	1	1	1	1	1
Today	1	1	1	1	1	4/5

linkages; (b) with product specifications for multiple markets; (c) with sales to other subsidiaries worldwide; (d) with technology sharing among subsidiaries; (e) with movement of intermediate and final products among subsidiaries; and (f) with centralization of production planning at headquarters.

The data in Table 4.10 provide a clear indication that the subsidiaries function as integral parts of multinational networks, not free-standing enterprises, although they have often achieved high levels of production planning autonomy in recent years. Beyond these numerical scores, some qualitative comments will assist in forming a richer understanding of the situation of MNE subsidiaries in this sector. Obviously, the central role of the parent in providing the international linkages for the subsidiary continues to prevail. In Ireland, the subsidiaries that belong to groups such as Dell, Intel and Microsoft, for example, do not relate directly with each other in Ireland. They relate at the parent level in the USA. In Ireland the relationship is primarily as a lobbying force to ensure that government policy is facilitative of the business environment. Most importantly, they lobby the government to act on their behalf at the EU level.

Product specifications are developed and coordinated by subsidiaries to serve many of the parent's markets. The subsidiaries sell a substantial part of their output to customers of other group subsidiaries globally. It is a complex picture, however. For example, Dell produces three products in Limerick. If customization is demanded, the product comes from the distribution centre in Central Europe. One could say that 80 per cent comes from Dell Ireland and 20 per cent from elsewhere. If one focuses on the 80 per cent of customers who do not require customization, one can say that the customers of this subsidiary are specific to this subsidiary and the score on this question should be 5 rather than 1.

Question (d) of Taggart's questionnaire is really a three-part question: is technology development carried out in many locations? Does each specialize in a specific technical area and/or product line? Is the output shared? Technology development is indeed carried out in many locations throughout the MNE, but each location does not

Table 4.11   Taggart's decision-making classification and the Irish ICT software sector

	5 years ago	Today
Market area	1 (n.a.)	1 (n.a.)
Product range	1/2 (n.a.)	2
Advertising	n.a.	n.a.
R&D	2–3	2–3
Product capacity	3	3
Process technology	3–4	3–4

Note: n.a. = not applicable.

specialize in a specific technical area and/or product line and the output is not shared by all subsidiaries.

There is substantial movement of semi-finished and finished goods between the different subsidiaries globally. While formerly production planning was centralized at the headquarters (HQ), today it remains the responsibility of the subsidiary, with HQ providing broad guidelines. Competitive threats notwithstanding, Ireland has manufactured ICT hardware well and continues to do so.

The ICT software sector based on the Taggart classification   Table 4.11 outlines the responses to the questions regarding decision making in the software sector. As mentioned above, MNE subsidiaries in Ireland have very little to do with market area, product range or advertising. These are generally parent functions. Software development is much like the hardware manufacturing sector discussed above in this respect: the subsidiaries operate as nodes in an international network.

The example of Motorola and the closure of its software development centre in Cork in January 2007 provides an insight. Subsidiary managers were informed of this decision with just 24 hours' notice. The operation was at the high end of software development, yet the parent decided to close due to the poor performance of its global cellular networks division. In this case the competitiveness of the subsidiary was challenged by loss of economic competitiveness in Ireland due to higher operating costs, and the competitive advantage of India (*Irish Times*, 2007).

The remaining three areas, which are more closely related to production, show somewhat higher levels of autonomy and therefore merit additional discussion. In the case of software, rather than R&D, it seems more accurate to refer to innovation. In process R&D, the subsidiary has a good deal of control, but since the product is primarily for the parent, the subsidiary has little scope to innovate new products. Production capacity and manufacturing technology fall more clearly within the role of subsidiaries in Ireland. In regard to production capacity, although in the early days of Microsoft Ireland, for example, all operational decisions were taken in the USA, this is no longer the case today. Operations technology is perhaps a more appropriate term than manufacturing technology when speaking of software. Process technology autonomy is high, with scores of 3 to 4. It has changed over a 15-year period, but this is not evident in the five-year period that was considered here.

Table 4.12 reports the results of the field research in the area of integration of the ICT

Table 4.12   Taggart's integration measure and the Irish ICT software sector

	a	b	c	d	e	f
5 years ago	1	1	n.a.	1	1	1
Today	1	1	n.a.	1	1	1

software sector. With the exception of question (c) ('the subsidiary sells a substantial part of its output to the customers of other group subsidiaries worldwide'), all values are at the level of 1, indicating very close integration of the subsidiaries into their parents' networks and very low levels of ability to function independently. The objective of the IDA has been international access to networks and to ensure that the global company configures more in Ireland rather than elsewhere. The key issue is embeddedness in the MNE's system, and accordingly systemic influence and interdependence are what counts, rather than geographical embeddedness and local autonomy. Ireland has become a good location to configure activities. MNE subsidiaries configure in Ireland; they do not embed locally.

A good example is SAP, the German software company, which has a number of subsidiaries in Ireland. They are a collection of different activities and they report independently to their parent – never to each other. There is no connection between SAP subsidiaries within Ireland. In contrast, Sage, a UK software accounting firm, is based in Ireland for the Irish market. It has strongly geographically segmented markets due to national differences in accounting rules.

One key issue in software development is the concept of mandate. Subsidiaries compete to get business, i.e. mandates. They want to win the parent's mandate and bring business to Ireland against competition from other international operations. Eriksson, for example, has a network of centres of excellence, with each centre bidding for technology development. In Ireland no sales are involved, so questions relating to subsidiary sales are irrelevant. The mandate is won, and then fulfilled on behalf of the parent. There is a substantial movement of semi-finished and finished goods between different subsidiaries. This characterizes nearly all the software subsidiary sector in Ireland. Sage, the UK software accounting firm mentioned above, is the exception.

Rather than the term 'production planning', 'operations planning' is the more appropriate term in software. Macro-level operations planning is done annually by the parent. Yet at a local level, the subsidiary deals with weekly and monthly targets and unexpected fluctuations. Newer subsidiaries tend to be managed centrally by HQ, while the older ones have more local responsibility.

The pharmaceutical sector based on Taggart's classification   Table 4.13 reports the responses from the field research regarding decision making in the pharmaceutical sector, disaggregated into production and sales and marketing. In most areas subsidiaries have only a consultative role.

The reason for the disaggregation in Table 4.13 is that global pharmaceutical companies generally have separate subsidiaries for production and sales & marketing. The production facilities usually have limited decision-making freedom. This is largely a consequence of the highly regulated nature of the industry. Before a product may be

Table 4.13 *Taggart's questionnaire responses on decision-making in the Irish pharmaceutical sector*

	Production		Sales and Marketing	
	5 years ago	Today	5 years ago	Today
Market area	2	2	1	1
Product range	2	2	2	2
Advertising	n.a.	n.a.	3	3
R&D	2	2	n.a.	n.a.
Product capacity	2	2	n.a.	n.a.
Process technology	2	2	n.a.	n.a.

manufactured or sold, the company needs to go through a long registration procedure in each of the nations where it wants to sell its products. This registration includes all details of the clinical trials and the clinical trial documents specifying the pilot plants, product characteristics and, importantly, the manufacturing process technology. These clinical trials are the most expensive part of the whole development cycle. Products are generally developed at corporate R&D facilities in the home countries. Process development is the responsibility of the chemical development groups at headquarters with the support of the pilot plants (which may be in Ireland). The high degree of regulation and the financial risks involved mean that it is a tightly controlled process. By the time the product is transferred to the commercial manufacturing plant in Ireland, most of the important decisions have been taken – unless the Irish subsidiary was initially involved in the pilot plant production. Even then, their decision making is far from autonomous. The local plant is typically only allowed to make suggestions, which are then decided on by the corporate development units.

The production subsidiaries' market is either the downstream sister plant or the MNE's marketing subsidiaries. In both cases they have little or no decision-making power, although top management of the subsidiary is generally part of the MNE's global commission or board. In such cases, the local manager can have some input. This is the same in regard to product range. Advertising is not relevant given that the outlet for the products is the MNE's internal market. R&D is discussed above. In the few cases where subsidiaries are involved in process development, their role is at most consultative.

Production capacity is all decided on a global basis, with some input by the local subsidiary. Manufacturing technology is highly regulated and specified by the licence, as already discussed. In regard to sales and marketing subsidiaries, the markets for products are decided on at a very early stage. However, regional marketing groups generally sit on corporate boards and in this way have the opportunity for input.

To sum up in terms of decision making, it has to be noted that some subsidiaries have increased the sophistication of their process technology, but decision making is still with the parent as the regulatory demands of the industry make the sector highly centralized. There has been an upgrading of activities in Irish subsidiaries, with definitely more high-value-added activities taking place, however, these subtle changes cannot be captured in a five-year period.

Table 4.14   Taggart's questionnaire responses on integration of activities in the Irish pharmaceutical sector

	a	b	c	d	e	f
5 years ago	2	3	3	2	2	1
Today	1	3	3	2	2	1

Table 4.14 summarizes the responses regarding integration of subsidiaries in the pharmaceutical sector.

A full appreciation of these responses requires some background on the sector. As mentioned above, the pharmaceutical sector in Ireland is divided into two main subsectors: the production of active pharmaceutical ingredients (API) and the formulation of drug products. API provides linkages with other global parts of companies. On the formulation side, the focus is not the local market. For example, Wyeth's subsidiary's market is Europe, North America and Japan. Headquarters manufacturing decisions are made to provide international linkages for this subsidiary and this has been increasingly the case, as the pharmaceutical sector serves many markets. Product specifications are developed and coordinated for different markets and then various plants are selected to produce them. Irish subsidiaries play an increasing role in process development

Production planning is managed at HQ. While 2/2 is the overall score, for the larger MNEs 1/1 is more accurate. In these firms production is managed by the parent. The parent's activities in Ireland take advantage of the low corporate tax rate, which attracts not just manufacturing but also R&D and some marketing functions.

A number of problems were highlighted above with respect to the use of Taggart's questionnaire in the Irish MNE subsidiary sector. Most notably, subsidiaries are not autonomous but are rather embedded as nodes in global networks. However, there are some key points that can be made based on the results of the field research.

With respect to decision making, in the ICT hardware sector, the role of the subsidiary is at its lowest in R&D, product capacity and manufacturing technology. It is somewhat more evolved in market area, product range and advertising. In ICT software, many of the questions are not applicable due to the nature of the sector, notably in regard to advertising. However, R&D and process technology score relatively high. In pharmaceuticals, production and sales & marketing are differentiated at the outset and scores differ in the two subsectors. In production there is very limited local decision making and no advertising. In sales and marketing, there is no real scope for local decision making in R&D, product capacity and process technology. Advertising does offer some latitude, as does (to a lesser extent) product range.

As regards integration of activities, the ICT hardware sector shows strong levels of integration with the exception of production planning, which is primarily the responsibility of the subsidiary. ICT software also demonstrates strong levels of global network integration with question (c) regarding sales to customers of other group subsidiaries not being applicable. In pharmaceuticals, the role of the parent is less pronounced. The subsidiary seems more autonomous, particularly in regard to production specifications and global sales to other subsidiaries. However, in the critical areas of manufacturing decisions and production planning, it is HQ that makes the decisions.

Choice of outward FDI destinations to strengthen domestic production and employment
The emergence of outward direct investment (ODI) as a new and rapidly growing phenomenon in Ireland has drawn attention to the international literature on home-country effects of FDI. Most of that literature identifies the effects as positive on balance. Blomström et al. (1997), for example, in a study on US firms, note that increased foreign production raises labour productivity and expands HQ services and high skill employment in the home base, while Desai et al. (2005) find that higher capital expenditures on the part of foreign affiliates of US MNCs are associated with higher parent-company investments in the USA. The implication drawn from this is that firms combine home production with foreign production to generate final output at lower cost than would be possible without ODI. This makes each stage of the production process more profitable and ultimately raises production in both locations, suggesting that home-country production and ODI are complements rather than substitutes.

Brainard and Riker (1997a; 1997b) provide some contrary evidence, however. While they find that the relationship between parent-firm employment in the USA and US affiliate employment in lower-wage economies is one of complementarity, affiliate employment in other high-wage economies appears to be to some extent substitutable for US employment. Braconier and Ekholm (2000) report a similar finding for Swedish MNCs. Such substitutability can arise if the FDI displaces exports from the firm's home base, in contrast to the type of FDI entailed in the offshoring of the labour-intensive segments of the production process.

In the Irish case, however, even though most ODI is directed towards developed countries, it does not typically entail the displacement of Irish exports. As Barry et al. (2003) point out, many of the largest Irish MNCs, which are thought to be responsible for the bulk of ODI, are in largely non-traded sectors. Of the top ten companies, as listed by Forfás (2000), Allied Irish Banks, Bank of Ireland and Irish Life are in financial retail services; Independent Newspapers is a media company; CRH (Cement Roadstone Holdings) and the Smurfit Group are in construction and packaging materials respectively. The only way these companies can expand on world markets is through FDI. This leaves only food companies Kerry and Greencore, glassware company Waterford Wedgwood and the pharma company élan operating in internationally traded sectors in which FDI might possibly substitute for exports.

Even if home- and host-country employment were substitutes rather than complements however, so long as the Irish economy remains at full employment the gains from ODI are likely to dominate the losses from any job displacement even in the short term.

Finally, it was pointed out that although Ireland tends to be associated globally with the strength of its FDI inflows, outward FDI has grown rapidly over the course of the 'Celtic Tiger' boom and in 2004, for the first time, outflows exceeded FDI inflows. This raises a new set of issues for Irish policy makers. The most difficult issues arise, however, when (a) outward FDI acts as a substitute for exports, and (b) unemployment prevails so that there are high adjustment costs associated with job displacement. Ireland faces neither of these difficult issues at present.

Clustering benefits of domestic production and employment in the industries studied
This section will initially consider the concept of a cluster from a theoretical perspective, and then move on to examine whether MNE subsidiaries exist spatially in clusters. The

Rugman–Verbeke (2003) classification of clusters will also be explored to ascertain to what degree, if any, it may characterize the spatial behaviour of MNEs in Ireland.

The term 'cluster' has a multitude of meanings in the literature and it is useful to discuss some of the competing definitions at this stage. The most basic definition is an industry or group of industries whose size within a region has been influenced by the playing out of Marshallian 'external economies'. These agglomeration-generating factors include technology spillovers, input–output linkages and thick markets for specialized factors of production. 'Bandwagon' or demonstration effects, whereby the location decisions of market leaders influence those of other firms in the sector, can have similar effects. Much of what Porter has written on clusters was articulated in the form of industrial districts by Marshall (1919), Piore and Sabel (1984) and Becattini (1990).

Enright (2000) defines more complex phenomena that fall within the broad Marshallian perspective. A 'working cluster', for example, exhibits 'dense patterns of interactions among local firms that differ quantitatively and qualitatively from the interactions that the firms have with those not located in the cluster'. He has in mind here the type of networking – involving cooperation in risk and innovation sharing and market stabilization – that prevails between competitor firms in Italian industrial districts. A region that contains not just a set of related industries, but complete or nearly complete supply chains, furthermore, he defines as a 'deep cluster'.

Markusen (1996) criticizes the focus of this literature on local networks of domestically owned SMEs, arguing that multinational firms can frequently shape and anchor successful industrial districts, that external networks are frequently as important as networks within the region, and that the external relationships in which firms, workers and public sector institutions and agencies are embedded condition the ability of the location to retain economic activity. In contrast to the Marshallian or Italian-type industrial district, this author identifies several other patterns of successful industrial regions. One is the hub-and-spoke district, whose structure is dominated by one or several large vertically integrated firms surrounded by their suppliers. Another is the state-anchored industrial district, whose structure is dominated by large government institutions surrounded by their suppliers and customers. A third, of particular interest in the Irish case, is the satellite industrial platform, based on large externally owned firms. Markusen points out that these can entail quite sophisticated operations, with the Research Triangle Park in North Carolina standing out as a prime example.

Amsden and Chu (2003), in a book on Taiwan, point to the important role that the public authorities often play in successful late industrializing regions, both in network development and, less controversially, in ensuring that the appropriate conditions are in place for agglomeration processes to take hold. Consistent with this, the notion of organizational learning within the Irish public sector bureaucracy – meaning the ability of the public administration system to extract, accumulate and use effectively the insights that become available to it – is a crucial element in the Irish story.

Rugman and Verbeke (2003) developed a two-stage framework to organizationally classify clusters with MNEs involved in local or trans-border clusters. Stage 1 is the geographical cluster, which may be domestic and symmetrical (Marshall, 1919; Porter, 1990; e.g. the Italian ceramics industry), domestic and asymmetrical (old economy and one industry, e.g. steel), trans-border and symmetrical (SMEs with competitive international linkages, e.g. the New Zealand dairy industry) or trans-border and asymmetrical (flagship companies, e.g. Toyota, with its high value added supplier network). This last category consists of 'core firms involved in purposive behaviour to optimize the value-added of clustering interactions and international linkages that are crucial to the cluster's success', and serves as a model and platform for the next stage. Stage 2 moves on from the cluster in geographical terms and characterizes it with respect to value added. Institutionalization and mutual adaptation are the two different logics that may characterize a cluster, and they may range in scope from narrow to broad. The Toyota supplier cluster is characterized as narrow in institutionalization scope in contrast to the (broader) flagship company concept with a greater variety of participants, such as local institutions and governments. The next cluster category is where 'flexible', adaptable MNEs are involved in R&D. And the final cluster category is where MNEs are so deeply embedded in the host country that their subsidiary-specific advantages may not be transferable back to the home-country cluster.

To see where the concept of the cluster fits in the Irish economy, a number of examples are appropriate. Hochtberger et al. (2004) present interesting case studies of three foreign firms engaged in software development in Ireland – Hewlett-Packard, Electronic Data Systems and IBM – which are summarized below.

Hewlett-Packard (HP) employs around 4000 people across three locations in Ireland, with its European Software Centre located in the west coast city of Galway. The various Irish divisions do not report to each other. They do not really have anything to do with each other, although they coordinate their efforts from the public relations point of view. Linkages are strong, however, with local tertiary educational establishments, particularly in terms of research carried out at the Digital Enterprise Research Unit of the National University of Ireland, Galway, and through a graduate recruitment programme and involvement in curriculum development at local institutes of technology.

US computer services firm Electronic Data Systems (EDS) first established an Irish presence in 1990. As the Irish affiliate performed well in its dealings with a number of EDS's most significant clients, the company came to appreciate more and more the skills that the Irish workforce offered, and the Irish affiliate was allowed to extend its scope towards greater process development. Interestingly, while EDS will often work with competitors on particular projects, these relationships emerge at the global corporate level rather than arising from the clustering of ICT MNCs in Ireland.

IBM has been manufacturing in Ireland since 1960, but most of its Irish workforce over the course of the 1990s came to be employed in services. Around one-third of its staff works in its sales and support centre for the EMEA region, while most of the remainder are employed on its technology campus outside Dublin. With the boom of the 1990s, the Irish subsidiary has become more involved in services provision in Ireland. The Irish ICT agglomeration is found to benefit IBM in an unusual way. According to the research interview of Hochtberger et al. (2004), the agglomeration means that Ireland is in some sense a microcosm of the global arena. The interviewee suggested that competing against other global firms in the Irish marketplace provides IBM with a close-up of other firms' global strategies, from which the entire corporation can learn.

The above examples are close to some of the findings based on the Taggart classifications that suggest that decision making and integration of activities are in essence limited in Ireland. The importance of linkages with universities is also noteworthy. But these cases also capture Markusen's ideas on the importance of external networks and the satellite industrial platform, based on large externally owned firms similar to the Research Triangle Park in North Carolina. IBM's experience of strong local competition in services in Ireland harks back to Porter's diamond in regard to competition and rivalry.

Other examples suggest greater embeddedness. Ó Riain (2004) notes that many Irish subsidiaries have been able to develop more sophisticated operations through what he terms corporate 'intrapreneuralism'. Intrapreneuralism is easier in more diverse parent corporations than in those such as Microsoft and Lotus, which concentrate on a relatively small number of strategic software packages. Their software development operations are highly concentrated, and the opportunities for building up capabilities around complex implementation, systems integration or sales support are limited. In contrast, there are significantly greater opportunities in companies such as Digital, Amdahl, IBM, Siemens, Nixdorf and Philips, which sell hardware and software in a variety of bundles, or in telecommunications companies such as Ericsson or ATT/Lucent Technologies, which have both hardware and software operations.

Despite the competitive attrition forcing ICT hardware makers to look East, many Irish-based ICT hardware companies have adjusted and carved out their own niche (Barry and van Egeraat, 2005). Apple, for example, shifted its focus from manufacturing to services. In this case, an Irish management team made a proposal to HQ, who concurred. Furthermore, when Intel decided to consolidate its cartridge assembly operation at its plants in the Philippines and Puerto Rico, the Irish plant was refitted to produce a higher-level wafer (Barry and Curran, 2004). Indeed, Intel decided to build its Fab 24 fabrication facility in Ireland, utilizing the most advanced 300 millimetre semiconductor manufacturing technology – as well as implementing a new IT innovation centre (Barry and Curran, 2004). These actions were viewed as a strong statement of intent with respect to Intel's long-term position in Ireland.

So, then, in geographical terms, how clustered are the three chosen sectors in Ireland? It should be noted first that economic activity in Ireland is much more clustered around the capital city, Dublin, than is the case in most of the rest of Europe. Hardware is even more tightly clustered around Dublin than is economic activity in general, and software substantially more so.

A common way to measure the extent of sectoral clustering is to compare a region's share of a particular manufacturing sector to its share of total manufacturing employment, and its share of software employment relative to its share of all market services. The Greater Dublin region accounts for around 40 per cent of all industrial employment and industrial establishments in the state. It also accounts for about 50 per cent of hardware employment and hardware firms. There are other smaller hardware clusters around second-tier cities such as Galway in the west and Limerick/Shannon in the mid-west.[8] Software, on the other hand, is almost completely clustered around the Greater Dublin region, which, while accounting for 40 per cent of aggregate services employment, accounts for a full 80 per cent of the country's employment in software.

Pharmaceuticals, by contrast, are primarily clustered around Cork in the southwest and County Dublin. This region accounts for 25 per cent of pharmaceutical employment compared to only 15 per cent of total industrial employment in the country (van Egeraat, 2006). This high level of concentration is sometimes attributed to the operation of agglomeration economies, notably Marshall's triad of localization economies. In fact, however, the concentration of the drug substance industry in these two particular urban centres has been largely driven by government intervention, especially environmental and regional planning policy, and the related spatially selective provision of well-serviced industrial sites and infrastructure. This is not to say that companies do not benefit from agglomeration economies. The point is that agglomeration advantages have not been the main factor driving the spatial concentration. Agglomeration economies are mainly of the urbanization type, relating particularly to the availability of labour supplies, although limited localization economies have recently been developing in the form of engineering services, tailored college courses and the supply of specialized qualified labour.

ICT hardware in general has a different geography to that of auto-manufacturing or traditional industries. Proximity and agglomeration do not seem to characterize this industry. Dell is headquartered at Cupertino, California, USA. There does not appear to be a cluster there as defined by Rugman and Verbeke (2003). A detailed survey of personal computer companies in the USA found little evidence of clustering either (Angel and Engstrom, 1995). The industry is characterized by high price competitiveness and outsourcing. It is not the nature of this industry to agglomerate. Dell in Limerick has very limited local sourcing (e.g. cardboard boxes and packing). Dell sources most of its product from Asia. Cost reduction is critical. The Dell subsidiary focuses on keeping operating costs below 10 per cent. It may be said that Dell has a low-value-added cluster in Limerick. With respect to the ICT hardware sector in general, R&D levels and linkages with research institutes or universities are limited. The Tyndall Research Centre at University College Cork does some research for Intel in the field of materials.

Clusters are characterized as having a set of related industries, to the point of having a deep supply chain. How evolved are the set of related industries and supply linkages of MNE subsidiaries in Ireland? Enterprise Ireland, a sister agency of the IDA, was tasked with the development of indigenous industry. It established national linkage programmes to further integrate foreign enterprises into the Irish economy and provide best practice in this area (UNCTAD, 2001, p. 185). The proportion of materials sourced locally by foreign MNCs in sectors other than food and electronics, for example, increased from 17 per cent in 1985 to 23 per cent in 2000, while in electronics (the key sector targeted), as mentioned earlier, the increase was from 10 per cent to 30 per cent (Ruane, 2001).

A recent survey of 12 pharmaceutical operations in Ireland (including ten subsidiaries of multinational operations) found that on average only 2 per cent of the value of the raw material inputs was manufactured in Ireland (van Egeraat, 2006). Nine of the ten foreign-owned pharmaceutical plants used no locally produced raw materials whatsoever. The only item that is typically sourced locally is packaging. On average, 65 per cent of the value of the packaging inputs is manufactured in Ireland. However, the same survey found that the pharmaceutical companies in Ireland have forged important local linkages with engineering companies (including many subsidiaries of large MNEs). Figures on the proportions of engineering services sourced in Ireland were not collected and absolute figures are, of course, a reflection of the size of the operation. However, to give an indication, the larger companies can spend tens of millions of euros per year on locally provided engineering services (excluding capital expenditures).[9]

Rugman and Verbeke (2003) provide a more evolved classification of clusters based on the Toyota supplier cluster in Japan and the concept of the flagship company. To what degree can we say that their classification helps explain the agglomerative tendencies or lack thereof of MNE subsidiaries based in Ireland? Irish MNE subsidiaries are not characterized as having a strong supply base like Toyota. Subsidiary R&D and innovation are still at a low level. While there are *in situ* flagship companies, they have limited local suppliers. Even when subsidiaries are perceived to be deeply embedded, ultimately they are dependent on their parent. The subsidiary itself may be highly competitive, but ultimately the perceived health of the parent will impinge on the subsidiaries. For example, Gateway closed its Irish operation in 2000. The Irish plant was efficient, but the company was unable to compete and pulled out of the European market (van Egeraat and Jacobson, 2004).

As described above, the evolution of the literature on clusters begins with the idea of the Marshallian industrial districts (later championed by Porter), characterizes the deep cluster by its evolved set of related industries, explores the role of the MNE, external networks and associated configurations, emphasizes the role of public authorities and organizational learning, and moves from geographical to an organizational understanding, with each phase suggesting different cluster types in value-added terms.

The examples given in this section demonstrate some elements of clustering dynamics in Ireland of MNE subsidiaries. Geographical concentration tends to take place in the main urban centres, with the role of government policy, notably in the arena of planning and the environment, being an important catalyst. Local sourcing of materials has increased in recent years in the ICT sector. But it would be difficult to suggest that there is an emergent cluster phenomenon *à la* Porter in Ireland. The examples given suggest a more nuanced dynamic. MNE subsidiaries in Ireland have strong external networks and configurations, with the parent company primarily making the decisions. The ICT hardware sector is highly competitive and increasingly looking eastwards for operating cost reductions. To remain competitive, Irish companies have had to move up the value chain from manufacturing to services provision. Increasing linkages are taking place with tertiary-level institutions by incumbent subsidiaries, notably MNE newcomers, with government policies and moneys in place to attract MNEs pursuing R&D. Markusen's satellite industrial platform and the Research Triangle Park in North Carolina seem to provide a deeper understanding of the concept of the cluster in Ireland.

In sum, the MNE presence and a government FDI-oriented strategy with strong regional and environmental planning objectives have proved to be the crucial ingredients of cluster development in Ireland, which is at variance with Porter's concept of cluster dynamics. Furthermore, unlike in Rugman and Verbeke (2003), purposeful cluster development or cluster-exploiting behaviour on the part of MNEs was not involved. The nature of the Irish clusters, based on the Taggart framework in the previous section, suggests that in ICT hardware and ICT software sectors, subsidiaries are nodes in global networks deferring to the decisions of the parent, rather than being independent actors. Nevertheless, the systemic influence of MNE subsidiaries in Ireland in the parent's decision-making process should not be overlooked.

The impact of government policy on the ICT hardware, ICT software and the pharmaceutical sectors

The role of government and government institutions has been at the heart of Ireland's success in attracting FDI. Ireland was one of the first countries globally to adopt an FDI-based development strategy. Its vehicle, the IDA, is widely recognized as one of the most effective investment promotion agencies in the world and operates at the level of 'best practices' (Loewendahl, 2001, p. 6).

(The IDA's *modus operandi* is described by former Irish Finance Minister and EU Commissioner Ray MacSharry and long-serving managing director of the IDA Padraic White, in MacSharry and White, 2000.)

The IDA first identifies and then targets, partly interactively, the high-growth sectors and subsectors that are thought to provide a good fit with Ireland's resources and development aims. Having attracted several computer and components firms in the 1970s, for example, and being favourably impressed by their performance *in situ*, the IDA launched a campaign in the early 1980s to develop Ireland as a major European location for electronics and computer software. Most MNEs that came to Ireland (*inter alia* Dell and Intel) were targeted. However, it was a chance encounter that led Apple to locate in Ireland.

The agency's next step involves approaching the strongest companies in these niche areas with a view to persuading them to locate in Ireland. Intel, for example, was pursued by the IDA for over a decade before deciding in 1989 to open a European plant, with Ireland ultimately emerging as the favoured location.[10] After maintaining contacts for more than two decades with IBM – a company that had traditionally shied away from export-platform activity – the IDA, partly on the basis of the success of the Software Development Centre that the company had set up in Ireland to meet its in-house development needs, eventually persuaded it that such a move could be beneficial, leading to the opening of an export plant in Ireland.

The sectors successfully targeted by the IDA all had relatively high skill intensities, medium as opposed to high plant-level economies of scale and relatively low transport costs, making them suitable for relocation to high-skill peripheral regions (Midelfart Knarvik and Tvedt, 2000). Targeting by the IDA helped capture these sectors for Ireland rather than having them go elsewhere, and the agency played a crucial role in advertising Ireland's advantages, in convincing potential investors that apparent difficulties could be overcome, and in capturing the important 'flagship projects' that appear to have been of importance in cluster development.

Crucially, however, experience and track record have given the IDA a degree of bureaucratic clout unusual for an investment promotion agency, allowing it to extend its influence into areas not traditionally recognized as lying within the industrial policy remit. By bringing the concerns of industrialists forcefully to government, for example, it played a major role in forcing through the modernization of the country's telecommunications infrastructure in the late 1970s and early 1980s, which allowed Ireland develop a head start in attracting IT-enabled services sectors, which had just begun offshoring.

When it noticed in the late 1970s a looming disparity between electronics graduate outflows and its own demand projections, it was able to secure rapid government action to institute one-year conversion courses to furnish science graduates with electronics qualifications. A huge expansion in the capacity of electrical engineering courses in the state followed, positioning the country well to profit from the subsequent explosion in the global software sector.

Enterprise Ireland also has a relatively strong involvement in venture capital. It is thought to account for 11 per cent of the funds under management in Ireland, compared to an average public sector involvement of 7 per cent across the rest of Europe. More recently, the development agencies have been to the fore in pushing for and overseeing the implementation of a new public emphasis on science, technology and innovation, once convergence with average Western European living standards had been achieved and the threat of increased corporation-tax competition from Central and Eastern Europe emerged.[11]

Recognition of the importance of these issues was heralded by the release in 1996 of the first-ever Irish government White Paper on Science, Technology and Innovation. It is underlined by the five-fold increase in investment in these areas under the current National Development Plan, by the funding by Science Foundation Ireland (SFI) of five joint partnerships between tertiary research institutions and industry, and by the introduction of a 20 per cent tax credit for incremental R&D in the Finance Act of 2004. Within ICT alone, the last few years have registered a number of significant developments under this new strategy, with companies such as Bell Labs, Hewlett-Packard and Intel establishing research institutes in partnership with several of the state's universities. Similarly, in the pharmaceutical sector an investment of $2 billion by Wyeth in 2006 has been notable, particularly given its interface with the Conway Institute of University College Dublin.

Conclusion
This chapter presented an analysis of three of the most successful international industries in Ireland through the prism of Porter's diamond determinants. The industries highlighted were the ICT hardware sector, the ICT software sector and pharmaceuticals. The first section profiled Ireland based on a Porter diamond perspective and the international sectors chosen. All sectors benefited from Ireland's main attractions for FDI, namely, the low corporate tax rate, EU membership, English-speaking environment with strong cultural connections with the USA, good business environment, responsive functioning of the labour market, high quality of public infrastructure, efficiency of public administration, availability of appropriate skills and the expertise of the IDA. In all sectors, demand was global rather than local. The ICT hardware sector had relatively limited supplier linkages and the pharmaceutical sector even fewer – but services linkages were important. The ICT software sector exhibited stronger linkages with the tertiary education sector and with Science Foundation Ireland through R&D. In regard to firm strategy, structure and rivalry, globalization, access to a low tax operating base and (formerly) relatively low-cost skilled labour characterized the ICT hardware sector. In software, there was strong competition among domestic SMEs but none among MNE subsidiaries. In pharmaceuticals, strategy was determined at global headquarters, but Ireland has become attractive for R&D due to government incentives. There was little evidence of rivalry between subsidiaries. The role of government, notably the IDA, was crucial in all sectors. The role of chance was limited due to the low tax environment and proactive IDA courtship.

When employment data were examined, the selected sectors had the highest share in the EU. In the computer hardware sector, employment in hardware was seen to be particularly important in two peripheral EU economies: Ireland and Scotland. Ireland's share of European exports in hardware is one of the highest in Europe, despite its small size. Software employment records its highest proportionate shares in Sweden, the UK and Ireland. Ireland was the largest global exporter of software, driven by the substantial presence of foreign software giants, *inter alia* Microsoft, Lotus and Oracle. Ireland's pharmaceutical employment as a share of manufacturing was the highest of any EU-15 country, illustrating that the sector is almost twice as important in Ireland (in employment terms) as in the Western EU as a whole.

The second section noted that while Ireland's inward stock of FDI is nearly twice its outward stock, outward flows have been strong in recent years. The importance of the USA as a source of inward FDI and also a destination for outward FDI was cited. The third section showed that inward FDI into Ireland was efficiency seeking. An analysis of decisionmaking and integration activities across the selected sectors showed that local decision-making was quite limited and that activities were quite integrated, though less so in pharmaceuticals. The fourth section noted that disaggregated data to examine outward direct investment were unavailable. Where acquisitions data were available, they reflected expansion of Irish companies in traditional sectors such as construction, packaging and food. Some software companies have begun to invest internationally, such as Riverdeep and Iona. In the other sectors, there is still limited outward FDI.

The penultimate section showed that MNE presence as well as a government FDI-oriented strategy with strong regional and environmental planning objectives proved to be the crucial ingredients of cluster development in Ireland, which is at variance with Porter's concept of cluster dynamics. The nature of the Irish clusters, based on the Taggart framework in the previous section, would suggest that in ICT hardware and ICT software sectors, subsidiaries are nodes in global networks, deferring to the decisions of the parent rather than being independent actors. Nevertheless, the systemic influence of MNE subsidiaries in Ireland in the parent's decision-making process should not be over-looked. The final section looked at the impact of government in general and the IDA in particular on the selected sectors. Without the prescience of government policy and the policy of the IDA to target selected companies in selected sectors over a number of years, the FDI-led success story that is the Irish economy today would never have happened.

Notes

1. Low corporate taxes in Ireland have led to the problem of transfer pricing where MNEs discount the value of what they are selling into industrial plants in Ireland.
2. Each cell therefore measures, for sector i and country j, $(L_{ij}/L_j)/(L_i/L_{EU})$.
3. Thus while Scotland in 1997 had only 8 per cent of UK manufacturing employment, it had 27 per cent of the UK's 63 000 jobs in computers and office machinery. Since Scotland is a region of the UK rather than an independent state, however, these data are harder to access than those on Ireland.
4. Data for European countries are only included if they record levels higher than Ireland's in one or both of the years shown.
5. Forfás is Ireland's national policy and advisory board for enterprise, trade, science, technology and innovation.
6. Exploiting the low corporate tax rate is an explanatory factor. This distortion has been addressed in recent years, showing that outward flows match inward ones. This supports Dunning's investment development path thesis (Barry et al., 2003).
7. Details on the field research can be obtained from the authors.
8. For an analysis of the emergence of an ICT cluster in Galway, see Green et al. (2001).
9. For further information on the low level of linkages in Irish MNE manufacturing, see van Egeraat and Jacobson (2004, 2005, 2006).
10. The story is told of how, at a late stage, the company became paralysed by fears that engineers with the requisite experience could not be found in Ireland. The IDA commissioned interviews with over 300 Irish

engineers, working mainly in the USA, who had the appropriate experience, and was able to report to Intel that over 80 per cent of them expressed a willingness to return to Ireland if offered a good career opportunity with a quality company. The IDA actually presented Intel with their hardcopy CVs to express their availability and readiness to move.

11. The development agencies comprise the IDA, Enterprise Ireland (the support body for indigenous industry) and Forfás, the national policy and advisory board for enterprise, trade, science, technology and innovation.

References

Amsden, A. and W. Chu (2003), *Beyond Late Development: Taiwan's Upgrading Policies*, Cambridge, MA: MIT Press.

Angel, D. and J. Engstrom (1995), 'Manufacturing systems and technological change: the US personal computer industry', *Economic Geography*, **71** (1), 79–102.

Barry, F. (ed.) (1999), *Understanding Ireland's Economic Growth*, London: Macmillan, and New York: St Martin's Press.

Barry, F. and D. Curran (2004), 'Enlargement and the European geography of the information technology sector', *World Economy*, **27** (6), 901–22.

Barry, F. and C. van Egeraat (2005), 'The eastward shift of computer hardware production: how Ireland adjusted', working paper, http://www.hwwa.de/etc/EI_WS_050916/WS-Papers.htm, retrieved on 6 March 2008.

Barry, F., H. Görg and A. McDowell (2003), 'Outward FDI and the investment development path of a late-industrialising economy: evidence from Ireland', *Regional Studies*, **37** (4), 341–9.

Bartlett, C.A. and S. Ghoshal (1989), *Managing Across Borders: The Transnational Solution*, Boston, MA: Harvard Business School Press.

Becattini, G. (1990), 'The Marshallian industrial district as a socio-economic notion', in G. Becattini, F. Pyke and W. Sengenberger (eds), *Industrial Districts and Inter-firm Co-operation in Italy*, Geneva: International Institute for Labour Studies, pp. 37–52.

Beije, P.R. and H.O. Nuys (eds) (1995), *The Dutch Diamond: The Usefulness of Porter in Analysing Small Countries*, Leuven–Apendoorn: De Garant.

Bellak, C.J. and A. Weiss (1993), 'A note on the Austrian diamond', *Management International Review*, **33** (2), 109–18.

Blomström, M., G. Fors and R.E. Lipsey (1997), 'Foreign direct investment and employment: home country experience in the United States and Sweden', *Economic Journal*, **107**, 1787–97.

Braconier, H. and K. Ekholm (2000), 'Swedish multinationals and competition from high- and low-wage locations', *Review of International Economics*, **8** (3), 448–61.

Brainard, S. and D. Riker (1997a), 'Are US multinationals exporting US jobs?', NBER Working Paper 5958.

Brainard, S. and D. Riker (1997b), 'US multinationals and competition from low-wage countries', NBER Working Paper 5959.

CFM Capital (2005), 'Acquisitions Survey', http://www.mazars.ie/about/media_publications.php, retrieved on 6 March 2008.

Clancy, Paula, Eoin O'Malley, Larry O'Connell and Chris van Egeraat (2001), 'Industry clusters in Ireland: An application of Porter's model of national competitive advantage to three sectors', *European Planning Studies*, **9** (1), 7–28.

Davies, H., P. Whitla, P. Kwok and H.K. Polyu (1995), *The Analysis of East Asia Competitiveness: Lessons from Hong Kong Experience*, Hong Kong: Hong Kong Polytechnic University and Lingnan College Hong Kong.

Deloitte and Touche (2005), www.deloitte.com.

Desai, M., C. Foley and J. Hines (2005), 'Foreign direct investment and the domestic capital stock', NBER Working Paper 11075.

Enright, M.J. (2000), 'Survey on the characterization of regional clusters: initial results', Working Paper, Institute of Economic Policy and Business Strategy, University of Hong Kong.

Florida, Richard (2002), *The Rise of the Creative Class: And How it's Transforming Work, Leisure, Community and Everyday Life*, New York: Basic Books.

Forfás (2000), *International Trade and Investment Report*, Dublin: Forfás.

Forfás (2001), 'Statement on outward direct investment', http://www.forfas.ie/publications/show/pub179.html, Retrieved on 30 January 2007.

Forfás (2007), 'Annual Competitiveness Report 2006, Volume 1: Benchmarking Ireland's Performance', http://www.forfas.ie/publications/show/pub243.html, retrieved on 30 January 2007.

Gambardella, A., L. Orsenigo and F. Pammolli (2000), *Global Competitiveness in Pharmaceuticals, A European Perspective*, Report for the Directorate General Enterprise of the European Commission.

Grant, R.M. (1991), 'Porter's *Competitive Advantage of Nations*: an assessment', *Strategic Management Journal*, **12**, 535–48.

Green, R., J. Cunningham, I. Giblin, M. Moroney and L. Smyth (2001), 'The boundaryless cluster: information and communications technology in Ireland', in *Innovative Clusters: Drivers of National Innovation Systems*, Paris: OECD.

Hochtberger, K., M.C. White and S. Grimes (2004), 'The evolution of multinational computer services affiliates in Ireland', CISC Working Papers No. 3, http://www.cisc.ie/documents/00013ciscwp.pdf, retrieved on 7 March 2008.

ICSTI (Irish Council for Science Technology and Innovation) (2003), 'ICSTI statement: embedding the pharmachem industry in Ireland', Dublin: Forfás.

ICT Ireland (2007), http://www.ictireland.ie/.

IDA Ireland (2006), www.idaireland.com.

IMD (2003), *IMD World Competitiveness Yearbook 2004*, Lausanne: Institute for Management Development.

Irish Times (2007), 'Motorola trouble is a warning, but the tech sector is not doomed', *Irish Times*, 3 February.

Kearny, B. (2003), 'Engineers ready to serve the world', *Pharmaceutical Engineering*, January/February, 63–66.

KPMG (2004), *KPMG's Corporate Tax Rates Survey*, http://www.us.kpmg.com/microsite/Global_Tax/CTR_Survey/2004CTRS.pdf, retrieved on 7 March 2008.

Lance, C. and J. Probert (2004), 'Between the global and local: a comparison of the German and UK clothing industry', *Competition and Change*, **8** (3), 243–66.

Lane, P.R. and F. Ruane (2006), 'Globalization and the Irish Economy', IIIS Occasional Paper No. 1, March.

Loewendahl, H. (2001), 'A framework for FDI promotion', *Transnational Corporations*, **10** (1), 1–42.

MacSharry, R. and P. White (2000), *The Making of the Celtic Tiger: The Inside Story of Ireland's Booming Economy*, Dublin: Mercier Press.

Markusen, A. (1996), 'Sticky places in slippery space: a typology of industrial districts', *Economic Geography*, **72** (3), 293–313.

Marshall, A. (1919), *Industry and Trade*, London: Macmillan.

Midelfart Knarvik, K.H. and J. Tvedt (2000), 'International trade, technological development, and agglomeration', *Review of International Economics*, **8** (1), 149–63.

O'Connell, L., C. van Egeraat and P. Enright (1997), 'Clusters in Ireland: the Irish dairy processing industry: an application of Porter's cluster analysis', *Research Series*, no. 1, Dublin: National Economic and Social Council.

OECD (2002), 'OECD Information Technology Outlook 2002', http://www.oecd.org/dataoecd/63/60/1933354.pdf

OECD (2006), 'Higher education in Ireland', *Review of National Policies for Education*, Paris: OECD.

O'Donnell, Rory (1997), 'International competitiveness in the context of peripheral regions', in B. Fynes and S. Ennis (eds), *Competing from the Periphery*, Dublin: Oak Tree Press, pp. 47–82.

O'Donnellan, Niall (1994), 'The presence of Porter's sectoral clustering in Irish manufacturing', *The Economic and Social Review*, **25** (3), 221–32.

O'Gorman, Colm, Eoin O'Malley and John Mooney (1997), 'The Irish indigenous software industry: an application of Porter's cluster analysis', National Economic and Social Council (NESC).

Ó Riain, S. (2004), *The Politics of High Tech Growth*, Cambridge: Cambridge University Press.

Pharmaceutical Ireland (2007), www.pharmaceuticalsociety.ie.

Piore, M. and C.F. Sabel (1984), *The Second Industrial Divide*, New York: Basic Books.

Porter, M. (1990), *The Competitive Advantage of Nations*, London: Macmillan Press.

Porter, M. (1998), *The Competitive Advantage of Nations*, Basingstoke: Macmillan Press.

Ruane, F. (2001), 'Reflections on linkage policy in Irish manufacturing – policy chasing a moving target?', mimeo, http://www.unece.org/ead/misc/ffd2001/ruane.pdf, retrieved March 2008.

Rugman, A. and R.D. D'Cruz (1993), 'The double diamond model of international competitiveness: the Canadian experience', *Management International Review*, **2**, 17–39.

Rugman, A.M. and A. Verbeke (2003), 'Multinational enterprises and clusters: an organising framework', *Multinational International Review*, Special Issue **3**, 151–69.

Smyth, J. (2006), 'EU court makes "artificial" companies liable to pay tax', *Irish Times*, 13 September.

Taggart, J.H. (1998), 'Strategy shifts in MNC subsidiaries', *Strategic Management Journal*, **19**, 663–81.

UNCTAD (1998), *World Investment Report 1998*, Geneva: United Nations.

UNCTAD (2001), *World Investment Report 2001: Promoting Linkages*, Geneva: United Nations.

UNCTAD (2004), *World Investment Report 2004*, Geneva: United Nations.

UNCTAD (2005), *World Investment Report 2005*, Geneva: United Nations.

UNCTAD (2006), *World Investment Report 2006*, Geneva: United Nations.
US Bureau of Economic Analysis (2006), http://bea.gov/bea/di1.htm, retrieved on 5 February 2006.
van Egeraat, C. (2006), 'The pharmaceutical industry in Ireland: agglomeration, localisation, or simply spatial concentration', NIRSA Working Paper 28, National Institute for Regional and Spatial Analysis, National University of Ireland, Maynooth, Ireland.
van Egeraat, C. and D. Jacobson (2004), 'The rise and demise of the Irish and Scottish computer hardware industry', European Planning Studies, **12** (6), 809–34.
van Egeraat, C. and D. Jacobson (2005), 'Geography of linkages in the Irish and Scottish computer hardware industry: the role of logistics', *Economic Geography*, **81** (3), 283–303.
van Egeraat, C. and D. Jacobson (2006), 'The geography of linkages in the Irish and Scottish computer hardware industry: the role of information exchange', *Journal of Economic and Social Geography*, **97** (4), 45–18.
van Egeraat, C. and P. Breathnach (2007), 'The manufacturing sector', in R. Kitchin and B. Bartley, *Understanding Contemporary Ireland*, London: Pluto Press, pp. 125–46.

5 Upgrading the international competitiveness of a transition economy: Slovenia in the European and global economy

Andreja Jaklič, Matija Rojec and Marjan Svetličič

Slovenia is a small economy that has almost accomplished the transition process and entered the EU (2004). With per capita GDP of €12 319 GDP in 2003 (€16 400 at purchasing power parity (PPP); IMAD, 2004) it is also the most developed among the new EU member states from Central Europe. With fewer than 2 million inhabitants, Slovenia could not survive without being an open, outward-oriented economy. Internationalization of operations is a critical factor for creating competitive firms and a strong economy. Traditionally the pattern of Slovenia's internationalization has been characterized by strong foreign trade and low FDI (foreign direct investment) penetration of the economy. The share of exports or imports in GDP is close to 60 per cent, while FDI inflows are only 3.5 per cent and the share of FDI outflows just 1.1 per cent. To put it into international perspective, in 2001, the share of trade in goods in Slovenia's GDP was 103.1 per cent, while the respective share for high-income countries was 37.9 per cent and 56.3 per cent for countries belonging to the European Monetary Union (EMU). The share of gross FDI in Slovenia's GDP was 3.8 per cent, while the respective share for high income countries was 5.3 per cent and for EMU countries 14.8 per cent (World Bank, 2003, p. 312). Slovenia's share in world trade flows is thus much higher than in world FDI stock and GDP. In these respects the Slovenian economy is somehow very Porterian: strongly integrated through international trade in a world (basically EU) economy based on a local and EU diamond (Rugman's 'double diamond'). Why refer to Slovenia as Porterian? Because he underestimates the role of FDI, or internationalization (Dunning, 1992). In Dunning's augmented Porter diamond Slovenia is much more weakly integrated due to its below average share of FDI in GDP.

This chapter aims to analyse the trends and determinants of international competitiveness of the Slovenian economy and evaluate the contribution of MNEs (multinational enterprises). MNEs and FDI significantly influenced the transition process and the country's competitive abilities, and their importance is expected to increase with EU membership. The analysis evaluates the impact of inward and outward FDI on the upgrading of international competitiveness, considering, like Porter, the role of demand as well as the role of chance and government in enhancing competitiveness. The chapter is structured as follows. After presenting the trends and determinants of the international competitiveness of the Slovenian economy, we deal with the role of inward and outward FDI in upgrading the parameters of Porter's diamond. Next follows an analysis of the impact of government policies in promoting competitiveness by upgrading the role of inward and outward FDI.

Competitive ability of the Slovenian economy
In static terms the achieved level of productivity (the right word for competitiveness according to Krugman, 1994) and real convergence of the Slovenian economy with the EU are relatively high. However, the indicators of competitiveness improvement reveal much slower dynamics than in other transition countries. After relatively fast productivity growth and decreasing unit labour costs in the second half of the 1990s, a slowdown in the 2000s was witnessed. This was reflected in Slovenia's world and EU market shares falling in 1998–2000, with a slow recovery since then. The reasons should be sought in the structural weaknesses and rigidities of the Slovenian economy, in particular in manufacturing. Labour costs are higher than in any other new Central European EU member state, but the share of labour-intensive products in Slovenia's exports is very high and the share of high-tech products on the other hand very low. The restructuring in the direction of products with higher value added is slow compared to other new EU member states and, in some cases, even the old EU member states. Slow structural and institutional changes in the country and in particular slow structural changes away from low-value-added activities constitute a serious problem for Slovenia's international competitiveness. This is clearly reflected in the declining rating of Slovenia in various international competitiveness rankings of countries. Such an outcome is to a large extent the result of the gradualist approach of Slovenia to the transition process.

In terms of economic development measured by GDP per capita at PPP, Slovenia is the most developed transition country (77 per cent of the EU-25 average in 2003)[1] and has made considerable progress since 1995, when it was 68 per cent of the EU-25 average (Eurostat, 2004). Other main macroeconomic indicators, such as the current account balance (mostly positive in the 1991–2004 period), general government balance (with the exception of 2002 never exceeding 2 per cent of GDP in the 1991–2004 period) and unemployment (6.7 per cent in 2004 according to ILO standard) have also shown good results. The exception has been inflation, which according to the Harmonized Index of Consumer Prices nevertheless decreased to 3.7 per cent in 2004 (IMAD, 2004; Mrak et al., 2004). Slovenia is also doing relatively well in terms of labour productivity. In 1995–2003 total productivity (GDP per employed person, on a full-time-equivalent basis) in Slovenia rose from 39.8 per cent to 50.5 per cent of the EU-15 average, followed by a certain slowdown of productivity growth in 2000–03. With these figures Slovenia stands much higher than any other new EU member state from Central Europe (IMAD, 2005).

Unit labour costs (the ratio of labour costs per employee to value added per employee) as a measure of cost competitiveness depict a similar trend. In 1996–99 they improved considerably, and then slowed down in 2000–03 (see Table 5.1). The trends in the Slovenian manufacturing sector are much better than for the economy as a whole. This points to the unfinished reforms and protectionism in the non-tradable sectors, where slow liberalization, deregulation and privatization allow them to increase wages and prices, while the manufacturing sector is fully exposed to international competition.

Comparison of unit labour cost trends in Slovenia and EU countries indicates fast convergence of Slovenia's cost competitiveness. It also shows that Slovenia has one of the highest unit labour costs among EU member states.[2] Thus, despite decreasing more rapidly, unit labour costs in Slovenia are still much higher than in other CEECs (Central and East European countries). As a consequence, Slovenia's share of world markets

*Table 5.1   Growth rates of unit labour costs*ᵃ *in Slovenia, 1996–2003*

	1996	1997	1998	1999	2000	2001	2002	2003
Slovenia – total economy	−3.8	−4.0	−2.1	−1.7	1.5	0.2	−1.9	−0.4
EU-25	−0.7	−0.4	−0.6	0.5	0.3	0.3	−0.7	−0.3
EU-12 (Euro area)	−1.1	−0.9	−1.0	0.4	−0.1	−0.1	−0.3	−0.1
Slovenian manufacturing sector	−7.1	−7.0	−1.7	−2.4	0.7	−0.8	−1.3	−3.5

Note: ᵃ Labour costs (compensation) per employee in current prices divided by value added per employee in current prices. Employment is measured in the equivalent of full-time equivalent.

Source: National Accounts Statistics SORS, Eurostat.

*Table 5.2   Slovenia's market share in most important trading partners*ᵃ *(%), 1996–2003*

	1996	1997	1998	1999	2000	2001	2002	2003
Totalᵇ	0.583	0.574	0.584	0.511	0.478	0.500	0.528	0.531
EU-7ᶜ	0.457	0.463	0.472	0.437	0.412	0.421	0.437	0.434

Notes:
ᵃ   Market share is calculated as a weighted average of shares of Slovenia's goods exports in the imports of its most important trading partners. The shares of individual trading partner in Slovenia's goods exports serve as weights for calculation of the weighted average (Fisher's formula).
ᵇ   Germany, Italy, France, Austria, the UK, Netherlands, Belgium, the USA, Switzerland, Croatia, Czech Republic, Hungary, Poland, Slovakia, Russia.
ᶜ   Germany, Italy, France, Austria, the UK, Netherlands, Belgium.

Source: IMAD (2005), based on SORS, Eurostat, WIIW, US Census Bureau.

has been declining (see Table 5.2). After hitting a record in 1998, Slovenia's share has dropped. By comparison, Hungary increased its market share in the EU by around 130 per cent, Slovakia by 90 per cent, Czech Republic by around one-third and Poland by one-fifth between 1995 and 2000 (IMAD, 2002, pp. 36–7).

Shift-share analysis of manufacturing exports of the CEEC-10 (Bulgaria, Czech Republic, Slovakia, Hungary, Poland, Romania, Slovenia, Estonia, Latvia and Lithuania) to the EU, decomposing the overall increase in their manufacturing exports to the EU into a general demand component, a structural effect component and a competitive effect component, helps reveal why the results were poor.[3] As much as 66 per cent of the total increase in the manufacturing exports of the CEEC-10 to the EU in 1995–99 was accounted for by the competitive effect component. This means that the CEEC-10 increased their market shares in the EU largely by raising their competitiveness against the other non-member states who were exporters to the EU. Slovenia was the only one of the CEEC-10 that recorded a negative contribution of the competitive effect component (competitive loss), with the loss amounting to −19.3 per cent (Havlik et al., 2001, pp. 20–24). In short, the competitiveness of Slovenian manufacturing exports to the EU in comparison with other (at that time) non-member exporting states has deteriorated. Given the fact that it was the technology-driven industries that contributed substantially to the overall competitive gains of the CEEC-10, the deteriorating competitiveness of Slovenian exports seems to be related to the slow pace of restructuring of manufacturing industry in the direction of technology-driven industries, which other CEECs achieved largely by relying on FDI in this sector.

Strojan-Kastelec (2001, pp. 10–14) explains the changes in Slovenia's exports of goods in 1994–99 as follows: (i) the major part of the annual change in Slovenia's exports of goods is explained by market growth; (ii) the structure of traded goods is unfavourable, with trade being concentrated in products whose demand in the EU rises at below-average rates; and (iii) the overall competitive position of the Slovenian economy has not deteriorated substantially, however the competitiveness in relation to CEFTA (Central European Free Trade Agreement) countries has clearly deteriorated. Demand conditions (in Rugman's sense) obviously played both a positive and negative role. Exports in general have been stimulated by demand growth, but this has not forced exporters to restructure fast enough. Therefore firms are facing restructuring changes with some delay and at higher costs.

Slovenia is not reducing its structural lag behind the EU-25 (natural-resource-intensive products being an exception, since they are already at the EU-25 level). The share of unskilled-labour-intensive products has been reduced considerably, yet this share is still almost twice as high as in the EU-25. Slovenia's structural surplus in unskilled-labour-intensive products versus the EU-25 was reduced by only 3.8 points in the 1995–2002 period. Slovenia has considerably increased the share of high- and medium-technology-intensive products. The share of low-technology-intensive products remains almost unchanged while its structural lag behind EU in exports of high-technology-intensive products increased. At the same time Slovenia increased its structural advantage *vis-à-vis* the EU-25 in exports of medium-technology-intensive products (see Table 5.3). The EU-25 is restructuring in the direction of high-technology-intensive products, while Slovenia is doing so more in the direction of medium-technology-intensive industries.

Why are there such differences among CEECs? There are two explanations. One is the better starting point of the Slovenian economy, which had a much longer tradition of exporting to the EU countries (extending back to socialist times) and developed its own competitive firms, some of which started internationalizing as early as the 1960s (see Jaklič and Svetličič, 2003). This stimulated more defence of existing market share in traditional, standardized products than changes in the export structure by increasing value added. Other CEECs previously exported more agricultural and resource-intensive products, which collapsed during the transition. In the manufacturing sector they mostly started immediately to seek affiliation with MNEs, which focused on more technology-intensive products. The lagging competitiveness of Slovenia is obviously an FDI-related issue.

Slovenia's problems with its international competitiveness are clearly reflected in various international competitiveness rankings. Slovenia fell from 35th position in 2002 to 45th position in 2004. According to IMD, Slovenia has the weakest performance in business and government efficiency, in particular in attitudes and values, company finances, fiscal policy, institutional framework, business legislation, etc. (IMD, 2004). In the WEF (World Economic Forum) competitiveness ranking of 103 countries, Slovenia

Table 5.3   Structure of exports of goods by factor content in Slovenia and the EU-25 (%), 1995–2003*

		1995	1996	1997	1998	1999	2000	2001	2002	2003
Natural-resource-intensive	Slovenia	16.6	16.1	16.6	15.4	15.1	15.3	15.1	14.6	14.6
	EU-25	20.0	19.7	19.0	17.5	17.5	18.0	17.6	14.8	n.a.
Unskilled-labour-intensive	Slovenia	25.6	24.2	23.0	22.5	22.8	21.7	21.4	20.1	18.6
	EU-25	12.1	12.0	11.9	11.6	11.2	10.6	10.6	10.4	n.a.
Low-technology-intensive	Slovenia	9.7	9.2	8.9	8.8	9.1	9.9	9.8	9.9	10.1
	EU-25	8.1	7.6	7.5	7.6	7.1	6.9	6.9	7.1	n.a.
Medium-technology-intensive	Slovenia	31.9	33.6	34.5	37.3	36.7	36.4	36.4	37.5	37.3
	EU-25	30.1	31.0	30.8	31.7	31.3	30.1	30.7	33.1	n.a.
High-technology-intensive	Slovenia	14.8	15.5	15.7	14.7	14.9	15.3	15.9	16.5	18.1
	EU-25	23.9	24.4	25.6	26.3	27.3	28.6	28.5	28.2	n.a.

Notes: * Classification does not entail all the products; therefore the total of shares for the five groups of products does not necessarily sum to 100 per cent.

Source: IMAD (2005), based on UNCTAD (2003).

is better positioned, i.e. in 33rd position as far as growth competitiveness is concerned, and in 31st position as far as business competitiveness is concerned (2004 ranking). Still, the country has seen its position slip in the last two years. According to IMD, some of the most problematic aspects of doing business in Slovenia are its inefficient bureaucracy, inflation, restrictive labour relations, tax regime, access to financing, and inadequate workforce and infrastructure (IMD, 2004). The reasons for such decreasing competitiveness lie in a gradualist approach to transition. This helped the economy to avoid unnecessary transition shocks, reductions in output and job losses, and has resulted in relatively high and stable economic growth. On the other hand, however, the gradualist approach has brought slow structural and institutional reforms, low involvement of foreign investors in the country, and consequently slower restructuring on the basis of global combinations of production factors and economies of scale and scope. As a result of this, firms were slower in adjusting to changes in the global economy due to the persistently protectionist government policy and lack of local competition (the small economy facilitates monopolization). Although the gradualist approach initially played a positive role, together with a floating exchange rate, it subsequently began to slow down some necessary reforms. Specifically: (i) it held back the privatization process, which failed to result in an efficient ownership structure, i.e. corporate governance in companies that would encourage restructuring; (ii) extensive state intervention in the economy persisted; (iii) liberalization, demonopolization and privatization of the financial, infrastructure and other non-tradable sectors were hesitant, which together with the existing rigidities in the labour market allowed continual increases in prices and, in turn, reduced the competitiveness of the corporate sector; and (iv) there was a costly and increasingly less efficient prevention of appreciation of the Slovenian currency, the tolar, which was supposed to solve the problem of marginal exporters, but in the long run in fact helped to maintain non-viable companies. Such an approach on the one hand enabled the inefficient non-tradable sector to survive and even expand and, on the other hand, by favouring quasi successful companies at the expense of efficient ones, held back restructuring within the tradable sector, most notably manufacturing (for more, see Rojec et al., 2004).

Inward FDI
Inward FDI is the most direct mechanism of dynamic integration effects and indicator of the contribution of MNEs to international competitiveness of a national economy. In spite of the relatively low penetration of FDI in the Slovenian economy, analysis and case studies show that FDI has had an impact on the upgrading of the four parameters of Porter's diamond. FDI has promoted restructuring and productivity upgrading in the Slovenian economy, and has been an important source of foreign technology and access to export markets. FDI in the Slovenian manufacturing sector has been distinctly of the factor-cost-advantage-seeking, export-oriented type, while in the service sector it has been distinctly local market oriented, which has brought about a broader and better supply of services. The impact of inward FDI on the development of local related and supporting industries has been modest since the foreign subsidiaries are clearly more import oriented than domestic companies, although recently they have tended to reduce their import propensity. Positive, but modest vertical spillovers confirm such a pattern. Horizontal spillovers of FDI in Slovenia are very small but in any case neutral, due to a low level of foreign penetration in the economy. Foreign investors also keep strategic and

marketing control in their hands and leave everyday operational functions to subsidiaries, which seem to be relatively independent only within the framework of their existing production mandate.

Further on, the impact of FDI on the four elements of Porter's diamond are analysed in more detail: (i) factor conditions are analysed by the level of FDI penetration, by the restructuring and productivity upgrading impact of FDI, and by the changes brought about by foreign investors in general; (ii) demand conditions are studied on the basis of the motivations and strategies of foreign investors and by the export orientation of foreign invested enterprises; (iii) the related and supporting industries parameter is analysed by the involvement of local suppliers in the supply networks of foreign investment enterprises and by spillovers; (iv) the strategy, structure and rivalry parameter is analysed by the pattern of decision making and control in foreign subsidiaries.

Inward FDI stocks and trends
The FDI stock in Slovenia at the end of 2004 amounted to €5633 million.[4] Inflows in 2004 were €421.6 million. The stock of inward FDI has increased approximately six times. However, the increase is mainly due to high FDI inflows in 2001 and especially in 2002, which were a consequence of one-off events, i.e. of several relatively big foreign acquisitions.[5]

FDI in Slovenia is distributed across a broad variety of industries. The main recipient sectors are trade (31.9 per cent of end of 2003 stock), financial intermediation (15.4 per cent), and other business services (10.2 per cent). In manufacturing, paper and paper products (4.8 per cent), rubber and plastic products (4.3 per cent), chemicals (3.9 per cent), machinery and equipment (3.5 per cent) and motor vehicles manufacturing (2.4 per cent) top the list. The manufacturing sector accounts for only 29.6 per cent of total inward FDI stock; the rest is in services. Investors from EU countries dominate FDI in Slovenia. Of the total end-of-2003 inward FDI stock, 65.6 per cent was accounted for by EU-15 countries, the major investors being Austria (with a 23.2 per cent share), Germany (7.8 per cent), France (7.5 per cent) and Italy (6.4 per cent).

Importance of FDI for the Slovenian economy
The penetration of FDI in the Slovenian economy (Table 5.4) is low compared to other EU countries. Thus, in terms of the quantity of inward FDI, the contribution of MNEs to the upgrading of factor conditions in Slovenia has been relatively low, and even more so if compared with those new EU member states that have gone through the transition process. With a 20.7 per cent inward FDI stock-to-GDP ratio in 2003, Slovenia lags behind all other EU countries except Greece with 9.8 per cent, and Italy with 11.8 per cent. The corresponding figure for the EU-15 is 32.8 per cent and for the ten new EU member states 42.5 per cent.

Foreign investment enterprises (enterprises with foreign equity share over 10 per cent – FIEs) active in Slovenia in 2003 accounted for only 5.1 per cent of the total population of Slovenian enterprises, but they have considerably higher shares in terms of employees, assets, sales and especially exports (Table 5.5). Comparison with other countries shows a comparatively low involvement of foreign investors in Slovenia. In 1999, the share of manufacturing majority foreign-owned FIEs in total Slovenian manufacturing turnover was 19.9 per cent (Bank of Slovenia, 2004). Of all OECD countries, only Portugal,

Table 5.4 Flows and stocks of inward FDI[a] in Slovenia (€ millions), 1993–2003[b]

	1993	1994	1995	1996	1997	1998	1999	2000	2001	2002	2003	2004
End year stock	851.3	1080	1376	1611	1999	2369	2675	3109	2952	3968	5069	5633
Annual inflow[c]	97.1	98.3	117.4	138.2	294.9	194.3	99.2	149.1	412.4	1750.4	298.8	421.6
Stock as % of GDP	7.5	9.2	9.5	10.7	12.4	13.6	14.2	15.1	13.5	16.9	20.7	21.7

Notes:
[a] FDI is defined as a foreign investor holding a 10 % or higher share in a company.
[b] From 1996 onwards direct investments with indirectly affiliated enterprises are also included.
[c] Inflows are in principle smaller than changes in stocks since international payments transactions comprise only part of the changes in stock; most notably inflow data do not include changes in net liabilities to foreign investors. Furthermore inflows do not include data on directly affiliated companies. From 1995 onwards data on reinvested earnings are also included in inflows and thus in the balance of payments.

Source: Bank of Slovenia (2004).

Table 5.5 *Share of foreign investment enterprises*[a] *in the total Slovenian non-financial corporate sector in terms of assets, employment, sales and exports (%), 2003*

	Assets	Employment	Sales	Exports
Total	18.9	12.6	20.9	32.1
Agriculture	0.7	0.4	0.8	4.3
Mining	0.1	0.1	0.6	9.8
Manufacturing	24.5	17.7	27.2	34.6
Electricity, gas and water	13.5	5.8	9.3	66.9
Construction	4.4	1.9	3.1	5.0
Trade and repairs	27.3	15.2	25.1	37.9
Hotels and restaurants	2.6	8.9	8.5	3.6
Transport, communication	8.3	7.5	10.6	12.0
Financial intermediation	43.6	22.0	37.7	42.1
Real estate, business services	16.2	8.5	10.1	17.7
M – Education	1.9	0.9	2.5	0.6
N – Health and social work	2.3	1.7	2.4	6.5
O – Other public/personal services	7.4	4.4	10.3	0.8

Note: [a] Enterprises with foreign equity share over 10 % throughout this text.

Source: Bank of Slovenia (2004), p. 83.

Finland, Turkey, Germany and Japan had lower foreign penetration in manufacturing (OECD, 2003, p. 55). Slovenia has by far the lowest level of foreign penetration and the lowest increase in penetration in 1993–2001 in all groups of industries, high-, medium- and low-tech. Consequently, the FDI impact on Porter's diamond can only be the weakest among all these CEECs.

Restructuring and productivity upgrading with FDI
In spite of the relatively low quantitative importance of FDI for the Slovenian economy, its impact on the restructuring and productivity upgrading has been important in Porterian terms (impact on the upgrading of factor conditions). Although foreign investors have brought mostly positive changes in the companies in which they invested, increasing their volume and scope of operation, increasing productivity and introducing new technology, the impact of FDI in the manufacturing sector is smaller in Slovenia than in other CEECs. Particularly worrying is the shift of FDI from medium-high into medium-low and low-tech industries (see Table 5.6).

The different industrial distribution of FIEs compared to domestic enterprises (DEs) indicates that FDI is having an important impact on the industrial restructuring of the Slovenian economy. FDI tends to concentrate in financial intermediation, trade and manufacturing. Table 5.6 confirms that, in terms of technology intensity, FIEs are superior to DEs; the share of value added produced in high- and medium-high-tech industries is much higher for FIEs than for the overall Slovenian manufacturing sector. Altogether the share of high- and medium-high-tech industries in manufacturing FIEs' value added in Slovenia in 2001 was 48.9 per cent,[6] while in the overall Slovenian manufacturing sector it was only 40.0 per cent.

Table 5.6   Distribution of value added of all and of foreign investment enterprises in the Slovenian manufacturing sector by level of technology (%), 2001

	High-tech	Medium-high-tech	Medium-low-tech	Low-tech
All enterprises	6.8	33.2	24.2	35.7
Foreign investment enterprises	11.2	37.7	18.7	32.4

Source: Damijan and Rojec (2004).

Table 5.7 summarizes structural changes in six Central European countries (CECs). The cumulative change in the distribution of value-added shares in the manufacturing sector over the period 1993–2001 again confirms the comparatively relatively lower gain of Slovenia. With exception of Estonia, in all the other CECs manufacturing activity has shifted away from low-technology industries towards either medium-low or medium-high-technology industries. Second, in all the above-mentioned countries the restructuring processes have been much more intensive in FIEs than in DEs in terms of the weighted measure of restructuring. Figures show not only the extent but also the direction of change, where larger weights are assigned to higher-technology groups. In Slovenia, FDI has moved away from medium high into medium-low and low-tech industries. Hence the overall positive technological restructuring in the Slovenian manufacturing sector seems to stem more from restructuring among domestic firms (Damijan and Rojec, 2004).

FDI and productivity growth
Another positive contribution of FDI to the factor conditions in Slovenia is the higher productivity level of FIEs than DEs, but DEs are gradually catching up with FIEs due to the situation in medium-tech industries. In high- and low-tech industries FIEs outperform DEs not only in terms of productivity level, but also in productivity growth.

In 2003, value added per employee in FIEs in the overall Slovenian non-financial corporate sector was by 37.2 per cent higher than in DEs, while in the manufacturing sector the margin in favour of FIEs was 29.3 per cent (Bank of Slovenia, 2004). DEs are gradually reducing their productivity gap with FIEs, from 63.0 per cent of FIEs' value added per employee in 1994 to 77.3 per cent in 2003. Table 5.8 shows that FIEs achieved the highest productivity growth in high-tech industries, followed by low-tech industries, in the 1995–2001 period in the Slovenian manufacturing sector. Productivity growth in medium-high- and medium-low-tech industry FIEs has been much lower. In high- and low-tech industries FIEs exhibit much higher productivity growth than DEs, while in medium-high- and medium-low-tech industries the trends are quite the opposite. In high-tech industries FIEs outperformed DEs 2.34 times and in low tech industries 1.46 times, while in medium-high-tech industries and in medium-low-tech industries DEs slightly outperformed FIEs (1.133 and 1.02 times respectively).

Table 5.8 demonstrates that manufacturing productivity growth in CECs during the 1990s has on average been largely due to FDI. Productivity growth of FIEs in terms of value added per employee is on average much higher than in DEs. The highest productivity growth is recorded by FIEs in high-tech industries followed by low-tech industries.

Table 5.7   Changes in the distribution of manufacturing value added[a] by technology intensity in Central European Countries:[b] all enterprises and FIEs (percentage points), 1993–2001[c]

	All enterprises						FIEs					
	CZ	ES	HU	PL	SL	SK	CZ	ES	HU	PL	SL	SK
High-tech	1.1	2.7	11.8	1.7	0.7	-0.3	2.6	14.2	16.3	0.0	1.7	0.2
Medium-high-tech	2.7	-12.1	8.2	1.5	1.3	-1.2	3.1	-17.5	11.6	3.1	-12.7	0.6
Medium-low-tech	-0.9	8.0	-5.1	-3.1	3.4	8.0	1.5	3.3	-11.5	11.2	6.8	14.5
Low-tech	-2.9	1.5	-14.9	-0.1	-5.4	-6.5	-7.3	0.0	-16.4	-14.4	4.2	-15.2
Absolute-change[1]	7.6	24.2	40.0	6.3	10.9	15.9	14.5	35.0	55.8	28.8	25.3	30.5
Weighted-change[2]	2.6	-2.7	15.6	1.6	2.7	1.6	5.2	3.6	20.2	5.9	-4.5	5.4

Notes:

a   For Hungary and Poland sales data have been used.
b   CZ – Czech Republic, ES – Estonia, HU – Hungary, PL – Poland, SL – Slovenia, SK – Slovakia.
c   Czech Republic, Hungary and Slovakia for 1993–2001, Estonia for 1995–2001, and Slovenia for 1994–2001.
1   Sum of absolute changes: $|\Delta S| = \sum_i |(S_{it_1} - S_{it_0}|$ over i technology groups.
2   Weighted change: $\Delta S*tech = \sum_i (S_{it_1} - S_{it_0})*w_t$, where $w_H = 1$, $w_{MH} = 0.67$, $w_{ML} = 0.33$, and $w_L = 0$.

Source: Damijan and Rojec (2004).

*Table 5.8   Cumulative changes in labour productivity (value added per employee[a])
by technology intensity of industries in FIEs and DEs in six CECs (%),
1995–2001*

	High-tech		Medium-high-tech		Medium-low-tech		Low-tech	
	FIEs	DEs	FIEs	DEs	FIEs	DEs	FIEs	DEs
Czech Republic	46	99	77	92	95	64	97	106
Estonia		166	95	118	239	133	341	141
Hungary	422	60	136	103	147	63	125	140
Poland	270	180	174	141	374	126	240	138
Slovenia	330	141	130	147	125	127	177	121
Slovakia	120	122	173	102	138	86	167	97
Average	238	128	131	117	186	100	191	124

Note: [a] Average cumulative growth rates of individual sectors within respective technology sectors. In the case of Hungary and Poland sales instead of value added data have been used.

Source: Damijan and Rojec (2004).

However, the comparatively very high labour productivity growth of FIEs in high-tech industries is to a great extent influenced by an outlier in the Hungarian data (Damijan and Rojec, 2004).

The factors behind the superior productivity level and productivity growth of FIEs were studied using a sample of 72 FIEs in the Slovenian manufacturing sector. Changes classified into five areas demonstrate that foreign investors in general had a positive impact (Table 5.9). Spearman's coefficients of rank correlation between the magnitude of changes in individual areas are positive and significant. This demonstrates not only that changes in one area are positively correlated with changes in other areas, but also that when changes are introduced this does not happen only in one or two areas but on a broad scale within the company's operations and with similar intensity. The highest correlation is between changes in productivity and quality (0.710), and productivity and technology (0.692), which indicates that changes in productivity go along with changes in technology and quality (Majcen et al., 2004).

Damijan and Majcen (2004) claim that FDI is an important source of technology transfer in the Slovenian manufacturing sector (2001). However, this technology is on average relatively standardized (Rojec and Stanojević, 2001). The most frequent changes introduced by foreign investors in the companies they invested in are: (i) increased product quality as a result of changes in the production and technological process; (ii) increased specialization of companies by concentrating on their core activity; (iii) changes in the organizational structure of a company in a way that reflects business methods in a foreign parent company; (iv) increased training of management and other employees; (v) improved information systems (new accounting and financial reporting systems, investment in internal informatization and control); (vi) reduction of employment, mostly using 'soft' methods, such as early retirement, assistance to former employees in

Table 5.9   *Magnitude of changes in 72 sample FIEs in the Slovenian manufacturing sector after the enterprises were registered as FIEs*

Magnitude of change	Value of sales	Share of exports	Level of produc- tivity	Level of technology	Level of quality	Overall
Sample FIEs distribution by magnitude of change						
Considerable reduction	1.4	1.4	0.0	0.0	0.0	n.a.
Reduction	2.8	2.8	0.0	1.4	0.0	n.a.
No change	13.9	22.2	19.4	22.2	29.2	n.a.
Increase	38.9	27.8	43.1	44.4	44.4	n.a.
Considerable increase	43.1	45.8	36.1	30.6	23.6	n.a.
No response	0.0	0.0	1.4	1.4	2.8	n.a.
Total	100.0	100.0	100.0	100.0	100.0	n.a.
Indicator of magnitude of change[a]	0.597	0.569	0.585	0.528	0.471	0.550

Note: [a] Calculated so that answers 'considerable reduction' are weighted by −1.0, 'reduction' by –0.5, 'no change' by 0, 'increase' by 0.5 and 'considerable increase' by 1.0. The higher the indicator, the more a particular business function is controlled by foreign parent companies.

Source: Majcen et al. (2004).

establishing their own businesses, etc.; (vii) major improvements in the role and quality of management;[7] and (ix) introduction of ecologically friendly products and processes.

Motivation and strategies of foreign investors

Although local and adjacent (neighbouring) markets are important motives for investing in Slovenia (see Table 5.10), case studies of foreign investors' strategy in Slovenia and especially the actual very high export orientation of FIEs in the manufacturing sector support the view that factor cost advantage seeking coupled with the market-seeking motive dominate in the manufacturing sector of Slovenia. Quite the opposite is true in the service and public utilities sector, where the market-seeking motivation clearly prevails.

This is strongly confirmed by the data on the export propensity of FIEs. In 2003 FIEs in Slovenia on average exported 43.2 per cent of their sales, the proportion in manufacturing industry being as high as 73.2 per cent.[8] The situation in the non-manufacturing sector is very different, with an exports to sales ratio in FIEs of only 16.9 per cent. FIEs are distinctly more export oriented than DEs: in 2003, DEs on average exported 24.2 per cent of their sales, the ratio in the manufacturing industry being 51.8 per cent and in the non-manufacturing sector 10.6 per cent (Bank of Slovenia, 2004). A higher export propensity of FIEs than DEs is a general feature in CECs (see WIIW database).

The export orientation of FIEs in the Slovenian manufacturing sector is the highest in the medium-high-tech industries, followed by high-tech industries. FIEs in the low-tech industries are clearly the least export oriented. Slovenia lost competitiveness in these industries long ago. They have survived only due to strong protection and government

Table 5.10   Motivations of foreign companies to invest in Slovenia[a]

Motive	Importance
Long-term cooperation	3.4
Access to Slovenian market	3.2
Quality labour force	3.2
Technology and know-how	2.7
Low cost of labour force	2.4
Recognized trade mark	2.3
Access to Southeast European markets	2.3
Supply of material and components	1.8
Access to EU markets	1.8

Note: [a] 251 FIEs answered the question. Each respondent was asked to assess each motive as: 1 = not important, 2 = less important, 3 = important, 4 = crucial.

Source: AGPTI in Gral iteo (2003).

Table 5.11   Exports-to-sales ratios of FIEs in the Slovenian manufacturing sector by technology intensity (%), 1994–2001

	High-tech	Medium-high-tech	Medium-low-tech	Low-tech
1994	58.5	69.8	69.6	46.7
1995	59.7	71.0	68.2	45.8
1996	66.9	72.6	68.6	42.3
1997	65.4	76.8	71.2	47.9
1998	73.8	78.4	71.3	52.7
1999	58.8	75.4	66.5	51.4
2000	73.7	80.0	70.5	61.1
2001	76.2	80.7	74.5	55.7
Change in %	17.7	10.9	4.9	9.0

Source: Damijan and Rojec (2004).

subsidies, which have allowed managers to delay restructuring in these industries, a process that should have begun in the 1970s. On the other hand, the very high increase in the exports-to-sales ratio for high-tech industries may indicate the increasing competitiveness of these industries (see Table 5.11; Damijan and Rojec, 2004).

The sample of 72 manufacturing FIEs analysed by Majcen et al. (2004) reveals that on average as much as 37.1 per cent of FIEs' sales goes directly to foreign parent companies and 35.8 per cent to other foreign buyers. The high percentage of sales going to foreign parent companies indicates that a number of FIEs in the Slovenian manufacturing sector are part of the integrated international production networks of their foreign parent companies.

Case studies of manufacturing FDI have disclosed a variety of motivations and strategies of foreign firms when investing in Slovenia (Lorentzen et al., 1998; Rojec and

Table 5.12   *Imports to sales ratios of FIEs in the Slovenian non-financial corporate*
            sector (%) (1996–2003)

	1996	1997	1998	1999	2000	2001	2002	2003
All FIEs	46.9	46.9	46.7	46.0	47.4	43.5	41.0	39.3
Manufacturing FIEs	52.5	53.5	53.6	51.8	52.8	49.8	48.6	49.5

Source: Bank of Slovenia (2004).

Stanojević, 2001; Rojec and Svetličič, 1998). The pattern of foreign investors' motivations and strategic behaviour is characterized by the following: (i) investing in Slovenia is a part of foreign investors' strategy of internationalization and relocation/restructuring via FDI in the context of globalization; (ii) foreign investors do not follow a single motive but, in principle, a multiple set of market-seeking, factor-cost-advantage-seeking and strategic motives; (iii) in spite of the relevance of local market as a motive, factor-cost advantage-seeking FDI is predominant in Slovenia, perhaps due to access to the markets of the countries of former Yugoslavia; (iv) cheaper labour is an important motive but the focus is always on the favourable price of skilled labour; and (v) often the deciding factor was a good opportunity, especially the possibility to buy a company in the privatization process where there has been good previous cooperation between the prospective foreign investor and the target company/local joint venture partner. In spite of the relevance of the local (ex-Yugoslavian) market as a motive, the factor-cost-advantage-seeking FDI based on quality and delivery time/proximity has been predominant in Slovenia.

Local suppliers and spillovers
The role of FDI in the development of related and supporting industries in Slovenia relates to the importance of local suppliers and to the extent of imported inputs. If FIEs are, on the one hand, much more export oriented than DEs, they are, on the other hand, also much more prone to import. In 2003, FIEs in Slovenia on average had an imports-to-sales ratio of 39.3 per cent, while the ratio for DEs was only 19.5 per cent. Ratios in the manufacturing sector were 49.5 per cent for FIEs and 28.8 per cent for DEs, and in the non-manufacturing sector 30.3 per cent for FIEs and 14.9 per cent for DEs. A positive feature is that imports-to-sales ratios in FIEs seem to have been gradually decreasing, which suggests the development of local suppliers: in 1996–2003 the ratio for all FIEs decreased by 7.6 per cent and for FIEs in the manufacturing sector by 3.0 per cent (see Table 5.12).

The data on imports to sales ratios of FIEs, however, only indirectly indicate the extent of imported inputs, which compete with domestic suppliers, i.e. domestic-related and supporting industries. This is because FIE imports not only contain inputs for their basic activity but also goods that are directly sold in the Slovenian market. Table 5.13 shows that most of the input supplies of sample FIEs come from other foreign suppliers, followed by foreign parent companies. There are considerable differences in the supply pattern of FIEs according to the technology intensity of their industry. High-tech FIEs get far more supplies from their foreign parents, the opposite situation being true in low-tech FIEs, while medium-low-tech FIEs get far more of their supplies from other

Table 5.13   Structure of input supplies of 72 sample FIEs in the Slovenian manufacturing sector by technology intensity (%)

Suppliers	Foreign parent company	Other foreign suppliers	Other local subsidiaries of foreign parent	Other local suppliers
Total	23.5	34.6	0.5	41.3
High tech	33.8	32.2	0.0	34.0
Medium-high-tech	23.0	38.4	1.3	37.3
Medium-low-tech	23.5	29.2	0.0	46.9
Low-tech	18.8	40.2	0.0	41.0

Source: Majcen et al. (2004).

domestic suppliers. As expected, high-tech FIEs are the most integrated into parent companies' network, as far as input supplies are concerned (Majcen et al., 2004).

The impact of FDI on the development of a host country's related and supporting industries is probably best indicated by the so-called vertical spillover effects, which measure the extent of FIEs' backward and forward linkages, i.e. the impact of FIEs on the structure of their suppliers and customers. On the one hand, FIEs can include local suppliers in their supply networks, with many positive impacts on these and other local suppliers, but, on the other hand, a foreign acquisition could also result in the displacement of previous domestic suppliers by new foreign suppliers brought in by the foreign parent company (e.g. the integration of a new subsidiary into the existing supply network of an MNE). Analysis of a large sample of manufacturing firms in ten transition countries by Damijan et al. (2003) shows positive but modest vertical spillovers of FDI in Slovenia for domestic firms.[9] This means that FDI has not disrupted the existing vertical linkages among enterprises in Slovenia, and there even seem to be certain positive effects on the development of local suppliers.

FDI spillover effects can also be horizontal.[10] Damijan et al. (2003) claim that horizontal spillovers in Slovenia are very small, varying by type of activity.[11] This outcome would be expected due to the low level of foreign penetration in Slovenia. Effects on related industries and spillover effects depend to a large extent also on the organization and management of FIEs. Majcen et al. (2004) distinguish 13 business functions of FIEs, which they classify into three groups: operational, marketing and strategic. They analysed the decision-making and control patterns in 72 FIEs in the Slovenian manufacturing sector in terms of who undertakes individual business functions. It was expected that foreign parent companies would exercise less control in operational functions, followed by stronger control in marketing, and the strongest influence would occur in strategic functions. Since sample FIEs are on average highly export oriented (the exports-to-sales ratio is on average 72.9 per cent), it was also expected that foreign parent companies would want to retain a relatively higher level of control in the marketing functions.

Table 5.14 fully confirms the above expectations. It is somehow surprising that, in general, the vast majority of business functions are undertaken only or mainly by the sample FIEs themselves. There is not a single business function predominantly undertaken only or mainly by foreign parents.[12] Foreign investors are eager to retain more

Table 5.14   Who undertakes individual business functions in a sample of FIEs[a] in Slovenia?

Business functions	Only/mainly FIE (%)	Only/mainly foreign parent company (%)	Not defined (%)	Total (%)	Indicator of foreign parent company influence[b]				
					Average	High-tech ind.	Medium-high-tech ind.	Medium-low-tech ind.	Low-tech ind.
Operational Management	97.2	2.8	0.0	100.0	0.111	0.222	0.123	0.071	0.121
Process engineering	83.3	16.7	0.0	100.0	0.278	0.389	0.284	0.238	0.303
Supply and logistics	90.3	9.7	0.0	100.0	0.194	0.278	0.173	0.167	0.273
Accounting and finance	94.4	5.6	0.0	100.0	0.083	0.167	0.099	0.036	0.121
Operational functions	91.3	8.7	0.0	100.0	0.167	0.264	0.170	0.128	0.205
Distribution, sales	69.4	30.6	0.0	100.0	0.319	0.500	0.333	0.238	0.394
Advertising	65.3	29.2	5.6	100.0	0.333	0.556	0.333	0.267	0.364
After-sales services	69.4	27.8	2.8	100.0	0.305	0.444	0.358	0.222	0.300
Marketing	59.7	40.3	0.0	100.0	0.403	0.500	0.370	0.381	0.485
Market research	52.8	47.2	0.0	100.0	0.463	0.444	0.444	0.440	0.576
Marketing functions	63.3	35.0	1.7	100.0	0.365	0.489	0.368	0.310	0.424
Determining the product price	70.9	29.1	0.0	100.0	0.315	0.500	0.272	0.226	0.545
Investment finance	79.2	20.8	0.0	100.0	0.269	0.333	0.259	0.238	0.333
Product development	54.2	45.8	0.0	100.0	0.454	0.444	0.444	0.405	0.606
Strategic management and planning	68.1	31.9	0.0	100.0	0.398	0.333	0.383	0.393	0.485
Strategic functions	68.1	31.9	0.0	100.0	0.359	0.403	0.340	0.316	0.492
Overall	73.4	26.0	0.6	100.0	0.302	0.393	0.298	0.256	0.377

Notes:
[a] FIEs = foreign investment enterprises, i.e. enterprises with foreign equity share over 10 %.
[b] Alternatively, this can also be called an indicator of subsidiary autonomy. It is calculated so that answers 'Only FIE' are weighted by 0.0, 'Mainly FIE' by 0.33, 'Mainly foreign parent company' by 0.66 and 'Only foreign parent company' by 1.0. The higher the indicator, the more a particular business function is controlled by foreign parent companies.

Source: Majcen et al. (2004).

control in two areas of strategic and long-term importance, i.e. in product development and marketing, including market research. The fact that foreign parent companies want the highest control in the marketing functions could be explained by the high export propensity of FIEs and, perhaps, the relatively larger lag in domestic expertise in this area.

Spearman's coefficients of rank correlation between individual business functions according to who undertakes them show positive and significant correlations. Marketing functions are particularly highly correlated with each other. It seems that individual foreign investors do have their own patterns of control, some preferring tighter control than the others. If they are keen to exercise tighter control, they do that in most business functions, and conversely, if they exercise a lower level of control, then this is the case in most business functions.

Comparison of decision-making and control patterns in FIEs according to the technology intensity of industries presents a mixed picture. The indicator of foreign parents' influence on decision making (see note to Table 5.14) shows, as expected, the highest foreign control in high-tech industries, followed by low-tech industries, and somehow a lower level of control in medium-high- and medium-low-tech industries. The normal expectation would be that a foreign parent would reduce its influence on decision making in FIEs in line with decreases in the technological level of the industry, but the high indicator of foreign parent control in low-tech industries does not support this view. Obviously there are other more important factors that determine the influence of foreign parents on decision making in FIEs. What is especially interesting in this context is that FIEs in high- as well as in medium-high-tech industries exhibit a lower-than-average level of foreign parent influence on product development and on strategic management and planning, which are rather important business functions for technological development. Low-tech FIEs exhibit much above average foreign parent influence in these two business functions. For strategic functions in general, foreign parent control is the highest in the case of low-tech FIEs.

The regression model used by Majcen et al. (2004) suggests that the level of foreign parent companies' overall control and the level of their control of marketing and strategic functions are the most important determinants of productivity growth in foreign subsidiaries in Slovenian manufacturing. The higher the foreign parent's control overall, as well as of marketing and especially of strategic functions, the higher the productivity growth in subsidiaries. Foreign parent companies seem to seek control of strategic and marketing business functions and leave operational control to subsidiaries themselves. The level and mechanisms of control of individual business functions seem not to be related to the level of foreign equity share. Foreign parent companies are eager to exercise control over marketing and strategic functions, regardless of whether they hold a majority or minority equity share. The conclusion of the impact of governance of FIEs on competitors in the Slovenian economy through micro-enhancing of competitiveness is mixed. The relatively low level of control indicates that weak foreign control can strengthen local human resource capabilities (factor conditions) and facilitate spillover effects in related industries and competition, but the strong positive correlation between foreign control and productivity growth, particularly in high-tech and low-tech sectors, suggests that maintaining a high local ownership share may result in substantial opportunity costs in terms of forgone productivity.

Outward FDI

As in all transition economies, Slovenia lags behind in outward internationalization, especially in the more demanding entry modes such as direct investment abroad and entry to more distant markets. Yet, compared to other transition economies, Slovenia has relatively more home-grown MNEs. One explanation is that the initially more open economy during the pre-transition period led to a stronger export orientation and consequently an earlier start to direct investment abroad. Slovenian enterprises started to invest abroad as early as the 1960s, yet the real take-off of outward investment activity took place at the end of 1990s and the turn of the millennium. However, the initial advantage in outward investment activity that placed Slovenia in the 1990s among the top CEC outward investors (in terms of outward FDI stock relative to GDP or per capita, not in absolute value terms) has recently vanished. One reason may be the modest share of foreign capital, since they could be among the important agents of outward internationalization.

In transition economies, investment abroad is generally much more modest in volume and in terms of number of firms engaged than inward FDI, and its impact has also been less examined. Studies (Jaklič and Svetličič, 2003) show that the contribution of outward FDI and own MNEs to national economic success has been important and has strengthened the 'competitive diamond' of Slovenia. As trends of inward FDI slow down and reflect low penetration compared to other transition economies, the role of home-grown MNEs becomes even more important. The impact of outward FDI is similar to that of inward FDI analysed on the four elements of Porter's diamond. The importance of home-grown MNEs in the Slovenian corporate sector clearly illuminates their role in the competitiveness of the Slovenian economy. Both the extension of the factor conditions and demand conditions will be studied, first by analysing the level of outward FDI and its geographical distribution to illustrate the extent and locations to which proprietary resources have been transferred and exploited. The geographical allocation of outward investment also suggests the location advantages sought. The analysis of the motivation and strategies of Slovenian investing firms reflect their home diamond as well as the diamonds of destination countries (Rugman and Verbeke, 2001). As market-seeking investment dominates, the impact on demand conditions is very important. The type of affiliates and the changing pattern of investors' trade further explains Porter's next element: related and supporting industries. Although domestic suppliers have retained their positions, the structure of intra-firm trade has been changing and increasing in volume and diversity. Upgrading of all four elements has been further demonstrated by the positive impact on the growth of domestic MNEs due to investment abroad. Being present abroad means importing international competition and sharing the strategy, structure and rivalry of foreign markets, and thus expanding the fourth element of the diamond.

Outward FDI stocks and flows

During the 1990s, three stages of the internationalization process can be identified, predominantly characterized by institutional/legal and political developments, and consisting mainly of privatization and accession to the EU (Jaklič and Svetličič, 2003, p. 52–63):

1. An early wave of internationalization (1990–93), marked by a rapid increase in outward investment on the one hand, and divestments and restructuring on the other.
2. A consolidation phase (1994–98) characterized by slow progress in outward investment activity mostly carried out by existing multinational companies.
3. A new wave of internationalization at the end of the 1990s (from 1999 onwards) that sped up the outward investments of existing multinationals and newcomers in terms of broadening and strengthening their foreign affiliate networks, and rapid expansion in the former Yugoslav markets and after 2001 in CECs.

The value of Slovenian outward FDI increased 7.3 times from 1993 to 2003, and amounted to €1849 million in 2004 (see Table 5.15). Relatively high growth was recorded for the fourth consecutive year. Outward FDI increased also as a percentage of GDP and gross fixed capital formation.

Trends in Slovenian outward FDI demonstrate the relevance of stage of development or evolutionary models (Johanson and Vahlne, 1977; Johanson and Wiedersheim-Paul, 1975; Vernon, 1966; Welch and Luostarinen, 1988). Previous exporting experiences have proven to be very important. Those Slovenian firms that were once major exporters (or direct investors) in the socialist era were among the first to start internationalizing their activities after transition started. Firms first entered foreign markets through exports and then continued with outward FDI, initially mostly by establishing trading units abroad and, later, production facilities.

The most important exporters and existing investing firms were considerably more important for progress in outward investment volume than the newcomers. Newcomers have arisen very slowly. According to the 1999 Survey (Jaklič and Svetličič, 2003), foreign affiliates' growth in Slovenia in the 1990s was higher than the growth of companies investing abroad. The second wave of internationalization brought an increase in the number of foreign affiliates and investing firms. The 1999 Survey indicated an expansion in the average affiliate number per investor from 2.8 to 4.3 in the 1995–98 period (see Table 5.16), while the 2001 Survey (Jaklič and Svetličič, 2003) showed an increase from 3.6 to 4.4 in the 1997–2000 period.[13] On average, foreign affiliates grew as measured by all business indicators (equity, assets, turnover, number of employees, exports).

By cooperating with foreign multinational corporations, firms enhance their capabilities and thus become able to invest abroad at a later stage. In some countries, foreign-owned firms are even the major investors abroad. The influence of inward FDI on outward internationalization as predicted in the evolutionary models (the inward–outward linkages explained in Ozawa's dynamic paradigm (1992) and in the investment development path) is not so strong in Slovenia. Major investors abroad are indigenous Slovenian firms, although inward FDI has started to assist substantially in restructuring the corporate sector. Inward FDI, i.e. foreign-owned companies, increased allocation efficiency by concentrating in activities with above-average profitability, value added and capital intensity as well as improving technical efficiency by increasing productivity and competitiveness (Rojec, 1998).

Foreign-owned companies that invest abroad – so-called indirect investors – have represented a small share of companies that invest abroad. In 1999, only 11 per cent of companies that invested abroad were foreign owned. Inward processing traffic, long-term

Table 5.15 Flow and stock of outward FDI[a] from Slovenia (€ millions), 1993–2003

	1993	1994	1995	1996	1997	1998	1999	2000	2001	2002	2003
Year-end stock (total)	251	289	382	371	416	519	603	854	1140	1417	1849
Equity and reinvested profits	216	279	286	277	294	314	359	501	692	894	1150
Net claims to foreign investors	35	10	97	94	122	206	244	353	414	523	699
Claims on foreign investors	227	216	275	280	365	355	401	526	594	686	883
Liabilities to foreign investors	192	207	178	186	243	149	157	174	130	163	184
Annual outflow	0.9	−2.5	−3.9	4.8	31.9	−1.8	35.7	71.7	161	168	413.7
Growth rates year-end stock total in %	n. a.	15.1	32.5	−3.0	12.1	24.7	16.3	41.5	34.3	31.6	30.4
Outward FDI stocks as % of GDP	2.2	2.5	2.6	2.4	2.5	3.1	3.0	4.4	4.9	6.8	6.5
FDI outflows as % of gross fixed capital formation	0.04	−0.1	−0.1	0.2	0.7	−0.2	0.6	1.3	3.1	1.9	4.8

Notes:
n.a. = not available.
[a] FDI is defined as an investment with a foreign equity share over 10 %. Negative value means disinvestment.

Source: Bank of Slovenia (2004).

Table 5.16   Number of outward investing companies and their foreign affiliates in Slovenia (1992–98)

	1992	1995	1998	Index 95–92	Index 98–95
No. of investors (current year)	25	29	32	116.0	110.3
No. of foreign affiliates	67	91	137	135.8	150.5
Average no. of foreign affiliates	2.1	2.8	4.3	133.3	153.6

Source: 1999 Survey (Jaklič and Svetličič, 2003).

co-production, licences and strategic alliances played a more important role in strengthening the capabilities of Slovenian firms for their investments abroad. They stimulated firms to follow their customers or competitors. The emergence of MNEs in Slovenia is on the whole more a result of the liberalization, privatization and revived growth in the period of transition than of interaction with inward FDI. In an examination of investment determinants, inward FDI was not recognized as an incentive to outward FDI (Jaklič, 2004).

Sectoral and geographical allocation
Both the industrial distribution and geographical dispersion of outward FDI confirm the relevance of internationalization as a gradual learning process in terms of entry modes, market choice and the outward orientation of industries. Outward FDI follows exports and the most important trading partners are important host locations for outward investments, while activities experiencing the most intense competition are among the first to invest abroad.

The industrial distribution of outward FDI is determined by a handful of large investors.[14] Since manufacturing has always largely depended on exports, while services suppliers have concentrated on the domestic market with its high level of protection, the manufacturing sector is far more active in outward investment activity than the services sector. Services firms indeed started to invest abroad only in the late 1990s and after 2000, frequently following their (manufacturing) clients or following their competitors in the closest markets, trying to profit from first-mover advantages. This is one example of upgrading the competitiveness of a sector by supported and related industries.

The most important services investors are financial intermediaries, the retail trade and suppliers of other business-related services. In manufacturing, the most important areas are chemicals and chemical products, especially pharmaceuticals, machinery and equipment, food products and beverages, and fabricated metal products. Except for pharmaceutical firms, the most important home-grown MNEs are those involved in intermediate products. These capital-intensive sectors started internationalizing through traditional exports and continue to contribute the lion's share of Slovenian exports even today (such as machinery and equipment, chemical products, various manufactured goods). The industries that were the first to start internationalizing using traditional exports were also the first to use advanced modes of doing business abroad. These industries are in addition more advanced in inward internationalization, especially as regards experiences with subcontracting, licensing, outward processing and inward FDI.

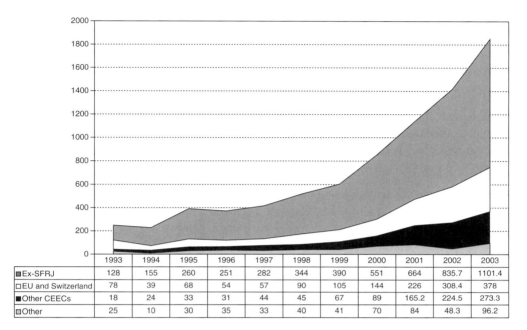

	1993	1994	1995	1996	1997	1998	1999	2000	2001	2002	2003
▣Ex-SFRJ	128	155	260	251	282	344	390	551	664	835.7	1101.4
▢EU and Switzerland	78	39	68	54	57	90	105	144	226	308.4	378
▪Other CEECs	18	24	33	31	44	45	67	89	165.2	224.5	273.3
▢Other	25	10	30	35	33	40	41	70	84	48.3	96.2

Source: Bank of Slovenia (2004).

Figure 5.1   Geographical allocation of Slovenian investment abroad (€ millions), 1993–2003

An evolutionary pattern of expansion could also be seen in the 'geographical bias' of outward investment. In value terms outward FDI is particularly concentrated in countries that are less developed than Slovenia. While Slovenian exports are concentrated in developed EU markets, outward investment is mostly located in low- and middle-income countries (mostly in former Yugoslavia and Central and Eastern Europe). Less than 20 per cent of the outward investment stock is located in countries with a higher income level. Firms claim that a combination of market penetration methods is increasingly being used in a number of markets, though less-developed markets where the competitive advantages of Slovenian firms are more easily exploited need even more direct penetration, as developed markets that (at least those that are closer) are still served by traditional exports.

In the 1993–2003 period, the former Yugoslav markets received 50 per cent to 70 per cent of the total outward FDI stock (see Figure 5.1). A very similar picture of concentration emerges if one considers the number of Slovenian companies with outward investments (see Table 5.16), or the number of outward investments by country.[15] In 2000, the former SFRY (Socialist Federal Republic of Yugoslavia) countries attracted 65 per cent of FDI in terms of value, or 1441 out of a total of 2160 outward FDI cases[16] (Bank of Slovenia, 2004, p. 66). In 2003 the region of the former SFRY still hosted 60 per cent of Slovenian outward FDI.

The dominance of successors to the SFRY has historical reasons. Before independence, the SFRY market was the most important one for Slovenian companies. In the former common market, Slovenian companies' investments 'served for trade promotion and for a vertically organized production process with large intra-firm trade, as is typical for vertical multinational companies'. Slovenian firms mostly carried out the lower stages of the production process in other republics, imported raw or intermediate products and remade them into final products before exporting or (re)selling them in other Yugoslavian republics. Intra- and inter-firm trade was seriously interrupted when Slovenia gained its independence. In the 1990–93 period, Slovenian sales to the successor states of the SFRY fell from US$6662 million to US$965 million (Damijan and Majcen, 2001). Exports were redirected to Western markets but the majority of Slovenian companies wanted to (re-)establish and (re)gain their market shares in the former SFRY countries. Liberalization of trade in this region began only in the second half of the 1990s. Trade relations were also very unbalanced, with a large trade surplus in Slovenia's favour with each former republic (see Mrak et al., 2001). Outward FDI has therefore proven to be an especially appropriate entry mode for gaining domestic producer status and easing local pressures to reduce exports from Slovenia. FDI ties have reduced information gaps and economic distrust, and been an effective long-term way of linking countries economically, socially and politically.

The second-most important country grouping involves other CEECs, which are increasingly attracting Slovenian investors. Due to its market size, Poland is growing in appeal. Outward FDI has been steadily increasing there: by 2001 it amounted to 8 per cent of the aggregate stock.[17] The most important recipient in Eastern Europe is Russia, with 2 per cent of the outward stock.

These two groups of countries were gaining in importance in terms of the amount invested and the number of investing firms while EU countries were, contrary to expectations, losing their attractiveness in the mid-1990s. The orientation to less-developed markets suggests that the knowledge, experience, or more generally firm- or ownership-specific advantages of Slovenian companies have generally been sufficient in less-demanding markets, but are not so in industrial countries compared to the strong firm-specific advantages possessed by large multinationals. While EU countries have been the main destination for traditional export sales, a direct market presence has been put into place in less-developed markets for (re)gaining market share and strengthening market positions. Apart from those that find a global niche or have entered the network of another global MNE (becoming the supplier of a global MNE and then following its expansion), the strategy of most Slovenian direct investors abroad is to become a regional MNE.

Although investing in the EU to become a local producer was regarded as a very effective *ex ante* adaptation to EU integration, in the late 1990s the anticipation of membership in fact reduced outward FDI there by reducing the incentive for tariff jumping. Trade liberalization and the Single Market made exports by would-be members an efficient enough entry mode during the period leading up to membership. As a result, outward FDI seems to have become a less attractive entry mode for EU markets. Despite the falling number of investors in the EU, the outward FDI stock in the majority of EU countries increased in the 1994–2001 period. Germany, along with neighbouring Austria, Italy and France, dominate both as outward FDI destinations and as trading partners. These four countries are also the most important inward investors in Slovenia. The importance of Austria as a location for Slovenian outward FDI can be explained not only by traditional internationalization patterns (a neighbouring country with strong historical ties), but also by the 'origin-covering' or 'window-dressing' factor during the war in Croatia, when a Bosnia-Herzegovina embargo on Slovenian goods was declared by the Milošević regime in Serbia. Slovenian firms tried to continue doing business there by establishing a presence in Austria to disguise their origins.[18] In the mid-1990s this motive lost importance. Since 1996 the number of companies investing in Austria and Germany has been falling, yet the investment value in these two countries has grown significantly since 1998. EU countries in general became more important again after 2000, and also became the top planned host locations for investment in the near future.

Among factors affecting a locational decision, market determinants play the main role, followed by cost determinants and, lastly, institutional factors as a reflection of geographical proximity. As shown by our sample of companies with outward direct investments, the locations of recently established foreign affiliates were mostly chosen to serve the local market rather than to export to third markets (Jaklič and Svetličič, 2003, pp. 137–47).

Motivations and advantages of outward investment
The most important motives for outward direct investment from Slovenia have been market seeking, followed by strategic asset seeking, increasing efficiency and, lastly, resource seeking (Figure 5.2). Thus outward FDI reflects the double-diamond paradigm: investors are responding to demand conditions in major markets. The small domestic market effect, the loss of the former Yugoslav market at the beginning of the 1990s, and increased competition from foreign companies in the domestic market has put pressure on Slovenian firms to internationalize. According to Dunning (1993), this kind of motivation is strongest in the second stage of the investment development path. An evaluation of Slovenia's investment development path at the end of 1990s found that Slovenia was somewhere between the second and third stages (Svetličič and Bellak, 2001).

Outward FDI is primarily aimed at expanding demand and is less influenced by factor conditions. The explanatory power of differences in factor abundance seems to be weak in explaining the observed patterns of outward FDI. Although Slovenia is small and, therefore, in terms of factor endowments, a relatively poor country with high labour costs, resource-seeking incentives surprisingly proved to be the least important (Figure 5.2).

Unit labour costs were only slightly more important than other factors. That is surprising as average Slovenian labour costs are relatively high, the highest among transition economies. Countries that appear to be the main destination of Slovenian outward investments have much lower labour costs, but also lower productivity. The biggest consequence of the low importance of resource-seeking motives is the fact that 90 per cent of Slovenian affiliates abroad are trading affiliates and only 10 per cent are production oriented. Another explanation for the smaller role of lower labour costs could be the lack of knowledge of what a global combination of factors (globalization) can offer in terms of strengthening competitiveness, together with the lack of capacity to achieve such globalization. The situation has been gradually changing since 2002, as almost half of all indicated investments are motivated by low labour costs and are in production (authors' own media survey).

The fact that the market potential outweighs factor price differences (such as labour costs or natural resources) suggests that firms realized that exports by themselves are

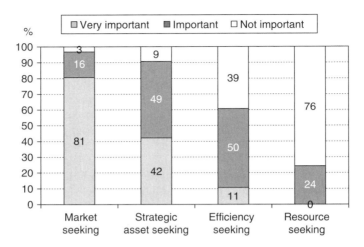

Source: 1999 Survey (Jaklič and Svetličič, 2003).

Figure 5.2   The relative importance of different motives to invest abroad for Slovenian firms (%)

no longer sufficient to retain their existing market shares abroad, let alone increase them. It also demonstrates that Slovenian MNEs are more of a horizontal than a vertical type. Vertical multinationals dominate when countries are very different in relative factor endowments (e.g. capital/labour, skilled/unskilled labour), while horizontal FDI predominates between similarly endowed, similar-sized countries in the presence of relatively high trading costs (Markusen, 1997). The major locations of Slovenian outward FDI are not very different in factor endowments and production costs, except for labour costs.

Slovenian firms have also followed their competitors that invested abroad. They needed a local presence to adapt their product to local tastes and to improve after-sales services. Some outward FDI has also followed Vernon's product life cycle (Vernon, 1966). Companies seek to capitalize on their technology, which is not very new, but is suited to the needs of local factor configurations. A number of Slovenian firms are investing abroad in kind, transferring to their affiliates their own technology while, at the same time, starting to upgrade themselves. The share of high-tech firms among investing firms is above the Slovenian average. Their firm-specific advantages are adapted technology and adapted products together with organizational know-how, rather than very new products and very recent technology.

Strategic-asset-seeking motives proved to be the second-most important incentive. Growth of a company and strengthening its overall competitive position were assessed as particularly important incentives for outward FDI. The strategic-asset-seeking investment orientation is a reflection of a long-term and internationally oriented strategy (growth, strong competitive position, high profits). This is encouraging, although strong demand for strategic assets could also be stimulated by the unavailability of other resources. Strategic-asset-seeking investments are frequently manifested through mergers and acquisitions (M&As). Although M&As save time in the process of a firm's growth and asset creation, and offer quick technology and knowledge transfers, companies at the early stage of the internationalization process (such as transition economy firms) are often unable to cope with them. The surveys showed that M&As indeed were quite rare in the case of Slovenian outward FDI in the 1990s. Instead, greenfield investments predominated,[19] and an increase in acquisitions was seen only after 2001. Yet after 2002 M&As became almost as important as greenfield investments. This latter change partly reflects more advanced privatization in Bosnia-Herzegovina as well as Serbia and Montenegro recently becoming, after Croatia, the second-most important outward FDI destination for Slovenian companies.

The firm-specific strategic advantages of Slovenian firms consist of specific products or services adapted to and already well known in established markets, along with the know-how for doing business there. Less-developed markets also offer the opportunity to exploit first-mover advantages. After they have strengthened their market position and acquired market knowledge, their motivations may diversify. Strategically, outward FDI goes hand in hand as firms restructure their assets to meet their objectives (Dunning, 1993, p. 60).

The efficiency-seeking incentive for outward FDI, the third-most important group of motives, is common for investors already established abroad and less important for the new outward investors. The sequential internationalization pattern suggests that the efficiency-seeking motive will gain in importance in future by enhancing investments abroad. Although the affiliate network of the average company in the sample is expanding, there are only a few companies in a position to invest abroad for this reason. The important explanatory variable in this respect is the size and international experience of a company. Slovenian MNEs are on average bigger and more experienced than companies not involved in direct investment abroad. However, they are still relatively small and inexperienced compared to Western MNEs. The overall size of a home economy influences international business activities. Mass consumption enables economies of scale, low costs, and standardized mass-market products. The domestic market does not offer such possibilities to Slovenian firms due to its small size and high labour costs; therefore achieving economies of scale and scope and exploiting surplus production facilities was identified as an important incentive for outward investment for more than half of the sample.

Investment motivation is one reflection of a firm's advantages. Next comes the perception of its position in comparison to its close competitors (2001 Survey, in Jaklič and Svetličič, 2003) in domestic as well as in the host-country market(s). Competitive advantages can serve as a proxy for ownership-specific advantages. Slovenian firms feel that their strongest advantage is in marketing knowledge, followed by technological and organizational knowledge. When interpreting the results, the geographical concentration of Slovenian outward FDI should be considered as it illustrates which location advantages could be complemented.

Surprisingly, the analysis of competitive advantage according to the location of outward FDI found no statistically significant differences in competitive advantages between those firms that invest exclusively in the region of former Yugoslavia, those that invest in former Yugoslavia and elsewhere, and those investing exclusively elsewhere. The insignificant results might be the consequence of overly similar 'geographical diversification' of foreign affiliates of the sample companies on the one hand and an unbalanced sample on the other hand.[20]

Table 5.17   The functional orientation of foreign affiliates of Slovenian investing firms, 1998

Functional orientation of foreign affiliate(s) related to	No. of investors transferring the function	No. of affiliates providing the function	As a percentage of all foreign affiliates[a]
Production (production, assembly)	11	15	10.9
Sales and marketing	29	130	94.9
R&D	2	3	2.2
Administration	11	70	51.1
Purchasing and logistics	14	78	56.9
Accounting, financial and fiscal	12	67	48.9

Note: [a] The combined total of the shares exceeds 100 since each foreign affiliate can perform more than one function.

Source: 1999 Survey (Jaklič and Svetličič, 2003).

Types of MNE organization/foreign affiliates and the changing pattern of trade

The nature of foreign affiliates differs across different foreign markets and, as Yeaple (2003) predicted, firms often follow the strategy of complex integration by integrating horizontally in some markets and vertically in other markets, although theory would – considering country size and factor abundance – predict vertical integration of Slovene MNEs. In the 1990s the majority of Slovenian investors mostly moved their sales and marketing function abroad, while this was rarely the case for the production function. According to the survey, only about 10 per cent of investors moved the production function abroad. This suggests that investors are mainly market seekers, with labour costs proving to be among the least important motives for investment. The sales and marketing function was the first to be internationalized. In 1998 some 95 per cent of foreign affiliates carried out sales and marketing functions, 56 per cent purchasing and logistics functions, and approximately 50 per cent accounting, financial and fiscal functions. Affiliates related to the R&D function were very few (Table 5.17).

The 2001 Survey[21] revealed a similar dominant functional orientation of foreign affiliates, with 72.1 per cent of foreign affiliates related principally to sales and marketing. Affiliates related mainly to production represented only 9.3 per cent, while affiliates related to other business functions represented 22.6 per cent of all foreign affiliates. Among the other functions, companies specified R&D (3 per cent), design (3 per cent), set-up and repair (4.1 per cent), financial and accounting functions, and logistics.

A comparison of the surveys shows that the share of investors moving the production function abroad is slowly increasing. Foreign affiliates are gradually growing in size and also broadening their functional orientation. According to their plans, the share of foreign affiliates related to production and assembly is set to increase in the future. Data after 2002, when firms started to relocate labour-intensive production abroad, confirm this. By value, almost one-third of production OFDI was intended to reduce the cost of labour in 2003, and almost 50 per cent in 2004. Market-seeking investments are still important but production ones became dominant in 2004.[22] This suggests a shift toward vertically integrated MNEs, which is in line with the propositions of the knowledge-capital model and empirical simulations (see, e.g., Markusen, 2001).

Effects

Unlike the impacts of inward FDI on a host country, which have attracted much research, the home-country effects of outward FDI have received much less attention, both empirically and theoretically.[23] Small countries' situations have been particularly neglected,[24] one reason being that the modest volume of outward FDI makes it difficult to identify the direct impacts of such flows in the short run. In any case, the effects of outward FDI take place only after a certain time has elapsed and after a certain volume threshold has been reached, as generally applies to any investment. It is much easier to check the impacts of such investment at the firm level, whereas sectoral and macroeconomic effects are more difficult not only to detect, but especially to distinguish from other influences. Generally, FDI theories along with the new trade theories predict positive net effects of outward FDI. The same prediction also arises from internationalization theories. The results of empirical studies vary somewhat, but the authors generally agree that the effects are difficult to measure econometrically.

Particularly relevant impacts of outward FDI from the transition economies' point of view are those of restructuring, growth and development in general. The most frequently mentioned are effects on trade and competitiveness, domestic production and employment. Estimates of the macroeconomic impacts of outward FDI are limited, particularly due to the short time series and still modest value of such flows. Therefore, the effects of outward FDI are evaluated mostly at the firm level based on the firms' own perceptions. Since the trade effect on the investing (parent) firm proved to be the most important one, the link between exports and outward FDI is especially emphasized. In spite of methodological difficulties, an attempt to briefly evaluate the development impact of outward FDI and externalities on the national economy is presented.

Effects of outward FDI on investing firms   The experience of Slovenian direct investors abroad is generally positive. According to the 1999 Survey, 85 per cent of sample companies assessed the success of outward FDI to have been in line with their expectations, while for 10 per cent the results even outperformed their expectations. Only 6 per cent were negatively surprised (Figure 5.3). The results were somewhat less enthusiastic two years later (2001 Survey, in Jaklič and Svetličič, 2003), which may easily be explained by the many new investments made in additional ventures to the SFRY during that period. These cannot yet yield results and are by definition more risky as they involve a region that features uncertainty. Nevertheless, even for the great majority of these investors in an unstable and unpredictable environment the outcome of outward FDI was still in line with their expectations.

From a policy point of view, it is crucial to understand why some investors produced results that were below their expectations. The failure of outward FDI was most commonly attributed to failures of management, particularly an unsuitable choice of personnel and a lack of information. The lack of capital (in the case of SMEs) and an unfavourable political climate or unforeseen political changes were mentioned as the two next most-important barriers or reasons why some outward FDI failed.

For Slovenian firms the key determinants of outward FDI success (ranked by

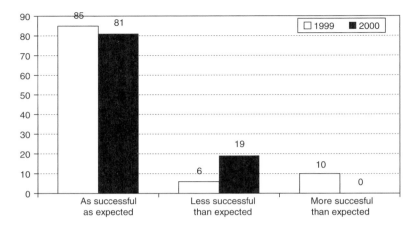

Source: 1999 and 2001 Surveys (Jaklič and Svetličič, 2003).

Figure 5.3   The success of Slovenian outward FDI (% of investing firms)

importance) are ownership-specific advantages that create non-price competitiveness, i.e. the quality of products, knowledge about the competition and foreign markets, personal contacts, international experience and skilled personnel, especially managers. The common denominator of all these factors is their human resource or skill intensity. Skills and knowledge have proved a precondition for the success of outward investments. Apart from such firm-specific factors, location-specific determinants such as foreign market conditions and political and economic changes in the host country have also played an important role. Cooperation with foreign partner(s) was judged to be relatively less important for a foreign investment's success.[25]

The effects of outward FDI on parent companies largely reflect the initial motives for such an investment (see Table 5.18). As a reflection of the prevailing market-seeking investment pattern, sample firms in both surveys and case studies particularly stressed the trade and competitiveness effects (see Figure 5.4). The effect on the improvement of strategic assets, such as a better international image and higher quality, increased product variety and efficiency (i.e. strategic-asset-seeking and efficiency-seeking aims) follow as the second-most important group of impacts. In line with the finding that resource-seeking investments were considered the least important, most companies investing abroad have not improved their access to cheaper imports (inputs) due to outward investment. The employment effect was also not significant, as lower labour costs were not among the main considerations.

Trade, competitiveness and home production effects   The linkage between trade and FDI is an important topic in several international business theories[26] and has often been empirically studied. While Mundell (1957) regarded trade and investments as substitutes, subsequent theoretical and empirical work has clearly established that the neoclassical framework is unrealistic. In the mid-1980s, Markusen (1997, p. 1) described these relationships as complementary. Empirical evidence and theoretical insights now predominantly support a complementary relationship between outward FDI and exports,

Table 5.18   Effects of foreign affiliates on the Slovenian parent company (% of investors)

Effects on	Strong increase	Increase	Unchanged	Decrease	Strong decrease
Market share	26	53	18	3	0
No. of employees	0	24	59	12	6
Exports	9	74	18	0	0
Imports	0	29	53	6	12
Production volume	9	68	24	0	0

Source: 2001 Survey (Jaklič and Svetličič, 2003).

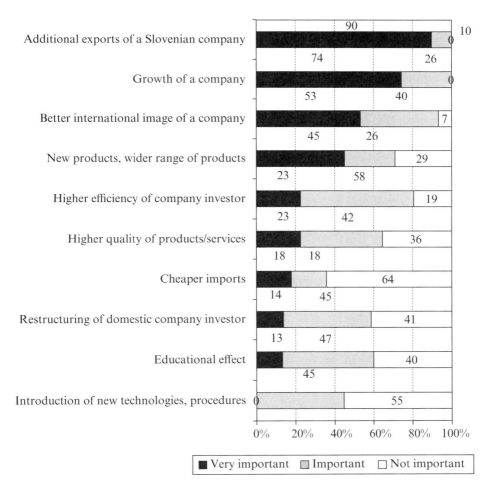

Source: 1999 Survey (Jaklič and Svetličič, 2003).

Figure 5.4   The importance of outward FDI's effects on a parent company

Table 5.19   Intra-firm trade of Slovenian outward investors, 1992–98

	1992	1995	1998
Intra-export (as % of total exports)	14.6	23.3	28.2
Intra-import (as % of total imports)	7.8	10.3	13.6

Source: 1999 Survey (Jaklič and Svetličič, 2003).

although the direction of causality has not yet been agreed on: does outward FDI depend on exports or vice versa? The new theories of trade that introduced product differentiation and economies of scale into the study of multinational companies and international trade (Helpman, 1984; Helpman and Krugman, 1985) explain that a substitutive or complementary relationship between outward FDI and trade is not defined *a priori*, but depends on a number of additional assumptions (whether the FDI is vertical or horizontal, the income level of a host country, the type of intra-firm transactions, etc.).

For Slovenia, by far the most important effects of outward FDI have been increases in exports and foreign market shares and access to markets. Among investing companies 79 per cent increased their foreign market share(s) and 83 per cent increased their exports. Such substantial effects on exports were anticipated since almost half of all exports from the Slovenian corporate sector derive from firms with outward FDI. The move from tapping foreign distribution channels to building their own channels helped firms to retain market share.

To a large extent this was the result of substantially increased intra-firm trade. From 1992 to 1998, intra-firm exports doubled on average and amounted to 28 per cent of total exports (see Table 5.19). Most investments abroad did not have any impact on imports whatsoever; imports remained the same in 53 per cent of cases. When there was an impact, intra-firm imports increased only modestly. Foreign affiliates have therefore not been a significant vehicle for gaining access to cheaper inputs. Foreign affiliates were on average net importers, mostly from the parent's home market. Their sales were also realized in the local market. Sales units, which dominate among foreign affiliates, operate as export promoters. Outward FDI therefore enhanced the export capacity and positive trade balance of the parent companies. This has already started to be a problem in some countries, where regular trade has now created huge trade surpluses (see Mrak et al., 2001). Outward FDI may in such cases be regarded as a way to reduce the danger of protectionist measures being taken by deficit countries to reduce imports. Investing abroad can thus be regarded as a macroeconomic remedy for reducing trade deficits, at least in final goods, since some intermediate goods would nevertheless also be exported in the case of investing in such a country.

The structure of intra-firm trade revealed that foreign affiliates mostly import final products from their parents. More than three-quarters of the sample companies exported final products to their foreign affiliates in 1998 (46 per cent of them exported exclusively final goods), more than one-third exported services and knowledge, while one-fifth of investors exported intermediate goods. Exports of raw materials were the lowest. Imports from foreign affiliates by investing companies were smaller and also increased more slowly in the period studied. The structure of parents' imports from affiliates again shows the prevalence of final goods, while the differences in the shares of services, inter-mediate goods or raw materials are much smaller (for details see Jaklič and Svetličič, 2003). Since the main result of outward FDI for a parent company was induced exports of mainly final products, exports and outward FDI seem to be complementary. There are relatively few investments aimed at least partly at substituting earlier exports with local production. The structure of intra-firm trade showed that the production process is still mostly kept in the parent firms.

Among the advantages of the investment entry mode over the export mode, proxim-ity to customers, adaptation to the local market, a personal 'touch' and contacts with local authorities and administrators that make export operations easier proved to be the most important. Factors such as the possibility of avoiding high entry costs, cheaper local labour and materials, getting subsidies, tax exemptions etc. to start up operations were less important. Customer feedback had improved as a result of foreign affiliates' activities according to 84 per cent of investors, and 60 per cent broadened their product portfolio (production range). Consequently, after establishing foreign affiliates the production volume of parent companies increased in size and variety for 77 per cent of investors. With the improved access to foreign markets, investing firms produce more output, which pushes down their average cost and also improves cost competitiveness. Thus outward FDI has created economies of scale for home production and increased efficiency, even though most investment was not of the efficiency-seeking type. The increased efficiency seen was more the result of scale economies, rationalization and competitive pressures.

In the case of production-oriented foreign affiliates, the expected effect on a parent firm following the theory would be restructuring through relocation, since the firm can reduce labour-intensive domestic production and consequently reduce the export of such goods and open doors for higher-value-added products. According to the interviews and survey, existing production affiliates have not (yet) influenced home production, but have above all been a way to raise foreign sales by establishing sales affiliates. They mostly complement existing home production facilities, especially when local conditions improve competitiveness. No respondent company reduced the level of its production as a result of outward FDI. Greater changes and reorganization are expected with the advance of internationalization, when investments could become more efficiency- than market-seeking.

The complementary relationship between outward FDI and exports can also run in the other direction; that is, an increase in exports may lead to an increase in outward FDI. Investment in the successors to the SFRY certainly had such a character since sales (and later exports) there were big enough to guarantee a stable level of demand. The situation was similar in other CEECs and the CIS (Communist Independent States), where local production at lower prices filled the growing local (and neighbouring countries') demand. On the basis of such arguments, in the future outward investment can also be expected in these currently important export markets. Future investment plans of Slovenian exporters confirm this.

Since export growth was evaluated as the most significant impact on the investing (parent) firm, the linkage between exports and outward FDI was also analysed at the aggregate level for all exporting Slovenian outward investors. The relationship between exports and outward FDI, analysed on the basis of an augmented Cobb–Douglas production function, produced positive and statistically significant coefficients, consistent with a complementary relationship, although the values of the coefficients were low (Jaklič, 2001). Outward FDI has obviously not substituted for exports but served as a complementary foreign market penetration mode.

Asset creation, learning effects and technology transfer   In the knowledge economy, which has become the major long-term development objective of all countries and hence also of Slovenia, the impacts of outward FDI on asset creation, learning effects and knowledge and technology transfer are becoming the most important. A better international image of the parent company (i.e. the creation of an intangible asset) was regarded as an important consideration when investing abroad. The image of being or becoming a multinational company helped them to improve sales opportunities (in foreign and domestic markets) and to stabilize sales revenues. Companies gained valuable market information and improved their ability to respond to customers' needs promptly. Better sales possibilities and an improved image resulted in a better financial position and greater solvency. In the 2001 Survey 90 per cent of investors stated that outward FDI had contributed positively to the parent company's financial position (although financing investments abroad is a financial burden). This often also resulted in a better credit rating.

These results reflect the ability of investors to differentiate their product and adapt it to local tastes and needs. The improved quality of products and services is a sign of technological restructuring. According to the interviews, many firms increased investments in R&D for process, product and quality improvement simply as a result of their direct presence in a foreign market. International competition thus motivated a parent company to strengthen its firm-specific advantages by investing abroad. This confirms the thesis that today companies invest abroad not only to utilize their existing advantages but also to strengthen or even develop them from scratch. Nowadays, firms start investing abroad not only because they possess firm-specific advantages but also 'from a position of weakness' (Dunning and Narula, 1996, p. 15), that is, because they seek to obtain advantages they do not currently have but which are available abroad in order to bolster existing competitive advantages or to speed up the process of catching up to their competitors.

This was also the case in the past, as demonstrated by the eclectic paradigm. Firms might be strong in one area (firm-specific advantages), but weak in terms of local factor conditions. By investing abroad, companies benefited from the factor endowments available abroad and thereby strengthened their factor conditions (see Rugman and Verbeke, 2001). Therefore they went abroad to benefit from the 'foreign diamond'. Since natural assets are nowadays losing their relative importance and human resources (created assets) are becoming crucial, knowledge-seeking outward FDI is gaining in importance. Firms also tend to start investing abroad much earlier than they used to (see Tolentino, 1992) in order to acquire assets abroad.

Slovenian companies regarded learning effects as important, but not in every field. The introduction of new technologies or processes, for example, was evaluated as not having an important effect for most investing companies. Knowledge acquired in the field of technology was assessed as the lowest priority (Table 5.20). The most significant was knowledge transfer in the field of marketing; some knowledge was also acquired in the

Table 5.20   Knowledge acquired as a result of outward FDI by Slovenian firms

	Technology	Marketing	Management	Organization
Average	2.2	4.0	3.6	3.3
Mode	3	4	4	3
Std dev.	0.9	0.7	0.9	0.7
Minimum	1	3	2	2
Maximum	4	5	5	4

Note: 1 – no transfer, 5 – very large knowledge transfer.

Source: 2000 Survey (Jaklič and Svetličič, 2003).

field of management and organizational capacity. Among other types of acquired knowledge stemming from direct investing abroad, companies mentioned financial knowledge and improving cash flow management.

The modest extent of technological learning is a result of the geographical distribution of outward FDI and its concentration in countries that are less developed compared to Slovenia. Slovenian firms are technologically more developed than host-country firms. Another explanation might be the short time lag involved, which has not allowed companies to realize potential technological effects that are long term by definition. Investors have also not been motivated to invest abroad to achieve certain technological results. These results do not fully correspond with the results of previous studies (Blomström and Kokko, 1994; Borenzstein et al., 1995), which suggest that positive FDI spillovers benefiting home firms are only generated if the technology gap between the foreign and domestic firm is not too large and if there is a certain threshold of human capital in the investing country. The gap between Slovenia and its investors' major host countries, the successors to the SFRY, has not been too wide, and thus stronger technology spillovers could have been expected, according to this theory. But the gap has widened during the transition and has become more like that seen between Slovenia and developed countries.

Employment effects   The employment effect of outward FDI is probably the most controversial and therefore the most-discussed aspect in the literature on outward FDI. The general belief of trade unions is that investing abroad means the exporting of jobs and thus reduces domestic employment, although this has not been empirically proven. Theoretically, foreign production can substitute for or complement domestic employment. Most often, the growth of a company and increased foreign production require increased employment by the parent company, which may be the result of a need to provide supervision and services to foreign operations, not to mention greater production of intermediate products made at home for export to the foreign affiliate for final assembly. Apart from that, it has to be taken into account what would have happened if such outward FDI had not taken place. In many cases of labour-intensive production, a potential investor abroad could face the danger of closing down its activity as a consequence of the erosion of comparative advantages of his country, usually manifested by increasing labour costs. Frequently an investing firm can argue that it couldn't have withstood the competition or would have been driven out of the market causing job and export losses. Competitive pressures, rationalization and restructuring could reduce employment or even force a company to close down.

The overall picture is that the share of outward investors in the entire Slovenian corporate sector's employment in the 1994–2002 period slowly increased, parallel to increasing shares in exports and sales. However, a loss of jobs could be attributed not only to investing abroad (relocation of production) but also to the general restructuring process accompanying the economy's transition to capitalism. This suggests that a restructuring process was under way (with value added and profits rising) in parallel with the movement to invest abroad, and firms investing abroad restructured more efficiently than the others. The 2001 Survey basically confirmed such aggregate tendencies by indicating that only 18 per cent of investing firms reduced the parent firm's employment as a result of outward FDI, while 24 per cent increased home employment, and employment did not change in the majority of cases (59 per cent). The employment effect was therefore quantitatively relatively lower compared to other effects. In qualitative terms it was, however, more important. The employment of skilled labour in outward investing firms rose from 1997 to 2000 much more steeply than the Slovenian average.

As case studies and interviews with managers demonstrated, a presence in Central and Eastern Europe (CEE) expands the personnel base of investing firms. Lack of skilled personnel prepared to work abroad was among the major barriers to outward internationalization. Affiliates from the CEE (especially in the region of former Yugoslavia and Poland) provided some new potential for international expansion.

Macroeconomic effects   All evolutionary models[27] predict a strong dynamic link between economic development and FDI. The relationship with FDI (inward or outward) is two-way: a higher development level increases FDI flows and vice versa, increased FDI stimulates growth spillovers with an important development implication. Although there is the possibility of asymmetry between the micro interests of investing firms and their home economy's macro interests, the number of investing companies might also be a measure of national competitiveness (Jones, 1996, p. 212). National economies have not competed exclusively through traditional exports for a long time (Quinlan and Chandler, 2001).

Investing firms may promote economic restructuring, trade performance, the level and structure of domestic production, investment and employment. The effects on a home economy are stronger the more investing firms have established linkages with other home firms.[28] FDI studies, so far deeply tied to viewing outward FDI as the transfer of resources from home to other economies, mostly neglect the other impacts of outward FDI. They see only an outflow of resources, with no positive impact on a home country's income of earned dividends, royalties and incomes generated abroad. They tend to forget that such investments contribute to the asset creation, technology and knowledge transfer that was described for the firm level.

Slovenian managers believe that internationalization through outward FDI strongly influences the domestic economy, improving its competitiveness and transformation (Figure 5.5). Restructuring and the competitiveness impact of outward investing was also seen as a significant contribution to the EU integration process. FDI linkages are

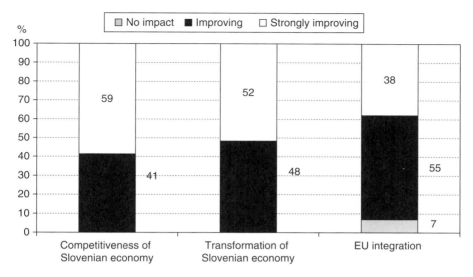

Note: Scores: 1 – no impact; 2 – hindering; 3 – improving; 4 – strongly improving.

Source: 2000 Survey (Jaklič and Svetličič, 2003).

Figure 5.5   Opinions of managers about the impact of outward FDI on the Slovenian economy (%)

an effective long-term method of linking countries economically, socially and politically (Lall, 1996).

Although Slovenian companies investing abroad represent a very modest share (about 2.4 per cent) of the total business sector, they have the highest growth potential and a significant influence on the total corporate sector, and may therefore be regarded as a significant qualitative growth pole. Analysing their share in selected aggregate categories of Slovenian corporate sectors shows that their importance is increasing (Figure 5.6). Improved exports, sales and efficiency are the next three elements where outward investing companies performed better than non-investing ones. Outward investors currently provide almost half of Slovenian exports, an indicator of their competitiveness that is reflected in the national economy's positive trade balance. Exports alone can no longer ensure efficient market access or the maintenance of foreign market shares. Outward FDI significantly improves market penetration and the stability of foreign market shares.

As a vital part of the Slovenian economy, outward investors heavily influence domestic industrial production in terms of both volume and structure. So far production volume has increased, although significant changes to the structure have not been found. Investing abroad in areas of the core competences of firms has proved to be too small to have an important effect on the overall economic structure, yet case studies have demonstrated advancement and diversification.

Investment abroad has also not crowded out domestic investment activity as some have feared.[29] Outward investment activity is stimulated above all by the desire to improve access to foreign markets. This stimulates investment at home and abroad.

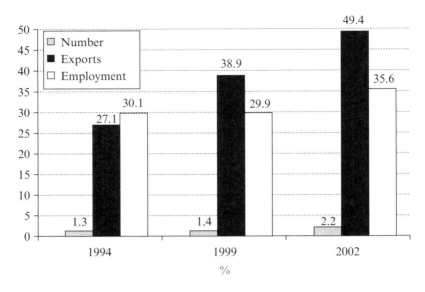

Source: Jaklič (2005).

Figure 5.6   *The importance of outward investors in the Slovenian corporate sector,*
1994–2002

Even more important than the quantitative changes found in production volume and domestic investment are qualitative changes within outward investors. These companies are the most exposed to competitive pressures in both the domestic and foreign markets; therefore they have constantly to improve their efficiency and productivity. They learn to improve their flexibility and develop capabilities to swiftly adapt to changes. Especially important effects are the ongoing improvements in quality, product differentiation and adaptation as a response to the closer links with customers that a direct presence in foreign markets provides. In the long run this will result in technological restructuring.

The educational effects of outward investment are significant not only for outward investing firms but also for the rest of the economy. These companies' growing demand for higher skills in the domestic labour market slowly builds up an awareness of the need to improve the knowledge and skills of labour. The surveys demonstrated the above-average and growing R&D activity of investing firms, which stimulates innovatory capacity. Since companies investing abroad are often domestic market leaders, they also introduce higher standards to the domestic economy and stimulate other companies to follow. Outward FDI firms enhance competition, including in the home market. Investment abroad enables firms to exploit the advantages of globalization and to draw on factor endowments found abroad. All these changes influence the industrial structure of the home economy and help bring about changes that better reflect what the international division of labour under globalization pressures shows to be the optimal allocation of resources. Low-value-added activities might be shifted abroad to improve cost competitiveness, while higher-value-added activities might be retained in the home country. Companies that invested abroad did indeed increase value added per employee and innovation potential in the 1990s (Jaklič, 2004). Accordingly, OFDI companies play a very important role in a home economy's innovatory activity, knowledge transfer and restructuring.

Outward FDI is therefore growth promoting. As endogenous growth theory (Romer, 1986; Lucas, 1988) predicts, welfare depends much more on innovation, knowledge creation and the accumulation of human capital than the accumulation of physical capital. The development impact could be stronger if, instead of a small group of 'national champions' with investments abroad, there are a number of firms at a similar internationalization level. Such capabilities are the key to the appropriate absorption potential of firms, industries and the economy in general. This absorption potential depends on the development of related industries or a supplier network in the home economy. With an increasing number and volume of outward investments, the potential to absorb will also be enhanced, as will the positive growth effects of outward FDI.

Outward FDI and exposure to foreign competition have substantially improved the Slovenian economy's restructuring and transformation. Firms investing abroad estimated the evolution of corporate learning in a more complex international environment as crucial for staying competitive, maintaining responsiveness and surviving. Those firms had an important demonstration effect on the rest of economy. Outward FDI has thus stimulated the transition process and helped close the gaps between Slovenia and developed industrial countries. While differences in development levels remain, investing abroad might be treated as a catching-up tool since it helps to narrow the gap in productivity, efficiency, knowledge (above all in marketing, organizational and management) and information. The most successful Slovenian outward investors can already compete in the world market with multinationals from developed economies, which is not the case for all or most companies that do not invest abroad or those still shielded from international competition.

Government policies related to inward and outward FDI

Inward FDI
The low level of FDI penetration in the Slovenian economy, and relatively limited scope of FDI in upgrading the parameters of Porter's diamond in the case of Slovenia, point either to low attractiveness of Slovenia as a location for FDI, or to an unreceptive inward FDI policy or general attitude towards FDI in Slovenia. This is clearly confirmed by comparing Slovenia's Inward FDI Performance and Inward FDI Potential Index (as defined by UNCTAD), the latter being constantly much higher than the former. The partial reduction of the lag of the Performance behind the Potential Index in 2000–02 was only a consequence of one-off events, i.e. of several big foreign acquisitions in 2002.

The low level of FDI penetration in Slovenia raises two issues. The first relates to the reasons for the relatively low FDI penetration in Slovenia, which persists in spite of a number of factors making Slovenia an attractive and friendly environment for investment and in spite of the fact that Slovenia fully applies the national treatment principle for foreign investors and foreign-controlled enterprises. The second issue relates to the government's policy towards FDI. Examination of studies of the reasons behind the relatively low level of FDI penetration in Slovenia (Dedek and Novak, 1998; FIAS, 1998, 2000; IMAD, 1999; OECD, 2002; Rojec, 1998) suggests the following factors:

Table 5.21   Inward FDI Performance and Inward FDI Potential Index of Slovenia in ranking among 140 countries (1990–2003)

	Inward FDI Performance Index[a]	Inward FDI Potential Index	Lag of performance behind Potential Index
1990–1992	84	117	+33
1994–1996	96	48	−48
1999–2001	109	29	−80
2000–2002	59	27	−32

Note: [a] Inward FDI Performance Index is calculated as the ratio of a country's share in global FDI inflows to its share in global GDP. See definitions in UNCTAD (2004).

Source: UNCTAD (2004).

1. Small local market.
2. Privatization and enterprise restructuring. There are several reasons why privatization has not contributed enough to FDI inflows. The first was the (mass) privatization concept in industry and trade, which implicitly favoured internal (employee and management) buy-outs. Foreign acquisitions were only exceptions in the privatization process, which was dominated by distribution through the use of ownership certificates and internal buy-outs at considerable discounts. The second factor was the slowness of the restructuring process in the privatized enterprises, which did not encourage them to search for strategic foreign partners. The third factor was the hesitant privatization of state ownership in the financial and public utilities sector, where only later some modest moves have been initiated.
3. Monetary considerations have for a long time been one of the major reservations of the Bank of Slovenia about foreign capital inflow. The bank embarked on various measures to cope with the risks associated with capital inflows. Although these measures have served their monetary purpose, i.e. preventing a negative impact of excessive speculative capital inflows, and although they were not directed directly at FDI, they have in practice tended to discourage it.
4. Administrative barriers to investment and the operations of companies are a relevant constraint to more active engagement of domestic and foreign investors since they increase the costs of establishing and operating a company. In a number of areas administrative procedures are long and complicated (especially in land and site development, some registration and approval requests, and employment-related issues).
5. Problems in acquiring industrial locations. Access to business premises and land to do business, especially for industry, getting clear title to it, and getting the necessary permits to build and operate a factory, are often complex and time consuming. The high price and low availability of land and industrial and business premises in general are also problems.
6. Relatively rigid and protective labour legislation that does not take sufficient account of the interests of employers, i.e., in general, the rules governing the relationship of employers and employees are biased towards employees.

7. Relatively rigid labour market. Slovenia has a well-educated and productive labour force, but labour costs are relatively high compared to the level in competitive investment locations, and the mobility of the labour force in Slovenia is relatively low (in certain regions there is a shortage of certain professions that are in surplus in other regions).

Most of the above factors, which represent barriers to inward FDI, and the hesitant attitude of political and economic policy to incoming FDI are basically integral parts of the Slovenian gradualist approach to transition. All these have reduced the pressures to restructure in the enterprise sector and, consequently, the need to attract strategic foreign partners. This was compounded by FDI policy, which has long been more concerned with how to prevent the 'cheap sale of the family silver' to foreign investors than with how to attract foreign investors. In other words, Slovenian policy towards attracting FDI has been rather passive, without a clear concept and commitment, and with insufficient funds and people for the serious targeting and attraction of FDI projects.

Outward FDI
At the beginning of the economic transition process, the government was not fully aware of its role with respect to outward internationalization and its reaction to outward FDI was rather defensive. Although the strategy of an outward-oriented economy has been followed from the outset of the new state, the emphasis has been on exports as the principal form of outward internationalization. Other entry modes such as international production, capital linkages or strategic alliances, or the holistic perception of internationalization of the economy, have mostly been neglected. Most of the factors mentioned above as reasons for low FDI inflows (slow privatization and restructuring, dispersed ownership and rigid labour markets) actually also influenced outward internationalization and hindered firms' development and outward expansion. The first incentives to develop a more active attitude to outward FDI can be traced to 1993, and were followed by a series of development strategies[30] and more developed proposals. The proposal for a more elaborated strategy by Šušteršič et al. (2001) was based on the new internationalization paradigm, yet implementation was poor. Consequently, outward investment was driven by companies in a bottom-up fashion, rather than involving a top-down national strategy in the sense of 'implementing plans to achieve set goals'.

The initial policy of mistrust of capital exports immediately after gaining independence, which was marked by various restrictions, began to soften and was formally transformed in 1999 (with the new Foreign Exchange Act) into an internationally compatible system of regulating international long-term capital flows. Although an unfriendly public mood towards outward FDI and fears about the exporting of jobs and capital were present, they did not translate into policies that restricted Slovenian outward FDI. The initial attitude, which viewed direct investment abroad as an unpatriotic act since it involved capital flowing abroad, has slowly changed and outward investment has gradually begun to be treated as a normal, 'non-contaminated' business activity, even though a certain scepticism remained.

Following the requirements of the Europe Agreement, the Organization for Economic Co-operation and Development Code and the European Union's *acquis*, Slovenia in 1999 removed all foreign exchange restrictions, retaining for its foreign exchange authority only the power to monitor transactions. The legislation adopted was therefore not a product of autonomous beliefs within the government, but rather was very much the product of EU accession (harmonization with the EU and OECD standards) on the one hand, and the bottom-up pressure of companies on the other.

The Slovenian government assisted outward investment by building an institutional framework including bilateral investment treaties (BITs) and double taxation avoidance treaties (DTTs) as an elementary FDI institutional environment. BITs were primarily stimulated by the need to ensure protection of inward FDI. Later on, with the increasing importance of outward FDI, BITs have also been oriented to major destinations of outward FDI. The signing of a BIT usually follows investments and not vice versa. Therefore it is hard to assert that BITs have played any significant role in the initial decisions to invest abroad. Much the same could be said for DTTs, since the number and the dynamics of these agreements were very modest and sometimes they were not even efficient (for more, see Jaklič and Svetličič, 2003, pp. 278–85). Promotional measures, started systematically only after 2000, also did not imply a strong incentive for initial decisions to undertake outward FDI.

From Slovenian firms' point of view, one of the more important instruments for facilitating outward FDI has been the existing export credit and insuring (guarantee) agency, the Slovenian Export Corporation (SEC), which was eventually able to provide at least some of its services to outward-investing firms. Its activities are predominantly oriented towards export promotion. However, since the most important outward investors have often also been the most important exporters, the guarantees and loans given for export promotion also facilitate investment activities. Enterprises have identified three basic weaknesses of institutional services: (i) the unavailability and high price of financing; (ii) the low quality and poor availability of information necessary for outward internationalization; and (iii) absence of or inefficient institutional environments/agreements. The companies have called for improved financial support at lower cost, improvement of informational support and promotion activities, greater availability of financial resources and better coverage with BITs and DTTs.

Conclusions

The aim of this chapter was to analyse trends and determinants of international competitiveness of the Slovenian economy and to analyse the role of inward and outward FDI in the upgrading of the four sets of parameters of international competitiveness as defined by Michael Porter, i.e. factor conditions, demand conditions, related and supporting industries, and strategy, structure and rivalry.

While the achieved level of productivity and real convergence of the Slovenian economy with the EU are relatively high, however, the indicators of competitiveness improvement reveal much slower dynamics than in other transition countries that entered the EU in 2004. The reasons should be sought in the structural weaknesses and rigidities of the Slovenian economy, in particular of manufacturing. Slow structural and institutional changes constitute a serious problem for Slovenia's international competitiveness. This is clearly reflected in the worsening rating of Slovenia in various international competitiveness rankings of countries.

Inward FDI is the most direct mechanism and indicator of the contribution of MNEs to the international competitiveness of a national economy. In spite of the relatively low penetration of FDI in the Slovenian economy, i.e. smaller than in the majority of the other EU-25 countries, statistical data, existing analysis and case studies show that FDI had an important impact on the upgrading of the four parameters of Porter's diamond for Slovenia. FDI has been one of the drivers of restructuring and productivity upgrading in the Slovenian economy, and it has been an important source of foreign technology and of access to export markets. FDI in the Slovenian manufacturing sector has been clearly of the factor-cost-advantage-seeking, export-oriented type, while in the service sector it has been typically local market oriented. These inflows have sped up the internationalization of the manufacturing sector and have brought about a broader and better supply of services for companies and the public at large. As far as the impact of inward FDI on the development of local related and supporting industries is concerned, the fact is that foreign subsidiaries import most of their inputs and that they are distinctively more import oriented than domestic companies. It seems, however, that foreign subsidiaries have recently tended to slow down their import propensity. Positive but modest vertical spillovers confirm such a pattern. Horizontal spillovers of FDI in Slovenia are very small but in any case neutral, due to the low level of foreign penetration in the economy. Similar is the impact of FDI in terms of the type of subsidiaries. Foreign investors keep strategic and marketing control in their hands and leave everyday operational functions to subsidiaries, which seem to be relatively independent only within the framework of their existing production mandate.

The low level of FDI penetration in the Slovenian economy and relatively limited scope of FDI in upgrading the parameters of Porter's diamond point to an inefficient inward FDI policy. The main barriers have been the small local market, the specific type of privatization and enterprise restructuring, the administrative barriers to the investment and operation of companies, problems in acquiring industrial locations, high taxes and non-transparent tax procedures, and relatively rigid and overly protective labour markets. Moreover, these disadvantages were compounded by weak FDI policy, which has long been more concerned with how to prevent the 'cheap sale of the family silver' to foreign investors than with how to attract foreign investors. In other words, Slovenia's policy towards attracting FDI has been rather passive, without a clear concept and commitment, and with insufficient funds and people for a serious targeting and attracting of FDI projects.

Defensive and non-supportive policy was also typical for outward investment. Outward FDI has grown as a result of changes in the business environment and bottom-up pressure from companies that were threatened with losing market shares abroad. Due to the lack of governmental strategy on outward FDI, investment abroad was not accompanied by any effective governmental measures. The liberalization of legislation and financial flows that took place in the mid-1990s was primarily the result of harmonization with EU and OECD standards, and was complemented by a national strategy of outward internationalization and supportive programmes (BITs, DTTs, and some common promotion and insurance activities) only at the end of the 1990s.

Although the policy incentives were lacking, outward FDI has made a very important contribution to national economic success. Compared to other transition economies, Slovenia has relatively more indigenous MNEs. This can be explained by Slovenia's relatively earlier entry into foreign markets, its more open economy (even in the pre-transition period) and its stronger export orientation. However, this initial advantage in outward investment activity has been vanishing, since the incentive for outward internationalization from inward FDI is much lower compared to that of other transition economies. As the outward-investing firms are the major providers of exports, the major employers with the most skilled employees, and are more technology intensive and innovative, they are a vital part of economy. By going abroad they have learned to adapt to the international environment and competition much more quickly, have restructured more efficiently than the rest of economy and have thus set new benchmarks for other domestic firms. Creation of Slovenia's own MNEs has therefore helped to speed up its transition process. By investing abroad, these companies have expanded the 'domestic diamond' in a significant way. Investments abroad that were primarily market seeking succeeded in providing access to foreign markets and in retaining foreign market shares, expanded factor conditions (especially by gaining marketing and organizational knowledge) and broadly improved demand conditions, resulting in a broadening product portfolio and improved quality. The impact on related and supporting industries has been more modest, in terms of both inward and outward FDI. One explanation is that a small economy lacks suppliers of an adequate size to support large MNEs. In some cases such linkages have been induced. Finally, many inward and outward investors have been pulled abroad by large MNEs' activities. Slovenian suppliers of intermediate products have followed such MNEs as they expanded abroad. By 'importing a more developed institutional environment', outward investing firms have sped up institutional changes in the domestic environment, enhanced competition and rivalry, and demonstrated how important the building of one's own strategy is.

In spite of numerous positive effects and qualitative changes that have been identified through restructuring and productivity upgrading, increasing innovative activity and knowledge building, the potential of FDI and MNEs in the case of Slovenia has not been fully exploited and leaves room for additional development incentives. Without relying on home-grown and foreign MNEs, Slovenia stands to see its competitive position weaken further.

Notes

1. The average for the ten new EU member states was 53 per cent (Eurostat, 2004).
2. In 2003, unit labour cost ratios in Slovenia were 0.72, in the EU-25 0.66 and in the EU-12 (Euro area) 0.64.
3. The general demand component indicates how a given country's exports would evolve if they were growing at the same rate as total EU imports; the structural effect component shows to what extent a given country's exports grow because they are centred on goods that are in above-average import demand in the EU; the competitive effect component shows whether a country increased the exports of certain goods to the EU more than its competitors from outside the EU. The competitive effect component is the main indicator of trends in competitiveness.
4. The number of MNEs in Slovenia at the end of 2003 was 2720. Of that total, 64.5 per cent were greenfield FDI and 30.0 per cent were acquisitions. In terms of equity the situation was the opposite, due to some large organizations; acquisitions accounted for 58.4 per cent of all foreign equity, while greenfield FDI accounts for only 30.0 per cent (Bank of Slovenia, 2004).
5. Pharmaceutical company Lek was acquired by Swiss Novartis, Belgium KBC bank acquired a 34 per cent share in NLB bank, Austrian Mobilkom acquired Simobil, French Société Générale made an additional investment in SKB Banka, Banka Koper was acquired by Italian San Paolo IMI, etc.
6. The share of these industries in Hungary was 59.1 per cent, in the Czech Republic 44.3 per cent, in Poland 36.2 per cent, in Slovakia 34.3 per cent and in Estonia 32.4 per cent (Damijan and Rojec, 2004).
7. Management has mostly been kept on, but strategic decisions are taken by the MNC headquarters, while subsidiaries are mostly independent in everyday operations.
8. The higher export propensity of FIEs as compared to DEs is also confirmed by panel analysis of the

export propensity of enterprises in the Slovenian manufacturing sector. The analysis found that FIEs have significantly higher export propensity than DEs, even after controlling for the different industrial distribution of FIEs and DEs, and for the impact of sample selection bias. Thus the higher export propensity of FIEs as compared to DEs in the Slovenian manufacturing sector is the result of differences in structural operational characteristics of the two types of enterprises (Rojec et al., 2000).

9. Similar results were found also for the Czech Republic and Poland, but in Bulgaria only for foreign subsidiaries. The analysis did not find negative vertical spillovers, except in Lithuania and Latvia for foreign subsidiaries.

10. These arise from: (i) increased competitive pressures on domestic enterprises, which would lead to their increased efficiency; (ii) movement of FIEs employees, who have received quality training and education, to DEs; and (iii) the fact that FIEs attract other foreign consulting, financial and auditing firms whose quality services may also be used by domestic enterprises. Horizontal spillovers could also be negative if DEs are not able to cope with the increased competition of FIEs and go bankrupt, or if quality employees of DEs are drawn away by FIEs.

11. Positive horizontal spillovers were found in the Czech Republic, Poland, Romania and Slovakia.

12. Since it was FIEs' representatives who answered the questionnaire, the answers may be biased in favour of higher decision-making power of subsidiaries. Therefore one should interpret the results more in terms of comparison of subsidiaries' decision-making power in various business functions.

13. 'New entrants' that have only just begun investing abroad mostly have only one or two foreign affiliates (the mode value was 1), while the 'early transition multinational birds' are rapidly expanding their foreign affiliate networks, not just in terms of number, but also size. The most internationalized firms owned up to 30 foreign affiliates in 2003.

14. Affiliates' industry data are not available.

15. The concentration in successor states of the SFRY is partly a reflection of inherited investments and partly the result of new FDI flows into this region.

16. Croatia is the top host country with 440 affiliates, followed by Bosnia-Herzegovina, and Serbia and Montenegro.

17. The most representative investments in Poland are in the pharmaceutical industry. Well-known investors there are the biggest Slovenian pharmaceutical companies Krka d.d. and Lek d.d., now Novartis.

18. Austria was always among the top countries as to profits realized by outward FDI. In 1998 it dropped to second place.

19. More that 85 per cent of foreign affiliates of the 1999 Survey sample companies were established as a greenfield type, 11.7 per cent were through acquisitions and 2.9 per cent through mergers.

20. Apart from small sample (Valid N = 34), the three selected groups of investors (namely in the region of former Yugoslavia, those that invest in the region of former Yugoslavia and elsewhere and those investing exclusively elsewhere) might be too similar to reveal differences in competitive advantages.

21. In the 2001 Survey, only the dominant business function of a foreign affiliate was noted.

22. The authors' own evaluation of media reports estimates the total value of outward FDI in production in 2004 at €316 million and only €23 million in trade affiliations, but with very high plans (€124 million) for subsequent years.

23. The amount of research undertaken on the impact of MNCs on a home economy is surprisingly small (Jones, 1996, p. 214). Some authors who have addressed this issue are: Aitken and Harrison (1999); Blomström and Sjoholm (1998); Blomström and Kokko (1994); Borenzstein et al. (1995); Konings (1999); Lall (1996). Increasing attention has recently been devoted to the home-country effects, i.e. Kokko (2000); Konings and Murphy (2001); Lall (2000).

24. Except for Sweden, which has extremely good research in this area (Braunerhjelm and Ekholm, 1998; Blomström and Kokko, 1994).

25. This is in line with the ownership structure of foreign affiliates that are usually wholly or majority owned by Slovenian investors.

26. See Mundell (1957), Vernon's product life cycle (1966) and, later, Helpman (1984), Helpman and Krugman (1985).

27. For example, the investment development path (Dunning, 1981), product life-cycle model (Vernon, 1966), 'flying geese' model (Akamatsu, 1961), Ozawa's dynamic paradigm (1992), the Uppsala model (Johanson and Vahlne, 1977; 1990).

28. These linkages are strongly industry-specific and vary by the activity of the investor.

29. Regression analysis showed a positive and statistically significant correlation between outward FDI and investment in a parent firm (Jaklič, 2001).

30. 'The Strategy for Economic Development. Approaching Europe, Growth, Competitiveness and Integration' (1995) was followed by 'International Economic Relations Strategies' (1996) and, finally, 'Slovenia in the Next Decade: Sustainability, Competitiveness, EU membership' (2001). On the basis of such studies, several sectoral strategies have also been elaborated (see Svetličič, 1998).

References

AGPTI in Gral iteo (2003), *Raziskava podjetij s tujim in mešanim kapitalom v letu 2003*, Ljubljana: Agencija za gospodarsko promocijo Slovenije in tuje investicije pri Ministrstvu za gospodarstvo in Gral iteo.

Aitken, B. and A.E. Harrison (1999), 'Do domestic firms benefit from direct foreign investment? Evidence from Venezuela', *American Economic Review*, **89** (3), 605–17.

Aitken, B., G. Hanson and A. Harrison (1994), 'Spillovers, foreign investment, and export behavior', NBER Working paper 4967.

Akamatsu, K. (1961), 'A theory of unbalanced growth in the world economy', *Weltwirtshaftliches Archiv*, **86** (2), 196–217.

Bank of Slovenia (2004), *Direct Investment 1994–2003*, Year 8, No. 1 Ljubljana.

Blomström, M. and A. Kokko (1994), 'Home country effects of foreign direct investment: Sweden', NBER Working Paper, No. 4639.

Blomström, M. and F. Sjoholm (1998), 'Technology transfer and spillovers: does local participation with multinationals matter?', NBER Working Paper, No. 6816.

Borenzstein, E., J. De Gregorio and J. Wha-Le (1995), 'How does foreign direct investment affect economic growth?', NBER Working Paper No. 5057, Cambridge, MA.

Braunerhjelm, P. and K. Ekholm (1998), *The Geography of Multinational Firms*, Dordrecht: Kluwer Academic Publishers.

Damijan, J.P. and B. Majcen (2001), 'Transfer of technology through FDI and trade, spillover effects, and recovery of Slovenian manufacturing firms', Ljubljana: Institute for Economic Research, mimeo.

Damijan, J.P. and M. Rojec (2004), 'Foreign direct investment and the catching-up process in new EU member states: is there a flying geese pattern?', Research Reports, no. 310, October. Vienna: The Vienna Institute for International Economic Studies (WIIW).

Damijan, J.P., B. Majcen, M. Rojec and M. Knell (2003), 'Technology transfer through FDI in top-10 transition countries: how important are direct effects, horizontal and vertical spillovers?', William Davidson Working Paper Number 549 (February), Ann Arbor, MI: The William Davidson Institute.

Dedek, F. and J. Novak (1998), *Raziskava podjetij s tujim in mešanim kapitalom (Research of Companies with Foreign and Mixed Capital)*, Ljubljana: Gral iteo, Urad za gospodarsko promocijo in tuje investicije pri Ministrstvu za ekonomske odnose in razvoj.

Dunning, J.H. (1981), 'Explaining outward direct investment of developing countries – in support of the eclectic theory of international production', in K. Kumar and M.G. McLeod (eds), *Multinationals from Developing Countries*, Lexington, MA: Lexington Books, pp. 1–22.

Dunning, J.H. (1992), 'The competitive advantage of countries and activities of transnational corporations', *Transnational Corporations*, **1** (1), 135–68.

Dunning, J.H. (1993), *Multinational Enterprises and the Global Economy*, Wokingham, UK: Addison Wesley.

Dunning, J.H. and R. Narula (1996), *Foreign Direct Investment and Governments, Catalysts for Economic Restructuring*, London and New York: Routledge.

Eurostat (2004), *New Cronos*, 3 December.

FIAS (1998), *Slovenia – Promoting Foreign Direct Investment*, Washington, DC: Foreign Investment Advisory Service.

FIAS (2000), *Administrative Barriers to Foreign Investment in Slovenia*, Washington, DC: Foreign Investment Advisory Service.

Havlik, P., M. Landesmann and R. Stehrer (2001), 'Competitiveness of CEE industries: evidence from foreign trade specialization and quality indicators', Research Reports, no. 278, July. Vienna: The Vienna Institute for International Economic Studies (WIIW).

Helpman, E. (1984), 'A simple theory of international trade with multinational corporations', *Journal of Political Economy*, **92**, 451–62.

Helpman, E. and P. Krugman (1985), *Market Structure and International Trade*, Cambridge, MA: MIT Press.

IMAD (1999), *Autumn Report 1999*, Ljubljana: Institute of Macroeconomic Analysis and Development.

IMAD (2002), *Development Report 2002*, Ljubljana: Institute of Macroeconomic Analysis and Development.

IMAD (2004), *Autumn Report 2004*, Ljubljana: Institute of Macroeconomic Analysis and Development.

IMAD (2005), *Development Report 2005*, Ljubljana: Institute of Macroeconomic Analysis and Development.

IMD (2004), *IMD World Competitiveness Yearbook 2004*, Lausanne: Institute for Management Development.

Jaklič, A. (2001), 'Internationalization of Slovenian companies during transition', in K. Liuhto (ed.), *East goes West: The Internationalization of Eastern Enterprises* (Studies in industrial engineering and management, 14). Lappeenranta: Lappeenranta University of Technology, Department of industrial engineering management, pp. 380–405.

Jaklič, A. (2004), *The impact of firms' factor endowments on the creation of multinational enterprises*, Ph.D. dissertation, University of Ljubljana, Faculty of Economics.

Jaklič, A. (2005), 'Creating multinational enterprises in transition economies; examining the case of Slovenia', in *Enterprise in Transition: Full Texts of Papers*, Split; Bol, CD-ROM, pp. 1591–606.

Jaklič, A. and M. Svetličič (2003), *Enhanced Transition Through Outward Internationalization*, Aldershot, UK, Burlington, USA, Singapore and Sydney: Ashgate Publishing.

Johanson, J. and F. Wiedersheim-Paul (1975), 'The internationalization of the firm – four Swedish cases', *Journal of Management Studies*, **12**, 305–22.

Johanson, J. and J.E. Vahlne (1977), 'The internationalization process of the firm – a model of knowledge development and increasing foreign market commitments', *Journal of International Business Studies*, **8** (1), 23–32.

Johanson, J. and J.E. Vahlne (1990), 'The mechanism of internationalization', *International Marketing Review*, **7**, 11–24.

Jones, G. (1996), *The Evolution of International Business: An Introduction*, London: Routledge.

Kokko, A. (2000), 'FDI and the structure of home country production', Policy Discussion paper No. 0018, Centre for International Economic Studies, University of Adelaide, Australia.

Konings, J. (1999), 'The effect of direct foreign investment on domestic firms: evidence from firm level panel data in emerging economies', Discussion Paper No. 86/1999, Centre for Transition Economics and Central European Policy Research, London; LICOS Centre for Transition Economics, Katholieeke Universiteit Leuven.

Konings, J. and A. Murphy (2001), 'Do multinational enterprises substitute parent jobs for foreign ones? Evidence from firm level panel data', Discussion Paper No. 100/2001, LICOS Centre for Transition Economics, Katholieeke Universiteit Leuven.

Krugman, P. (1994), *Peddling Prosperity: Economic Sense and Nonsense in the Age of Diminished Expectations*, New York: Norton.

Lall, S. (1996), 'Transnationals from developing countries. Impact on home economies', Background Paper for the FIAS High Level Roundtable on Outward Foreign Investment from Newly Industrialized Economies in Asia, Bangkok.

Lall, S. (2000), 'FDI and development: research issues in the emerging context', Policy discussion paper No. 0020, Centre for International Economic Studies, University of Adelaide, Australia.

Lorentzen, J., P. Moellgaard and M. Rojec (1998), 'Globalization in emerging markets: does foreign capital in Central Europe promote innovation?', *Journal of International Relations and Development*, **1** (1–2), 84–105.

Lucas, R. (1988), 'On the mechanics of economic development', *Journal of Monetary Economics*, **22**, 3–42.

Majcen, B., M. Rojec, A. Jaklič and S. Radošević (2004), 'Functional upgrading and productivity growth in foreign subsidiaries in the Slovenian manufacturing sector', 8th EACES Conference 'EU Enlargement – What Comes After 2004?', Belgrade: Faculty of Economics, 23–25 September, pp. 120–21.

Markusen, J. (1997), 'Trade versus investment liberalization', NBER Working Paper 6231.

Markusen, J. (2001), *Multinational Enterprise and the Theory of International Trade*, Cambridge: MIT 2001.

Mrak, M., A. Jaklič and D. Veselinovič (2001), 'Financial aspects of Slovenia's economic cooperation with the countries of the former Yugoslavia: current trends and perspectives', *Economic Business Review*, 3 (3), 271–97.

Mrak, M., M. Rojec and C. Silva-Jauregui (eds) (2004), *Slovenia: From Yugoslavia to the European Union*, Washington, DC: The World Bank.

Mundell, R. (1957), 'International trade and factor mobility', *American Economic Review*, **47** (2), 321–35.

OECD (2002), *OECD Investment Policy Reviews – Slovenia*, Paris: OECD.

OECD (2003), *Indicators of Economic Globalization*, Paris: OECD.

Ozawa, T. (1992), 'Foreign direct investment and economic development', *Transnational Corporations*, **1**, 27–54.

Quinlan, J. and M. Chandler (2001), 'The U.S. trade deficit: a dangerous obsession', *Foreign Affairs*, **80** (3), 87–97.

Rojec, M. (1998), *Restructuring with Foreign Direct Investment: The Case of Slovenia*, Ljubljana: Institute for Macroeconomic Analysis and Development.

Rojec, M. and M. Stanojević (2001), 'Slovenia: factor cost-seeking FDI and Manufacturing', in Grigor Gradev (ed.), *CEE Countries in the EU Companies' Strategies of Industrial Restructuring and Relocation*, Brussels: European Trade Union Institute, pp. 137–71.

Rojec, M. and M. Svetličič (1998), 'Short overview of the Slovenian economy and foreign investment in Slovenia', *Eastern European Economics*, **36** (6), 60–72.

Rojec, M., J.P. Damijan and B. Majcen (2000), 'Export propensity of foreign subsidiaries in Slovenian manufacturing industry', Paper for 6th EACES conference 'Globalization and European Integration', Barcelona.

Rojec, M., J. Šušteršič, B. Vasle, M. Bednaš and S. Jurančič (2004), 'The rise and decline of gradualism in Slovenia', *Post-Communist Economies*, **16** (4), 459–82.

Romer, P.M. (1986), 'Increasing returns and long-term growth', *Journal of Political Economy*, **94**, 1002–37.

Rugman, A. and A. Verbeke (2001), 'The generalized double diamond approach to the global competitiveness of Korea and Singapore', in D. Van den Bulcke and A. Verbeke (eds), *Globalization and the Small open Economy*, Cheltenham, UK and Northampton, MA, USA: Edward Elgar, pp. 36–53.

Strojan-Kastelec, A. (2001), 'Ocena konkurenčne sposobnosti slovenskega gospodarstva', *Prikazi in analize*, IX/I, Ljubljana, Bank of Slovenia, 5–24.

Svetličič, M. (1998), 'Slovenian state strategy in the new Europe', Paper for Workshop on 'State Strategies and International Regimes in the New Europe', 15–16 May 1997, South Yutland University Press.

Svetličič, M. and C. Bellak (2001), 'Investment development path of small transition conceptual background and empirical evidence', Göteborg: Conference 'Small States in World Markets – Fifteen Years Later', 27–29 September.

Šušteršič, J., M. Rojec and M. Mrak (2001), 'Slovenia in a new decade: sustainability, competitiveness and EU membership: the strategy of economic development 2001–2006', Instutitute for Macroeconomic Analysis and Development, Ljubljana.

Tolentino, P.E. (1992), *Technology Innovation and Third World Multinationals*, London and New York: Routledge.

UNCTAD (2004), *World Investment Report 2004*, New York and Geneva: United Nations.

UNCTAD (2003), *Handbook of Statistics, 2003*, New York and Geneva: United Nations.

Vernon, R. (1966), 'International investment and international trade in the product cycle', *Quarterly Journal of Economics*, **80**, 190–207.

Welch, L.S. and R. Luostarinen (1988), 'Internationalization: evolution of concept', *Journal of General Management*, **14**, 36–64.

World Bank (2003), *World Development Indicators 2003*, Washington, DC: The World Bank.

Yeaple, S.R. (2003), 'The complex integration strategies of multinationals and cross-country dependencies in the structure of foreign direct investment', *Journal of International Economics*, **60** (2), 293–314.

6 Multinational enterprises from small economies: the internationalization patterns of large companies from Denmark, Finland and Norway*

*Gabriel Robertstad G. Benito, Jorma Larimo,
Rajneesh Narula and Torben Pedersen*

It is generally accepted that, *ceteris paribus*, firms from small open economies (SMOPECs) tend to demonstrate a higher propensity to internationalize their operations than those from larger home economies (Bellak and Cantwell, 1998). The most obvious factor is market size, and the tendency for SMOPEC firms to venture to foreign markets is often explained primarily by this constraint.

At the same time, many industries are increasingly becoming global. Factors such as increasingly rapid technological change, convergence of consumers' tastes and increased worldwide competition have led to a quest for scale, scope and learning economies that, in turn, has motivated the development of increasingly larger corporations through international mergers and acquisitions (Ghoshal, 1987; Yip, 1989; Kozul-Wright and Rowthorn, 1998). These are the factors that act as centrifugal forces in the internationalization process. Indeed, as firms are becoming increasingly global, the question is whether there remains a role to be played by the local environment.

In this chapter it is proposed, along with Porter (1990), that centripetal forces are at play as well. Institutions, support infrastructure and related companies exist around, and because of, firms in a given location (Markusen, 1996). The ability of such factors to meet the needs of the multinational enterprise (MNE) play a crucial role in determining the extent of their internationalization (Narula, 2002). For this reason, it has been argued that the home base plays a continued or possibly increasingly important role for the global firm (Porter, 1990; Porter and Sölvell, 1998).

Thus there is an important interface between the micro-level (firm-specific) issues and the macro-level (country-specific) issues in firm internationalization that is not well understood. In addition to the issues of internationalization being a matter of understanding the centripetal and centrifugal forces, there is a symbiotic relationship between the MNE and its environment that has become exceedingly complex. This is not to say that there is no role for idiosyncratic behavior of firms due to differences in strategy (Shaver and Flyer, 2000). Rather, as suggested in Figure 6.1, the strategy of the MNE is formulated within the framework of the micro–macro interface.

This interaction between firms and locations is axiomatic for all countries, regardless of size. However, the micro–macro interaction is likely to be much more pronounced in the case of MNEs from SMOPECs, since they outgrow their home base more easily, and small countries are more dependent on their large companies (Kozul-Wright and Rowthorn, 1998). A major strategic error by management in a single enterprise can create a substantial shock wave to the total economy. Therefore the main issue for small

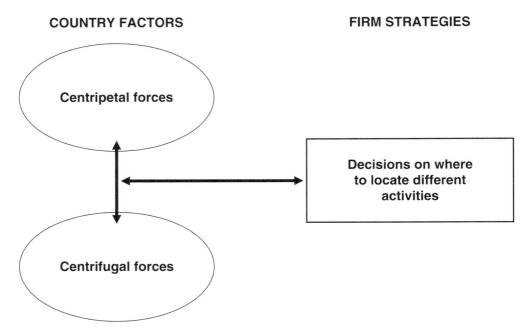

Figure 6.1   The interface between micro- and macro-level factors

countries is whether the centripetal forces stemming from the quality of the location-bound assets compensate for the centrifugal forces stemming from the limited size of the local market. Or, put differently: can the limited size be traded off by a higher quality of locally bound assets?

The firm's international activities can be divided into operations (such as production and sales abroad) and strategic activities (such as internationalization of capital, R&D and headquarter functions). It is expected that the internationalization has, over time, moved from being predominantly 'operations' oriented to becoming more strategic in the sense that it involves the ownership and decision-making entities of the companies, and that development patterns will differ across companies and countries depending on the nature and strength of various centrifugal and centripetal forces.

In this chapter these issues will be investigated for three SMOPEC countries: Denmark, Finland and Norway. These three countries compose a particularly interesting set since they share many features: they are affluent neighboring countries of about the same size, they belong to the same cultural 'block' (Ronen and Shenkar, 1985), and their political institutions and traditions share many characteristics. Sweden and Iceland – the two other Nordic countries – were left out because they are markedly different in terms of size.

In each country the focus will be on the ten largest companies over the period 1990 to 1999, since these companies are those that are particularly exposed to the dilemma of retrieving local roots while globalizing. These companies basically make up the set of large companies in Denmark, Finland and Norway, and they are commonly regarded as the economic locomotives of their home countries.

The remainder of the analysis proceeds as follows. To begin with, a brief overview is provided of the possible implications of globalization on the behavior of MNEs originating from small economies. The data are then described. The two following sections then report and discuss the findings of the study, with an emphasis on the implications for home countries.

Globalization, small economies and MNEs: centrifugal and centripetal forces

There is considerable evidence (e.g. Freeman and Lundvall, 1988; Dunning and Narula, 1996; van Hoesel and Narula, 1999; Bellak and Cantwell, 1998; Van Den Bulcke and Verbeke, 2001) that there are certain common characteristics of the small open economy that cause its firms to be more globalized than firms from larger countries. Globalization as used here will refer to economic globalization, which is defined as the increasing cross-border interdependence and integration of production and markets for goods, services and capital. This process leads both to a widening of the extent and form of international transactions, and to a deepening of the interdependence between the actions of economic actors located in one country and those located in other countries (Narula and Dunning, 2000). The literature has illustrated that small open economies tend to be more internationalized, with a relatively large share of the value-added activity being conducted with the explicit purpose of serving overseas markets. Furthermore, firms from these countries tend to be competitive in a few niche sectors, as small countries are likely to have limited resources and prefer to engage in activities in a few targeted sectors, rather than spreading these resources thinly across several industries.

At the same time, there is considerable variation between countries: SMOPECs are by no means a homogeneous group. It is useful to analyze the determinants of internationalization of SMOPEC-based multinational firms from two perspectives: factors that encourage internationalization (centrifugal forces); and factors that encourage concentration of these firms' activities in their home location (centripetal forces).

Some of the characteristics of small economies are a function of size *per se* (Krugman, 1991). The limited domestic market size means that if such firms are to achieve economies of scale in production, they must seek additional markets to that of their home location in order to increase their *de facto* market size (Walsh, 1988; Narula, 1996; Bellak and Cantwell, 1997). The demand conditions at home may constrain the sectors and kind of ownership advantages that firms of a particular nationality develop. First, small market size constitutes a disadvantage in the development of process technology as economies of scale are not present, but may provide a competitive advantage in product innovation (Walsh, 1988). Second, firms from small countries have access to fewer kinds of created location advantages at home. That is, the infrastructure and national business systems tend to be focused in fewer industrial sectors. Globalization has also meant that firms increasingly need to maintain competencies in several areas, as products become increasing multi-technology in nature (Granstrand et al., 1997). A benefit of industrial concentration is that it supports 'thick labor' markets locally, particularly for specialized skills, so that employers and employees find each other more easily (Krugman, 1998). Thus, if firms from SMOPECs require technological inputs not available locally, they must seek these in overseas locations (see Narula, 2002 for a discussion). Also, companies seek out capital markets outside their home country for equity as well as for loan capital with the aim of lowering their cost of capital (Oxelheim et al., 1998). All in all, the limited size of the home market works as the main centrifugal force of the companies located in SMOPEC countries (Krugman, 1998). It should be noted that globalization has resulted in *de facto* economic integration – at least amongst the Triad countries – in addition to *de jure* economic integration projects such as the Single European Market. These exogenous developments have further enhanced the centrifugal forces on companies located in SMOPEC countries (Kozul-Wright and Rowthorn, 1998).

On the other hand, the main centripetal forces are the kinds and quality of assets that are bound to the home country. Industrial specialization in a given location is often associated with the kinds of assets that it possesses (or possessed) in abundance. Such asset advantages lead to a specialization of domestic firms in particular niche sectors (Soete, 1987; Archibugi and Pianta, 1992; Narula, 1996), and those firms that survive the intense rivalry that commonly exists in such sectors are likely to develop strong competitive (or so-called ownership) advantages. Hence, as pointed out by Cantwell and Narula (2001), the ownership advantages underlying firms' internationalization tend to reflect the particular location advantages of their country of origin. Obviously, these assets also tend to attract inward investment in these same sectors. Such specialization over a long period often leads to a development of successful clusters of firms and institutions that support a given industry, creating agglomeration economies in production and technology (Krugman, 1998). For instance, in Denmark, the food sector has the features that characterize a strong cluster: several highly competent companies, strong links with suppliers, internationally competitive related industries – e.g. manufacturing specialized machinery – and a variety of supporting institutions and organizations in the areas of research, teaching and quality control. In Finland, the forestry and pulp and paper industries constitute a particularly strong sector (Hermesniemi et al., 1996; Moen and Lilja, 2001), whereas in Norway clusters can be found in the oil and gas, offshore and maritime sectors (Benito et al., 2000; Reve and Jakobsen, 2001; Reve et al., 1992).

So far, the discussion has focused on the macro-level implications of increasing global competition, rapid technological change and economic integration, including the possible impact of these forces on the economies of small countries. However, the forces of globalization also shape decisions and processes at the firm level. In order to understand the strategic moves by companies, it is necessary to distinguish between the degree of mobility of tangible assets (such as materials, components, blueprints and products) and of intangible assets (such as business practice, expertise and supporting institutions). Whereas companies can access global markets for most tangible assets, the intangible assets that are critical to such activities as R&D, design and core manufacturing are typically more embedded in the local clusters (Porter and Sölvell, 1998).

Even where strong clusters do not exist, firms are often most familiar with their home-country situation, creating inertia. This inertia is associated with the nature of the national business systems of their home countries, and the level to which these firms are locally embedded. The level of internationalization reflects the extent to which firms are interdependent and co-dependent on domestic institutions and policies that have not only formed them – and with which they are most familiar – but which they have also helped create (Narula, 2002). Clusters are strongly path-dependent, and companies that operate in clusters have tended to maintain their strategic activities at home despite the internationalization of their production and sales. As argued by Porter and Sölvell (1998), while the MNEs may have global networks of subsidiaries involved in operating activities (such as sales, service, local assembly and production), typically, strategic activities (such as R&D laboratories, design and headquarters functions) are much less dispersed.

However, this implies a view of the MNE as a traditional unitary firm in which the headquarters of the parent firm constitutes the center and other units – domestic or foreign – make up the periphery. In the past, the distribution of power and authority within the corporation, the control over critical resources and the location of strategic activities versus operational activities have been depicted as a center–periphery pattern with corporate headquarters firmly 'planted' in the home country of the MNE as the unchallenged center. Even though such a description of an MNE may still find proponents, and perhaps even provides a sufficiently accurate description of some companies with international activities, it is a view that is now increasingly challenged (Forsgren, 1990; Forsgren et al., 1995; Zanfei, 2000). Companies are becoming more complex, less hierarchical, and less dependent on firm-specific advantages based on location-bound assets in their home countries (Hedlund, 1986). Several important developments have been identified: the move towards more 'geocentric' mind-sets, structures and policies (Perlmutter, 1969), the evolution towards multi-center or network structures in MNEs (Forsgren, 1990; Ghoshal and Bartlett, 1990), and the emergence of subsidiaries – so-called 'centers of excellence' – that enjoy positions and roles of substantial strategic character and weight in a corporation (Birkinshaw and Morrison, 1995; Holm and Pedersen, 2000).

The ongoing transformation of MNEs is likely to affect companies from large as well as from small countries, but the impact and speed of change could differ. The relative importance of foreign activities is likely to be greater, on average, for companies based in small countries. Hence small-country MNEs may have had to respond more quickly and make more substantial changes than their large-country based competitors. Likewise, small countries are hit harder than large countries by adverse home-country effects. Also, because small-country MNEs typically take up a larger part of the economic activities, strategic misjudgment by their management may have severe implications for the national economy of a country. This chapter is particularly interested to investigate to what extent the internationalization development of small-country MNEs in recent years has followed the patterns described above. Based on the preceding discussion, the propositions are that:

1. Large companies have expanded their international activities at a greater rate than their home countries.
2. Their internationalization has, over time, moved from being predominantly 'operations' oriented – that is, selling and/or producing goods and services abroad – to becoming more strategic in the sense that it involves the ownership and decision-making entities of the companies.
3. Development patterns will differ across companies and between industries and countries depending on the nature and strength of various centrifugal and centripetal forces.

Data

For each of the three Nordic countries, Denmark, Finland and Norway, the ten largest companies were selected. These are the companies that are particularly exposed to the dilemma of retaining local roots while globalizing. The group of 'top-ten' companies was chosen on the basis of total sales figures in 1999. In addition, the following selection criteria were observed. First, the companies should be predominantly nationally owned: i.e. the largest owner group should be domestic or, alternatively, home-country nationals should own the majority of stock.[1] Second, because state-owned companies usually have rather restricted scope for strategic action, especially with regard to internationalization, such companies were excluded.[2] Third, companies in the financial services sector (banking and insurance) and in food retailing typically have restricted market scope. Historically, most companies in these sectors have focused exclusively on domestic markets, and even though an increasing internationalization has been observed in these sectors in recent years (see Benito and Strøm, 2000 for a discussion of internationalization in food retailing), the scale of international operations has been modest so far. These sectors were therefore excluded.

Once the companies were selected, the bulk of data was taken from company annual reports.[3] Additional sources of data were the companies' web pages and company directory services such as General Business File International. Furthermore, the companies were also contacted to obtain information unavailable elsewhere (such as data on R&D). For all companies, data were collected for the years 1990 and 1999, thus making it possible to track the internationalization of companies over time.

The information collected can be put into three broad categories: (1) general company information, such as number of employees, type and number of industries; (2) accounting data such as annual sales, profits, return on equity, return on assets; and (3) a wide range of data regarding their international activities (see Dörrenbächer, 2000 for a discussion of internationalization indicators). Data in the latter category included, *inter alia*, foreign sales, number of foreign subsidiaries and international joint ventures (IJVs), number of divisions, business area, and/or corporate headquarters located abroad, and the share of equity held by foreigners. Also, information on R&D employment at home and abroad was obtained for Danish and Norwegian companies, but such data were unfortunately unavailable for Finnish companies.

Results and analysis

The Nordic economies in the 1990s
Table 6.1 shows that these three economies share many similar features at the macro level, but also have considerable differences. First, they are roughly the same size in terms of overall GDP and population. They have also shared a similar high growth rate over the whole decade in question, but all three countries experienced some level of recession in the early 1990s, with high unemployment and economic crises resulting in industry restructuring by policy makers.

In the case of Finland, the recession was associated with an exogenous shock. There was a collapse of the Finnish trade with Eastern European countries, especially with the former Soviet Union. In 1990, exports to the Soviet Union still represented almost 13 percent of total exports, but because of the economic and political changes in Russia and the abandonment of the earlier bilateral trading system, the share export to Russia dropped to 2 percent in 1992. That, and the reduction in domestic demand, implied considerable restructuring in several industries and caused a number of bankruptcies.

Table 6.1 Macroeconomic indicators, Denmark, Finland and Norway, 1990 and 1999

	Denmark	Finland	Norway
GDP			
● 1990 (current US$)	133430	136911	115430
● 1999 (current US$)	173830	129677	152926
GDP growth, 1990–99			
● At current prices/US$ rates (%)	30.3	−5.3	32.5
● At 1990 prices/US$ rates (%)	25.8	19.0	35.4
External trade and investment			
Exports			
● 1990 (current US$)	36892	31152	46925
● 1999 (current US$)	48993	48520	59681
Imports:			
● 1990 (current US$)	33353	33443	39354
● 1999 (current US$)	44274	37996	50481
External trade (% of GDP)[a]			
● 1990	52.6	47.2	74.7
● 1999	53.7	66.7	72.0
Stock of outward FDI (million US$)			
● 1990	7342	11227	10888
● 1999	42035	31803	38423
Stock of FDI (% of GDP)[b]			
● 1990	5.5	8.2	9.4
● 1999	24.2	24.5	25.1
Employment			
Total employment			
● 1990	2605700	2504000	2054200
● 1999	2678700	2296000	2280600
● Growth, 1990–99 (%)	2.8	−9.1	11.0
Manufacturing industries			
● 1990	479500	556000	294500
● 1999	447100	488000	311000
● Growth, 1990–99 (%)	−6.8	−12.2	5.6

Notes:
[a] Calculated as: [Export$_t$ + Import$_t$]/GDP$_t$ × 100
[b] Calculated as: [FDI$_t$/GDP$_t$] × 100

Sources: Statistics Denmark, Bank of Denmark, Statistics Finland, Bank of Finland, Statistics Norway, Bank of Norway, UNCTAD, *World Investment Report 2000*.

The Finnish currency was devalued in 1991 and the exports to other markets than Eastern Europe grew steadily. The recovery of the Danish economy was associated with a substantial increase in Danish exports (up 33 percent from 1990 to 1999) resulting in a significant surplus on the trade balance. In the case of Norway, the recession in the early 1990s was gradually overcome through, principally, disciplined fiscal policies, a centralized system of wage bargaining that was able to agree on fairly moderate wage increases, and a consistently high demand for oil and gas in a period that saw high prices for these commodities.

Although all three economies have always had a dependence on a natural-asset base, Norway has remained more dependent on natural resources, due largely to the discovery of significant offshore petroleum reserves in the late 1960s. However, it has also managed to maintain a strong position in the fishing industry. It is a peculiar feature of the Norwegian economy not shared to the same extent by the others that the Norwegian state has always taken a strong interventionist position. There have been several waves of infant-industry development implemented through various degrees of import-substituting policies. During the early part of the postwar era, the focus had been on scale-intensive process sectors such as chemicals, while in the 1970s its focus was electronic-based industries. The late 1960s was associated with a strong emphasis on fostering firms in this industry during the following decade. In some cases, the state has intervened through ownership of 'strategic' firms, and in others they have fostered national champions. In most cases, institutions and infrastructure were built to support the targeted sectors. National control was retained through stringent state controls on inward and outward capital movements, although there has been a gradual phasing out of these institutions. Its membership of the European Economic Area has affected the Norwegian state's continuation of its interventionist policies, as it must abide by EU regulations on subsidies and competition policy. Contrary to the situation in both Finland and Norway, state ownership of manufacturing companies has always been insignificant in Denmark. The Danish state has also consistently followed a strategy of no direct intervention in industry. However, it has been active in shaping the conditions for developing the manufacturing sector, including educational policy, tax policy, competition policy, and as a large demanding customer.

Finnish exports were dominated by metals, engineering, and paper and pulp from the 1960s until the mid-1990s. Since then there has been a clear change in the structure of exports. Electronics and electro-technical industry have become the largest export sectors, accounting for close to 30 percent of the total manufacturing exports in 1999. Nokia has played a central role in this change – and even in the whole recovery of Finland. The growth of Nokia, and its main suppliers, has been exceptional even by global standards. It has been calculated that in 1999 Nokia accounted for more than 3 percent of Finnish GDP and 20 percent of total exports (Ali-Yrkkö et al., 2000).

All the countries in question are highly dependent on external trade and outward FDI (see Table 6.1), with trade accounting for more than 50 percent of GDP, and outward FDI at roughly 25 percent of GDP. It is important to note that the significance of trade has remained stable over the 1990s, while the importance of FDI has grown considerably, although there are important differences between the countries. Norway has remained outside the EU, rejecting membership twice, first in 1972 and again in 1994. This has 'pushed' Norwegian firms to internationalize more strongly than might otherwise have been the case. In contrast, Denmark joined the EU as the first Nordic country in 1972, and membership of the EU has since then been the main gateway for the integration of the Danish economy into the global marketplace. In the 1990s, almost two-thirds of Danish exports went to other EU countries and more than 70 percent of the total imports came from other EU countries. Finland became a member of the EU in 1995, and this has played an important role in its economic recovery.

Table 6.2   The ten largest private, non-financial companies in Denmark: some characteristics, 1999

Company	Main industry	Total sales, 1999, in million US$	Foreign sales (% of total sales, 1999)	Number of employees in 1999	Foreign employment (% of total employment, 1999)
Carlsberg	Brewery	4671.5	70	21 906	49
MD Foods	Dairy products	3790.0	64	13 604	35
FLS Industries	Special machinery	3134.7	80	14 140	65
Novo Nordisk	Organic chemicals	3124.4	99	15 184	38
Danisco	Sugar	2869.8	77	15 413	60
Danfoss	Valves and compressors	2152.9	90	18 860	58
Egmont	Publishing	1221.3	75	4 164	47
Grundfos	Pumps and compressors	1122.9	92	9 699	57
Rockwool	Non-metallic minerals	1076.9	91	7 346	81
Lego	Manufacturing of toys	954.8	94	6 284	28

Large companies in the Nordic countries

Denmark   Historically the agricultural sector has been important in Denmark, both politically and economically. This is reflected in the composition of the largest Danish firms by industry (see Table 6.2), where food-related sectors including food manufacturing and their suppliers (e.g. farmers and manufacturers of machinery) make up a large share of the economy. The vertical links between suppliers and production companies are often strengthened by an ownership link where the production company is owned by the suppliers as a cooperative, as is the case with the second-largest Danish company (see Table 6.2), MD Foods. MD Foods is a dairy company owned by the farmers delivering the raw milk to be manufactured into all types of dairy products. Over the years many supporting institutions, such as research and quality control centers, have been developed around these companies to constitute a food cluster.

Three of the ten Danish companies belong to the food cluster. These are Carlsberg (the sixth-largest brewery in the world), MD Foods (the largest dairy company in Northern Europe), and Danisco (the largest sugar company in Northern Europe). The remaining companies are more scattered in terms of industry category or cluster, although four companies are included in activities related to construction; namely FLS Industries (cement factories), Danfoss (valves), Grundfos (pumps), and Rockwool (insulation).

In the last decade, most of the companies have been involved in substantial global restructuring in their industry, where the name of the game has been either to grow by acquisition and thereby become one of the big global players, or be acquired by others. Several of the companies have made substantial acquisitions abroad – such as MD Foods' acquisition of Swedish Arla Foods, and Danisco of Finnish Cultor – thus becoming the market leader in their industry.

There is a distinction between the highly internationalized companies with a foreign sales to total sales ratio above 90 percent and the companies in the food cluster that are more domestically oriented with a foreign sales ratio below 80 percent (see Table 6.2). However, it is the companies in the food cluster that have been most active in foreign acquisitions in the last decade. This is illustrated by the foreign employment ratio of 49 percent for Carlsberg and 60 percent for Danisco, which clearly exceeds the foreign employment ratio of some of the highly internationalized companies such as Novo Nordisk (38 percent) and Lego (28 percent).

The companies in the food cluster serve as an illustration of the interplay between the centripetal and centrifugal forces, where the centripetal forces consist of the strengths of the Danish food cluster and the centrifugal forces stem from international competition and pressure for restructuring the industry. The question that remains to be answered is whether the expansion of international activities will be at the expense of strong roots in the Danish cluster or whether it will strengthen the competencies in Danish companies by tapping into other knowledge bases.

A survey of the internationalization patterns of Danish companies indicates that Danish companies had, until quite recently, mainly internationalized their 'operations' (Pedersen et al., 1998). Sales and service activities were internationalized to a large extent in the sense that these activities are located abroad. Production activities (including assembly and packaging) were also highly internationalized, but at a somewhat lower rate than for sales and service. Activities that were least internationalized were the highest-value-adding activities such as design, marketing, R&D and headquarters activities.[4]

Finland   Although foreign trade has historically been very important, the more intensive internationalization of Finnish companies started only in the 1960s and 1970s. Truly active internationalization began in the 1980s. The 1990s saw a great deal of restructuring taking place in several of the largest Finnish companies, but companies continued to internationalize in those business sectors that they had not divested. In 1990, the mean foreign sales ratio in the ten largest Finnish companies was close to 70 percent (see Table 6.5). The highest ratio was 93 percent in Outokumpu and the lowest – 40 percent – in Metra. Table 6.5 shows that by 1990 the sales of Finnish companies were highly internationalized, reaching a mean foreign sales ratio of 88 percent in 1999. This figure indicates the critical role of foreign sales in the largest Finnish companies. A typical example of significant increases in foreign sales is the Metra Corporation, where foreign sales increased from 40 percent in 1990 to 95 percent in 1999 because of the substantial restructuring of operations over those years (see Table 6.3).

The expansion of production abroad lagged behind foreign sales throughout the decade: the share of foreign employment remained clearly lower than the share of foreign sales (see Tables 6.3 and 6.5). In 1990, the mean foreign employment ratio was about 36 percent, or half of the foreign sales ratio. The mean employment ratio had increased to about 55 percent in 1999, a rate of increase in the mean value about the same as the rate of increase in foreign sales.

Table 6.3 *The ten largest private, non-financial companies in Finland: some characteristics, 1999*

Company	Main industry	Total sales, 1999, in million US$	Foreign sales (% of total sales, 1999)	Number of employees in 1999	Foreign employment (% of total employment, 1999)
Nokia	Communication equipment	21 067.9	98	55 260	58
Stora-Enso	Paper and pulp	11 333.2	93	40 226	62
UPM-Kymmene	Paper and pulp	8 802.5	87	30 963	32
Metsäliitto	Paper and pulp	6 077.6	82	20 854	47
Metso	Special machinery	3 609.0	90	23 274	52
Outokumpu	Non-ferrous metals	3 099.6	92	11 972	45
Metra	Engines and equip.	2 876.9	95	15 551	76
Kemira	Fertilizers	2 691.6	82	10 743	53
Kone	Elevators	2 570.1	96	22 630	93
Rautaruukki	Steel and iron	2 544.4	69	12 491	38

All the largest Finnish companies have traditionally preferred acquisitions to green-field investments. In the case of Nokia, there was also an intensive network of strategic alliances and other cooperative arrangements. The considerable growth in foreign sales of Nokia also increased the internationalization of the company's main Finnish subcontractors, with subcontractors establishing and acquiring their own foreign manufacturing units close to Nokia's main foreign units. The internationalization and foreign establishments by other large Finnish firms have not had similar effects to those of Nokia. In Kone and Nokia about half of the sales were from European countries and half from outside Europe, whereas in the other large companies at least two-thirds, in some cases even over 80 percent, were from European countries. Hence most of the top Finnish firms are mainly European oriented in their operations, and some companies – e.g. Metsäliitto and Rautaruukki – did not own manufacturing units outside Europe in 1999.[5]

Norway The sample of Norwegian firms is an eclectic collection, including their industry, size, and degree and rate of internationalization. From Table 6.4, three main observations can be made. First, there are no clear cases of companies that are dependent upon a single industrial cluster. Three companies in the set are, at least partly, involved in industries that have cluster-like characteristics, namely Norsk Hydro, Kværner and Aker, which operate in the petroleum and offshore sectors. A much more obvious feature is the fact that the companies, including those just mentioned, are almost without exception 'old-fashioned' conglomerates that operate in a variety of industries and product categories. Second, there seems to be a distinction between those companies that operate in sectors that traditionally have been highly internationalized, and sectors that have

Table 6.4   The ten largest private, non-financial companies in Norway: some characteristics, 1999

Company	Main industry	Total sales, 1999, in million US$	Foreign sales (% of total sales, 1999)	Number of employees in 1999	Foreign employment (% of total employment, 1999)
Norsk Hydro	Fertilizers, oil, metals	13 132.4	90	37 900	53
Kværner	Oil field machinery	9 085.1	76	61 955	85
Orkla	Food	3 952.9	58	25 037	56
Aker RGI	Oil and gas services	3 673.8	51	18 995	44
Norske Skog	Paper and board	2 314.6	85	6 315	23
Dyno Industrier	Explosives	1 377.3	91	7 757	81
Elkem	Metals	1 228.6	93	4 030	23
Merkantildata	Computers, software	1 294.4	65	3 830	67
Rieber & Søn	Food	988.8	67	8 428	74
Schibsted konsern	Media and publishing	963.3	44	4 910	55

been domestically oriented. This dichotomy is not unrelated to the predominance of resource-based advantages, which has been the mainstay of the Norwegian economy throughout the twentieth century. Companies in resource-based sectors such as petroleum, metals, and pulp and paper (i.e. Norsk Hydro, Elkem and Norske Skog) are all dependent on foreign customers – as indicated by foreign sales ratios ranging from 85 to 93 percent (see Table 6.4). However, as expected, given their reliance on local resource advantages, the foreign employment ratios of these companies are considerably lower, ranging from 23 percent in Norske Skog to 53 percent in Norsk Hydro.

The traditionally high degree of state involvement in business (both as an owner and as a proactive regulator) has resulted in a certain tolerance for monopoly-like market structures in some sectors and the targeting of others through various levels of import-substituting policies. For some companies the tendency for home-market orientation is also associated with their protection from international competition. These firms have gone abroad relatively later than the resource-oriented firms that have had to face international competition much earlier. This can clearly be seen from Table 6.4, where companies such as Orkla, Mekantildata, Rieber and Schibsted have a substantially lower foreign sales ratio on average than 'traditional' industrial firms.

Third, there were no distinctively large firms within the Norwegian sample by international standards. The largest company in the Norwegian top ten – Norsk Hydro – had total worldwide sales in 1999 of US$13.1 billion. In general, though, compared with other small countries such as the Netherlands – or Belgium, Sweden and Switzerland – Norwegian firms were predominantly small, with nine of the ten firms in Table 6.4 having

Table 6.5   *Large companies in Denmark, Finland and Norway: mean values (1990 and 1999)*

	Denmark Mean	Finland Mean	Norway Mean
Total sales 1990, in million US$	1 336.52	3 452.09	2 022.78
Total sales 1999, in million US$	2 411.90	6 467.28	3 801.14
Percentage growth, 1990–99 (%)	80.5	87.3	87.9
Foreign sales ratio, 1990	0.75	0.69	0.45
Foreign sales ratio, 1999	0.83	0.88	0.72
Number of employees, 1990	8 317.00	21 382.00	9 060.00
Number of employees, 1999	12 660.00	24 396.00	17 916.00
Percentage growth, 1990–99 (%)	52.2	14.1	97.7
Foreign employment ratio, 1990	0.34	0.38	0.27
Foreign employment ratio, 1999	0.51	0.56	0.56

less than US$10 billion in annual sales, and eight out of ten having annual turnover of less than US$4 billion.

Large companies in the Nordic countries: similarities and differences

Firms from all three Nordic countries tend to demonstrate some similarities, as shown in Table 6.5. First, there is a predominance of resource-based firms. This is due, in part, to the traditionally strong clusters found in these countries in the resource-intensive sectors (see Hermesniemi et al., 1996; Reve et al., 1992). Second, Table 6.5 shows that there were no truly large companies – or 'global giants' – in these countries. In fact, with the possible notable exceptions of Nokia and Stora-Enso in Finland and Norsk Hydro in Norway, the top ten firms really consist of companies that in other contexts would probably have been termed medium-sized. One possible explanation may be that in all three countries governments have had an inclination to encourage and support the development of 'national champions', albeit less so in Denmark. Even though such companies have come to dominate their domestic markets, barriers to and/or lack of incentives to internationalize and the restricted sizes of these markets have prevented them from developing into large companies with worldwide presence.

Third, a general observation from Table 6.5 is that companies in the top ten league in each of the countries have became more internationalized across a number of relevant dimensions over the 1990s, especially in terms of foreign sales and employment rates. Moreover, their internationalization has been much stronger than the corresponding international trade figures at the national level. Internationalization patterns in Table 6.6 were measured by 'operation' and 'strategic' variables, which show that the top ten Danish and Norwegian firms have predominantly grown by expanding their international operations. This pattern was less easily observed in the case of Finnish firms, where the number of subsidiaries remained stable and the number of IJVs actually fell, although both the foreign sales and employment ratios increased between 1990 and 1999.

Internationalization patterns in Table 6.6 also revealed interesting differences

Table 6.6   Internationalization of the ten largest companies in Denmark, Finland and Norway: mean values

Dimensions of internationalization	Denmark			Finland			Norway		
	1990	1999	Percentage change, 1990–99	1990	1999	Percentage change, 1990–99	1990	1999	Percentage change 1990–99
'Operations oriented'									
Foreign sales ratio	0.75	0.83	10.7	0.69	0.88	28.8	0.45	0.72	60.0
Foreign employment ratio	0.34	0.51	50.0	0.38	0.56	47.4	0.27	0.56	107.4
No. of subsidiaries	38.70	68.30	76.5	82.80	88.70	7.1	29.80	62.80	110.7
No. of IJVs	7.00	10.80	54.3	12.80	11.90	−7.0	8.60	13.20	53.5
'Strategic'									
Foreign R&D ratio	0.22	0.23	1.2	n.a.	n.a.	n.a.	0.09	0.37	298.2
Foreign equity share	3.50	4.70	34.0	2.80	40.6	1350.0	13.70	23.00	67.9
No. of division HQs abroad	0.10	0.40	300.0	0.30	0.10	−66.7	0.10	2.70	2600.0
No. of corporate HQs abroad	0.00	0.00	0.0	0.00	0.00	0.0	0.00	0.10	0.0

Note: 'n.a.' denotes that data were not available.

between the national samples. First, the Norwegian companies have on average experienced a higher rate of internationalization during the 1990s than their counterparts from Denmark and Finland. This is true for most indicators of internationalization used in the study apart from growth in the number of IJVs, where the Danish companies display a marginally higher percentage change over the 1990 to 1999 period. The fact that the Norwegian companies on average were less internationalized in the early 1990s than their Danish and Finnish counterparts suggests that the Norwegian companies experienced 'catch-up', which in turn may partly explain their quicker internationalization pace through the decade. However, as argued by Oxelheim and Gärtner (1994), their stronger internationalization also reflects Norway's decision to stay outside the EU, thereby promoting the relocation of value-added activities to units within the EU.

Second, there are also important differences between the countries with regard to the extent to which their companies have internationalized beyond merely gaining a larger market presence abroad or relocating production to foreign locations. For example, while the average number of foreign subsidiaries of Danish and Norwegian companies increased by 76.5 percent and 110.7 percent respectively from 1990 to 1999, the corresponding figure for Finnish firms is only 7.1 percent (see Table 6.6). In the case of Norway, Table 6.6 shows that there is also a clear development towards internationalizing strategic activities such as R&D, and the ownership of their largest companies has also become increasingly international. Even though there has also been a strong internationalization of Finnish companies' equity, other measures of strategic internationalization have been less pronounced in the case of Finland, and almost absent among Danish companies. The internationalization of strategic activities is best illustrated by the increasing number of division or business area headquarters located abroad, which has gone from 1 in 1990 for Norwegian companies to 27 in 1999. The corresponding figures for Danish firms are 1 and 4, respectively (see Table 6.6). By contrast, the number of foreign-located divisional headquarters declined over the same period among Finnish companies. In addition, the only company in our sample that had moved their corporate headquarters to a foreign location was the Norwegian company Kværner.

The overall impression is clearly that for all three countries the largest companies have expanded their operations activities abroad, but whereas Danish and Finnish companies have concentrated their strategic activities at home, several exceptions to that rule can be found among Norwegian companies. This may reflect a number of developments, of which two appear particularly important. First, the outsider status of Norway *vis-à-vis* the EU has pushed some Norwegian firms to relocate strategic activities to take advantage of benefits that accrue to firms based within the EU. Second, Norwegian firms have tended to internationalize more as a result of weaker clusters at home. One example is the forest, pulp and paper sector that, in striking contrast to Finland, did not develop into a competitive cluster in Norway, leaving the only remaining major company, Norske Skog, alone on the international scene. Norske Skog has been successful in its internationalization, recently becoming the second-largest newsprint producer in the world through a series of acquisitions, but the company is much less nationally anchored than the Finnish-based firms (Moen and Lilja, 2001). Another example is the Norwegian metals sector, which has lost many of its former cluster characteristics (Reve et al., 1992). There is also evidence that the traditional strong linkages between various maritime sectors – e.g. between shipping, ship yards and ship equipment – have eroded over time (Benito et al., 2000). Companies have been obliged to seek access to clusters in other locations, and therefore tended to relocate strategic aspects of their activity more than Finnish or Danish firms.

Summary and discussion

This chapter has investigated the internationalization patterns of the top ten companies from three small Nordic countries – Denmark, Finland and Norway – over the period 1990 to 1999. Most companies in the sample have become more international over the last decade across all investigated dimensions of internationalization. This finding holds across the three countries, but is particularly accentuated in the case of Norwegian firms, partly due to their lower degree of internationalization at the beginning of the period.

Small nations are becoming more dependent on their MNEs, yet find themselves in an exceedingly vulnerable position. On the one hand, the growth rates of their largest companies are typically vastly superior to the growth of the national economies, and as a result, the relative importance of the activities of such companies has increased. On the other hand, increased globalization pressures have forced MNEs to reconfigure their activities worldwide. In order to survive, companies base their actions on what makes sense from a business perspective, and sometimes these actions may be in conflict with home-country goals and policies.

Globalization is characterized by increased cross-border interaction, but that does not necessarily imply a simple unidirectional outward movement. While MNEs may be forced to internationalize their activities and hence 'grow' out of their home countries, at the same time they also tap into local clusters and knowledge and resource pools. Differences between the internationalization patterns of the top ten firms in the three Nordic countries investigated suggest that centrifugal and centripetal forces are working with varying strength across countries. Norway seems generally to have been hit harder than Denmark and Finland over the last decade by the centrifugal forces of globalization and/or, conversely, by a lack of correspondingly strong centripetal forces. The findings in this study regarding 'operational' versus 'strategic' internationalization are of particular interest. The high degree of 'operational' internationalization can largely be explained by the needs to seek markets, lower costs and access resources outside the home country. Scale, scope and cost pressures act as strong centrifugal forces that, in an increasingly liberalized and global economy, largely drive 'operational' internationalization. There has been a convergence across the countries through the 1990s for all investigated dimensions of 'operational' internationalization, and the average values for the Danish, Finnish and Norwegian datasets turn out to be very similar at the end of the period.

'Strategic' internationalization is less a function of exogenous factors such as country size *per se*. A strong home-country 'embeddedness' counterbalances or neutralizes the motives for moving strategic activities and units to foreign locations. Such 'embeddedness' is the result of strong linkages to government and to state and local authorities, of cultural affinity, the existence of well-developed and well-functioning national innovation systems and infrastructure, and the existence of strong industrial and local clusters. The essence is that such factors work as centripetal forces keeping certain types of activities in a given location. Of course, in the absence of sufficiently strong centripetal forces, internationalization of a 'strategic' kind becomes more likely.

Overall we find that a low degree of 'strategic' internationalization typifies the top ten MNEs, especially those from Denmark and Finland. There has been some relocation of strategic activities among the top ten Norwegian companies. Our results indicate that this cross-country variance between MNEs reflects not just varying firm-specific strategies. Although our analysis here is necessarily tentative, it suggests that important idiosyncratic differences exist between the three Nordic home countries, which are ultimately reflected in the activities of their MNEs. A more detailed analysis is called for to separate these various influences. For instance, the dichotomy between Finland and Denmark on the one hand, and Norway on the other, is influenced by the integration of the former in the EU, while also reflecting the latter's less-developed clusters. The behavior of MNEs involves a complex set of issues, and the macro–micro interface deserves more careful study than has hitherto been the case.

Notes

*   From *International Studies of Management & Organization*, vol. 32, no. 1 (Spring 2002): 57–78. Copyright © 2002 by M.E. Sharpe, Inc. Reprinted with permission. All rights reserved. Not for reproduction.
1. In the cases of Denmark and Finland, none of the foreign-owned firms was large enough to be considered for inclusion, whereas in Norway several large companies are foreign owned (e.g. ABB Norge, Esso Norge, Norske Shell, Elf Petroleum Norge). This is largely due to the importance of the oil and gas sector in Norway, in which some of the biggest oil companies in the world operate.
2. In the case of Norway, that means that companies such as Statoil (oil and gas) and Telenor (telecommunications) were not included in the sample.
3. The companies were selected from the following lists; *Børsens Nyhedsmagasin: Danmarks 500 største koncerner* in Denmark, *Talouselämän 500 suurinta yritystä* in Finland, and *Kapitals 500 største* for Norway.
4. An econometric analysis of the Danish survey data shows that the number of white-collar workers in Denmark is significant and positively related to FDI, while the number of blue-collar workers in Denmark is negatively related to FDI (Pedersen et al., 1998). This indicates that the Danish companies are structuring their international network with operations activities dominated by blue-collar workers increasingly located abroad at the expense of their activities in Denmark, while strategic activities associated with innovation and value adding are retained in Denmark.
5. The large acquisitions made by Stora-Enso in the summer of 2000 in the USA have led to an expansion of sales to cover more of the Triad area, and may be indicative of a future trend among other large Finnish companies as well.

References

Ali-Yrkkö, J., L.Paija, C. Reilly and P. Ylä-Anttila (2000), *Nokia – A Big Company in a Small Country*, Helsinki: ETLA series B 162.

Archibugi, D. and M. Pianta (1992), *The Technological Specialization of Advanced Countries*, Dordrecht: Kluwer.

Bellak, C. and J. Cantwell (1997), 'Small latecomer countries in a globalising environment: constraints and opportunities for catching-up', *Development and International Cooperation*, **13** 139–79.

Bellak, C. and J. Cantwell (1998), 'Globalization tendencies relevant for latecomers: some conceptual issues', in M. Storper, S. Thomadakis and L. Tsipouri (eds), *Latecomers in the Global Economy*, London: Routledge, pp. 40–75.

Benito, G.R.G. and Ø. Strøm (2000), 'Chain strategies and modes of foreign market penetration in agribusiness', *Journal of International Food and Agribusiness Marketing*, **11** (2) 1–21.

Benito, G.R.G., E. Berger, M. de la Forest and J. Shum (2000), *Den maritime sektor i Norge sett i et klyngeperspektiv* [A Cluster Perspective on the Norwegian Maritime Sector], Sandvika: Norwegian School of Management BI, Research Report 8.

Birkinshaw, J. and A.J. Morrison (1995), 'Configurations of strategy and structure in subsidiaries of multinational corporations', *Journal of International Business Studies*, **26** (4), 729–53.

Cantwell, J. and R. Narula (2001), 'The eclectic paradigm in the global economy', *International Journal of the Economics of Business*, **8** (2), 155–72.

Dörrenbächer, C. (2000), 'Measuring corporate internationalisation: a review of measurement concepts and their use', *Intereconomics*, **35** (3), 119–26.

Dunning, J.H. and R. Narula (eds), *Foreign Direct Investment and Governments: Catalysts for Economic Restructuring*, London: Routledge.

Forsgren, M. (1990), 'Managing the international multi-centre firm: case studies from Sweden', *European Journal of Management*, **8** (2), 261–67.

Forsgren, M., U. Holm and J. Johanson (1995), 'Division headquarters go abroad: a step in the internationalization of the multinational corporation', *Journal of Management Studies*, **32** (4), 475–91.

Freeman, C. and B. Lundvall (eds), *Small Countries Facing the Technological Revolution*, London: Pinter.

Ghoshal, S. (1987), 'Global strategy: an organizing framework', *Strategic Management Journal*, **8** (5), 425–40.

Ghoshal, S. and C.A. Bartlett (1990), 'The multinational corporation as an inter-organizational network', *Academy of Management Review*, **15** (4), 603–25.

Granstrand, O., P. Patel and K. Pavitt (1997), 'Multi-technology corporations: why they have "distributed" rather than "distinctive" core competencies', *California Management Review*, **39** (4), 8–25.

Hedlund, G. (1986), 'The hypermodern MNC – a heterarchy?', *Human Resource Management*, **25** (1), 9–35.

Hermesniemi, H., M. Lammi and P. Ylä-Antilla (1996), *Advantage Finland – The Future of Finnish Industries*, Helsinki: ETLA Series B113.

Holm, U. and T. Pedersen (eds) *The Emergence and Impact of MNC Centres of Excellence: A Subsidiary Perspective*, London: Macmillan.

Kozul-Wright, R. and R. Rowthorn (1998), 'Spoilt for choice? Multinational corporations and the geography of international production', *Oxford Review of Economic Policy*, **14** (2), 74–90.

Krugman, P. (1991), 'Increasing returns and economic geography', *Journal of Political Economy*, **99**, 483–99.

Krugman, P. (1998), 'What's new about the new economic geography?', *Oxford Review of Economic Policy*, **14** (2), 7–17.

Markusen, A. (1996), 'Sticky places in a slippery space: a typology of industrial districts', *Economic Geography*, **72**, 293–313.

Moen, E. and K. Lilja (2001), 'Constructing global companies: contrasting national legacies in the Nordic forest industry', in G. Morgan, P.H. Kristensen and R. Whitley (eds), *The Multinational Firm: Organizing Across Institutional and National Divides*, Oxford: Oxford University Press, pp. 97–121.

Narula, R. (1996), *Multinational Investment and Economic Structure: Globalisation and Competitiveness*, London: Routledge.

Narula, R. (2002), 'Innovation systems and "inertia" in R&D location: Norwegian firms and the role of systemic lock-in', *Research Policy*, **31**, 795–816.

Narula, R. and J. Dunning (2000), 'Industrial development, globalisation and multinational enterprises: new realities for developing countries', *Oxford Development Studies*, **28** (2), 141–67.

OECD (1992), *Economic Surveys. Finland. 1991–1992*, Paris: OECD.

OECD (1999), *Economic Surveys. Finland. 1999*, Paris: OECD.

OECD (2000), *Economic Outlook. No. 67*, Paris: OECD.

Oxelheim, L. and R. Gärtner (1994), 'Small country manufacturing industries in transition – the case of the Nordic region', *Management International Review*, **34** (4), 331–56.

Oxelheim, L., A. Stonehill, T. Randøy, K. Vikkula, K.B. Dullum, and K.-M. Modén (1998), *Corporate Strategies to Internationalise the Cost of Capital*, Copenhagen: Copenhagen Business School Press.

Pedersen, T., A.H. Jespersen, T.L. Hoppe and S. Fangel (1998), *Danske Virksomheders Etableringer i Udlandet* [Danish Companies' Establishments Abroad]. Copenhagen: Dansk Industri.

Perlmutter, H. (1969), 'The tortuous evolution of the multinational corporation', *Columbia Journal of World Business*, **4**, 9–18.

Porter, M.E. (1990), *The Competitive Advantage of Nations*, New York: The Free Press.

Porter, M.E. and Ö. Sölvell (1998), 'The role of geography in the process of innovation and the sustainable competitive advantage of firms', in A.D. Chandler, P. Hagström and Ö. Sölvell (eds), *The Dynamic Firm: The Role of Technology, Strategy, Organization, and Regions*, Oxford: Oxford University Press, pp. 440–57.

Reve, T., T. Lensberg and K. Grønhaug (1992), *Et konkurransedyktig Norge* [A Competitive Norway], Oslo: Tano.

Reve, T. and E.W. Jakobsen (2001), *Et verdiskapende Norge* [A Value-Creating Norway], Oslo: Universitetsforlaget.

Ronen, S. and O. Shenkar (1985), 'Clustering countries on attitudinal dimensions: a review and synthesis', *Academy of Management Review*, **10** (3), 435–54.

Shaver, J.M. and F. Flyer (2000), 'Agglomeration economies, firm heterogeneity, and foreign direct investment in the United States', *Strategic Management Journal*, **21** (12), 1175–93.

Soete, L. (1987), 'The impact of technological innovation on international trade patterns: the evidence reconsidered', *Research Policy*, **16**, 101–30.

Van Den Bulcke, D. and A. Verbeke (eds), *Globalization and the Small Open Economy*, Cheltenham, UK and Northampton, MA, USA: Edward Elgar.

Van Hoesel, R. van and R. Narula (eds) (1999), *Multinationals from the Netherlands*, London: Routledge.

Walsh, V. (1998), 'Technology and the competitiveness of small countries: a review', in C. Freeman and B.-A. Lundvall (eds), *Small Countries Facing the Technological Revolution*, London: Pinter, pp. 37–66.

Yip, G.S. (1989), 'Global strategy . . . in a world of nations?', *Sloan Management Review*, **30**, 29–41.

Zanfei, A. (2000), 'Transnational firms and the changing organisation of innovative activities', *Cambridge Journal of Economics*, **24** (5), 515–42.

7 The competitive advantage of Canada: a firm-level analysis
Wenlong Yuan and Alain Verbeke

International business is very important for Canada. With a population of approximately 33 million people, Canada exports between 40 and 50 per cent of its GDP, while gross imports represent 30 to 40 per cent of GDP. However, Canada's potential to attract FDI has been falling. For example, its share of inward FDI as a percentage of total global flows fell from 7.1 per cent in 1985 to 3.1 per cent in 2002 (Sanford, 2005).

Opinions have varied widely as to what impact international linkages have on the Canadian economy and Canada's international competitiveness. Researchers have investigated the competitiveness of the Canadian economy from a macroeconomic perspective, based on either Michael Porter's 'national diamond' framework or the revised 'double diamond' framework (Rugman and D'Cruz, 1993; Rugman and Verbeke, 1993).

For example, in 1991, Michael Porter published a report entitled 'Canada at the Crossroads' that analysed Canada's international competitiveness, based on his 'national diamond' model of competitiveness. According to Porter, a country's standard of living is based on its productivity and international competitiveness, which in turn are determined by the quality of the macro-level and microeconomic business environments within the country. The macroeconomic environment encompasses such factors as government budget deficits or surpluses, government debt, tax rates, and the regulation of trade and investment policies. At the microeconomic level, a combination of four interrelated components comprises Porter's diamond of competitiveness, namely factor conditions, demand conditions, related and supporting industries, and firm strategy and rivalry. Porter concluded that while Canada had prospered economically in the past based on the wealth provided by its natural resources, well-educated citizens, and close proximity to the USA, it faced a number of substantial challenges leading into the 1990s that were likely to bring about a decline in overall competitiveness within the context of free trade. In a follow-up report a decade later, Martin and Porter (2001) found that Canada had made some progress, most notably at the macroeconomic level, with the elimination of the federal deficit, lower interest rates and inflation, and a more export-oriented economy.[1] However, they found that Canada's overall prosperity had declined relative to the USA and other Organization for Economic Co-operation and Development (OECD) countries, largely as a result of poor productivity growth.

In contrast, Rugman (1991, 1992) noted, after the release of the initial Porter report, that in the context of a small, advanced open economy such as Canada's with significant interests in the much larger US market, Porter's diamond framework might be flawed. Specifically, Porter's approach does not adequately represent the complexities and realities of global strategic management by multinational enterprises (MNEs) today, especially those based in smaller countries such as Canada (Rugman and Verbeke, 1993). In a scenario where the regional, rather than national, context is most important, Rugman and D'Cruz (1993) argue that it is more appropriate to consider a "double diamond" framework of factors (i.e., from two countries: Canada and the USA) that shape the competitiveness of Canadian businesses. In the case of Canada, a small open economy that is heavily reliant on the USA for trade and growth, the reality is that firms, by necessity, must take into consideration the competitive forces in the US market.

While a wealth of macroeconomic data and research exists at the national level, there is a real need to understand the micro- or firm-level drivers. Specifically, strategic motivations of foreign MNEs setting up operations in Canada and the roles of such Canadian operations reflect the competitiveness of the Canadian economy as perceived by foreign MNEs. In the context of the integrated North American Free Trade Agreement (NAFTA) region, changing strategies of MNEs and Canadian subsidiary roles should also reveal changes in Canadian competitiveness as a result of international linkages. Thus an in-depth analysis and understanding of a set of large MNEs will help to evaluate the Canadian economy correctly.

The intention of this chapter is to answer the following research questions:

1. What are the foreign direct investment (FDI) motivations for foreign MNEs operating in Canada?
2. What are the roles of the Canadian subsidiaries?
3. What is the impact of the increased regional integration on these foreign subsidiaries in Canada?

To answer these questions, the corporate strategic responses are investigated of these MNEs to NAFTA, and the resulting implications for Canada's competitiveness. Specifically, in-depth analysis will be conducted on the foreign trade and investment strategies of MNEs, and on the changing role of foreign-owned subsidiaries in Canada – an aspect that is often overlooked in the existing literature. The impact of these changes on Canadian competitiveness will also be assessed. Our research demonstrates that an in-depth understanding of MNE strategies, especially regarding the role and management of subsidiaries, is critical to evaluating correctly the significance of NAFTA to Canada and its competitive position in the global economy.

The remainder of this chapter proceeds as follows. First, the different perspectives on the competitiveness of Canada are briefly reviewed in the regional context. Second, the conceptual framework, which links MNEs' strategies to Canadian competitiveness, is discussed. Third, the research methodology is presented, as well as the findings based on an empirical analysis of 50 Canadian subsidiaries of foreign MNEs and 12 Canadian firms. The implications of this research for evaluating the competitiveness of Canada are taken up in the conclusions.

Competitiveness of Canada in the regional context
While Porter states that firms can selectively tap into the diamonds of other nations, it is predominantly the diamond forces of the firm's home country that are responsible for determining its global competitiveness. However, as noted earlier, Porter's approach does not adequately represent the complexities and realities of global strategic management by MNEs today, especially those based in smaller countries such as Canada.

Rugman and Verbeke (1993) refer to the work of Bartlett and Ghoshal (1989), with their 'transnational solution', Reich (1991), with multiple centres for MNEs, and Ohmae (1990), portraying firms in a borderless world, as examples where research demonstrates that a firm's national home base has become less important, and in some ways immaterial, to business strategy in an international context.

Rugman's critique of the national diamond framework and his development of the double diamond have been subsequently expanded by Rugman and Verbeke and others in various contributions. Rugman and Verbeke (1993) extend Porter's diamond framework by introducing four additional geographic levels – local, regional, foreign and global – which, together with the national level, comprise a more flexible and realistic scope of analysis for determining competitiveness. Moon et al. (1995, 1998) note that the national diamond does not adequately account for the international activities of MNEs, which exploit factor advantages across various countries and not just primarily through a national home base. Their work develops a generalized double diamond model, which allows small open economies to compare the shapes and sizes of both domestic and international diamonds, thus highlighting the most important factor variables requiring government policy intervention.

In the case of Canada, access to factors in the US diamond play just as significant a role in shaping the competitiveness of business in Canada as the domestic diamond does. Similar to the case in Europe, where the home-national diamond may not be the most relevant factor for many of the smaller countries in close proximity to larger economies, Canada must build competitive advantages derived from accessing and competing in the national diamonds of the USA within an increasingly integrated NAFTA region. Hence, in a double diamond framework, the competitiveness of Canada and its MNEs depends partially on the make-up of the Canadian domestic diamond but also significantly on access to the USA, which acts as a crucial partner in terms of interconnected trade and investment.

Overall, the above research stresses three important points for the analysis of Canadian competitiveness. First, researchers should pay more attention to international linkages and the impact of other countries' national diamonds when analysing Canadian competitiveness. With deep integration in the NAFTA region, analysing the competitiveness of Canada should incorporate the influence of the USA, as the regional diamond factors also play an important role.

Second, researchers should investigate the major international economic actors, namely the MNEs, and examine their perceptions of Canadian competitiveness. Such an analysis will reveal the micro-level factors that drive changes in Canadian competitiveness.

Third, researchers should focus more on how MNEs have responded to changing international linkages, such as increased integration within the NAFTA region. Such responses will reflect the perceived changes in Canadian competitiveness from the perspective of MNEs.

Conceptual framework
This chapter aims to fill the gap in the current understanding of MNEs' perceptions of Canadian competitiveness in the context of increased regional integration in the NAFTA region. The MNEs' activities are analysed, mainly from the following three angles: FDI

motivations, subsidiary roles and the impact of NAFTA. FDI motivations demonstrate the location advantages of Canada as perceived by MNEs; subsidiary roles reflect both the competitive advantage of Canada compared to advantages of other locations and subsidiary competences compared to other subsidiaries inside the MNEs; and the impact of NAFTA reveals the changing competitive advantages of Canada.

FDI motivations

Four major FDI types have conventionally been identified in the mainstream international business literature (Dunning, 1993): natural resource seeking, market seeking, efficiency seeking, and strategic asset seeking. In the case of Canada, FDI motivations reflect the specific characteristics of Canada that attract foreign MNEs to invest in Canada rather than other countries.

For MNEs as natural resource seekers, subsidiaries are set up to gain access to physical resources, capital, labour, and technological, managerial and organizational expertise, typically at a lower cost or with higher quality than in the home country. Market seekers invest abroad to supply final goods and services to foreign markets, and typically engage in horizontal integration. Efficiency-seeking FDI leads to the concentration of MNE activities in particular countries, starting from an existing, more dispersed, activity base. This occurs for one of two reasons. First, the MNE may want to benefit from differences in input markets among countries, thus leading to the geographic concentration of specific value-added activities in the vertical chain. Second, the firm may choose to take advantage of economies of scale and scope in countries with 'broadly similar economic structures and income levels' (Dunning, 1993, p. 60), thereby leading to the concentration of complete value chains in specific countries. Finally, strategic asset seekers expect to acquire the assets of foreign organizations to promote the acquirers' long-term strategic objectives, typically by deriving synergies from complementary assets.

Subsidiary roles

A subsidiary facing a specific environment with unique challenges and possessing an idiosyncratic set of competences should be managed differently from other subsidiaries. Specifically, MNE corporate management should allocate different roles and responsibilities to different subsidiary types (Bartlett and Ghoshal, 1986, 1989). In addition, a number of researchers (Birkinshaw, 1997, 2000; Paterson and Brock, 2002; Rugman and Verbeke, 2001; Taggart, 1997a, 1997b, 1998) have also argued that subsidiary management may sometimes have considerable latitude to pursue its own initiatives as it sees fit, thereby driving the subsidiary's charter extension.

Thus subsidiary roles reveal not only the competitiveness of Canadian subsidiaries inside their MNE networks, but also the contribution of subsidiaries' endeavours and Canadian location advantages to subsidiary roles mentioned above. In some cases, both favourable environments in Canada and subsidiary endeavours have contributed to unique expertise held by the Canadian subsidiary. In other cases, the Canadian subsidiary's entrepreneurial management has been instrumental to an important role of the subsidiary in the MNE, even if it does not benefit from the assumed strategic importance of the Canadian environment.

To identify subsidiary roles and subsidiary strengths, a differentiation is first made among four types of subsidiaries, following Bartlett and Ghoshal (1986):

A. Strategic Leader: The subsidiary plays a critical role because of both the strategic importance of the Canadian environment and a high level of unique competences developed by the subsidiary (high level of strategic importance of the Canadian environment and high level of firm-specific competences).
B. Contributor: The subsidiary is important, not so much because of the Canadian environment *per se*, but because it has worked hard at developing unique expertise that no other subsidiary possesses (low level of strategic importance of the Canadian environment and high level of firm-specific competences).
C. Implementer: The subsidiary is important because it is a 'team player' within the global company network and contributes substantially to the parent firm's cash flow (low level of strategic importance of the Canadian environment and low level of firm-specific competences).
D. Black Hole: The subsidiary is doing a good job given the limited resources at its disposal, but there is much more potential in the Canadian market that could be exploited if the subsidiary were given more resources or if its responsibilities were extended (high level of strategic importance of the Canadian environment and low level of firm-specific competences).

Type A represents those subsidiaries that rely on both strong internal capabilities and a strategically important national environment, and Type B reflects subsidiaries that have attained their present role in the MNE mainly through their entrepreneurial endeavours. In Type C, the subsidiary is supposed to engage in induced activities, that is, activities decided upon in a top-down fashion by the MNE parent company, as a team player in the MNE network, but it cannot pursue any autonomous activities because of a lack of entrepreneurial capabilities or slack resources in an environment not considered critical to the MNE as a whole. In Type D, the Canadian market may be viewed as critically important, but again, the limited entrepreneurial capabilities or slack resources at its disposal inhibit the pursuit of opportunities in this market.

The perceived capabilities of the Canadian subsidiaries (or the most important foreign subsidiaries in the case of Canadian-based MNEs) are also examined. These capabilities are assessed by comparing the subsidiary's strengths with those of the most admired other subsidiary in the multinational group. In the two comparisons the following value chain activities are included: innovation, purchasing, logistics (transport, warehousing and distribution), production, sales and marketing (including advertising), after-sales service (including distributor support), financial management, management information systems, human resources management, management of political issues, coordination/ control of the international operations, and management of stakeholders (other than shareholders).

The internal comparison between the subsidiary that is surveyed and the most respected subsidiary inside the MNE allows for both a comprehensive evaluation and a sophisticated understanding of subsidiary competences. It is intended to identify the strengths and weaknesses of the Canadian subsidiary, to highlight the possible existence of a capability gap between the surveyed subsidiary and the remainder of the MNE (Rugman and Verbeke, 2001, p. 244), and to uncover any unique, specialized resources at the subsidiary level.

The effect of regional integration on subsidiary strength
Regional integration may expose national subsidiaries to more internal competition and lead to rationalization within MNEs. Building upon the hypothetical comparison between the subsidiary's present position after NAFTA, and its assumed position if NAFTA had not come into existence, we examine whether there has been a positive, negative or negligible impact on subsidiary activities. We expect that the explanation from the respondents may shed light on whether the Canadian subsidiary has been able to develop any unique advantages as a result of NAFTA.

Research methodology
A list of 100 foreign subsidiaries in Canada was developed from the population of 157 foreign subsidiaries included in the *National Post Business 500* (2003). In addition to the 50 foreign-owned subsidiaries, 12 of the largest Canadian-based MNEs were also surveyed as a separate group, with the intention of discerning whether domestic MNEs displayed responses regarding their Canadian operations that were unique or distinct from the foreign subsidiaries.

Substantial background information was collected on each firm included in the sample for the period 2004 to 2005, with a focus on corporate history, strategy and organizational structure. We then personally contacted the senior managers (typically the chief executive officer or chief operating officer) of all the subsidiaries on the list and conducted interviews with them to complete the questionnaire, often complemented with open-ended questions on the Canadian subsidiary's capabilities so as to check the reliability of the data provided.

The Canadian firms were interviewed using a separate survey that retained the core questions but with slightly adjusted wording to account for the fact that operations in Canada were controlled by the domestic head office rather than being operated as a subsidiary. Results from the Canadian MNEs are presented separately from the foreign-owned subsidiaries and not bundled together unless expressly noted otherwise.

The resulting usable dataset includes 12 Canadian firms and 50 foreign subsidiaries operating in Canada, with 37 from the USA and 13 from the European Union (EU). Of the 50 foreign subsidiaries, 22 (44 per cent) reported sales of over $1 billion in Canada in 2004, including three with sales over $15 billion. This is estimated to represent approximately half of all such foreign-owned firms of this size and accounts for a significant portion of sales by MNEs in Canada. In terms of industry representation, there are 19 companies in manufacturing (30.6 per cent), 21 in oil and gas (33.9 per cent), eight in financial services and insurance (12.9 per cent), five in transportation and utilities (8.1 per cent), five in services (8.1 per cent), two in wholesale and retail trade (3.2 per cent), and two additional companies in mining and construction, respectively. The subset of 12 Canadian MNEs surveyed reflects a more narrow industry sample, comprised of four energy firms, three in manufacturing, three in financial services and one mining company.

Survey results
The results from the survey conducted with 50 subsidiaries of foreign-owned MNEs and 12 Canadian MNEs have been grouped according to the three key issues outlined in the conceptual framework: the strategic motivations that led to the establishment

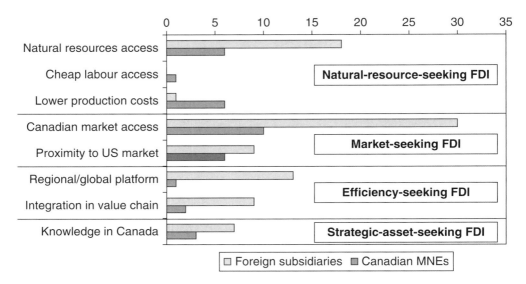

Figure 7.1   Initial strategic reasons for establishing operations in Canada

of the Canadian subsidiary, subsidiary roles, and the effect of regional integration on subsidiary competences.

FDI motivations
The average year of establishment of operations in Canada by the US-owned subsidiaries was 1956, ten years earlier than those based in the EU, while the average for the Canadian MNEs was 1930. These results are consistent with historical investment patterns where global interregional investment coming from Europe has grown more recently over the past few decades compared with traditional intraregional investment from the USA over the past century, while many of the Canadian MNEs have a long-established presence in their home base, sometimes dating back to the nineteenth century.

Figure 7.1 shows the results, with the strategic reasons grouped according to the four FDI types. It is apparent that the majority of foreign subsidiaries entered Canada for market-seeking reasons, with 60 per cent (30/50) indicating that access to the local Canadian market was a motivation and another 18 per cent (9/50) indicating that the close proximity to the US market was also of strategic importance. This motivation was most prevalent among manufacturing firms, with 87 per cent (13/15) of the foreign manufacturing subsidiaries citing access to the local Canadian market, and was less important among energy firms, with only 24 per cent (4/17) citing this as a strategic reason. However, none of the foreign manufacturing subsidiaries listed proximity to the US market as a strategic motivation, while two of the four Canadian manufacturing MNEs did. This probably reflects traditional differences in administrative heritage and firm structure as Canadian subsidiaries of foreign MNEs would be tasked with focusing primarily on the Canadian market, with the US market managed by a counterpart American unit within the MNE's network (or head office in the case of US-based MNEs), while Canadian MNEs evolved from a heritage of exporting into the US market. Nearly one-third (5/17) of the foreign energy subsidiaries and three of the four Canadian energy MNEs cited access to the US market as a strategic factor in their Canadian operations, with many noting that the Free Trade Agreement (FTA) and NAFTA had removed export restrictions and created a truly integrated North American energy market with the free flow of oil and gas across the border.

Access to natural resources was the second-most commonly cited reason for establishing operations in Canada. However, strong industry differences are once again observed as 76 per cent (13/17) of energy subsidiaries stated that access to natural resources in Canada was a motivation, along with all four of the Canadian-based energy companies, compared with only one manufacturing subsidiary. This result is not unexpected given the strong upstream motivations for energy firms to seek Canadian oil and gas resources. What is surprising is that manufacturing subsidiaries, and foreign subsidiaries as a whole, did not cite any of the other forms of resource-seeking motivations, with only one listing lower production costs and none citing access to cheap labour as a strategic reason for establishing operations in Canada. In contrast, half (6/12) of the Canadian-based MNEs cited lower production costs as a strategic factor in their operations.

In terms of efficiency-seeking motivations, just over one-quarter (13/50) of foreign subsidiaries listed Canada as an attractive platform from which to conduct regional or global operations and product mandates. In addition, nearly one-fifth (9/50) stated that the Canadian operations created value for the parent company through integration in a tightly coordinated international value chain. These results were similar across the range of industries and firm sizes.

Lastly, strategic-asset-seeking motives in the form of value creation through access to unique knowledge in the Canadian environment was cited by 14 per cent (7/50) of the foreign subsidiaries. In comparison, 25 per cent (3/12) of the Canadian MNEs cited this as an important strategic reason for conducting operations in Canada.

In all, given the strong importance placed on market-seeking reasons for FDI in Canada and the lesser importance on resource or strategic-asset-seeking motives, these findings indicate that a likely priority in the initial role of foreign subsidiaries was to bypass existing trade tariffs and develop downstream customer-end competences in order to successfully carry out their mandates.

Subsidiary roles and revealed competences
Figure 7.2 transposes the responses obtained from the foreign subsidiaries and Canadian MNEs, utilizing the general framework where the strategic importance of the Canadian environment is either high or low and the subsidiary's level of developed competences is high or low. The results[2] show that approximately half of the subsidiaries describe the Canadian unit as an 'Implementer', as 24 selected response C. These Canadian subsidiaries are useful for cash flow purposes and make contributions to value creation within the MNE (otherwise they would not be operating in Canada in the first place), but these contributions are the result of operational strengths developed through induced activities rather than the result of unique subsidiary-specific advantages (SSAs) developed through strong entrepreneurial capabilities and autonomous activities.

The second-most common response was A, with ten subsidiaries stating that both the Canadian environment and the unique SSAs developed in the Canadian operations are of high importance to the firm (as shown in the upper-right quadrant). These 'Strategic

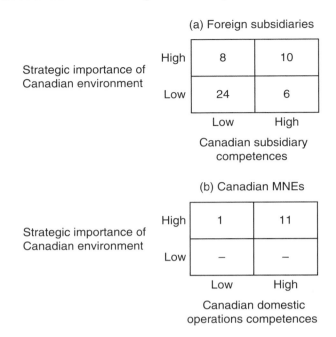

Figure 7.2   Strategic role of Canadian operations and environment in the global firm

Leaders' represent the optimal outcome envisioned by long-term government objectives in policy initiatives such as NAFTA.

Eight of the subsidiaries selected response D (upper-left quadrant), indicating that the subsidiary has not been able to develop strong entrepreneurial competences, and probably lacks slack resources in the Canadian environment in spite of the potentially high strategic importance of this environment for the company.

Finally, six subsidiaries indicated that the Canadian unit plays an important role because it has developed SSAs and expertise that are unique among other subsidiaries in the global MNE (response B as represented in the lower-right quadrant), despite the Canadian environment being of lower strategic importance to the parent company. These 'Contributors' are perhaps of most interest, as they represent success stories of Canadian subsidiaries that have established an important role in the MNE primarily through strengths in entrepreneurial activities within the Canadian environment, despite this national market not being perceived as the most strategically important within the global context (a plausible scenario for Canada as a small open economy situated next to the world's largest market in the USA).

Further analysis shows some significant differences between US- and EU-based firms. Of the ten subsidiaries with the role of 'Strategic Leaders', nine are US companies and only one is European. This represents 24 per cent (9/37) and 8 per cent (1/13) of these firms by region, respectively. On the other hand, five of the eight subsidiaries with the "Black Hole' role are EU-based, representing 42 per cent (5/13) of this subset, while the remaining three are US-based firms representing only 8 per cent (3/37) of this group. These regional differences appear to reflect and support the argument for home-region

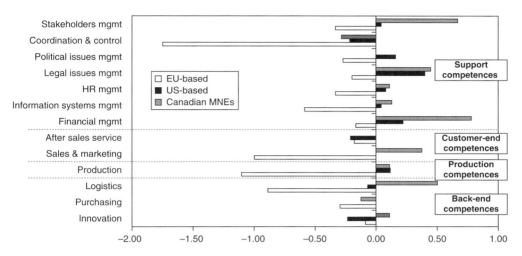

Figure 7.3   *Comparative ranking of Canadian operations versus most respected subsidiary*

bias, that the majority of larger MNEs remain strongest and attach the highest strategic importance to their home region rather than being truly global and equally strong in each of the triad regions (Rugman and Verbeke, 2004).

Not surprisingly, nearly all (11/12) of the Canadian-based MNEs selected response A, ranking both the strategic importance of the Canadian environment and the development of unique competences in the domestic operations to be high. However, one Canadian manufacturing firm conceded that its domestic operations had not achieved a high level of competences despite the strategic importance of the home market, when compared to how well its foreign subsidiaries in the USA and Europe had performed in developing their own unique SSAs.

Comparing Canadian subsidiaries with their peers   The results of the internal comparison replicate and magnify the differences observed above between subsidiaries from the USA and the EU. Canadian subsidiaries of US-owned MNEs generally ranked themselves on a par with other most-respected international subsidiaries within the company, whereas those of EU-owned firms tended to score themselves much lower. This is particularly evident in the areas of production, sales and marketing, logistics, and coordination and control. Scores for the Canadian-based MNEs were generally the highest of the three, but cannot be directly compared as they reflect the strengths of the parent operations versus those of a subsidiary.

Overall, if these competences in the Canadian units are viewed as the result of forces driving subsidiary roles within the MNE, these results are consistent with the present role of the Canadian operations. There, nearly 80 per cent of the EU-based subsidiaries had described their role as either a team player or could do better if given more resources (i.e. low subsidiary competences), while this figure was closer to 50 per cent for US-based subsidiaries, as more of them described their role as being critical or important because of the development of unique SSAs (i.e. high subsidiary competences).

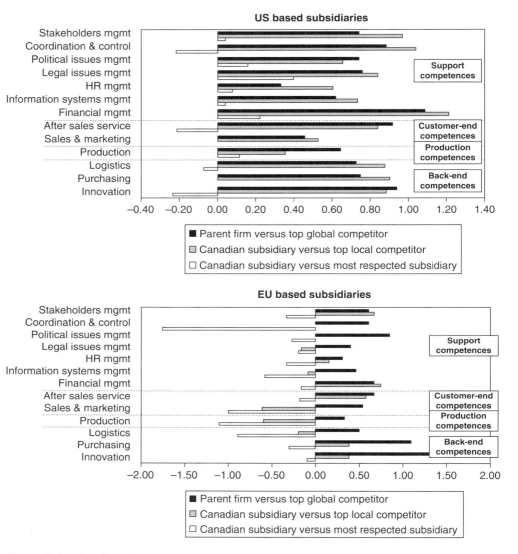

Figure 7.4   Combined comparative rankings of foreign subsidiaries in Canada

The above comparison of the subsidiary's competitiveness internally versus other sub-sidiaries offers an understanding of the unique strengths or gaps in capabilities that exist in the Canadian operations and their role inside the larger MNE. Comparison of differences in how the subsidiary and how the parent company rank against their respective competitors offers insights into whether the Canadian subsidiary has been able to benefit from the unique firm-specific advantages (FSAs) of the MNE as a whole and whether it has compensated in the Canadian environment for weaknesses at the parent level. In Figure 7.4, the three combined comparative rankings are presented in distinct graphs for the US-based and EU-based subsidiaries.

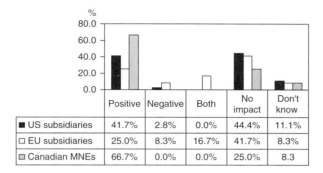

	Positive	Negative	Both	No impact	Don't know
■ US subsidiaries	41.7%	2.8%	0.0%	44.4%	11.1%
□ EU subsidiaries	25.0%	8.3%	16.7%	41.7%	8.3%
▨ Canadian MNEs	66.7%	0.0%	0.0%	25.0%	8.3

Figure 7.5   Impact of free trade on domestic and foreign firms in Canada

From this perspective it can be seen that US subsidiaries in Canada have been successful in transferring FSAs from the parent, and even augmenting these strengths or developing unique SSAs in the Canadian environment, as they rank themselves higher *vis-à-vis* their local competitors than the US parent versus its rivals for nine of the 13 value-added activity areas. Furthermore, these Canadian units generally rank themselves on a par with other subsidiaries considered to be the most respected in the firm, implying that the Canadian operations are equal to, or in effect are, the most-admired subsidiaries in the company's global network. In contrast, the EU subsidiaries lag behind their parent firm in nearly all categories, and rank themselves far below the most-respected subsidiaries in the firm, suggesting that they have not been able to successfully absorb and exploit existing company FSAs or develop unique competence areas within the Canadian environment. These results imply that the integrated NAFTA region has enabled US-based firms to more easily transfer FSA knowledge and skilled personnel within their home region to Canada compared to EU-based firms, which are NAFTA 'outsiders'.

Effects of regional integration
In this third section an examination is carried out on the effect of regional integration through free trade and NAFTA on subsidiary strengths, particularly in terms of entrepreneurial versus operational strengths and upstream or back-end versus downstream or customer-end strengths.

As Figure 7.5 shows, Canadian-based MNEs are the most positive regarding the impact of the FTA and NAFTA, with 67 per cent of respondents indicating that free trade has had a positive impact and another 30 per cent saying it has had no impact. None of the Canadian MNEs believe that free trade has had a negative impact on their company. In comparison, executives from the foreign subsidiaries are somewhat less positive. Responses from the US-based subsidiaries were evenly split between positive (42 per cent) and no impact (44 per cent), while the EU-based subsidiaries showed the least optimism, with only 25 per cent saying that free trade has had a positive impact, 8 per cent a negative impact, 17 per cent both positive and a negative impact, and 42 per cent saying it has had no impact.

Relating this back to the results in the previous section regarding comparisons of subsidiary and parent competences, it is reasonable to posit that US-based subsidiaries, which have been enabled by NAFTA to more easily receive knowledge and transfer skilled personnel from the home country, would view free trade as having a more positive impact than the EU-based subsidiaries, which have not been as successful at absorbing company FSAs or developing unique competences in Canada. For example, some of the US energy firms noted that free trade has allowed for the easier interchange of personnel and ideas between the USA and Canada, enabling them to fit the right skills in the right place. A number of firms also mentioned the positive impacts in terms of a free flow of intraregional oil and gas exports, with one executive stating that 'the energy industry relies on a free flow of energy across the border and improved ability to move people back and forth'. Another subsidiary manager stated that NAFTA 'allows regional/ continental economics to work without as many regulatory bottlenecks and allows easier interchange of people and ideas in both directions across the border'.

Further, the effect is analysed of regional integration on back-end subsidiary strengths and customer-end strengths by asking executives to assess if they would have been in a worse position, better position, or same position in each of the 13 activity areas had the FTA and NAFTA not been signed by Canada. Three main findings were observed. First, the benefits of NAFTA for foreign subsidiaries are identified primarily in product-related back-end activities including purchasing, logistics, innovation and production. This is consistent with the conceptual arguments presented earlier, that there may be stronger effects of regional integration on back-end rather than customer-end subsidiary activities, although some further extensions may be required to reflect the empirical results. Other support-related activities including financial management, management information systems (MIS), management of human resources (HR), management of legal issues, management of political issues, coordination of the international operations, and management of stakeholders appear to be less affected by NAFTA for most subsidiaries. This scenario may reflect the possibility that the benefits associated with product-related back-end activities are more readily evident to senior managers than other upstream or support-related activities. Thus the integration of other activities may be viewed as being less significant or result in a lower level of focus on such activities.

Second, relatively fewer benefits are reported from free trade for customer-end activities, in the sense that sales and after-sales services do not benefit as noticeably from regional integration. This indicates that local responsiveness is still needed in accessing customers, and that the firms have been cautious not to over-integrate in these areas.

Third, a limited number of subsidiaries reported positive benefits from free trade in the area of innovation, while most said that they would have been in the same position in this area regardless of NAFTA. These results differ somewhat from the earlier formulated hypothesis that firms would allocate entrepreneurial responsibility, and often, entrepreneurial resources, to regionally based subunits. Thus former national subsidiaries, if not functioning as regional business centres for specific product lines, would then play a less important role in the search and pursuit of new business opportunities. In this sense, a small proportion of subsidiaries would be strengthened in the area of innovation, while most would see their innovation capabilities curtailed. These results indicate that a small number of subsidiaries may have been able to gain the responsibility of a regional business centre. However, we have not found the weakening of innovation competences among a large number of subsidiaries. This probably reflects the difficulty of moving some of the former mandates away from the subsidiaries.

Finally, we enquired whether the Canadian operations have been able to develop any

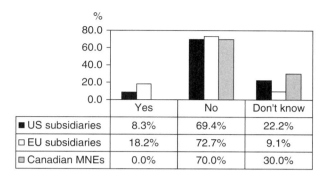

%	Yes	No	Don't know
■ US subsidiaries	8.3%	69.4%	22.2%
□ EU subsidiaries	18.2%	72.7%	9.1%
▣ Canadian MNEs	0.0%	70.0%	30.0%

Figure 7.6   Development of unique advantages by Canadian MNEs and foreign subsidiaries from NAFTA

unique advantages as a result of the FTA and NAFTA (see Figure 7.6). It is interesting to note that 70 per cent of the Canadian MNEs said that they have not and 30 per cent were unsure, while none indicated that they have developed unique advantages from free trade, despite two-thirds having said that free trade has had a positive impact on their firm. Approximately 10 per cent of the foreign subsidiaries mentioned that they have been able to develop unique advantages from free trade, but 70 per cent also reported that they have not, and the remainder were unsure.

These results reveal a number of points. First, for Canadian-based MNEs it appears that the immediate benefits of NAFTA have focused more on securing stable access to US markets rather than on the ability to develop new FSAs. As one respondent stated, NAFTA has ensured national treatment and continued protection of open market access rather than providing anything new. A Canadian auto parts manufacturer stated that NAFTA has been positive because it maintained benefits already established under the Auto Pact, and it opened up access to Mexico, so as to benefit both production and sales.

Second, on the surface, it appears that the prevailing perception that free trade has had a positive impact is rooted more in improvements in macro-level economic growth rather than in firm-specific adaptations. However, a more likely explanation is that company managers may not think in terms of direct links between NAFTA and its resulting impacts on company operations and strategic responses in terms of FSA development. In other words, business executives often look at the outcome of free trade as being positive, but do not deliberately associate the strong strategic changes developed in response to it over the past decade and a half as being directly tied to it. As it relates practically to government policy, there is a need for further research and deliberation among business executives and managers in Canada – of both Canadian MNEs and foreign subsidiaries – to discuss the linkages between government economic policy and resulting corporate strategy, so as to understand better how an institutional context such as NAFTA affects Canada's regional and global competitiveness.

Conclusion

Overall, the results from the survey provide a new perspective on the competitive advantages of Canada. By analysing FDI motivations, subsidiary roles and the impact of NAFTA on Canadian subsidiaries, we investigate the micro-level drivers of Canadian competitiveness, thereby providing a complementary perspective to mainstream macro-level analysis of Canadian competitiveness.

First, international linkages do affect the competitiveness of Canada, as both Canadian subsidiaries of foreign MNEs and Canadian organizations have benefited from deep regional integration in the NAFTA area. However, such benefits mainly accrued to product-related, back-end activities such as purchasing, logistics, innovation and production.

Second, NAFTA has helped to facilitate the transfer of FSAs to Canadian subsidiaries, particularly for insider US-owned firms. For many of the US-based firms, the Canadian operations are among the most-respected subsidiaries in the company's global network. The picture is somewhat less conclusive for European firms. EU-based subsidiaries in Canada appear predominantly to be Implementers rather than Strategic Leaders. In this regard, Canada must do a better job at defining and communicating the unique benefits of the Canadian environment within the wider North American region and the effects of NAFTA on Canada's regional and global competitiveness.

Third, the role and position of the Canadian subsidiaries within the overall firm is determined both by the strategic importance of the Canadian market and the level of competences developed by the subsidiary. Although a large group of Canadian subsidiaries take the role of either Implementer or Black Hole, the eight Contributors represent success stories of Canadian subsidiaries that have established an important role in the multinational group, primarily through strengths in entrepreneurial activities within the Canadian environment, despite the position of Canada as a small open economy situated next to the world's largest market – the USA.

Notes

1. Martin and Porter (2001, p. 6) state that between 1991 and 1999, the federal budget improved from a deficit of 6.6 per cent of GDP to a surplus of 0.9 per cent, the best position among all G-7 countries. Interest rates (three-month Treasury bills) fell from an average of 11.55 per cent (1988–90) to 4.97 per cent (1998–2000). Inflation declined from 4.6 per cent (1988–90) to 2.1 per cent (1998–2000). Exports as a percentage of GDP increased from 25.2 per cent (1989) to 43.2 per cent (1999).
2. Two firms did not answer this survey question, with 48 foreign subsidiaries left for our analysis.

References

Bartlett, C.A. and S. Ghoshal (1986), 'Tap your subsidiaries for global reach', *Harvard Business Review*, **64** (6), 87–94.
Bartlett, C.A. and S. Ghoshal (1989), *Managing Across Borders: The Transnational Solution*, Boston, MA: Harvard Business School Press.
Birkinshaw, J. (1997), 'Entrepreneurship in multinational corporations: the characteristics of subsidiary initiatives', *Strategic Management Journal*, **18** (3), 207–29.
Birkinshaw, J. (2000), *Entrepreneurship in Global Firms*, London: Sage Publications.
Dunning, J.H. (1993), *Multinational Enterprises and the Global Economy*, Wokingham: Addison Wesley.
Martin, R. and M. Porter (2001), *Canadian Competitiveness: A Decade after the Crossroads*, Toronto: Rotman School of Management, University of Toronto.
Moon, C., A. Rugman and A. Verbeke. (1995) 'The generalized double diamond approach to international competitiveness', in Alan M. Rugman, Julien van den Broeck and Alain Verbeke (eds), *Research in Global Strategic Management. Volume 5: Beyond the Diamond*, Greenwich, CT: JAI Press, pp. 97–114.
Moon, C., A. Rugman and A. Verbeke (1998) 'A generalized double diamond approach to the global competitiveness of Korea and Singapore', *International Business Review*, 7, 135–50.
National Post Business (2003), 'Canada's 500 largest corporations', *National Post Business*, 86–105.

Ohmae, K. (1990), *The Borderless World: Power and Strategy in the International Economy*, New York: Harper Business.

Paterson, S.L. and D.M. Brock (2002), 'The development of subsidiary-management research: review and theoretical analysis', *International Business Review*, **11**, 139–63.

Porter, M. (1991), *Canada at the Crossroads: The Reality of a New Competitive Environment*, Ottawa: Business Council on National Issues and Ministry of Supply and Services.

Reich, R. (1991), 'Who is them?', *Harvard Business Review*, **69** (2), 77–89.

Rugman, A. (1991), 'Diamond in the rough', *Business Quarterly*, **55** (3), 61–4.

Rugman, A. (1992), 'Porter takes the wrong turn', *Business Quarterly*, **56** (3), 59–64.

Rugman, A. and R.D. D'Cruz (1993), 'The double diamond model of international competitiveness: the Canadian experience', *Management International Review*, **2**, 17–39.

Rugman, A. and A. Verbeke (1993), 'How to operationalize Porter's diamond of international competitiveness', *The International Executive*, **35** (4), 283–99.

Rugman, A. and A. Verbeke (2001), 'Subsidiary-specific advantages in multinational enterprises', *Strategic Management Journal*, **22**, 237–50.

Rugman, A. and A. Verbeke (2003), 'Multinational enterprises and clusters: an organising framework', *Multinational International Review*, Special Issue **3**, 151–69.

Rugman, A. and A. Verbeke (2004), 'A perspective on regional and global strategies of multinational enterprises', *Journal of International Business Studies*, **35**, 3–18.

Sanford, Jeff (2005), 'Trade winds', *Canadian Business*, **78** (3), 23–4.

Taggart, J.H. (1997a), 'Autonomy and procedural justice: a framework for evaluating subsidiary strategy', *Journal of International Business Studies*, **28** (1), 51–76.

Taggart, J.H. (1997b), 'An evaluation of the integration-responsiveness framework: MNC manufacturing subsidiaries in the UK', *Management International Review*, **37** (4), 295–318.

Taggart, J.H. (1998), 'Strategy shifts in MNC subsidiaries', *Strategic Management Journal*, **19**, 663–81.

8 Chile as an example of the augmented diamond
Robert Grosse

The Chilean economy: clusters, competitiveness and the augmented diamond

Chile is an emerging market characterized by 30 years of free market economic policies and a well-developed private sector that produces a wide range of goods and services. It has been the most open economy in Latin America (recently rivalled by Mexico), since the Pinochet government's decision to adopt (University of) 'Chicago style' free market policies in 1976. Per capita income by 2005 had reached over US$6000, putting Chile at the top of the range of emerging markets worldwide.

Even before the 1970s Chile had demonstrated a recurring preference for open market economic policy, probably because the country's market is so small, and the most viable transportation has been via ocean routes, which easily include products from other countries as well as from within Chile.

A comparison of some macro characteristics of Chile and other Latin American countries appears in Table 8.1. Note that Chile eclipses the other Latin American countries overall, falling just slightly behind Argentina in education and literacy. Chile leads by far in having the lowest level of perceived corruption in the region, and also leads in the Human Development Index (which takes into account life expectancy, literacy and income). Venezuela leads in GDP growth due to the huge oil price increases in 2006, though Chile's growth rate outperforms all of the countries over the past two decades.

The country extends along the Andes mountains in southern South America for more than 6000 km (3500 miles). The northern part of the country is mostly desert, with very little population. The central part of the country is where most of the people live, from Santiago at the foot of the Andes to Valparaiso on the Pacific Ocean about 70 miles west. The southern part of the country is largely sub-arctic tundra, with very little population. Chile overall had just over 16 million people in 2007.

The economy is largely service-based, as with most countries in the early twenty-first century. Services ranging from financial services to tourism to transportation constitute about 60 per cent of GDP, with manufacturing a distant second at about 38 per cent of GDP. Agriculture constituted only about 6 per cent of GDP, but it was the source of key clusters of firms in such industries as wine production, fruits and vegetables, and wood products. The traditional largest sector during the twentieth century was copper mining, and a copper-producing cluster also exists.

As far as the four sets of parameters that help determine country competitiveness are concerned, Chile stacks up quite impressively. With respect to factor conditions, Chile is a world leader in production of copper, grapes and other fruits and vegetables, salmon, and lumber and wood products. Indeed, Chile could be accused of facing the 'Dutch disease'[1] of having abundant mining resources (i.e. copper), which could distract the economy from diversifying and building new competitive advantages. Despite the major significance of copper in Chile's exports, the country has moved far beyond dependence

Table 8.1   Comparison of six Latin American countries, 2006

	Chile	Argentina	Brazil	Colombia	Mexico	Venezuela
GDP per capita[a]	$8864*	$5458*	$5716*	$2887*	$8066*	$6736*
Education index[b]	0.91	0.95	0.88	0.86	0.86	0.87
Literacy rate (% over age 15)[b]	95.7	97.2	88.6	92.8	91.0	93.0
Perceived level of corruption[c] (rank out of 163 countries)	7.3 (21/163)	2.9 (93/163)	3.3 (70/163)	3.9 (59/163)	3.3 (75/163)	2.3 (141/163)
GDP – real growth rate (%)[a]	4.0	8.5*	3.7	6.8*	4.8	10.3
Human Development Index[b]	0.859 38/177	0.863 36/177	0.792 69/177	0.790 70/177	0.821 53/177	0.784 72/177

Notes:
[a]   IMF, *World Economic Outlook*, 2006 (*estimates).
[b]   UNDP, *Human Development Report 2006*. Data are from 2004.
[c]   Transparency International; *Corruption Perceptions Index 2006*.

on that natural resource by entering into downstream production of refined copper products, and by diversifying into other sectors that take advantage of other natural resources. Perhaps Chile could be viewed as economically weak because of its overall dependence on natural-resource-based industries – and this issue is certainly a major one in the early twenty-first century.

As far as created factors, or specialized factors, are concerned, Chile has made major inroads in the development of skills and knowledge. The education system is highly regarded in Latin America, although that is not nearly as high in the rankings as that of a number of industrial countries such as the Netherlands or New Zealand.[2] Chilean management is viewed as possibly the most competitive in Latin America, with a dispro-portionate number of Chilean firms in the list of Latin America's largest, in comparison with Chile's ranking by population or GDP.[3]

As far as demand conditions go, Chile has had a relatively open economy for more than a quarter of a century, and prices are largely market determined, with companies compet-ing freely in most products. Thus demand is sophisticated, because consumers are used to having choices between products and services, and the market plays the major role in balancing supply and demand. Per capita income is high for emerging markets, though low relative to the Triad countries. With a relatively small population of just 16 million, Chile's market is certainly limited in its ability to offer firms scale economies in serving domestic demand. With national GDP on the order of US$108 billion in 2006, and no regional market of the significance of NAFTA or the EU, Chile is clearly too small to attract industries such as auto assembly, computer manufacturing or biotech research.

Considering related and supporting industries associated with those in the clusters of copper, fruits and vegetables, salmon, and wood products, there are relatively few down-stream producers of processed goods using these raw material inputs. Certainly copper

Table 8.2   Chilean wine exporters, 2000

Company	Nationality	Products	Comments
Concha y Toro	Chile	Almaviva, Don Melchor	Chile's biggest vineyard
Santa Rita	Chile	Casa Real, Triple C, Pehuén Floresta	
William Cole	Chile	Cabernet Sauvignon, Carmenere	
Caliterra	Chile	Shiraz Reserve, Merlot	
Chateau Los Boldos	France	Merlot, Chardonnay, Syrah	
Torres	Spain	Grans Muralles, Mas Borres	
Franciscan	California, USA	Napa Valley Cabernet Sauvignon, Napa Valley Chardonnay	
Casa Lapostolle	France	'Classic' Sauvignon Blanc, 'Classic' Chardonnay	Founded in 1994 with a joint venture

Source: http://news.bbc.co.uk/1/hi/business/1943461.stm.

is refined and used in the production of wire and some other products, but the economy remains based primarily on raw materials for export. It seems that there should be room for downstream food processing, and for manufacture of wood products such as furniture, but neither of these directions has been followed in any significant way to date.

As far as company strategy, structure and rivalry are concerned, Chile is intensely competitive, and firms that succeed are necessarily quite adept at responding to rivals' threats. The four clusters clearly demonstrate the characteristics of intense domestic competition and survival of multiple rivals in each of the sectors. In addition, other sectors such as supermarkets, banks, department stores and other services tend to be highly competitive, pitting domestic and international rivals against each other.

For example, in the wine cluster, competition among the dozen main producers has led to several highly successful wineries producing and exporting red and white wines, under the names of Concha y Toro, Santa Rita, Undurraga, Santa Emiliana – all locally owned; and Miguel Torres (Spanish), Robert Mondavi (US) and Rothschild (French). The leading Chilean wine exporters are listed in Table 8.2.

Figure 8.1 shows the distribution of these wine exporters according to the percentage of wine exports that each sold in 2001.

Chilean firms as a group are probably the second-most active in international business among Latin American firms, following firms from much larger Mexico. That is, Chilean firms in all industries tend to be more outward-looking than their counterparts in other Latin American countries, with the exception of Mexican firms (which have a 2000 km border with the USA and face an enormously powerful demonstration effect there).

Inward FDI in Chile: a focus on copper, wine and salmon
Foreign direct investment (FDI) into Chile has played a major role in the development of the key industrial sectors such as copper, wine, salmon and other agriculture. The

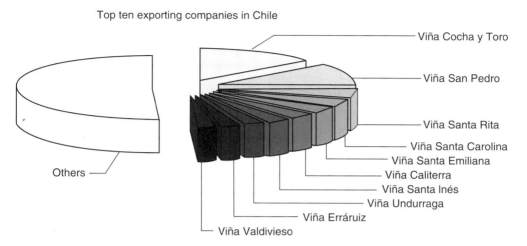

Top ten exporting companies in Chile

Viña Cocha y Toro

Viña San Pedro

Viña Santa Rita

Viña Santa Carolina

Viña Santa Emiliana

Viña Caliterra

Viña Santa Inés

Viña Undurraga

Viña Erráruiz

Viña Valdivieso

Others

Source: *Nuevos Mundos* (2002).

Figure 8.1 *Structure of the Chilean wine industry, by export value, 2001*

earliest activity was in the metal-mining sector, which was temporarily surpassed by nitrates (saltpetre[4]) as far back as the late nineteenth century. While copper far and away dominates Chile's mining exports today, that role was played by nitrates in the period between the 1880s and the First World War, before the discovery in Europe of processes to manufacture synthetic fertilizers. And in the late 1800s, gold and silver production and export often surpassed copper in value, though not in quantities. At the turn of the twentieth century, Chile's main export activities were as shown in Table 8.3.

The key industries in which FDI took place during the 1800s were mining, railways, and nitrates. The copper and other mining investments came largely from British firms, which often were not actually direct investors but rather investment groups that were formed in London for the specific purpose of investing in Latin American gold/silver/ copper mines (Stone, 1968; Wilkins, 1988). Similarly, British companies invested in railway construction and operation in Chile in the latter part of the nineteenth century, accumulating over £10 million of railway investment by the end of the century.

During most of the twentieth century FDI in Chile was concentrated in the copper industry and in other natural resource sectors. While some manufacturing investment was attracted, the relatively small national market, and the great distances to other, more attractive markets, discouraged this kind of activity. Despite a very favourable regulatory climate, low wage costs and an abundance of high-quality labour, virtually no offshore assembly (*maquila*) investment has taken place in Chile, in contrast with Mexico and other countries around the Caribbean.

In the past quarter-century, FDI into and out of Chile has grown quite importantly, with the largest amount of value still involved in the natural resource sectors. Figure 8.2 shows the FDI inflows and outflows from 1970 to 2004.

Note that the FDI inflows began earlier than the FDI by Chilean firms going overseas. The graph does not show the inflows from earlier in the twentieth century or even earlier,

Table 8.3   Mining exports from Chile, 1903

Mineral/metal	Quantity	Value in pesos (then worth 18d. – or 7½ p – in UK currency)
Gold, grammes	1 424 625	1 745 115
Silver, grammes	39 012 382	1 284 308
Copper, kg	29 923 132	21 438 397
Lead, kg	70 984	9 097
Cobalt ore, kg	284 990	99 695
Lead and vanadium ores, kg	2 000	n.a.
Manganese ore, kg	17 110 000	682 400
Coal, metric tons	827 112	8 250 720
Nitrates, metric quintals	14 449 200	140 102 012
Iodine, kg	157 444	1 687 327
Borates, kg	16 878 913	2 363 048
Salt, quintals	162 635	324 270
Sulphur, kg.	3 440 642	337 515
Sulphuric acid, quintals	1 600 000	176 000
Guano, metric quintals	111 335	267 466

Source: http://www.1911encyclopedia.org/Chile#Mining.

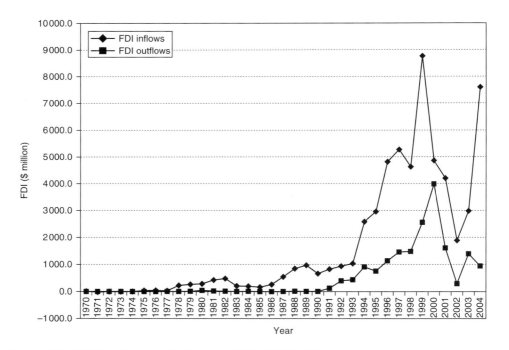

Figure 8.2   FDI outflows and inflows in Chile, 1970–2004

since the available aggregate data only begin in 1970. Even so, it is clear that Chile is an emerging market, and that foreign firms investing in Chile entered long before Chilean firms began looking abroad.

FDI in the Chilean copper industry
While nitrates were the most important export industry in Chile during the late 1800s, mining dominated exports before and after that time. In addition to copper, gold and silver have been mined in Chile for centuries, although the amounts of the precious metals are far smaller than the copper deposits and exports. During the period before independence from Spain, direct investment in mining companies was realized through 'crown companies' authorized by the Spanish government to conduct mining business and export to Spain from Chile.

Domestic firms were the initial exporters of copper in the early 1800s. During colonial times copper exploitation remained a small industry, but this began to change during the nineteenth century. In 1810, the year Chile became independent, the country had a production of 19 000 tons of copper. Production grew to several times that amount later in the century, until the boom in nitrate production siphoned away investment to that industry, and copper production declined for more than a decade.

Copper has played a large role in the Chilean economy since at least 1800, when British and American investors were already competing with other foreign investors to control Chile's copper, gold and silver markets. By 1835, Chile was exporting 12 700 tons of copper a year, much of it to the USA. Copper accounted for 55 per cent of the country's economy by 1860, and Chile was the world's largest source country for copper at that time. The copper mines were operated by domestic firms in the early years; major international copper refiners entered only at the beginning of the twentieth century.[5]

FDI in Chilean copper production began in 1904, when the US-based Braden Copper Co. started the exploitation of the El Teniente mine. The Braden investment was sold to the Kennecott Corporation, also a US company, in 1916. Kennecott remained the number one or number two producer of copper in Chile up until the nationalization of the industry in 1971.

The Chile Exploration Company, owned by the New York Guggenheim family (and ASARCO), started mining the vast reserves at Chuquicamata in 1910. In 1923, the Chile Exploration Company was sold to the Anaconda Copper Company, another US firm. Anaconda also owned the Andes Copper Company, which operated the Salvador deposit. Anaconda became the largest copper producer in Chile until the nationalization of the mines in 1971. The Cerro de Pasco copper company, also based in the USA, operated mainly in Peru. This company invested in Chilean production only in 1967. Then for the remaining few years until the nationalization of the industry in 1971, Cerro de Pasco remained the third-largest copper producer in Chile.[6]

During the twentieth century the foreign copper companies dominated Chilean copper production until the 1960s, when a wave of inward-looking nationalism took hold in most countries throughout Latin America. As part of this wave, in 1967–69 Chile's government under President Frei required the foreign copper companies to sell 51 per cent of their ownership in Chilean mines to the government. The government initially created an agency called the 'Copper Department', and in 1966 converted it into a state-owned

Table 8.4   Ownership structure of the main mining companies in Chile (2000)

Name	Owners	Production (thousand tons/ year in 1999)	Chile market share (%)
Codelco-Chile	Government of Chile	1520	32
S.C.M. El Abra	Phelps Dodge (51%); Codelco (49%)	225	4
S.C.M. Candelaria	Phelps Dodge (80%), Sumitomo (20%)	199	4
Minera Escondida	BHP Billiton (57,5%), RTZ (30%); Consorcio japonés (JECO, liderado por Mitsubishi 10%) y IFC del Banco Mundial (2.5%)	758	22
Cia. Minera Cerro Colorado Ltda	BHP Billiton (100%)	128	2
Empresa Minera Mantos Blancos S.A.	Anglo American (100%)	153	3
Cia. Minera Disputada Ltda.	Anglo American (100%)	250	n.a.
Doña Inés de Collihuasi	Falconbridge (44%), Anglo American (44%) Nippon–Mitsui (12%)	434	9
Cía. Minera Lomas Bayas	Falconbridge (100%)	59	1
Minera Los Pelambres Ltda	Antofagasta Minerals (60%), Consorcio japonés (Nippon Mining, Marubeni, Mitsui, Mitsubishi Materials Corp. y Mitsubishi Corp, 40%)	336	7
Minera El Tesoro	Antofagasta Minerals (61%), Equatorial Mining (39%)	84	2
Minera Michilla S.A.	Antofagasta Minerals (74.18%), Otros (25.82%)	52	1
Cia. Minera Disputada	Exxon Minerals (100%)	253	n.a.
Cia. Minera Zaldívar	Placer Dome (100%)	148	3
Quebrada Blanca	Aur Resources (76.5%), Sociedad Minera Pudahuel (13.5%) y Enami (10%)	74	1
Carmen de Andacollo	Aur Resources (63%), Cia. Minera del Pacífico (27%) y Enami (10%)	22	n.a.

Source: Chilean Copper Commission, http://www.cochilco.cl/english/inversion/fr_proyectos.html.

company, the Corporación del Cobre, or Codelco. The foreign companies continued to control the operation of the business, but they had to contribute half of after-tax profits to the government.

When the extreme socialist government of Salvador Allende came to power in 1970, conditions immediately worsened for the foreign companies. All the copper companies were expropriated in 1971.[7] These holdings were consolidated into state-owned Codelco in that same year. Codelco remains today the largest copper producer in Chile, with ownership of the three key mines: Chuquicamata, El Teniente and Salvador.

In 1979, Minera Utah de Chile Inc. and Getty Mining (Chile) Inc. agreed to jointly pursue a mining exploration programme in northern Chile. The companies agreed to finance the project 50/50, with Minera Utah acting as the operator. On 14 March 1981, the joint venture discovered a commercially exploitable copper ore deposit that later gave rise to the Escondida mine. Rights to the ore deposit were subsequently transferred to the current owners, BHP, which holds a 57.5 per cent share, and Rio Tinto, which holds a 30 per cent share. In the early 2000s, Escondida was the world's largest copper mine.

In the 1980s and more recently, foreign and domestic private sector copper companies again entered Chile and began developing new mines both independently and in joint ventures with Codelco. These include the Luksic family's Antofagasta Copper Company, along with BHP Billiton, Anglo American, Rio Tinto (RTZ), Placer Dome, Phelps Dodge, Falconbridge, Barrick Gold and Newmont Mining. The main copper-mining companies in Chile in 2000 are listed in Table 8.4.

Technology and capital in the Chilean mining industry have traditionally come from abroad. Most of this knowledge and funding has come through FDI by the firms, starting with Anaconda and Kennecott, while some knowledge has been transferred to Codelco through licensing and other contracting as well. Over the past 30 years Codelco itself has developed its own group of engineers and managers who carry out R&D in copper-mining processes. According to public documents, it appears that Codelco still relies mainly on contracting out to obtain foreign technology for use in mining, information technology and other applications.

FDI in the Chilean wine industry
Although not quite as long lived as copper, the Chilean wine industry has existed for two centuries (Table 8.5 gives a timeline of wine production in Chile). Wine production has been distributed in various regions of the country, producing a wide variety of wines. While technology and know-how in the industry were initially imported by Spanish immigrants in the 1700s, a wave of French influence took place in the mid-1800s, with a number of French wines introduced at that time. Vines and winemakers from Bordeaux were brought in by wealthy Chilean landowners who sought to replicate that legendary French wine region in South America. Gradually, the simple black Pais grape which the Spanish had planted was replaced by Cabernet Sauvignon, Merlot, Semillon and Sauvignon Blanc (actually the related Sauvignonasse), all major Bordeaux varieties.

Ownership of the grape-producing fields, the wineries and local distribution was all in hands of Chileans (or immigrants living in Chile). Export to Europe was controlled by foreign distributors who purchased the wine from Chilean growers/vintners.

FDI of any significance in the wine industry in Chile is a very recent phenomenon. Through most of the twentieth century wine production was heavily regulated and oriented towards domestic consumption. Between 1938 and 1973 production was restricted, heavily taxed and almost exclusively aimed at local consumption. With the arrival of the Pinochet government and the dramatic process of market opening beginning in 1973, the wine industry was permitted to expand and to take on foreign owners. In 1978 the Spanish firm Miguel Torres entered and began producing wine in the Central Valley at Curicó.

Table 8.5   A history of wine in Chile in seven stages

1. Before 1850	• Spanish conquerors and Jesuits imported wine and later produced wine in the country (Pais) • First generation of big 'viñaderos' • Development of different wine areas in the country: Concepcion, Coquimbo, Region Central etc. • Low quality of wine and mainly domestic consumption
2. During the 1800s	• 1808: Independence, economic growth, arrival of EU and US people. French people generated appreciation by Chilean people and stimulated visits to Bordeaux • 1880: introduction of French wines • Improvements in techniques due to French experts coming to the country • Governmental support to the industry: infrastructure, human capital and credit • New structure of the industry: new wine areas founded by French oenologists • New investment by second-generation Chilean entrepreneurs operating on other sectors
3. 1880–1938	• Expansion and consolidation of existing firms • Foreign families concentrate in trade and retail (*bodegueros*) • Domestic consumption • Universities
4. 1938–73	• Ley of Alcoholes (1938) • Limited production (fines for extra planting), maximum prices controlled (1965) • High domestic consumption of wine • Tributes • Mechanization • Conflicting relations between big firms and small grape growers (upsurge of cooperatives and period of contestations and strikes) • Agrarian reform in the 1960s under Allende
5. 1973–90	• Military dictatorship (1973–89) • End of the Agrarian reform • Liberalization of markets • Miguel Torres (1973) and introduction of French methods of production
6. 1990–98	• Worldwide increase of production and consumption of wine • Development of 'boutique' wineries (SMEs, high quality) in Chile • Technological upgrading and international competitiveness of Chilean wines
7. 1998–present	• Slowdown of worldwide consumption • Worldwide oversupply of wine • Reduction of international prices and fierce competition

Source: Author's own based on Del Pozo (1998).

Table 8.6   FDI in the Chilean wine industry, 1974–98

(a) FDI in the Chilean wine industry (thousands of US$), 1974–98

Company name	Origin	Turnover
HAC Investments Ltd	USA	16 700
Marnier Investissement S.A.	France	5559
The Robert Mondavi Corp y R.M.E. Inc.	USA	5925
Les Domaines Barons de Rothschild	France	3524
European Wine Company B.V.	Netherlands	2411
Miguel Torre Carbó y Otros	Spain	2107
Baron Philippe de Rothschild S.A.	France	1989
C.N. Mariani y Otros	USA	2352
Magnota Winery Corp.	Canada	1277
Stimson Lane Ltd/Int. Wines & Spirits Ltd	USA	1066
Other	Various	7224
Total		50 135

(b) Joint ventures between Chilean and foreign wineries, 1974–98

Name of joint venture	Name of foreign/Chilean partner	Origin of foreign partner
Almaviva	B. Philippe de Rothschild-Mouton/Concha y Toro	France
Aquitania	F. Solminihac/B. Prats, P. Pontallier	France
Caliterra	Robert Mondavi/Viña Errázuriz	USA
Casa Lapostolle	Marnier Lapostolle/Rabat family	France
Dallas Conte	Mildara Blass/Santa Carolinia	Australia
De Larose	Larose Trintaudon/AGF/Familia Granella	France
Los Vascos	B. Philippe de Rothschild-Lafite/Viña Santa Rita	France
Mapocho	BRL Hardy/Viña Cánepa	USA
Veramonte	Franciscan State/A. Huneeus	USA
Villard Estate	Thierry Villard/Santa Emilliana	France
William Fèvre	W. Fèvre/Victor Pino	France

Source: Agosin et al. (2000).

In short order, additional foreign wine companies entered the Chilean market, with firms from the USA and France quickly following Miguel Torres. The main foreign investors in Chilean wine production are shown in Table 8.6(b). Foreign investors include: Eric von Rothschild (Los Vascos), Dominique Messeny (Chateau Los Boldos), Robert Mondavi (Caliterra), Kendall Jackson (Vigna Cali), Alexander Maria Lapostolle (Casa Lapostolle), Baron Philippe de Rothschild (mainly the two branches of the Rothschild Family, namely Baron Philippe de Rothschild-Mouton and Baron Philippe de Rothschild-Lafite), and William Cole, among many others. These winemakers from France, Spain, Australia, the USA and New Zealand brought with them know-how for managing the wine business as well as the most up-to-date technology. Table 8.6(a) lists major foreign wine producers that have invested in Chile.

During the approximately 20-year period from 1978 to 2000 Chile went from being a minor participant in the international wine business to becoming the fifth-largest exporter of wine in the world. The combination of good growing conditions, a favourable regulatory climate and a self-reinforcing group of wine producers has propelled Chile into this situation in the early twenty-first century. While the growing conditions existed for centuries or longer, the value-added conditions of skills, technology, funding and government policy were clearly added in an extremely brief period of time.

During the 1980s government policy was used to subsidize export-oriented production, and the wine industry was an early recipient of this support. Corfo specifically offered subsidies to small farmers who agreed to work together through cooperatives to develop better wine grapes, to improve the wine production process, and to find export markets for their wines. After the 1982–83 economic crisis, the government started a major technology transfer programme especially oriented to the agricultural sector called Technology Transfer Groups (GTT). The main purpose of the GTT was to create a formal link between organizations such as the Agricultural and Farming Research Institute (INIA) and agro-producers. The aim was to facilitate the dissemination of foreign knowledge and the use of new technologies by local farmers. Additional policy support came from the export promotion agency, ProChile. This agency was founded in 1974, and was charged with promoting exports by small and medium-sized Chilean companies. It financed nearly half of total costs related to promotional activities of the Chilean wine sector abroad, including trade fairs, travel costs and marketing brochures and equipment. This support was offered to all sectors of Chilean industry, so the wine sector was not singled out for either ProChile or Corfo assistance.

FDI in the Chilean salmon industry
Salmon fishing, like wine production, grew from almost nothing before the 1980s to become a world-leading industry in Chile in the 1990s and beyond. The cultivated salmon industry in Chile was initially developed through a technology transfer programme in collaboration with the Japanese government and Japanese companies. This programme began in 1969 and continued through 1987.[8] In 1974 the US chemical firm Union Carbide initiated production of cultivated salmon at Curaco de Velez in Chile on the basis of imported genetic material through its local subsidiary, Domsea Farms Chile. At around the same time a second venture, this time supported by Corfo – a public development agency of the Chilean government – began operating under the name Lago Llanquihue Ltd. Four years later this firm was exporting small quantities of trout and salmon to France. After a few years the firm was sold to the private sector.

In 1981 Foundation Chile – a private/public undertaking resulting from the reprivatization of ITT assets previously nationalized by the socialist government of Salvador Allende – bought Domsea Farms and created Salmones Antartica, still one of the biggest firms in the industry today. The Japanese firm Nishiro, in a joint venture with Pesquera Mytilus, started Mares Australes, which later merged with Marine Harvest, under the control of Nutreco, a large Dutch company.[9]

During the 1980s the industry saw increases in output and the number of (mostly

Table 8.7   The evolution of cultivated salmon and trout production in Chile and the world, 1961–2002

Year	World production of cultivated salmon and trout (000 tons)	Chilean production of cultivated salmon and trout (000 tons)	Percentage of world production	Total value exported (US$ millions FOB)
1981	17	–	–	–
1984	49	–	–	–
1987	136	2	1.1	8.0
1990	366	29	7.9	140.0
1993	448	77	17.1	291.4
1996	751	184	24.5	538.0
1999	1010	223	22.0	817.8
2000	1112	302	27.0	973.2
2001	1327	450	33.9	964.3
2002	1439	506	35.2	973.0

Source: Asociación de la Industria del Salmón de Chile (2003).

domestic and small) firms, and improvements in quality control of the salmon. Exports grew, and by the end of the decade Chile accounted for about 7 per cent of world salmon exports. Once the industry had become established and Chile became a significant exporter (see Table 8.7), foreign salmon cultivators began to enter and to acquire existing Chilean fisheries. A process of consolidation took place during the 1990s, leaving just half a dozen firms in control of 80 per cent of output by the end of that decade.

In fewer than 20 years Chilean salmon exports – almost entirely cultivated salmon – increased from about US$8 million in 1987 to around US$1200 million in 2003. Salmon exports now account for close to 6 per cent of Chile's total exports. From a negligible participation in the world's salmon production – 1.1 per cent in 1987 – Chile's share in global salmon production reached more than one-third by 2001.

The industry consolidated during the 1990s, due largely to the competitive pressures of needing to produce salmon at lower cost and in greater quantities. The small, family-owned firms mostly dropped out of the business by selling or closing their fisheries. By the early 2000s, most of the Chilean industry was owned by Norwegian and Dutch fishing companies, including Nutreco, Fjord Seafood and Statkorn Holding, as shown in Table 8.8.

These multinational fishing and fish-processing companies do more than simply harvest fish from Chilean waters. They also carry out extensive R&D in their Chilean affiliates, mainly in the area of aquaculture improvements, but also in fish packing, storage and other aspects of the business (Maggi, 2004). Despite their growing degree of technological sophistication, Chilean salmon-farming activities still continue to be based mostly on imported machinery and equipment and 'disembodied' know-how, marginally supplemented by *ad hoc* knowledge generation and adaptation efforts carried out locally by salmon farming firms. On the other hand, the know-how for operating salmon farms and international distribution activity is increasingly a strength of the Chilean firms, so

Table 8.8   The world's 25 largest salmon fishing companies, 2001

Company	Production, 2000 (tonnes)	Production, 2001 (tonnes)	Turnover 2000 (NOK)
1. Nutreco Holding N.V. (Neth)	141 500	165 000	7692 Aquaculture-division
2. Pan Fish ASA (No)	64 200	97 000	4740
3. Stolt Sea Farm S.A. (L)	47 000	55 000	2793
4. Fjord Seafood ASA (No)	39 120	102 000	2325 Including Q4 from Chile and UK
5. Statkorn Holding ASA (No)	35 000	53 000	1350
6. Salmones Pacifico Sur S.A. (Ch)	27 000	50 000	620
7. George Weston Ltd (Ca)	21 700	23 000	5000 Connors Bros.
8. Midnor Group AS (No)	19 300	26 000	500 Adjusted for assets in partially owned licences
9. Camanchaca S.A. (Ch)	19 000	25 000	630
10. Multiexport S.A. (Ch)	18 000	25 000	765
11. Dåfjord Laks AS (No)	17 000	23 000	300
12. Laschinger Holding (G)	17 000	21 000	500
13. Salmones Unimarc S.A. (Ch)	16 000	18 000	450
14. Hydrotech Gruppen (No)	15 100	20 000	400 Minority items not included
15. SalMar AS (No)	15 000	19 200	500 Adjusted for assets in partially owned licenses
16. Hydro Seafood GSP (No)	14 500	22 900	300
17. Follalaks Holding AS (No)	12 430	14 900	300 Adjusted for assets in partially owned licences
18. Trusal S.A. (Ch)	12 000	16 000	–
19. Invertec (Ch)	11 000	20 000	1260 Entire conglomerate
20. Cultivos Marinos Chiloé (Ch)	11 000	15 000	450
21. Aguas Claras S.A. (Ch)	11 000	13 000	387
22. Salmones Antartica S.A. (Ch)	11 000	13 000	270
23. Sjøtroll AS (No)	10 500	26 260	340
24. Seafarm Invest AS (No)	10 190	14 710	229
25. Los Fiordos (Ch)	10 000	16 000	–

Note: Neth – Netherlands; No – Norway; L – Luxembourg; Ch – Chile; Ca – Canada; G – Germany.

Source: Intrafish, http://www.intrafish.com/intrafish-analysis/Top30/index.php3?thepage=2.

technological development is far from completely imported. Appendix A sketches the development of the cultivated salmon industry in Chile during the past few decades.[10]

Appendix B describes the three stages of salmon growing, and the kinds of technology involved in each stage.

Natural-resource-seeking FDI in three Chilean industries
The three industries selected for discussion here are copper, wine and salmon. These are three of the four most important clusters of business activity in Chile, and they are

presented in order of their significance to the Chilean economy. In 2004 copper constituted about 43 per cent of Chilean exports and 12.7 per cent of GDP. Wine made up about 8.11 per cent of exports and 2.38 per cent of GDP, and salmon fishing accounted for 5.2 per cent of Chilean exports, as well as 1.53 per cent of GDP (World Bank Group, 2007).

All three of these industries and all of Chile's clusters are natural resource based. There are no market-seeking clusters or efficiency-seeking clusters in the overall group. Chile's economy, despite its strong performance in Latin America during the past 30 years, continues to produce competitive firms primarily in these natural resource sectors.

The Chilean copper-mining cluster has grown around the extraction of copper ore in which the country has strong comparative advantages. Over 25 per cent of the world's copper ore reserves are located in Chile. Domestic production currently supplies two-thirds of the inputs, 40 per cent of the equipment, 70 per cent of the engineering services and 60 per cent of the costs of inputs of machinery and engineering services for the copper industry.

Initial FDI into this sector occurred a century ago by US-based copper companies seeking the raw material for export to the US market and later to other world markets. When the industry was nationalized under the Allende government in 1971, these foreign investors lost their subsidiaries. When the Pinochet government came to power, the nationalized copper business was not privatized, but the sector was opened to foreign firms once again. This meant that other foreign companies entered Chile, and that they were again looking primarily for the raw material to sell in international markets. By the early 2000s production of copper in Chile had moved to a situation where state-owned Codelco only produced about one-third of total Chilean copper output, and a dozen or so foreign and domestic private sector firms produced the other two-thirds of total output.

Even in the twenty-first century the copper industry in Chile seems to present an 'enclave' kind of investment, where the foreign firms invest huge amounts of money in production facilities, but they then export the commodity raw material and have little additional impact on the domestic Chilean economy. While the mines today are far safer and more environmentally responsible, the economic impact remains largely in the form of direct employment and tax revenue.[11]

The countries of origin of the foreign copper companies have multiplied since the pre-Allende days. Now the main participants in the Chilean mines are BHP (Australia); Rio Tinto (UK, the present owner of Kennecott); Phelps Dodge (USA); and Falconbridge (Canada), along with the government-owned Codelco and the domestic, privately owned Antofagasta.

Wine is a relatively recent major export product from Chile. The economic opening of the mid-1970s and beyond has encouraged domestic and foreign firms to enter the wine production sector, given the ideal growing conditions in several locations within Chile. Government policy to stimulate incoming FDI has helped as well, with the investment promotion agency, Corfo, playing a major role in this effort. The foreign wine producers operate subsidiaries in Chile with no restrictions on foreign ownership. The vineyards operate to some extent as enclaves, given that the main funding and management come from abroad, and the main markets in Europe and the USA are served through the multinational firms' subsidiaries in those countries.

Salmon is the most recent major export product from Chile among the three clusters of firms/products discussed here. FDI in this sector provided some initial impetus to its development in the 1980s, and then during the 1990s, the largest global salmon-farming companies acquired much of the Chilean industry, leaving the majority in the hands of foreign direct investors today. The foreign firms initially brought technology and access to world markets, and they continue to provide these competitive elements to Chilean salmon production.

What the foreign MNEs offer in each of the three sectors under consideration here is roughly the same in each case. The foreign firms bring access to foreign markets, especially in the USA and the EU. They bring financial capital that permits investment in large-scale facilities, and they bring technology for developing high-quality, modern production facilities. And finally, they bring management know-how for operating globally competitive firms. These strengths are passed on to Chilean firms by various means, including acquisition by the foreign firms, strategic alliances with them, and movement of people from foreign to domestic firms in each sector.

The limited amount of outward FDI in three Chilean industries
Outward FDI in the copper industry is extremely limited in the Chilean case, with almost no activity. The main copper producer, Codelco, operates a joint venture in Mexico to produce silver with the Mexican firm, Peñoles. Otherwise, Codelco is present overseas only in copper selling and distributing ventures for its primary product from Chile. In downstream areas such as production of copper wire, tubing and sheet, the Luksic family's Madeco company has expanded into Brazil, Peru and Argentina.

Outward FDI in the wine industry is likewise very limited. The Concha y Toro company owns vineyards in Mendoza, Argentina, as does Viña Santa Carolina. The internationalization of this industry continues to be based on a push for export markets and a pull for technology and funding from abroad. The limited overseas expansion of Chilean wineries is thus mostly for establishing sales contacts in key markets such as the USA and the EU, and for production of wine in neighbouring Argentina.

In the salmon industry, the main salmon growers that remain in Chilean hands have production only in Chile. On the other hand, since the largest salmon growers are Norwegian and Dutch companies, it is clear that they also have production in those European countries, and are regularly importing new knowledge and access to foreign markets from their parent companies. The transfer of knowledge to Chilean firms occurs mostly through the competition of local and foreign salmon growers in the Puerto Montt area of southern Chile, with workers and managers moving between firms and with some degree of technology licensing.

Geographic distribution of the three Chilean clusters
The geographic distribution of each of the three sectors in Chile depends completely on the location of the raw material or the growing conditions. Copper mines are largely located in the Atacama desert in northern Chile; salmon farming is largely concentrated in the southern part of the country near the city of Puerto Montt; and wine grapes are grown in several fertile valleys in the central part of the country.

If downstream production of processed foods or manufactures based on mining resources were to be developed, then some additional locations would logically become centres for such production. Similarly, the production of related products such as machinery for fishing and fish processing, or copper-mining equipment, or wine-grape technology, could take place in Chile to a much greater degree than it does at present.

The impact of government policies on the three sectors in Chile

The Chilean government has the distinction of being the first in Latin America to reject the 'Cepalista'[12] economic policy direction of inward-looking development, and to embrace an outward-looking and open policy regime. Whatever its faults and imperfections, the military regime of Augusto Pinochet (1973–88) was characterized from the start as favouring open markets. The famous 'Chicago boys' (led by Arnold Harberger and Milton Friedman) trained a generation of Chilean graduate students both at the University of Chicago and by visiting at the Universidad Católica de Chile, teaching them the doctrine of free market economics. The government policy regime in Chile began to pursue such policies soon after Pinochet took power, with Chile leaving the protectionist Andean Pact, opening the economy to incoming FDI as well as to Chilean investment overseas, and then privatizing state-owned companies. Chile was the first Latin American country to privatize the national social security system, putting the management of retirement funds in the hands of private sector companies (AFPs) beginning in 1981. Even today this system remains a model for national pension plan management worldwide.

Following this same spirit of outward-looking industrialization, Chile's government under both Pinochet and subsequently three elected presidents has promoted competition and economic openness. The governments have initiated numerous policies to attract investment, from the rejection of the Andean Pact's protectionist Decision 24 in 1973 to more recent projects by the development agency, Corfo, to entice foreign companies to Chile. The results have been extremely impressive, with Chile occupying the position of the most successful Latin American country in economic growth and in several other measures of well-being during the past 30 years. For a smaller country to achieve this distinction (rather than Argentina, Brazil or Mexico) is quite striking, and the great successes of Mexico and Brazil in the early 2000s owe to an important degree to Chilean-style economic policy reforms.

The development agency, Corfo, has demonstrated numerous achievements in attracting domestic and also foreign direct investment, to build the industrial base of Chile.

Conclusions

Chile has been the most successful country in Latin America during the past half-century as far as internationalization is concerned. Even so, Mexico has been catching up quickly with the Chilean success story by joining NAFTA and continuing with an open market policy since then. The successes of Chile do not mean that the country has overcome all the problems of economic development or of unequal income distribution, etc. However, in terms of demonstrating success in building private industry, attracting FDI, building successful clusters of companies in key sectors, operating financial markets and many other areas, Chile is ahead of the pack.

The examples of salmon and wine both illustrate the ways in which Chile's governments over the past three and a half decades have made major commitments to open market economic policies in general, and also have supported the development of local sectors that could become competitive internationally. While wine and fishing were domestic industries that existed in limited form for many decades before the 1980s, it was only once the 'Chicago boy' policies were instituted that Chile developed world-class firms and competitiveness in these sectors. With a combination of foreign multinationals and domestic Chilean firms, today Chile is the world leader among salmon exporters and ranks fifth among wine-exporting countries.

Government policies have consisted of more than simply establishing rules for free competition and keeping the government largely out of business activities. The industrial promotion agency, Corfo, has actively courted foreign companies to invest in sectors such as wine and salmon growing, as well as a host of other industries, including wood products, fruits and vegetables, and even high-tech manufacturing.

A potentially useful avenue of future policy is the concept used by the Brazilian government to attract R&D activity to that country. Foreign (and domestic) investors are offered large tax incentives to invest in local R&D activity. For example, in the auto industry firms in Brazil are offered a 50 per cent reduction in corporate income tax if the firm invests at least 5 per cent of that saving in local R&D activity. A similar policy could benefit Chile, given that in the cases of all three sectors studied here, Chile has a large market share globally, and thus firms could justify the local R&D to serve the large-scale business in copper, wine or salmon production.

The greatest challenge to Chile's continued growth and development is the heavy dependence on natural resource industries as the engines of growth. Commodities have traditionally proven fickle sources of income and jobs, due to weather conditions, price shocks, and limits in extending success in producing a commodity to other business areas. By building its global competitiveness on such sectors, Chile runs the risk of global downturns that are outside its ability to control.

Notes

1. In the 1960s, the Netherlands experienced a vast increase in its wealth after discovering large natural gas deposits in the North Sea. Unexpectedly, this ostensibly positive development had serious repercussions on important segments of the country's economy, as the Dutch guilder became stronger, making Dutch non-oil exports less competitive. This syndrome has come to be known as the 'Dutch disease'.
2. Chile ranked 39th among 60 countries in 'educational system' in IMD (2005).
3. See *America Economia* (2007).
4. Saltpetre, or potassium nitrate, was discovered in enormous quantities in the northern Atacama desert of Chile in the nineteenth century. This mineral is used as a fertilizer. Chile was the world's largest producer of nitrate, which accounted for roughly 50 per cent of total Chilean exports around 1890. A collapse in the nitrate industry followed Germany's development of synthetic nitrate during the First World War.
5. 'A few foreign companies were active in Chile during [the 1860s], but 90% or more of production was controlled by Chileans' (Gedicks, 1973, p. 12).
6. When Cerro de Pasco was nationalized, it ultimately received US$59 million in 1974 in compensation – in comparison with Kennecott's US$68 million. See http://www.historicaltextarchive.com/sections.php?op=viewarticle&artid=671.
7. The expropriations were converted into nationalizations under the Pinochet government half a dozen years later, when compensation was paid to the former foreign owners. See, for example, OPIC (1979).
8. Montero (2004).
9. This paragraph and the previous one are adapted from Katz (2004).
10. The boom in salmon farming has brought new life to the economy of southern Chile, which was based on traditional fishing, mollusc farming and harvesting, traditional agriculture and summer tourism. According to estimates from SalmonChile, the salmon industry supports about 28 000 direct jobs and more than 12 500 indirect jobs in the region. Direct jobs are located in processing plants (50 per cent), fattening farms (33 per cent) and hatcheries (15 per cent). The indirect jobs are in direct supply businesses located around the hatcheries, farming centres and processing plants. In the last decade, there has been significant expansion of both commercial and personal services, established mostly in the cities of Puerto Montt, Puerto Varas and Isla Grande de Chiloé (Maggi, 2004, p. 2).

11.   This statement refers to the foreign-owned copper mines. The Chilean-owned mines of course produce revenues to Chilean owners, and knowledge and other spillovers to the domestic economy that are more extensive than those of the foreign-owned mines.
12.   CEPAL is the United Nations Center for Latin America and the Caribbean (Centro Economico para America Latina). It was led during the 1960s by Argentine Raul Prebisch, whose economic doctrine was highly nationalistic. His views and his analysis favoured local ownership of business, substitution of imports with local production, and generally an anti-MNE outlook. CEPAL produced many studies and treatises supporting this kind of economic policy regime from 1960 to about 1985.

References

Agosin, M.R., E. Pasten and S. Vergara (2000), 'Joint ventures en la industria vitivinícola Chilena', ECLAC working document, Santiago de Chile.

America Economia (2007), 'The America Economia 500', *America Economia Magazine*, 9 July.

Aquanoticias (1996), Journal of the Chilean salmon farming industry.

Aquanoticias (2004), Journal of the Chilean salmon farming industry.

Del Pozo, J. (1998), *Historia del Vino Chileno. Desde 1850 hasta hoy*, Santiago de Chile: Editorial Universitaria.

Gedicks, A. (1973), 'The nationalization of copper in Chile: antecedents and consequences', *Review of Radical Political Economics*, **5**, 1–25.

IMD (2005), *World Competitiveness Yearbook 2005*, Lausanne: IMD.

Katz, J. (2004), 'Economic, institutional and technological forces inducing the successful inception of salmon farming in Chile', Universidad de Chile.

Maggi, C.C. (2004), 'The salmon farming and processing cluster in Southern Chile', Interamerican Development Bank Working Paper, WP16/2004.

Montero, C. (2004), 'La transferencia de tecnología en los procesos de integración a la economía global: el cluster de salmon en Chile', New York: United Nations, UNCTAD/ITE/IPC/.

OPIC (Overseas Private Investment Corporation) (1979), 'Annual Report 37', Washington, DC: OPIC.

Stone, I. (1968) 'British long-term investment in Latin America', *Business History Review*, **42** (3), 311–39.

Wilkins, M. (1988), 'The free-standing company, 1870–1914: an important type of British foreign direct investment', *Economic History Review*, **41** (2), 259–82.

World Bank Group (2007), http://devdata.worldbank.org/AAG/chl_aag.pdf, retrieved March 2008.

Appendix A

Table 8A.1 Evolution of salmon farming in Chile, 1960–2000: major 'stylized facts'

Exports	1960–1973	1974–85	1986–89	1990–95	1996–2002
	-------	1000 tons	11000 tons	100000 tons	500000 tons
Main products and markets		Salmon (Coho), fresh or frozen. Trout	Salmon (Coho), beheaded, for Japanese mkt	Salmon (Coho) Japan. Atlantic salmon for USA	Diversification of markets. USA, Asia, L. America
Key event in marketing		Brokers buy directly from firms	Brokers buy from firms and wholesalers	'Collective' export activities	Large foreign retailers buy directly
Issues needing to be resolved	Transition from catch and release to cultivation tanks	Established know-how for freshwater and need to develop saltwater aquaculture	Rapid expansion in scale of production	Development of forward (eggs and smolts) and backward linkages (food, vaccines, etc)	Environmental control systems. Salmon food. Production of eggs, vaccines. Traceability
Government policies	Technology transfer under government cooperation. Support from Corfo, SAG	Regulation and technology from Corfo, Fundacion Chile SERNAPESCA JICA, others	Provision of basic road and ports infrastructure	Missions for market research, technology for supporting industries. Regulation	Missions for environmental managment. Sources of productivity growth
Typical type of firm in industry	External cooperation. No industry yet	Family-owned small firms. Few foreign companies	Local SMEs grow very fast.	Presence of foreign firms gets stronger	Mergers & acquisitions by foreign firms become strong

188

Intermediate suppliers	Very few	High degree of vertical integration. Few domestic input suppliers	Outsourcing expands and many new suppliers enter the market	'Cluster' gets stronger and service industries develop
Expected externalities		Supporting industries develop	'Clustering' forces become stronger	International norms and standards diffuse. Good manufacturing practices and traceability
Sources of competitiveness	Natural comparative advantage	Production	Mostly local quality standards	Productivity, local and international standards, ISO 9000 and 14000. Traceability
Relations among agents in the industry	International cooperation. Proactive state participation	Public/private cooperative actions, Corfo Fundacion Chile	Initial forms of globalization emerge	Full-scale globalization after M&As

Source: Based on M. Iizuka (2004), 'Organizational capability and export performance: the salmon industry in Chile', mimeo, taken from Katz (2004).

Appendix B: the technology of salmon farming

Salmon farming involves three quite different production activities. There is first hatchery and pisciculture, which is the area where salmon eggs, alevins (yolk sac fry) and smolts (juvenile fish) are produced. The set of activities involved is very demanding in terms of both high-quality natural resources – uncontaminated waters, climatic conditions – and skilled personnel capable of managing sophisticated quality control and environmental protection routines. This first stage in the salmon-farming process is then followed by the cultivation stage, where alevins and smolts are grown in captivity into fully grown fish, ready to go to the market. The size and quality of cultivation tanks, salmon-feeding equipment and salmon food play a crucial role in this part of the global production process.

Finally, there is a third stage, the processing industry, where different products and forms of packaging are developed – boneless, frozen fillets, smoked, sliced – for the market. Figure 8A.1 presents a simple description of the production process.

Although these three different industries can be vertically integrated under one single company roof, they can also develop as separate production units, trading among themselves and opening up opportunities for specialization, economies of scale and intra industry division of labor.

Each of these three industries employs its own specialized technology, capital goods and intermediate inputs. Each relies on specialized suppliers of capital goods, intermediate inputs and services. It should be noted that all three of them started up in Chile on the basis of high import content, which was then gradually reduced and substituted by local production. Salmon eggs and smolts, salmon food and salmon-processing equipment came mostly from abroad during the early stages of the industry. Some years later, as the industry gained in size and complexity, the demand for many of these intermediate inputs expanded and acquired economic significance, inducing domestic and foreign companies to establish local production capacity. Many firms entered the industry at that point, catering to a rapidly expanding demand for pesticides, chemicals, vaccines, nets, transport services, veterinarian services, production organization logistics, legal services and so forth.

Salmon food accounts for roughly 45 per cent of total production costs while salmon eggs and smolts add a further 18 per cent to 20 per cent to the above. In other words, the first two stages in salmon-farming production – hatchery and cultivation – account for roughly two-thirds of salmon unit production costs (*Aquanoticias*, 1996).

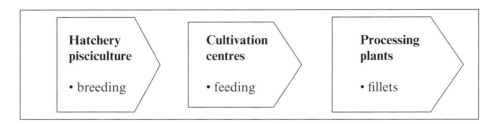

Figure 8A.1   Stages of production in salmon farming

Table 8A.2   Main businesses in the salmon cluster in Southern Chile

Name of business/group	Product (location)	Value of sales/ export 2001 (US$ mill. fob)	Capital structure/ recent changes
Grupo Trouw-Chile (Nutreco-Neth.)	Feed (Osorno). Fish farming, processing, commercialization (Lgo Llanquihue, Pto Montt, Chiloé)	240.0	Multinational corporation with Dutch capital. Trades on the Amsterdam Stock Exchange. It deals with sales to Trouw-Chile (feed) and Marine Harvest (salmon). Acquired production businesses in Norway, Scotland (Marine Harvest) and Chile (Mares Australes)
Ewos-Chile (Nor)	Feed (Chiloé and Coronel, VIII Region).	115.0	Multinational corporation with mostly Norwegian capital. It operates an R&D experimental station in Chiloé
Grupo Aqua Chile (Chl–USA)	Fish breeding, farming and processing, commercialization (Gala, Pto Cisnes, Chiloé, Pto Montt)	100.0	Holding company consisting of Chilean and US capital. Initially a joint venture between Pacífico Sur (Ch) and Aquafarms (USA). In 1998 they incorporated Piscicultura AquaChile and, in 2000 bought Salmopack (processing plant)
Camanchaca S.A.	Fish breeding, farming and processing (Pto Montt, Chiloé)	75.0	Firm associated with industrial fishing. Chilean capital. Publicly traded corporation
Multiexport S.A. (Ch–Jap)	Fish breeding, farming, processing, commercialization (Pto Montt, Chiloé)	60.0	Holding company. National capital. Recent strategic partnership with Grupo Mitsui Co Ltd (Japan)
Salmofood S.A.	Feed (Chiloé)	60.0	Created in 1993 with support from farming companies: Aguas Claras, Invertec, Aucar and Tecmar. Today Invertec is principal shareholder
Mainstream S.A.	Fish breeding, farming, processing (Chiloé)	56.3	National, S.A. Publicly traded. Eblen Fly. controls 70% of ownership. Bought assets from Aucar
Fjord Seafood Chile (Nor-Ch)	Fish breeding, farming, processing, commercialization	53.6	Norwegian Capital. Recently acquired by Tecmar Ltda and Linao Ltda

Table 8A.2   (continued)

Name of business/group	Product (location)	Value of sales/ export 2001 (US$ mill. fob)	Capital structure/ recent changes
	(Aysén, Chiloé, Pto Montt)		
Alitec (Neth)	Foodstuffs (Pargua, Chiloé)	50.0	Belongs to the Dutch corporation Provimi
Salmones Antártica (Jap)	Farming, processing (Aysén y Chiloé)	45.0	Created by Fundación Chile in 1981, sold to a Japanese corporation at the end of that decade
Biomar S.A.(Ch–Nor)	Foodstuffs (Pto Montt)	42.0	Principally Norwegian capital. Publicly traded
Cultivos Marinos Chiloé	Farming, processing (Chiloé, Aysén)	40.0	Belongs to a national holding company with investments in the real estate and hotel sectors. The group began in the 1980s thanks to Corfo loans
Aguas Claras S.A.	Fish breeding, farming, processing (smoked)	37.0	Acquired by Antarfish (Chilean holding). Founding partner of Salmofood
Invertec-Mar de Chiloé	Fish breeding, farming, processing (Chiloé)	35.0	National capital, family owned (Montanari family). Founding partner of Salmofood. Holding structure. Some of the larger ones not associated with SalmónChile
Los Fiordos Ltda	Fish breeding, farming, hatchery, processing, commercialization (Chiloé, Aysén)	35.0	Part of an agricultural industry national holding company, Agrosuper. Part of its production targets the national market. Commercializes the 'Super salmón' brand
Ventisqueros	Fish breeding, farming, processing (Pto Montt)	25.0	National capital
Trading Unimarc	Farming, processing, commercialization (Chiloé)	25.0	National, Errázuriz family

Source: Maggi (2004), p. 16.

Table 8A.3   Ranking of salmon-exporting companies in Chile, 2003

Company	% of total value
Marine Harvest S.A. (Nutreco, Netherlands)	14.7
Aqua Chile S.A. (Nacional, USA)	12.3
Camanchaca S.A. (Nacional)	8.4
Mainstream S.A. (Ewos, Norway)	7.2
Multiexport S.A. (Nacional, Japan)	6.4
Cultivos Marinos Chiloé S.A. (Nutreco, Netherlands)	5.9
Fjord Seafood Chile S.A. (Norway)	5.7
Salmones Antártica S.A. (Japan)	4.7
Pesquera Los Fiordos S.A. (Nacional)	4.6
Pesca Chile S.A. (Spain)	3.0
Others	27.1
Total	100.0

Source: *Aquanoticias*, March 2004.

9 The development trajectory of a small island economy: the successful case of Mauritius
Jahan Ara Peerally and John Cantwell

Mauritius is a fast-developing, small island economy, with characteristics of small developing countries in general. The Mauritian economy, which depended solely on sugar exports until 1970, has successfully diversified into two other sectors, namely textile manufacturing and up-market tourism. The last decade has seen the development of a freeport, an offshore business centre and an information and technology sector. The private sector has responded significantly to the challenge of sustainable development and growth of the economy. Today the business scene in Mauritius is one where there is a fast-expanding network of small, medium and large enterprises. The economic landscape was, however, not always as healthy and prolific.

During the pre-independence days of British rule the Nobel Prize winner and economist James Meade[1] predicted that if Mauritius were given independence, the economic prospects would be very dim. His assessment of Mauritius as being essentially a monocrop economy, vulnerable to terms-of-trade shocks, rapid population growth, and potential for ethnic tensions, provided a good example for a 'case study in Malthusian economics' (Meade, 1961, 1967). It is therefore rather ominous that a second Nobel Laureate, novelist V.S. Naipaul, described independent Mauritius in equally gloomy terms:

> an agricultural colony, created by empire in an empty island and always meant to be part of something larger, now given a thing called independence and set adrift, an abandoned imperial barracoon, incapable of economic or cultural autonomy. (Naipaul, 1972, p. 270)

Three decades later, defying all predictions, Mauritius has overcome economic stagnation and successfully embarked on a path of self-sustaining growth. It is now hailed as 'an economic success' (UNCTAD, 2001), a 'paradigm of fast sustainable growth' (Chernoff and Warner, 2002) and an 'outlier in sub-Saharan Africa' (Wignaraja, 2002). Such rapid and sustainable economic growth provides the basis for the primary aim of this chapter. It is geared towards presenting the development of a national diamond for Mauritius in an attempt to understand the foundations of this sudden sustainable growth.

The local economy has been based on three distinct industries, starting with the sugar industry, progressing to the industrialization phase through the textile industry and finally to a booming tourism industry. This industrial progression traces an unwitting developmental path from a resource-based economy to manufacturing and finally to services, which is an ideal trajectory for the economic success of developing countries. The secondary aim of the chapter is therefore to analyse the role of foreign direct investment (FDI) in the development and success of the textile and tourism industries.

The structural transformation of the Mauritian economy

Most small open economies share a number of specific economic problems such as vulnerability in world markets, low capacity to borrow on international capital markets and diseconomies of scale. Despite such inherent barriers, Mauritius is an exceptional case in point due to its successful economic structural transformation.

Mauritius remained a single-crop economy based on sugar well after independence in 1968. The initial economic importance of the sugar industry must not, however, be discounted despite the major phasing-out process it is now undergoing. The sugar industry occupied a prominent role in post-independence economic development with a GDP contribution of 25 per cent, employing 45 per cent of the labour force and representing 90 per cent of exports. Mauritius depended heavily on sugar for decades, but it was evident that sugar production would be unable to support any substantive economic growth for the country. Today's rising production costs,[2] labour shortages in the industry and increased competition from other less-developed countries[3] are forcing the speedy phasing out of the sugar industry. Sugar and sugar by-products accounted for only 4.2 per cent of GDP, 7 per cent of employment and 24.9 per cent of total Mauritian exports in 2005 (CSO,[4] 2006).

The country's overreliance on a sunset sugar industry and Meade's recommendations compelled the post-independence government to attach a high priority to industrial development in its economic strategy. The need for structural transformation of the economy was being felt and addressed as early as the 1970s with the setting up of the Mauritian export processing zone (MEPZ). The authorities were resolute in their determination to institutionalize a manufacturing sector by encouraging the development of an export-biased EPZ, thereby diversifying from a monocrop agricultural sector. The adjustment and stabilization period, more specifically, lasted from 1979 to 1986 and the number of firms and employment in the MEPZ rose threefold from 1983 to 1988. By 1993 the MEPZ superseded the sugar industry as the top foreign exchange earner and the economic transformation was considered as successfully implemented. The MEPZ led by textile firms is now considered as the second pillar of the Mauritian economy.

Thus Mauritius developed the most flourishing EPZ in Africa and attracted crucial FDI in the sector through aggressively pursuing a market-oriented strategy aided by beneficial trade agreements inherited from colonial ties. Following this strategy and the economic success it entailed, the country was able to further consolidate and expand its tourism industry. A similar pattern of development can therefore be witnessed in the latter.

Although the country is lacking in natural resources such as land and local raw materials, it is none the less endowed with a year-round tropical climate, sandy beaches, safe lagoons, a unique cultural setting and a bilingual population. With conscientious plans and policies the government developed the industry, and tourist arrivals per year have increased from a mere 48,797 in the early post-independence 1970s to a staggering 788,276 in 2006 (CSO, 2007a). Tourism, one of the sectors overlooked in the Meade Report, now constitutes the third pillar of the economy.

Since establishing the process for economic transformation in 1974, Mauritius has achieved steady economic growth of more than 5 per cent per annum, reaching one of the highest gross national incomes (GNI) per capita for small island development states (SIDS) in Africa (see Table 9.1). When comparing the various SIDS of similar

Table 9.1 *Gross national income per capita (1976–2006) and Human Development Index (HDI) (2005) for the small island developing states (SIDS)*

Region	Country	Population	GNI per capita (US $)					HDI 2005
			1976	1986	1996	2006		
Africa	Cape Verde	446000	109.5	187.3	498.0	1088.6		0.736
	Comoros	749000	59.3	161.1	230.9	396.6		0.561
	Guinea-Bissau	1257000	148.6	149.7	251.8	305.9		0.374
	Mauritius	1210000	718.7	1426.2	4378.0	6460.1		0.804
	Sao Tome and Principe	143000	30.6	57.5	40.2	55.3		0.654
	Seychelles	83000	47.1	200.4	484.4	659.4		0.843
Asia and the Pacific	American Samoa	57902	n.a.	n.a.	n.a.	n.a.		n.a.
	Bahrain	677886	1687.4	3461.6	6077.1	15228.6		0.866
	Commonwealth of the Northern Marianas	78252	n.a.	n.a.	n.a.	n.a.		n.a.
	Cook Islands	20000	13.4	32.1	94.2	n.a.		n.a.
	Fiji	832000	693.4	1259.6	2083.0	2928.8		0.762
	French Polynesia	266339	654.4	2119.7	3761.9	5642.8		n.a.
	Guam	166090	n.a.	n.a.	n.a.	n.a.		n.a.
	Kiribati	85000	39.6	31.3	76.3	130.1		n.a.
	Maldives	309000	29.2	139.4	428.5	869.9		0.741
	Marshall Islands	53000	18.3	56.4	111.6	191.0		n.a.
	Federated State of Micronesia	129000	47.5	117.7	231.4	256.3		n.a.
	Nauru	13000	37.0	53.9	58.8	79.4		n.a.
	New Caledonia	213679	798.3	1201.3	3607.0	4743.5		n.a.
	Niue	2156	n.a.	n.a.	n.a.	n.a.		n.a.
	Palau	20000	45.2	38.0	112.0	162.0		n.a.
	Papua New Guinea	5032000	1431.7	2203.8	4493.3	5522.9		0.530
	Samoa	159000	85.7	99.6	227.0	408.7		0.785
	Solomon Islands	479000	67.1	134.2	383.5	411.1		0.602
	Timor-Leste	1019252	n.a.	n.a.	367.5	847.4		0.514

	Tonga	100 000	30.6	70.5	184.3	230.0	0.819
	Tuvalu	10 000	2.4	4.4	12.5	25.6	n.a.
	Vanuata	207 000	83.5	119.6	230.1	343.5	0.674
Latin America and the Carribean	Anguilla	13 008	5.1	24.7	72.7	198.2	n.a.
	Antigua and Barbuda	65 000	58.9	209.9	514.8	915.7	0.815
	Aruba	108 000	305.3	513.2	1301.7	2244.1	n.a.
	Bahamas	312 000	740.6	2209.2	3483.0	6077.5	0.845
	Barbados	269 000	438.9	1279.4	1931.4	3307.4	0.892
	Belize	272 945	80.3	223.5	577.6	1002.6	0.778
	British Virgin Islands	22 187	16.3	55.1	403.0	973.5	n.a.
	Cuba	11 273 500	14 497.4	25 469.8	26 304.1	51 504.2	0.838
	Dominica	70 000	32.6	109.8	217.4	286.8	0.798
	Dominican Republic	8 639 000	3842.7	5727.8	13 182.9	29 890.2	0.779
	Grenada	94 000	40.0	128.7	245.7	419.4	0.777
	Guyana	705 803	421.6	453.1	653.4	856.6	0.750
	Haiti	8 400 000	871.8	2217.6	2742.6	4618.9	0.529
	Jamaica	2 621 000	2895.5	2479.8	6395.1	9448.1	0.736
	Montserrat	9425	10.3	38.7	47.5	43.3	n.a.
	Netherlands Antilles	219 000	531.9	1562.8	2718.9	3340.8	n.a.
	Puerto Rico	3 897 960	8091.0	17 007.0	32 093.0	58 418.3	n.a.
	Saint Kitts and Nevis	38 000	27.6	92.4	230.1	453.2	0.821
	Saint Lucia	151 000	56.9	265.5	546.2	872.3	0.795
	Saint Vincent and the Grenadines	115 000	32.3	123.8	269.6	423.6	0.761
	Suriname	436 935	529.9	995.3	853.6	2038.5	0.774
	Trinidad and Tobago	1 306 000	2391.8	4541.4	5237.4	17 541.9	0.814
	US Virgin Islands	124 000	n.a.	n.a.	n.a.	n.a.	n.a.

Source: United Nations Statistics Division; UNDP (2005).

population sizes,[5] Mauritius again shows one of the highest GNIs per capita and human development indexes.

Mauritian economic success has been attributed to various factors, including social, political and macroeconomic stability (see, e.g., Kearney, 1990; Durbarry, 2001; Andersson et al., 2005). Such multifactorial stability has contributed to FDI inflows and the development of export-oriented manufacturing such that Mauritius consistently showed the highest trends for FDI flows and stocks among African SIDS until 2005 when it was overtaken, only in terms of inward FDI flows and stocks, by Seychelles (see Table 9.2). The following discussion provides an insight into the two main sectors for FDI activity within the economy.

It must be noted, however, that information on the origin and amount of capital invested in both the MEPZ and the tourism industry is not easily obtained and is rather fragmentary in nature. As stated in a recent OECD publication (Goldstein, 2004, p. 42) on FDI in Sub-Saharan Africa,

> Data limitations make it almost impossible to have a clear view of the aggregate distribution of FDI flows and stocks in SADC[6] by investor countries and stocks . . . Many countries do not publish reliable data. In some cases only cumulated flows are available and in others there is information only on approved investments and not actual commitments.

Similar barriers were experienced with the data collected, but the FDI and country data presented in the chapter nevertheless allow for an adequate investigation into the role of FDI in the two industries under discussion.

The second and third pillars

Since the phasing out of the sugar industry, the Mauritian economy has relied on two of its most recent economic pillars, namely textile/garment exports and tourism. The following discussion traces out the evolution of these two industries and reviews the role of MNEs, if any, in relation to national competitive success.

The MEPZ and the textile industry

As discussed earlier, the impetus for industrialization in Mauritius has been provided by the manufacturing sector, led by the EPZ firms (see, e.g., Bheenick and Shapiro, 1989; Hein, C., 1988; Hein, P., 1989). The MEPZ, which contributes over 70 per cent of total exports, is dominated by the textile and apparel industry, which accounts for over 50 per cent of total firms within the zone. Moreover, textile and apparel firms, to date, account for 82 per cent of employment, 67 per cent of production output and 71 per cent of the exports of the MEPZ sector (CSO, 2007b). These firms also account for 72.8 per cent of cumulative FDI in manufacturing, more specifically in the EPZ (UNCTAD, 2001).

It can therefore be posited that the textile and apparel industry is unquestionably the manufacturing champion of the economy. Nevertheless, over the last decade, the authorities have been actively pursuing diversification away from textiles and apparel into more sophisticated industries such as information technology, light engineering and jewellery. Difficulties started to emerge in the late 1980s due to increasing international competition. With increased liberalization, especially in the 1990s, several textile firms in the MEPZ have closed down and the level of employment has declined. This marked a turning point in the performance of the textile industry as its contribution to economic

Table 9.2   FDI flows and stocks for African small islands development states (SIDS) (1980–2006)

African SIDS	FDI Category	Millions (US $)								
		1980	1990	2000	2001	2002	2003	2004	2005	2006
Cape Verde	Inflows	..	0	33	17	10	16	20	76	122
	Inward stock	..	4	173	190	199	215	235	311	433
	Outflows	..	0	1	1	0	..	0	0	0
	Outward stock	..	1	7	7	7	7	7	7	8
Comoros	Inflows	..	0	0	1	0	1	1	1	1
	Inward stock	2	17	21	22	22	23	24	25	26
	Outflows	0	1	0	0	0	0	0	0	0
	Outward stock	..	1	1	1	1	1	1	1	1
Guinea-Bissau	Inflows	..	2	1	0	4	4	2	9	42
	Inward stock	0	8	38	38	42	46	48	56	98
	Outflows	..	..	0	0	1	1	–8	1	–4
	Outward stock	0	0	0	0	1	1	–1	–1	–3
Mauritius	Inflows	1	41	266	–28	32	63	14	42	105
	Inward stock	26	168	672	645	677	739	753	795	900
	Outflows	..	1	13	3	9	–6	32	48	10
	Outward stock	..	1	132	135	144	138	170	217	227
Sao Tome and Principe	Inflows	..	..	4	3	3	1	–2	..	0
	Inward stock	..	..	11	15	18	19	17	17	16
	Outflows	0	0	0	0	0	0	0	0	0
	Outward stock	0	0	0	0	0	0	0	0	0
Seychelles	Inflows	10	0	24	65	48	58	38	86	146
	Inward stock	83	213	448	554	683	685	723	809	906
	Outflows	4	1	8	9	9	8	8	7	8
	Outward stock	16	64	114	132	160	155	163	178	169

Source: UNCTAD (2008).

growth and exports slowed down considerably. Now, with the implementation of the new WTO,[7] the Mauritian textile and apparel industry is at a crossroads and will undoubtedly be engulfed by the competition from larger, more powerful developing countries.

So far textile firms have adapted to the international competition and the unresponsiveness of wages to labour productivity through a process of capital deepening, technology upgrading and moving to higher-value-added products. The depreciation of the Mauritian rupee *vis-à-vis* the European currencies (i.e. the currencies of its main trading partners) has also helped in maintaining the industry's competitiveness. The firms' efforts have shown positive results and employment has risen within the clothing sector.

In spite of major readjustments, the textile industry remains the main manufacturing base of the economy and still dominates the MEPZ. The industry, when compared to other local industries, is also characterized by the highest levels of technology imports and FDI following a mushrooming of foreign subsidiaries since the 1970s (UNCTAD, 2001).

Consequently the Mauritian textile industry clearly provides a favourable setting for assessing Porter's determinants of national competitive advantage within a small open economy.

The tourism industry
The attractive climate and numerous beaches have proved a blessing in the development of a third economic pillar for the country. Though overlooked by the Meade Report of 1961, the tourism industry is considered as a significant growth sector and one ever more vital to the country's development.

Tourism was active in Mauritius as early as the 1950s, with a reported 1803 tourists visiting the island in 1954. Within a decade, the number of tourist arrivals increased to 10 000 and by post-independence 1972, the figure reached 48 797, with a total of 25 hotels and 1009 rooms. As shown in Table 9.3, the number of tourist arrivals in Mauritius is estimated at an astounding 788 276 for 2006, with about 98 registered hotels accounting for 10 666 rooms (CSO, 2007a).

Thus, since the 1970s the development and growth of the industry have proceeded at a steady rate. The industry contributed 8.5 per cent to GDP and employed over 8 per cent of the labour force in 2006 and is the country's second-largest foreign exchange earner after manufacturing (CSO, 2007a). Additionally, as can be seen from Table 9.3, Mauritius was hardly affected by the global slump in tourism following 9/11, nor did it suffer from the impact of high oil prices on the airline industry in 2003 and 2004. It is believed that the ability of the country to maintain a steadfast position in view of such global challenges is due to the fact that it caters to an up-market, middle- and high-income tourist segment, which is relatively insensitive to shifts in global demand (OECD, 2005).

Tourism in Mauritius comprises four sectors, namely restaurants, hotels, travel and tourism. The sector that has attracted the most inward FDI is the hotel sector. It must however be noted that the majority of hotels have been built with local capital and, in cases of FDI, the hotels are owned in joint ventures with local shareholders (Durbarry, 2002). The following section looks at the role of inward FDI in the textile and tourism industries and its contributions, if any, to the development of a national diamond.

Table 9.3   *Tourist arrivals, hotels and rooms in Mauritius (1972–2004)*

Year	Hotels	Rooms	Tourist arrivals
1972	25	1009	48 797
1973	29	1182	67 994
1974	30	1248	72 915
1975	34	1499	74 597
1976	37	1881	92 561
1977	37	1881	102 510
1978	38	1981	108 322
1979	38	2000	128 360
1980	43	2201	115 080
1981	51	2201	121 620
1982	51	2204	118 360
1983	55	2300	123 820
1984	54	2488	139 670
1985	55	2630	148 860
1986	56	2888	165 310
1987	60	3108	207 570
1988	64	3399	239 300
1989	67	3605	262 790
1990	75	4603	291 550
1991	80	5064	300 670
1992	84	5271	335 400
1993	85	5341	374 630
1994	90	5888	400 526
1995	95	5977	422 463
1996	90	6668	486 867
1997	87	6809	536 125
1998	90	7267	558 195
1999	92	8255	578 085
2000	95	8657	656 453
2001	95	9024	660 318
2002	95	9623	681 648
2003	97	9647	702 018
2004	103*	10 640	718 861
2005	99	10 497	761 063
2006	98	10 666	788 276

Note: *Excluding two hotels not operational because of renovation works.

Source: CSO (2007a).

MNEs and national competitiveness

Multinational enterprises (MNEs) have contributed significantly both to the development of the MEPZ and tourism. The MEPZ was initially able to attract export-oriented FDI in the early 1970s due to the preferential access agreements it had with the EU and the USA. The most significant agreement for local industrial development was the privileged, duty-free access granted to textiles and clothing products shipped to the EU market following the signing in 1975 of the Lomé Convention (now the Cotonou Agreement). This duty-free preferential access was an important factor in attracting significant foreign investors, largely from Germany, the UK, France, the Hong Kong Special Administrative Region (SAR), Italy and India, to the zone since its initial establishment (see Table 9.4 for cumulative inward FDI flows in the MEPZ by country of origin). Thus it can be inferred that the Asian and Indian MNEs have adopted a market-seeking strategy by investing in Mauritius. Although the island is not the final market for their products, it nevertheless allows them to reach their market more effectively.

The foreign investors profited from an abundant, cheap, literate and bilingual labour supply and also from loose labour legislations.[8] In fact, it was not until 1993 that legislation was passed to promote better working conditions in the MEPZ (ILO, 2001). Furthermore, the country offered a well-developed infrastructure including good roads, efficient communication, an excellent harbour and good air transportation. These advantages seem to determine the strategy of European MNEs, which is one mainly oriented towards resource seeking with particular emphasis on low-cost, skilled labour coupled with operational expertise seeking.

The presence of a skilled workforce and a well-developed infrastructure was an added benefit in targeting the tourism industry, which, like the MEPZ, also figured in the country's first five-year development plan (1971–1975) (Durbarry, 2002). The plan incorporated various incentives to attract both local and foreign investment into tourism as well as the 1974 Hotel Development Incentive Act, which served to consolidate the confidence of investors in the tourism industry. The incentives provided to investors were the free repatriation of profits, income tax concessions, advantageous corporate tax rates, import duty exemptions on capital equipment, and loans from the Mauritius Development Bank (Brown, 1997; Gabbay, 1988).

Although tourism did not attract as much inward FDI as the MEPZ and the textile industry, it is sufficiently sizeable to allow for some scrutiny. Table 9.5 shows the cumulative inward flows of FDI into the hotel sector for the periods 1990–95 and 2000–05 by country of origin. It can be seen that the portfolio of foreign investors is rather eclectic, with investors from all over the world, some from the region such as Réunion and South Africa, and some from other parts of the world such as Asia, Europe, the Far East and more recently the Middle East.

Attracting FDI into a developing economy is only one of the steps towards capability building and upgrading the industrial base. In order to secure long-term developmental effects by MNEs, it is paramount that the latter engage in substantial knowledge diffusion and technology transfer into the local economy.

The following discussion examines the effect of MNEs on these industries in Porterian terms, i.e. focusing on factor conditions, demand conditions, related and supporting industries, and strategy, structure and rivalry. It seeks to identify any building on existing indigenous skills, creation of local linkages or adaptation of MNEs to local conditions in the country.

Factor conditions
The MEPZ has been deemed the largest employer in the country, and more importantly it is viewed as having significantly contributed towards the emancipation of women

Table 9.4 Cumulative inward FDI flows in the MEPZ by country of origin (million rupees), 1990–95; 2000–05

Country of origin	1990–1995 (%)	2000–2005 (%)
Australia	9 (0.8)	–
Bermuda	35 (3.1)	–
British Virgin Islands	221 (19.8)	–
Channel Islands	18 (1.6)	–
China	31 (2.8)	51 (12.1)
France	119 (10.7)	12 (2.8)
Germany	96 (8.6)	–
Hong Kong	140 (12.5)	9 (2.1)
India	156 (14.0)	85 (20.1)
Isle of Man	7 (0.6)	–
Italy	11 (1.0)	199 (47)
Japan	41 (3.7)	–
Luxembourg	2 (0.2)	13 (3.1)
Macau	7 (0.6)	–
Malaysia	17 (1.5)	–
Réunion	5 (0.4)	–
Singapore	20 (1.8)	14 (3.3)
South Africa	5 (0.4)	–
Sweden	3 (0.3)	–
Switzerland	36 (3.2)	5 (1.2)
Taiwan	64 (5.7)	–
UK	72 (6.5)	35 (8.3)
Zimbabwe	3 (0.3)	–
Total	1116	423

Source: Mauritius Industrial Development Authority; CSO.

*Table 9.5   Cumulative inward FDI flows in tourism in Mauritius by country of origin
(million rupees), 1990–95; 2000–05*

Country of origin	1990–1995 (%)	2000–2005 (%)
Bermuda	6 (1.1)	–
British West Indies	30 (5.7)	–
Channel Islands	5 (0.9)	–
Dubai	0 (0.0)	68 (19.8)
France	36 (6.8)	8 (2.3)
Germany	48 (9.1)	37 (10.8)
Hong Kong	17 (3.2)	146 (42.4)
India	–	5 (1.5)
Japan	9 (1.7)	–
Malaysia	253 (48.0)	–
Réunion	53 (10.1)	5 (1.5)
Singapore	12 (2.3)	–
South Africa	0.3 (0.1)	2 (0.6)
Switzerland	10 (1.9)	5 (1.5)
Taiwan	29 (5.5)	–
UAE	0 (0.0)	5 (1.5)
UK	17 (3.2)	61 (17.7)
Other	1.5 (0.3)	2 (0.6)
Total	526.8	344

Source: Mauritius Industrial Development Authority; CSO.

workers. Women accounted for about 80 per cent of workers from the setting up of
the zone to 1985, when the proportion started to decline, dropping to 56 per cent. At
the onset of industrialization, the labour force, considered well educated and calling for
wage scales much lower than in developed countries and in competing locations in the
Far East, proved attractive to foreign investors.

Evidence as to the contribution of FDI to factor conditions in the zone is scant and also, to some extent, contradictory. Wignaraja (2002), for example, conducted a study of the impact of firm-level characteristics on the technological capabilities of 40 Mauritian garment firms. He found that firm size, technical manpower, employee training and foreign technical assistance were all significantly related to the technology index of Mauritian garment firms. However, firm age and foreign equity were not significant, implying that MNEs may not have played a significant role in building an integral technological capability infrastructure in the industry.

Sannassee (2002), on the other hand, found that all textile MNEs in the MEPZ, with the exception of one, have contributed towards upgrading skills by providing training, both in-house and overseas, to employees. He also states that the majority of textile MNEs (over 89 per cent) in the MEPZ were started as greenfield investments as opposed to acquisitions. This suggests that the MNE subsidiaries injected novel foreign managerial skills and knowledge into the sector as opposed to piggybacking on skills and knowledge built up by existing firms in Mauritius. The greenfield strategy pursued by the MNEs also leads to the conclusion that by setting up new plants, they have contributed to upgrading the manufacturing, building and plant-related infrastructure within the zone.

Nevertheless, governmental effort remains the primary driving force behind the textile industry. Such efforts include, for example, the setting up of a model factory at the Clothing Technology Centre[9] (CTC) to initiate local enterprises in the latest technologies and best-practices management. The centre comprises a state-of-the-art cutting room equipped with CAD/CAM facilities, coupled with the latest computerized spreading machines, servo cutters, and computer cutting equipment. The model factory also addresses the problems of multiskilling, reskilling and skills realignment in the clothing sector.

Porter posits that to 'form the backbone of any advanced economy, a nation does not inherit but instead creates the most important factors of production such as skilled human resources . . .' (Porter, 1990, p. 79). This particular point seems to be most applicable in terms of the factor conditions aspect of the tourism diamond. One of the main contributions of the tourism industry to the local economy is the expansion of the Hotel School of Mauritius, which was initially set up with funds from the UNDP, ILO and French government in 1971. What started off as a tentative project operating out of a small house in Mauritius was, due to the growth of the tourism industry, further expanded and transferred to the management of the Industrial Vocational Training Board (IVTB) and the aegis of the Ministry of Education in 1997. In the same year, the Hotel School of Mauritius also incorporated a tourism department. The school has been running two Higher National Diplomas (HND) in Hotel Management and Culinary Arts and is internationally recognized, with students regularly recruited by overseas hotels. The school also undertakes various tourism degree courses in collaboration with the University of Mauritius. As such, the growth and development of tourism have contributed to the improvement and upgrading of skills within the country; however, it is problematic to ascertain the real role of domestic enterprises versus MNEs in the process, since little research has been conducted on the subject.

In spite of the lack of research, it can be argued that the hotel- and hospitality-specialized and skilled labour force does provide some level of competitive advantage to the local tourism industry. In fact, it is noteworthy that in the African region, only

Seychelles and Mauritius have achieved such high levels in tourism development. It is argued that in the remaining three African SIDS, namely Sao Tome and Principe, Cape Verde and the Comoros, tourism is still very much in an incipient stage (UNEP, 1996). The success of tourism in Mauritius and Seychelles, compared to the other African SIDS, has been attributed to the development of social and physical infrastructures and human resources. In the case of Mauritius, it can also be hypothesized that the MEPZ was instrumental in laying down the physical infrastructural foundation that was a prerequisite for the healthy take-off and development of a tourism industry.

Demand conditions
In Porterian terms, demand conditions refer to the nature of home-market demand for an industry's product or service. As was traced earlier, the MEPZ and textile sector were born out of a need to industrialize based on an export-oriented strategy. The industry is not driven by an import-substituting strategy or the need to meet a rising local demand for textile products.

Demand conditions related to the zone and textile industry can therefore be interpreted within the context of the final markets for MEPZ products and the role of MNEs in supporting this process. It is believed that the main reason for the large influx of foreign investors since the late 1970s, especially from China and Hong Kong, has been their desire to gain entry to EU and US markets via the MEPZ.

As seen in Table 9.6, the main MEPZ export market is the EU, to which Mauritius enjoyed duty-free access under the terms of the Lomé Convention. The top two export markets have continuously been France and the UK for the last two decades. The demand for Mauritian textile products by the EU markets has been greatly enhanced by the major investments made by the French, UK and German MNEs in the MEPZ since its inception. The same trend has been aided by the Hong Kong and Chinese MNEs. Lately the emergence of other important European markets such as Belgium, Italy and Spain has been observed.

MEPZ exports to the US market have increased steadily over the past two decades and now account for the second-largest regional export destination. The demand from the Americans for Mauritian textile goods has been attributed in part to the country's political friendship with Western democracies and more importantly to the US effort to increase trade relations with Africa. The Africa Growth and Opportunity Act (AGOA), signed into law on 18 May 2000, is testimony to the commitment of the USA to promoting trade with Africa. Since then, the AGOA has undergone several amendments and has now: (i) extended preferential access for imports from beneficiary Sub-Saharan African countries to 30 September 2015; (ii) extended the third-country fabric provision for three years, from September 2004 to September 2007; and (iii) provided additional Congressional guidance to the Administration on how to administer the textile provisions of the bill.

The AGOA also provides reforming African countries with the most liberal access to the US market available to any country or region with which the USA does not have a free trade agreement. The US International Trade Commission (USITC, 2004) reports that the move towards higher-valued goods by the textile sector in Mauritius accounted for an increase of 29 per cent in US imports that entered free of duty under the AGOA in 2003. It is also stated that there are 49 textile and apparel firms that are registered

Table 9.6 *Mauritian EPZ exports by country of destination (million rupees), 1983–84; 2003–06*

Country of destination	1983	1984	2003	2004	2005	2006
Total EPZ exports	1306.8	2150.7	31 444	32 046	28 954	33 610
Europe	1041.6	1492.1	20 507	21 760	21 351	25 930
Belgium	67.6	70.8	646	1011	1279	1432
France	143.7	580.1	7253	6995	6045	6573
Germany	162.3	262.8	1176	1003	730	927
Italy			1196	1425	1190	1834
Netherlands	44.9	52.0	749	730	550	740
Spain			448	476	187	142
Sweden	0.1	0.1	67	18	898	1742
Switzerland			473	534	552	551
UK	226.2	352.4	7848	8895	9208	11385
Other	126.8	174.0	651	673	712	604
America, of which:	183.8	514.1	8722	7541	5338	4677
USA	183.8	514.1	8474	7306	5130	4404
Asia	13.5	22.0	399	793	342	255
Other (inc. Africa and Oceania)	67.9	122.4	1816	1952	1923	2748

Source: CSO.

Table 9.7 *African SIDS exports to the USA (million US$), 2002–06*

African SIDS	2002	2003	2004	2005	2006
Cape Verde	1.8	5.6	3.7	2.6	1.0
Comoros	5.3	4.0	16.5	1.4	1.5
Guinea-Bissau	0.0	1.9	26.6	0.1	0.3
Mauritius	280.6	297.9	270.4	221.9	218.9
Sao Tome and Principe	0.4	0.1	0.1	0.2	0.2
Seychelles	26.3	13.0	6.0	10.1	7.3

Source: Foreign Trade Statistics, US Census Bureau.

with the government of Mauritius for export to the USA under the AGOA. These firms employ about 50 000 workers and have a production capacity of 15 million pieces per month. To date, Mauritius accounts for the highest value of exports to the USA when compared to the other African SIDS, as shown in Table 9.7.

Despite the increasing trade with the USA, the EU remains the main commercial partner for both imports and exports, as well as the main destination for MEPZ exports.

The same pattern is seen with the tourism industry, as the main tourist market for the country is the EU. It is reported that since the early 1990s, the EU has accounted for over 50 per cent of tourist arrivals in Mauritius. As in the textile industry, demand for the Mauritian tourism product is also not related to home-country demand. Although local values and circumstances are undoubtedly instrumental in contributing to the industry's success, it is nevertheless the pressures and demands of tourists that induce the firms within the industry to be innovative and competitive.

As remarked earlier, Mauritius is marketed as a high-class destination and targeted at up-market tourism, thus it has always been an expensive tourist destination. While there are several low- and medium-priced hotels available on the island, the destination is still considered to be out of the standard tourist's reach. An important factor in making the destination inaccessible is airfare. Chartered flights are not allowed, and apart from flying with the national carrier, Air Mauritius, reaching the island at a favourable rate is difficult. With increasing competition in Europe from other affordable destinations, Mauritius has adopted a far more aggressive marketing strategy while also diversifying the tourism product in an attempt to maintain its European clientele. The current emphasis is on spa, golf and green ecotourism holidays, and ideas for the future include Mauritius as a tax-free shopping paradise. It has been suggested that both locally owned and multinational hotels are increasingly including truly ecological tourism structures, golf and spa within their facilities.

Related and supporting industries

Although there are some firms in the MEPZ that are vertically integrated, with spinning mills and dyeing plants, the textile industry is primarily geared towards manufacturing t-shirts, shirts, trousers and pullovers. The first three product types involve mainly CMT (cut, make and trim) in terms of manufacturing processes. Since Mauritius is a small remote island, lacking in natural resources, the bulk of raw materials and intermediate products, such as yarn and fabrics, needed by the industry is imported. Imports, mainly from China, India, Europe and South Africa, equal about half of exports (Anker et al., 2001).

More recently, there have been efforts by firms to engage in backward integration away from the traditional CMT and knitwear manufacturing. Emphasis is increasingly being placed on fabric manufacturing. This trend is attributed to the AGOA's rules of origin requirements, since Mauritius was not awarded the special third-country fabric provision until 2004 (Andersson et al., 2005). One of the country's leading domestic apparel manufacturers, CMT Ltd, is planning on opening a cotton-spinning mill that is expected to produce about 8000 tons of combed cotton yarns annually. Regarding foreign ventures more specifically, China's first cotton-spinning mill in Mauritius, Tianli Spinning Company, has been operational since March 2003 and has recently undergone an expansion. Further projects by Indian and Pakistani investors to set up spinning plants in Mauritius are in the pipeline and have been approved by the Board of Investment (BOI) (USITC, 2004).

In terms of other related industries, such as manufacturing labels or accessories (e.g. zips and buttons), the number of players remains low. Nevertheless, it is reported that the MEPZ sector has created a demand for services in packaging, consultancy, water and other utilities etc., and that local enterprises have benefited from spillover effects from MNEs (UNCTAD, 2001).

The Mauritian tourism industry is composed of an array of supporting sectors that include any player that primarily engages in meeting the needs of tourists, such as hotels, restaurants, banking and financial institutions, airlines, airports, travel and tours, and entertainment. Porter's (1990) argument for advantage building in downstream industries stemming from internationally competitive home-based suppliers does not seem to apply directly to the idiosyncratic case of the service-based tourism product. Yet the players from supporting sectors have as much of a stake as direct participants in delivering the most cost-effective service in an efficient manner to the country's tourists, in order to make Mauritius a competitive tourist destination.

As briefly stated earlier, Air Mauritius enjoys almost a monopoly as the main passenger carrier to the island. Although several major airlines[10] serve Mauritius, they tend to do so through code sharing with Air Mauritius. The situation is such that the airlines charge high prices, which uphold the high-class destination image that the island has and continues to project. However, with increasing global tourism competition, Mauritius faces the possibility of losing European tourists to more reasonably priced destinations, especially in terms of airfare. A case in point is the German market, representing the third-largest tourist group arriving from Europe. Most German tour operators felt that the airfare was not sufficiently reasonable to allow for a greater influx of tourists to the island. One such airline and budget tour operator, Lufttransport Unternehmen GmbH (LTU), planned to offer reasonable – not low-price – flights from Germany to Mauritius and to use the country's surplus medium-class hotel capacity. Although Mauritius will not open its air space to normally priced tour operators and charter flights, Air Mauritius signed a code sharing agreement with LTU in 2005. Thus the carriers will each have a hard block seat swap on the other's flights between Germany and Mauritius. The alliance will also allow Air Mauritius to commercialize seats on the Munich–Mauritius and Düsseldorf–Mauritius route, and to benefit from the market support of the German Rewe group, which is a major tour operator in Germany and a shareholder in LTU. In such low-key ways, some supporting sectors within the tourism industry find ways to leverage, if not increase, their competitive foothold within the global industry.

Another sector that has shown some penchant for innovative behaviour is local licensed tour operators. Maurisun Adventure and Tours, for example, claims to be a pioneer of ecotourism in Mauritius and helped in the tourism product diversification wave as put forward by the government. Maurisun aims, through its 'Rainbow package', to cooperate with businesses and individuals in developing tourism opportunities that foster the growth of the economy while minimizing negative environmental and cultural impacts. Maurisun suggests that since ecotourism was introduced by them, it has been adopted and applied by other stakeholders in the country.

The nature of tourism as a product is such that the dynamism and drive necessary to make the supporting sectors internationally competitive are different from the dynamism and drive clearly exhibited by manufacturing industries, for example. Further research, especially at the developing-country level, is required in order to assess and understand the role of related and supporting players in such a service-based industry. Similarly, the role of related and supporting industries in services seems to be very much industry specific, highly distinctive in nature, and dependent on the type of service offered.

Strategy, structure and rivalry
According to Porter (1990, pp. 181–2),

> [g]eographic concentration magnifies the power of domestic rivalry . . . The presence of domestic competitors automatically cancels the types of advantage that come from simply being in a particular nation – factor costs, access to or preference in the home market, or costs to foreign competitors who import into the market. Companies are forced to move beyond them, and as a result, gain more sustainable advantages.

Similarly, Jenkins (1990) argues that the competitive dynamics in an industry where foreign and domestic firms are on the same scale and produce similar products for the same market will push domestic firms to adopt similar production techniques to those of the MNEs. This imitative behaviour of local firms allows them to compete successfully against MNEs (Jenkins, 1990). From this position, it can be assumed that the long-standing industrial dynamics, in the form of both competition and linkages, in the Mauritian textile industry have allowed the capabilities of domestic firms and MNEs to be at par.

Empirical evidence on the Mauritian textile industry (Peerally and Cantwell, 2006) shows that both domestic and textile MNEs have above-average technological capabilities. Furthermore, the same study of textile firms demonstrates that both domestic firms and MNEs engage in advanced product innovation activities. The main difference between domestic firms and foreign subsidiaries is that the capabilities of the latter are highly significant over all levels[11] of product innovation activities, thus implying that they engage in the production of standardized, as well as horizontally and vertically differentiated, products, while for domestic firms, product innovation activities are significant only at the advanced innovation levels.

Furthermore, it was found that the development of capabilities in domestic firms has been principally reliant on their in-house R&D/sampling[12] activities. Recall that the textile firms are all based within the MEPZ, which implies that the products are targeted mainly at foreign markets. In the case of foreign subsidiaries, Peerally and Cantwell argue that searching out, finding and serving product markets is viewed as being primarily the responsibility of MNE headquarters. Since most headquarters are located within those final product markets, it is argued that foreign subsidiaries within the MEPZ have an inherent advantage over domestic firms. The latter have to establish their own network of customers in highly competitive global markets. Thus it was found that domestic firms rely primarily on introducing new products that are vertically differentiated in order to compete effectively against MNEs. Their overall technological capability is less dependent on improving their existing products, which can be assumed as being targeted at the local market. This seems to be their strategy for competition and survival.

Following the above, the structure of textile MNEs is such that the production units are localized in Mauritius, while the buying and marketing agents are very often located within the final markets or at headquarters. Procurement is considered mainly a centralized function and retained at headquarters. In terms of R&D or product sampling facilities, most MNE subsidiaries will have in-house facilities.

Domestic firms, on the other hand, tend to be fully centralized at the local level, with both primary and support activities – such as raw materials procurement, firm financing, planning, product marketing and development and human resource management – conducted at firm level within the zone. For some larger domestic firms, there is now an increasing trend towards shifting production units to cheaper producing areas in the regions, while retaining all support activities in Mauritius. It must however be pointed out that the bulk of production units are nevertheless maintained within the MEPZ, as the regionalization process is still in a tentative stage.

When looking at the behaviour and strategy of foreign and domestic firms in the tourism industry, the focus once again shifts to the hotel sector. Rivalry in the hotel sector can be assumed to be primarily between hotels of similar sizes and with a similar number of stars. Multinational hotels in the island tend to be in the 'large'[13] hotel category, and include the Sun International hotels, for example, which are South African owned. These large multinational hotels have noteworthy large locally owned competitors, as well as foreign hotels that are run as franchises or under licence. The interesting aspect of these large hotels is that they are in most cases managed under contract by a local team. Irrespective of whether the hotel is set up through FDI or under licence, the local team of managers always benefits from training by the parent company. The advantage of using a management contract is that the local teams also bring with them a profound understanding of the local culture and can thereby transmit a true Mauritian experience to tourists. Thus the multinational hotels not only follow a physical resource-seeking strategy, aimed at exploiting the naturally endowed tourism product, but also an expertise-seeking strategy aimed at using the local cultural know-how.

The marketing strategy of larger hotels in general is primarily focused on promoting their hotels and Mauritius as a high-class destination and is geared towards attracting tourists with high spending power. In the medium-sized hotel category, there is a larger proportion of locally owned and managed hotels, and although they are not directly competing with larger hotels, they tend to imitate, within feasible bounds, the strategy followed by larger hotels. Small hotels fall within the same category as other important accommodation providers in the tourism industry such as exclusive guest houses, bed and breakfasts, boarding inns, beach bungalows and self-catering beach bungalows and apartments. These types of accommodation each target a different tourist group that does not fall into the high-spending, high-class tourist category. With Air Mauritius's willingness to code-share and provide more reasonable airfares, this sector of the tourism industry is also flourishing.

Rivalry between the different types of similar hotels is not very apparent, although there are constantly various innovative packages that are designed to attract customers. In recent years hotels have tended to look more closely at the locals as a potential customer base. During off-peak seasons, hotels are designing packages exclusively targeted at locals in order to keep rooms at full occupancy all year round.

As might be expected, most hotels are geographically concentrated along the coastal regions and have thus contributed to the development of coastal villages. One such prominent example of tourism-induced growth relates to the town of Grand-Bay, where everything ranging from the number of shopping facilities and entertainment facilities to property prices has shot up. Similarly, hotels are linked to the development of supporting sector clusters in the coastal region, consisting mainly of restaurants and handicraft stores.

Table 9.8   Outward FDI flows in textiles and tourism from Mauritius (million rupees), 2000–04

	2000	2001	2002	2003	2004	2005*
Textiles, outward FDI flows						
Botswana	6	0	0	0	0	–
China	0	0	0	0	0	80
Madagascar	2	0	238	41	96	98
Mali	0	0	0	0	5	–
Total	8	0	238	41	101	178
Tourism, outward FDI flows						
Dubai	0	0	0	0	0	30
Maldives	0	0	0	0	333	103
Seychelles	68	0	0	130	75	90
South Africa	0	0	0	7	0	0
Thailand	0	0	0	0	14	0
Total	68	0	0	137	422	223

Note: * Jan.–June.

Source: Mauritius Industrial Development Authority; CSO.

Outward FDI and regional integration – substantial or trivial?
Most of the outward FDI from the two industries at hand has remained within the region (see Table 9.8). This suggests an increasing trend towards regionalization and is believed to have been enhanced by trade agreements such as the AGOA and regional trading blocks such as the SADC and COMESA.[14]

Although the textile industry has been unable to move entirely to value-added activities, its emphasis on volume production has pushed firms to move to Madagascar, India and Mozambique, suggesting resource-seeking behaviour. However, it is also argued that the AGOA has reinforced outward FDI in textiles, not only to SADC but also to Senegal and Ghana (Goldstein, 2004), which are not part of SADC or COMESA, the two main trading blocks in Africa. Recent investment in textiles includes, for example, Belin Textiles International, a Ghana–Mauritius joint venture established to export products to the US under the AGOA. The first subsidiary opened in July 2004. Domestically owned Floreal Knitwear Ltd, the second-largest woolmark knitwear supplier in the world, has operations in Madagascar, China and Bangladesh. However, it must be noted that the latter two are in the form of alliances, while the Madagascar facility is fully owned, again suggesting that the bulk of outward FDI is more regionally focused. Another domestic giant, the Compagnie Mauricienne de Textile, has recently started implementing alliances with Bangladesh- and China-based textile firms.

However, the main focus of outward FDI remains regional. Another example is that of the takeover by Mauritian investors of a ruined textile firm in Mozambique, Textil do Pungue. The investors reportedly plan to invest $3 million in renovating the facility and to employ 600 workers to produce 7000 pairs of jeans per day for the US market under the AGOA (USITC, 2004). Thus the outward foreign investment in the region by Mauritian investors also seems to be market-seeking in nature.

Table 9.8 shows that some rather important tourism investments have been made in the region and elsewhere. The Mauritian-owned leisure group, Beachcomber, has recently established a subsidiary in South Africa as the marketing arm of its local tour and hotel services. Another example of regional expansion is that of Naïade Resorts Limited. Incorporated in 1987, it currently runs five hotels and a nature reserve on the island, and has expanded in the region with one hotel in Seychelles and another in Maldives.

Although it may be argued that the amount of outward FDI flows by Mauritius in textiles and tourism is somewhat trivial when compared to other developing countries, the flows can also be viewed as being rather substantial in size when compared to other African SIDS. Irrespective of the industry at hand, the country has made regional cooperation and integration an important item on its agenda. Mauritius has taken measures to further aid regional integration by, for example, charting out the political framework for regional cooperation through the establishment of appropriate protocols and agreements such as the Double Taxation Avoidance Agreement and the Investment Protection and Promotion Agreement. An additional measure includes facilitating the process of regional integration at the administrative and diplomatic levels by, for example, simplifying administrative procedures in terms of visas and permits, facilitating access to external funding for feasibility and marketing studies, providing necessary information to potential investors, and mounting trade and investment missions to neighbouring countries.

One of the main goals at the regional level for Mauritius is to become a leading regional centre for international financial services, including banking, insurance and other consultancy services. It has been reported that of all the countries in COMESA, Mauritius is the leader in cross-border investments in banking, finance, hotel management and agriculture. Furthermore, it is also one of the eight African countries to have signed 29 bilateral investment treaties with developed and developing countries alike during the 2001 UN Conference on Trade and Development. These treaties are believed to be instrumental in paving the way for further FDI flows and regional cooperation in and from Mauritius.

Policy shifts for development
Although there are various views on the factors that contributed to the success of the Mauritian structural transformation, one area of general consensus is that its growth strategy has been based upon coherent policies and the presence of appropriate support institutions.

The initial, post-independence policies were greatly influenced by the Meade Report (1961), which predicted a bleak future for Mauritius based on the fact that it was a monocrop economy and vulnerable to terms-of-trade shocks, rapid population growth (and hence a rise in unemployment) and ethnic tensions. In an attempt to diversify the economic structure and create employment, the government adopted an import substitution strategy by setting up import-competing industries. Predictably, the opportunities provided by this approach were soon exhausted and the government implemented an outward-oriented development policy that led to the emergence of the export-oriented sector or the MEPZ in the early 1970s. The government, however, also maintained the import-substituting industries that had been established under the previous policy regime. As a consequence, a mixed policy approach of import substitution and export promotion was adopted. Eventually the mixed approach failed and the import regime was liberalized after facing various budgetary difficulties due to the expansionary fiscal policies of the 1970s.

The MEPZ firms were meanwhile benefiting from tax incentives, and duty-free access to imported inputs was granted to them. The policies devised by the government were targeted towards taking advantage of existing preferential trade agreements such as the Lomé Convention and attracting inward FDI. Historically, Mauritius has benefited from preferential arrangements for its two main products, namely sugar and textiles/clothing. Preferential arrangements in the sugar sector, granted since independence in 1968, guarantee a certain volume of sugar exports to the EU. Sugar trade between African, Caribbean and Pacific (ACP) countries and the EU has been regulated by two trade agreements: the ACP/EU Sugar Protocol and the Agreement on Special Preferential Sugar, and Mauritius has benefited substantially from the former.

As we know, the trade agreements governing textiles and clothing have proved most significant to economic growth and development. Following the economic boom driven by the MEPZ, further reforms were implemented in the early 1980s and that decade witnessed sustained growth, during which unemployment fell and inflation was negligible.

By the 1990s, Mauritius was considered as one of the most open economies as well as one of the main FDI recipients in Africa. Additionally, various measures were undertaken to streamline bureaucratic procedures and encourage further inward investments. These measures included, for example, adoption of double taxation agreements, the establishment of a one-stop-shop for investors, the setting up of the Mauritius Export Development and Investment Authority (MEDIA), and tax reforms (Andersson et al., 2005). Particular support is also provided to SMEs, which are mostly locally owned, through the Small and Medium Industries Development Organization (SMIDO). SMIDO's mission is to consolidate, expand and enhance SMEs' competitiveness through various training schemes and tax and fiscal incentives, including a venture capital scheme.

The presence of appropriate support institutions[15] has also been argued to have been fundamental in the structural transformation of Mauritius (Bonaglia and Fukasaku, 2002; Subramanian and Roy, 2001). Subramanian and Roy (2001) have attributed the success of the Mauritian EPZ, especially when compared to other African EPZs, to the quality of the institutions in terms of transparency and their ability to manage rent-seeking behaviour and corruption. Gulhati and Nallari (1990), for their part, have claimed that Mauritius was able to overcome its macroeconomic imbalances in the early 1980s due to its domestic institutions.

However, it is also argued that policy formulation with regard to technology and competitiveness for industrial development in response to the current challenges of globalization has been impeded partly due to the multiplicity of institutions involved, which has resulted in a lack of coordination and absence of overall strategic focus (World Bank, 1994). Following the global economic slump in 2000, the situation for the MEPZ has weakened, with declining textile exports. Nevertheless, the textile industry continues to seek opportunities to enhance growth and advancement in the current industrial and manufacturing structure. As seen earlier, the increasing trend towards regional integration and the textile industry's role as a major player in the region bodes well for the future of the industry. The private sector has also been active in the formulation of policies. A recent example of private sector involvement has been its push for the promotion of cluster formation for industries including textiles, regional integration, and linkages between SMEs and large companies. Technology improvement, creation of an efficient industrial environment and further export market penetration of firms have been particularly emphasized.

Policy decisions in tourism, as in the textiles industry, are made with a special effort to keep the local business environment always open to foreign investment. The government has continuously offered various fiscal and other incentives to investors in the tourism industry. Nowadays in the hotel sector, for example, investors pay a nominal corporate tax of 15 per cent[16] during the entire course of the business venture, with all dividends paid out being free from income tax for the first ten years. Other incentives include the duty-free importation of certain equipment, access to local sources of finance, through the Development Bank of Mauritius for example, and free repatriation of profits, capital and dividends (Durbarry, 2002). It is also suggested that the authorities are constantly striving to streamline procedures regarding foreign investment in order to fast-track the process.

More recently the government has formulated and implemented an integrated development strategy that takes into account the social and environmental aspects of tourism in the island. As part of this strategy, any hotel promoter investing in the island is also required to contribute US$1 million to a social fund. The fund is geared towards developing projects for the benefit of the community living in the coastal region of the hotel (WTO, 2003).

Support institutions for the industry also play a significant role in its development. The Mauritius Tourism Promotion Authority (MTPA), for example, through its offices in all the main tourist markets, is an ubiquitous promoter of the Mauritian tourism product as well as a source of information to potential tourists. A similar function is also fulfilled by the international offices of Air Mauritius. Other supporting bodies include the Association of Hotels and Restaurants in Mauritius (AHRIM) and the Tourism Advisory Council. The latter was set up by the government to aid in policy formulation and comprises representatives from both the public and private sectors.

A concluding note

As can be seen from the discussion in this chapter, Mauritius, though a small African developing economy, has made noteworthy economic progress despite the various inherent and inherited barriers it has faced before and since independence. This progress has been the centre of various debates and research interests alike. The multiple authors referred to in this work bear testimony to this fact. Similarly, academics have often compared the economic development, albeit gradual, achieved by the country to that of the Asian Tigers (see for example Kearney, 1990). Although it has not reached newly industrialized country status like the Asian Tigers, the country is one of two to have attained developing-country status in Africa.

The slowdown in the advancement of the island can be attributed to the challenges brought on with the new millennium such as the phasing out of preferential agreements under the World Trade Organization, the emergence of lower-cost producing countries and the world economic slump. Mauritius is determined and well positioned to overcome them. Both foreign investors and the government feel that Mauritius remains a lucrative investment location, and FDI in high value added and high-skilled activities will follow and play an important role in the future growth of the country. Mauritius is also exerting itself to become an important investor in the African Sub-Saharan region with increasing outward FDI in textiles.

Finally, the future of the country can be seen as optimistic since the foundations for success are well in place, as shown through the analysis of the elements of the national diamond. In addition to clear policy orientation, the small developing Mauritian economy has shown resolute consistency in terms of political stability, democracy, good governance, social cohesion in a multi-ethnic society (Subramanian and Roy, 2001) and belief in free enterprise.

Notes

1. Professor Meade was appointed by the British government to head the Economic Survey Mission to Mauritius from 1950 to 1961. The assessment and findings were presented in a series of papers and in a final report in 1961 that was dubbed the 'Meade Report' (Meade et al., 1961).
2. It has been estimated that for the Mauritian sugar sector to become internationally competitive, production costs would have to be reduced by at least 22 per cent in the medium term and by 45 per cent in the long term.
3. Increased competition is also felt from substitute products such as beet sugar, corn syrup and artificial sweeteners.
4. CSO – Central Statistics Office, Mauritius.
5. SIDS with a population ranging from 1 million to 3 million, including Guinea-Bissau, Timor-Leste, Jamaica and Trinidad and Tobago.
6. SADC – Southern African Development Community, of which Mauritius is a member.
7. The first Multifibre Arrangement (MFA) came to an end in 2005.
8. See, e.g., Hein (1989), Alter (1990) and Meizenhelder (1997) for details on labour conditions, especially for female workers within the MEPZ.
9. The CTC was set up by the government with the long-term objective of pushing the textile industry forward in their drive towards modernization of production operations.
10. Such as Air France, British Airways, Air India, Air Zimbabwe, Singapore Airlines, Aeroflot and South African Airways.
11. Product innovation activities are classified as basic innovation activities, intermediate innovation activities or advanced innovation activities.
12. Product 'sampling' means research activities involved in creating new product samples.
13. Large hotels are defined by the government as well-established beach hotels with more than 80 rooms.
14. COMESA – Common Market for Eastern and Southern Africa.
15. Various organizations have directly and indirectly played a key role in trade and investment promotion in Mauritius. These organizations include, for example, the Mauritius Industrial Development Agency, the Export Processing Zone Development Authority, the Small and Medium Industries Development Organization, the Board of Investment, the Mauritius Standard Bureau and the Development Bank of Mauritius. See Bonaglia and Fukasaku (2002) for a full description of these organizations and their roles.
16. Instead of the normal statutory rate of 30 per cent.

References

Alter, R. (1990), 'Export processing zones for growth and development: the Mauritian example', Working Paper No. 90/122, International Monetary Fund, Washington, DC.

Andersson, J., F. Bonaglia, K. Fukasaku and C. Lesser (2005), 'Trade and structural adjustment policies in selected developing countries', OECD Development Centre, Working Paper No. 245.

Anker, R., R. Paratian and R. Torres (2001), 'Mauritius: studies on the social dimensions of globalization', Geneva: ILO.

Bheenick, R. and M. Shapiro (1989), 'Mauritius: a case study of the export processing zone', in *Successful Development in Africa, EDI Development Policy*, K series No. 1, Economic Development Institute, Washington, DC.

Bonaglia, F. and K. Fukasaku (2002), 'Trading competitively: trade capacity building in Sub-Saharan Africa', OECD Development Centre Studies.

Brown, G. (1997), 'Tourism in the Indian Ocean: a case study of Mauritius', in D.G. Lockhart and D. Drakakis-Smith (eds), *Island Tourism Trends and Prospects*, London: Pinter, pp. 229–48.

Chernoff, B. and A. Warner (2002), 'Sources of fast growth in Mauritius: 1960–2000', mimeo, paper prepared for the conference on 'Iceland and the World Economy: Small Island Economies in the Era of Globalization', Center for International Development, Harvard University, May.

CSO (2006), 'National accounts of Mauritius 2006', also available from the Central Statistics Office of Mauritius website, http://statsmauritius.gov.mu/, retrieved December 2007.

CSO (2007a), 'Selected tourism statistics, international travel and tourism', also available from the Central Statistics Office of Mauritius website, http://statsmauritius.gov.mu/, retrieved December 2007.

CSO (2007b), 'Export processing zone, 3rd quarter 2007', also available from the Central Statistics Office of Mauritius website, http://statsmauritius.gov.mu/, retrieved in December 2007.

Durbarry, R. (2001), 'The export processing zone', in R. Dabee and D. Greenaway (eds), *The Mauritian Economy: A Reader*, Basingstoke, UK: Palgrave Macmillan.

Durbarry, R. (2002), 'The economic contribution of tourism in Mauritius', *Annals of Tourism Research*, **29** (3), 862–5.

Gabbay, R. (1988), 'Tourism', in R.T. Appleyard and R.N. Ghosh (eds), *Indian Ocean Island Development*, Canberra: National Centre for Development Studies, Australian National University, pp. 205–33.

Goldstein, A. (2004), 'Regional integration, FDI and competitiveness in Southern Africa', OECD Development Centre Studies.

Gulhati, R. and R. Nallari (1990), 'Successful stabilization and recovery in Mauritius', EDI Development Policy Case Series, World Bank.

Hein, C. (1988), 'Multinational enterprises and employment in the Mauritian EPZ', International Labour Organization, Geneva.

Hein, P. (1989), 'Structural transformation in an island country: the Mauritius export processing zone (1971–1988)', *UNCTAD Review*, **1** (2), 41–57.

ILO (2001), *Towards a Socially Sustainable World Economy: An Analysis of the Social Pillars of Globalization*, Geneva: ILO.

Jenkins, R. (1990), 'Comparing foreign subsidiaries and local firms in LDCs: theoretical issues and empirical evidence', *Journal of Development Studies*, **26** (2), 205–28.

Kearney, R. (1990), 'Mauritius and the NIC model redux: or, how many cases make a model?' *Journal of Developing Areas*, **24**, 195–216.

Meade, J.E. (1961), 'Mauritius: a case study in Malthusian economics', *Economic Journal*, **71**, 521–34.

Meade, J.E. (1967), 'Population explosion, the standard of living and social conflict', *Economic Journal*, **77**, 233–55.

Meade, J.E. et al. (1961), *The Economics and Social Structure of Mauritius – Report to the Government of Mauritius*, London: Methuen.

Meizenhelder, T. (1997), 'The developmental state in Mauritius', *The Journal of Modern African Studies*, **35** (2), 279–97.

Naipaul, V.S. (1972), *The Overcrowded Barracoon*, London: André Deutsch.

OECD (2005), 'African economic outlook 2004/2005', OECD Publishing, African Development Bank, OECD Development Centre.

Peerally, J. and J. Cantwell (2006), 'The dynamism between product innovation capabilities and technological capabilities in low-R&D industries: evidence from the Mauritius textile industry', University of Mauritius, mimeo.

Porter, M.E. (1990), *The Competitive Advantage of Nations*, New York: The Free Press.

Sannassee, R.V. (2002), *Analysing the Presence and Contribution of Wholly Owned Subsidiaries and Foreign Joint Ventures in the Mauritian Export Processing Zone – A Case Study of the Textile and Wearing Apparel Sector*, Ph.D. Dissertation, University of Reading.

Subramanian, A. and D. Roy (2001), 'Who can explain the Mauritian miracle: Meade, Romer, Sachs or Rodrik?', IMF Working Paper, WP/01/116.

UNCTAD (2008), 'FDI indicators', *Foreign Direct Investment Statistics*, http://www.unctad.org/Templates/Page.asp?intItemID=2921&lang=1.

UNCTAD (2001), *Investment Policy Review: Mauritius*, Geneva: United Nations.

UNDP (2005), *International Cooperation at a Crossroads: Aid, Trade and Security in an Unequal World*, Human Development Report.

UNEP (1996), *Sustainable Tourism Development in Small Island Developing States, Commission on sustainable development*, fourth session, Progress in the implementation of the programme of action for the sustainable development of small island developing states, Report of the Secretary General, addendum.

USITC (2004), *US Trade and Investment with Sub-Saharan Africa*, Fifth Annual Report, Investigation Number 332-415, USITC Publication 3741.

Wignaraja, G. (2002), 'Firm size, technological capabilities and market-oriented policies in Mauritius', *Oxford Development Studies*, **30** (1), 87–104.

World Bank (1994), *Mauritius: Technology Strategy for Competitiveness*, Report No. 12518-MAS, Washington, DC.

WTO (2003), *World Tourism Organization in Africa, 1996–2003*, Madrid: UNWTO.

10 New Zealand and the challenge of global competition
Peter Enderwick and Joanna Scott-Kennel

With a population of just 4 million and a location on the geographical periphery of the world economy, New Zealand certainly qualifies as a small economy. Its historical and economic development, heavily dependent on the inflow of foreign resources (capital, technology and migration), and the export of primary commodities, means it is also an open economy. However, its economic structure, with a small domestic market and traditional reliance upon natural-resource-based industries (tourism, dairy, meat, forestry, fruit and aluminium), means that it is primarily a trade-based economy. While inward investment flows and stocks in New Zealand are well above the average for all developed countries, the absolute amounts of such investment are low and have declined markedly since the late 1990s (Enderwick, 1998). On the other hand, outward investment flows and stocks are well below those of comparable developed economies, reflecting the commodity- and trade-based nature of the economy. While there is a high level of foreign ownership of New Zealand industry, particularly among larger manufacturing firms (Rosenberg, 1998), few New Zealand-based companies appear able to sustain successful international operations (Akoorie, 1993).[1]

The intention of this chapter is to examine three of the most internationally successful New Zealand industries – forestry, export education and information and communications technology (ICT) – and to consider the role that international investment plays in these sectors. The choice of industries for New Zealand is not straightforward. The largest export earners – dairy, meat and tourism – are either subject to considerable barriers to foreign investment (in the case of dairying) or are primarily trade based (meat and tourism). For these reasons the focus here is on industries that are significant and have considerable future potential, but are not necessarily the dominant international sectors. Forestry has attracted a high level of inward investment and experienced a considerable increase in outward investment as restrictions were eased in the mid-1980s. Export education is a much newer industry that has experienced extremely rapid growth and is now the fourth-largest source of foreign exchange earnings for New Zealand. ICT has been identified as a high-growth sector expected to double its contribution to GDP and employment by 2012 (BCG, 2001; ICT Taskforce, 2003).

Nature of the New Zealand economy
The competitiveness of New Zealand business is of considerable concern because, on a number of measures, the New Zealand economy has underperformed over several decades. While New Zealand enjoyed the world's second-highest per capita income level in the 1950s, it has now slipped far behind comparable developed economies. Per capita income in 2002, at US$14900, was just 73 per cent of that of Australia and 41 per cent of the US level. This relative decline has occurred over a considerable period: for the last

Table 10.1   New Zealand's selected exports by commodity, 2003

	NZ$ million	% of all merchandise exports
Milk powder, butter and cheese	4679	16.0
Meat and edible offal	4112	14.1
Logs, wood and wood products	2386	8.1
Mechanical machinery and equipment	1358	4.6
Fish, crustaceans and molluscs	1215	4.1
Fruit	1032	3.5
Aluminium and aluminium articles	980	3.4
All merchandise exports	29 278	

three decades both income and multifactor productivity growth in New Zealand have been among the lowest of all OECD nations (OECD, 2003). The result of these trends is that New Zealand's international competitiveness is comparatively low: the 2004 World Competitiveness Scoreboard ranks New Zealand at 18th, down from 16th the previous year, and well below other small open economies such as Singapore, Hong Kong, Denmark, Finland, Luxembourg, Ireland, Switzerland and the Netherlands, all of which are within the top 15 (IMD, 2004).

The weaknesses of the New Zealand economy have been attributed to a number of factors, including size (Simmons, 2001), location (McCann, 2003) and economic structure (Crocombe et al., 1991). Given the success of many other small open economies, it is difficult to argue that size is a disadvantage. New Zealand's location on the periphery of the world economy certainly adds to transport costs but innovations in information technology have made distance less of a constraint. An economic structure heavily biased towards natural resource commodities provides perhaps the strongest explanation. As Table 10.1 highlights, New Zealand has a production and trade structure more characteristic of a poorer developing economy.

This table shows that resource-based commodities constitute a very significant proportion of merchandise export earnings: dairy, meat and forestry alone account for almost 40 per cent of export earnings. Of these industries, forestry is characterized by the highest levels of internationalization, with significant inward and outward investment and product exports. It is also one of the fastest growth sectors with considerable export earning potential. Forestry is one of the three industries discussed in this chapter.

The resource dependence of the New Zealand economy is reflected in other ways. The most significant foreign exchange earning sector is tourism, a resource-based service industry contributing directly 3.4 per cent to GDP. The limited manufacturing capability of the New Zealand economy means that resource and service industries are the primary economic drivers. Within the service sector, one of the fastest-growing and most international areas is export education. This is the second industry profiled in this chapter. Third, we consider ICT, a technology-based industry that has carved out a niche position in global markets on the basis of local entrepreneurship and inward FDI.

It is important to note that while New Zealand is a small and relatively open economy,

Table 10.2   Outward investment position of selected small open economies, 2000

Country	Outward FDI flows 1992–97 as % of all developed countries	Outward FDI stock as % of all developed countries, 2000	Outward FDI flows as % of GFCF,* 2000	Outward FDI stock as % of GDP, 2000
New Zealand	0.017	0.14	13.3	14.1
Belgium and Luxembourg	2.7	3.5	164.3	72.4
Finland	0.9	1.0	95.1	43.3
Ireland	0.2	0.63	20.2	33.9
Netherlands	7.1	5.9	92.3	81.4
Sweden	2.3	2.4	95.8	51.4
Singapore	2.0	1.1	19.3	61.3
Hong Kong	7.5	6.6	133.2	234.9
Average all developed countries			20.8	21.4

Note: * Gross fixed capital formation.

Source: UNCTAD (2004), appendix tables B.2, B.4, B.5 and B.6.

it is principally a trade-based economy historically characterized by high levels of inward investment but little outward investment. Exports as a percentage of GDP are 35 per cent. This is lower than almost any other small economy, only one-third the level of Belgium, Luxembourg and Ireland, and a fraction of the figures for the most open economies such as Singapore or Hong Kong. When broader measures of openness such as a transnationality index are used, similar findings emerge (UNCTAD, 2004). The international investment position of New Zealand is also skewed (Enderwick, 1998). New Zealand is highly dependent on inward investment. Inward FDI as a percentage of gross fixed capital formation or GDP in New Zealand is some six times above the average for all developed economies. Low levels of inward investment in recent years suggest that dependence on inward investment is a long-established feature of the economy (Enderwick, 1998). The result is a high level of foreign ownership, particularly among the largest firms. Enterprises with at least 10 per cent foreign ownership accounted for 6.9 per cent of all enterprises and 6.1 per cent of full-time-equivalent employment in 2002. The control of the largest firms is most apparent within manufacturing, where foreign owners account for 1.7 per cent of enterprises but almost 74 per cent of manufacturing employment. Three-quarters of the New Zealand wine industry is now in foreign hands; foreign ownership also dominates in banking, insurance, power, railways and telecommunications (Enderwick, 1998).

A different situation exists with regard to outward investment, with New Zealand levels well below the developed-country median, as Table 10.2 highlights (UNCTAD, 2004). This table makes clear New Zealand's weak performance in terms of outward investment. On all four measures it underperforms other small open economies and even the average for all developed countries. The only other country that shows a similar imbalance in terms of reliance on inward investment and limited outward investment

Table 10.3   Harvest from New Zealand's planted forests (actual to 2000 and forecast to 2040)

Year	Volume (million m³)
1950	0.9
1960	3.0
1970	6.8
1980	9.4
1990	11.1
2000	18.0
2010	31.3
2020	34.6
2030	43.3
2040	52.5

Source: MAF (2000).

is Ireland. The expectation that there will be a positive correlation between inward and eventually outward FDI, encapsulated in the concept of the investment development path, does not seem to hold for New Zealand. New Zealand appears to be far less open than other small economies when assessed on trade or investment measures (AT Kearney/Foreign Policy, 2004).

Forestry
Forests constitute one of New Zealand's key resources, contributing 4 per cent of GDP. Forests cover 30 per cent of New Zealand's land mass, a total of 8.2 million hectares, of which 1.8 million are planted forests. In 2001 these forests yielded 18.5 million cubic metres of wood, almost all from planted forests. Nearly 70 per cent of this harvest was processed onshore by New Zealand's four paper and pulp companies, eight panel board companies, more than 350 sawmillers and approximately 80 remanufacturers. Given the size of the New Zealand economy, much of this product is exported, and forestry ranks third in terms of New Zealand's commodity exports. However, in global terms New Zealand is a small player, accounting for 1.1 per cent of the world's total output and 1.3 per cent of world trade in forest products. This is much lower than Sweden's 8.2 per cent and Canada's 18.8 per cent of world trade. The global market for forest products is very competitive. New Zealand faces considerable competition from Australia, Chile, Finland, Sweden, Indonesia, the USA, Canada and Russia. Australia and Chile have planted forest estates of radiata pine comparable in size to those of New Zealand. However, forecasts suggest that New Zealand forestry will grow significantly and could become the country's number one source of foreign exchange (see Table 10.3). Due to heavy planting in previous decades, the volume of wood available for export is expected to increase dramatically, with a 74 per cent increase between 1996 and 2010.

Factor endowments
New Zealand's forestry industry derives strong factor endowment advantages from its temperate climate, considerable past plantings of radiata pine, and ability to grow wood

quickly and efficiently. Plantation trees are young on average: 60 per cent are 15 years old or younger (average harvest age is 27). Much of the country's competitive advantage comes from the forest-growing, as opposed to the processing, sector. However, the forest sector suffers two disadvantages. First, it is extremely concentrated by species – 90 per cent of the plantation forest comprises one species, radiata pine. This raises potential problems of biosecurity: disease or a similar catastrophe could devastate the entire industry. There are only a few market segments where radiata pine has advantages over other species. One is medium-density fibreboard (MDF), where radiata pine has a colouring advantage, and paperboard and newsprint, where radiata's long fibres give additional strength. In markets for sawn timber, radiata pine is simply one of a number of substitute woods, and its acceptance as a structural timber does not really extend beyond Australasia.

Second, plantation forests are regionally distributed within New Zealand, a country with a similar landmass to the UK. Their wide dispersion throughout the two major islands makes it difficult to build large-scale processing plants and encourages production for niche markets.

Less clear is whether or not New Zealand has a cost or labour skill advantage in forestry. Labour costs in New Zealand are mid-range, lower than those of forest product competitors such as Sweden and the USA, but higher than those of Chile and Russia. There is a similar picture with regard to labour skills and productivity – better than developing countries, but inferior to the USA, Finland and Sweden. Labour availability is an ongoing concern in the forestry industry. In some regions it is limited and nationally there is concern about the quality of labour attracted to the industry, which does not enjoy a positive reputation as an employer.

Demand conditions
The New Zealand market for processed wood products is largely saturated and characterized by intense competition. Further growth and higher returns are more likely to be secured from overseas markets. New Zealand's primary export markets for wood products are Australia, Japan, Korea and the USA, which together account for three-quarters of forestry exports by value. Future growth is expected in Asian markets, particularly China.

Related and supporting industries
The forestry industry in New Zealand is characterized by a number of value-adding processors – sawmillers, paper and pulp manufacturers, panel board producers and remanufacturers. Many of these are foreign owned, including all seven paper and pulp mills and the largest panel facilities. Forestry also depends on a number of key supporting industries – road transport, ports and sea freight and electricity. The industry is also characterized by a large number of groupings representing various sectoral interests. Forestry operates under the umbrella of the Ministry of Agriculture and Forestry (MAF) and utilizes the services of Trade New Zealand, which promotes trade and international investment. The major industry associations include Forest Research, Forest Industries Training, the New Zealand Forest Owners' Association and the pan-industry New Zealand Forest Industries Council.

One problem facing the industry is regional variation in the provision and quality of capability and infrastructure. For example, softwood drying and processing technology in New Zealand is generally world class, but exists in only some regions. A similar imbalance applies to the quality of infrastructure such as road transport, which is considerably underdeveloped in regions such as Northland, the East Coast and the west coast of the South Island. Shipping links to second-tier markets are generally poor and traffic congestion substantially raises the costs of using the Port of Auckland (in New Zealand's largest city).

Firm structure, strategy and rivalry
Since privatization (the government now owns only 3 per cent of plantation forests), the New Zealand forestry industry has generally been characterized by considerable competition. Average returns have been low, to the extent that a number of major players have withdrawn from the industry, or at least from forest ownership. In recent years there has been a significant change in the structure of major forestry firms. The traditional form has been the large, vertically integrated corporation encompassing both forest ownership and further processing. The primary link between forest ownership and downstream processing has been security of wood supplies. Vertical integration has been the conventional solution to the problem of securing supplies. However, recent forest sales by a number of debt-ridden corporations have increased the diversity of forest ownership. The purchasers have been overseas investors of various forms, including endowment, pension and investment funds. Their business model is quite different from that of the large, publicly quoted corporations, some of whom found forestry increasingly inconsistent with shareholder demands for short-term returns. Debt-free investment funds are likely to focus more on long-term capital growth and to adhere to consistent strategic goals, which is more compatible with the notoriously cyclical forestry industry. This change is positive from the perspective of independent processors being protected from dominant suppliers, but may inhibit the establishment of very large-scale plants. A further downside of this change in structure is a concern over the extent to which such investors will be involved in 'industry good' activities such as research, lobbying and training.

    As Table 10.4 illustrates, foreign ownership of New Zealand plantation forest is considerable, particularly US ownership. Recent purchasers have been largely US-based institutional investors.

Role of foreign investment in forestry
As the above discussion suggests, inward investment has been vital to the development of the New Zealand forestry industry, particularly in forest ownership and further processing. Traditionally these two have been linked through large corporations that have brought capital, technology and market access to wood processing and secured supplies through the purchase of formerly state-owned plantation forests. Early investors, such as Nelson Pine Industries (Japanese), Pan Pac (Japanese) and Winstone Pulp (Indonesian), typically formed joint ventures with New Zealand companies. Recent forest sales have seen substantial transfers of the resource from largely foreign-owned corporations to foreign-based institutional investors. Much of the processing capacity is foreign controlled. A number of foreign investors – Brightwood, Grand Pine Enterprises, Gunns, Panahome Innosho and Tachikawa – have made substantial investments in wood processing without ownership of plantation forests (MAF, 2001).

Table 10.4 Ownership of major plantation forests in New Zealand by area, 2002

Ownership	Area (ha)	Percentage of area
Foreign-owned	845 000	46.6
of which: USA	623 000	34.3
Japan	88 000	4.9
Malaysia	81 000	4.5
China	25 000	1.4
Indonesia	17 000	0.9
UK	11 000	0.6
Domestic-owned	262 000	14.4
Others	707 000	39.0
Total	1 814 000	100.0

Source: New Zealand Forest Owners Association (2004).

Table 10.5 Forestry processing and export earnings in New Zealand (%), 2001

Form of processing	Harvested volume, %	Export earnings, %
Logs	32	21
Paper and pulp	23	33
Plywood, veneer, sawmills	41	36
Other forestry products	4	10
	100	100

However, in the past two decades, investment in forestry processing has not kept pace with the growth of the wood harvest and there is concern about how the industry will cope with the imminent 'wall of wood'. One result is the export of much of the harvest in unprocessed form. For example, of the 2002/3 harvest of 23 million cubic metres, 10 million cubic metres, or 44 per cent, was exported in log form. In this situation, much of the further processing and value added occurs overseas. In some cases, for example Japan, many of these logs are simply chipped overseas and yield little additional value.

Even where further processing occurs, unlike for rivals such as Sweden or Finland, there is little sophisticated value added, as Table 10.5 suggests.

The most sophisticated value adding occurs in the form of paper and pulp and other forestry products. While paper and pulp accounts for 33 per cent of forestry export earnings, only 23 per cent of the harvest is processed in this way. Exporting in the form of logs or even sawn timber creates little value added.

Outward investment by New Zealand forestry firms occurred soon after liberalization in the mid-1980s. The two major (then) domestically owned firms, Fletcher Challenge (now having substantially divested) and Carter Holt Harvey (now US owned), acquired overseas forest resources largely in an attempt to diversify their sources of supply and to be closer to developing markets. In the case of Fletcher Challenge, its major newsprint buyers in Australia expressed concern about vulnerability to disruption of supplies from their New Zealand base in the event of labour disputes or a natural disaster such as an earthquake, encouraging them in 1987 to purchase British Columbia Forest Products. Investments of this type were promoted by uncertainty regarding access to the domestic resource as the government privatized its holdings and by the desire to secure access to overseas markets. For Fletcher Challenge these investments were not profitable, as the company incurred huge losses on its purchase of UK Paper (Stride, 2000a, 2000b). More recently, the company has substantially pulled back to New Zealand, has sold off its forest holdings and has recreated itself as a value-added wood products company.

Forestry clusters
There is little evidence of strong clustering in the New Zealand forestry industry. The geographical dispersion of the forest resource and processing capacity discourages effective clustering. Indeed, a listing by Trade and Enterprise New Zealand identifies forestry specializations in 11 regions in New Zealand. These are very small and, in most cases, inactive. Few have achieved a meaningful degree of specialization and all lack critical mass. In terms of value added, there is some potential within the forest engineering group at Rotorua, and for furniture manufacturing in Porirua and South Canterbury. However, these represent small groupings of similar firms and are not clusters in the sense of integrated groups of related businesses capable of driving innovation and growth (Porter, 1998). In terms of the industry's need to move into higher-value-added processes, there is considerable potential for 'extended' clusters where, for example, wood is seen as an integral part of construction and design, panel products are linked to furniture design and manufacturing, and paper and pulp explores emerging needs within the packaging industry.

Role of government
Government is of considerable importance to the New Zealand forestry industry. In the past four decades the role of government has changed significantly. Three distinct periods can be identified (Thorpe, 2003). Traditionally, the government's role was central as a key player in the establishment of plantation forests and as a major owner of this resource. With privatization of the forest resource this role changed dramatically and became effectively 'hands off'. This is reflected in the decline in government ownership of the plantation forest resource from 51 per cent of the total in 1987 to less than 5 per cent today. A third stage, apparent since 2000, has seen the government playing a more facilitative role and providing leadership through the Wood Processing Strategy, for example. In addition, the government has major responsibilities with regard to sustainability and biosecurity, infrastructure development and certification.

Sustainability and biosecurity
The Resource Management Act (RMA) of 1991 provides the legislative basis for environmental management in New Zealand and is of obvious importance to an industry such as forestry. The Act has been subject to considerable criticism and is seen as a major impediment to further processing investment. The principal concerns relate to the time burden and costs of the process, inconsistency in its application between councils, delays in reaching the Environmental Court, objections processes and high degrees of risk and uncertainty. A significant example of the impediments created by the RMA is provided

by a proposed investment by Chinese-owned Wenita Forest Products, which sought to establish a new MDF plant at Allanton on the South Island. The company's inability to obtain air discharge consent led to the shelving of the project.

Carbon taxes are an emerging issue for the forestry industry, and the New Zealand government moved early to ratify the Kyoto Protocol on Climate Change at the end of 2002. If this raises costs for forestry processors it could become an impediment to further investment. Biosecurity is a major concern for the New Zealand forestry industry because of its dependence on a single species and also has implications for the assessment of investment in wood processing. Recent scares such as Asian Gypsy Moth have seen the government commit considerable additional resources to this area.

Infrastructure

With regard to infrastructure, the forestry industry faces problems with regional variations in the quality of road transport and access as well as concerns about the availability and cost of electricity. The establishment of further processing investments depends, in part, on the ease with which forest resources can be transported both to mills and to ports for export. A number of the more remote regions of New Zealand that have increasing wood harvests suffer from poor roads and transport links. A widespread concern is the fact that the funding criteria for roads are not particularly favourable to forestry. Funding for road projects is based on cost–benefit ratios. Unfortunately, the benefit parameters place little weight on economic or industrial development.

Privatization and reform of the electricity sector have not been a clear success and many investors worry about the cost and availability of future power supplies. Power shortages and price spikes in recent years have led to temporary closures of major mills. Environmental concerns have also caused the cancellation of recent projects to increase power generation capacity. These concerns certainly influence potential new investment in the forestry industry.

Certification

Certification offers the possibility of competitive advantage in an industry subject to growing environmental sensitivity. There is a need for the adoption of an internationally recognized certification process acceptable to all interests in the New Zealand industry. Government may need to play a role in this. Recent decisions by major retail chains such as the US-based Home Depot and Lowe's, and Sweden's IKEA mean that certification is a pressing concern. Certification is intended to ensure that wood is tracked from the forest to processing and distribution to the customer, and must ensure an appropriate balance of social, economic and environmental concerns. This basis for certification tends to favour companies that own their own forests or vertically integrate wood supplies and further processing, to the disadvantage of independent processors who rely on a variety of raw material suppliers.

In terms of legislation and investment screening there are few problems for the forestry industry. New Zealand's Overseas Investment Act of 1973, which assesses applications for foreign investment, is not seen as particularly onerous and the threshold criteria mean that it applies only to relatively large-scale processing investments. The Commerce Act of 1986 addresses anti-trust and competition legislation. The key restrictions are in Section 47, which deals with business acquisitions and potential market monopoly.

However, a decision in March 2001 permitting the acquisition of a large kraft mill by a major competitor suggests that the Act does not really constrain new investment decisions. One area where there could be some impact is in long-term supply contracts, which may be desired by independent wood processors. The Act interprets any such contract that substantially lessens competition as unenforceable. This could be a disincentive to processing investments.

Export education
The export education industry in New Zealand has experienced rapid growth in recent years and in 2002 was worth NZ$1.7 billion, placing it fourth in terms of foreign exchange earnings, just behind forestry. Growth has been remarkable. In 1959 there were 590 international students in New Zealand; by 2003 there were almost 80 000. Worldwide, in 2000 there were some 1.8 million students involved in international education; by 2025 this number could be as high as 7.2 million. As well as attracting a large number of students to the country, New Zealand tertiary education providers also catered to 2200 students in overseas locations. The principal markets are in Asia – China, South Korea and Japan in particular.

New Zealand's remarkable growth is attributable to three principal factors. The first was a 1989 government policy shift that allowed state-owned education providers to charge full fees for international students. This strongly encouraged institutions to attract such students, particularly when coupled with a decline in state funding. Second, changes in immigration policy placed greater weight on a New Zealand education for those seeking residence. Third, both China and India relaxed controls on international travel and foreign exchange, enabling many of their students to seek an overseas education.

Export education is delivered through four principal modes. The most popular is consumption abroad, whereby the student moves to the supplier country. Cross-border supply involves international provision of the service without movement of the student or teacher. Distance education is the most widely used example of this mode. Third, a commercial presence can be established in the country in which the student resides. New Zealand institutions have used this approach in the form of offshore campuses or 'twinning' arrangements. Finally, educational professionals can be moved to the country of student residence. This is most practical for short-term intensive programmes.

Like many other English-language countries, New Zealand has been able to capitalize on the considerable potential offered by the international education industry. While international students are found at the primary, secondary and tertiary levels, the following discussion focuses on the tertiary sector.

Factor endowments
In factor terms, New Zealand has three major advantages in export education. First, it is an English-speaking nation with strong social, legal and cultural influence from the UK. This is attractive for many students seeking to improve their English-language skills and acquire knowledge of Western business and society. Second, New Zealand is perceived as having a high-quality education system drawing on the Anglo-Saxon model. To the extent that this is seen as student centred and conducive to independent thinking and learning, it is highly regarded. Third, New Zealand is seen as an attractive and safe place to study. In addition, potential students from countries such as China find it much easier

and quicker to obtain permission to study in New Zealand than in competing locations such as the UK or the USA. At the tertiary level at least, New Zealand is seen to be a lower-cost destination than the four major English-speaking alternatives, Australia, Canada, the UK and the USA (IDP Australia, 2002). The majority of international students are found in business and related subjects as well as the vocational areas of nursing, medicine and trades.

Demand conditions
The demand for international education from Asian countries, and in particular China, is the result of economic development, a cultural recognition of the importance of education, and ease of travel. Demand from China increased significantly after 1999 when China endorsed New Zealand as an acceptable education destination (Asia 2000 Foundation, 2003). Demand for overseas education has also been stimulated by domestic policies regarding education. Discriminatory access to tertiary education, a long-standing problem for Malaysian Chinese, as well as insufficient capacity in countries such as China and Korea, creates demand for overseas programmes.

Related and supporting industries
A number of related and supporting organizations have assisted the growth of the export education industry. From the tertiary sector perspective, language schools can be seen as supportive. Many students for whom English is not their first language spend an average of six months on language preparation before entering a tertiary institution. A number of industry bodies also play a role. Education New Zealand was created in 1998 as the successor to New Zealand Education International Limited and took over responsibility for facilitating the recruitment of international students to New Zealand. The country's trade development organization, Trade New Zealand, also supports the education industry in a variety of ways. Marketing is coordinated through New Zealand International Education Marketing Network (NZIEMN), which is developing a generic brand for education. Different segments of the tertiary industry also undertake student recruitment activities, including the New Zealand Vice Chancellors Committee International Advisory Group, the Polytechnic International Managers Group, APPEL (Association of Providers of English Language) and NZAPEP (NZ Association of Private Education Providers). Quality assurance in the university sector is undertaken by the New Zealand Vice Chancellors Committee and the Universities Academic Audit Unit.

Firm structure, strategy and rivalry
Globally, international education is characterized by increasing competition. As well as strong marketing efforts by well-established export countries such as the USA, the UK, Canada and Australia, there are important changes occurring within countries that were traditionally major suppliers of students (Ministry of Education, 2001). Both Malaysia and Singapore have become major host nations in recent years. Singapore, using alliances with top US universities, has become a strong regional centre for postgraduate study. Malaysia has capitalized on changes in the post-9/11 world by creating a large number of places for Muslim students uncomfortable in a number of Western nations.

In comparative terms, using the percentage of tertiary students who are not citizens of the country of study, New Zealand is an average performer, comparable to the USA and

Canada, but far below Ireland, the UK and Australia (Ministry of Education, 2001). A number of institutions such as the University of Auckland have attempted to overcome the constraints through participation in international consortia such as Universitas 21. As a general rule, New Zealand is behind its competitors in the provision of distance education programmes (Ministry of Education, 2002a).

One feature of the industry that may have disadvantaged New Zealand is the fact that the earliest and most ambitious players in the international education sector were non-traditional universities, particularly upgraded polytechnics and 'new universities'. This favours the UK and Australia, which experienced widespread upgrading. In contrast, New Zealand has upgraded only one institution to university status in recent years.

At first glance, the export education industry of New Zealand appears very fragmented, with over 1100 providers for international students. However, at the tertiary level, there are 36 providers, of which the eight universities and 21 polytechnics and institutes of technology accounted for 95 per cent of the 12 649 international students studying at this level in 2001. The level of involvement in overseas markets also varies greatly. Of the 63 offshore programmes offered by New Zealand universities in 2001, more than half were provided by just three institutions. At the same time, many institutions have just a single programme. New Zealand providers offered an average of one to two programmes in 2001, compared with 23 for Australian providers (Ministry of Education, 2002a).

By far the largest number of international students – perhaps as many as 65 000 – are enrolled in English-language schools, which have grown dramatically in recent years. The most important providers in terms of tertiary student numbers are state owned or rely on the state for the majority of their funding. For them international education is a marginal, albeit lucrative, part of their business. However, declining real levels of government funding mean that greater dependence is now placed on international students, and a sudden collapse in numbers could threaten the viability of some institutions[2] (Ministry of Education, 2004).

Role of foreign investment in export education
There has been limited inward investment into the New Zealand market. A number of Australian and some UK business schools have attempted to tap both the domestic and international student market, particularly in Auckland. However, New Zealand's Education Act of 1989 places a number of non-tariff restrictions on inward investors. The use of terms such as 'university' or 'degree' are protected and foreign service providers cannot assume that they will be able to operate in New Zealand on the same basis that they enjoy in their home country. This, coupled with the small size of the New Zealand market, discourages such investment.

A growing aspect of the international education industry is overseas investment. New Zealand educational institutions have made significant investments in recent years. In 2001, of the 36 tertiary providers, 17 offered offshore programmes, with 63 programmes in total, a tenfold increase from the six offered in 1997. These programmes focused on China, South East Asia and the Pacific, with total enrolments of 2200.

The methods of overseas market entry highlight the problems of cultural sensitivity and quality assurance in the delivery of international services (Enderwick, 2005). Of the 63 programmes, 26 were delivered through an offshore campus, 20 were distance learning and 16 were a combination of these approaches (Ministry of Education, 2002a). The financial risks and regulatory barriers to establishing offshore campuses, as well as evidence that purely distance learning programmes are not well received by students, have encouraged joint venture arrangements such as 'twinning' and 'joint delivery'. These factors might also be expected to encourage collaborative approaches to offshore provision, allowing the sharing of risk and expertise, but these are rare. To help overcome some of the problems and increase consistency, the New Zealand government is exploring the possibility of creating an Offshore Education Network (Ministry of Education, 2002b).

The offshore experience of New Zealand educational providers suggests that the problems they encounter are not dissimilar to those identified in the broader literature. Case studies of Lincoln University and UNITEC Institute of Technology highlight problems of adapting to local laws and regulations, selecting and managing with an appropriate partner and maintaining service quality at a distance (Ministry of Education, 2003). More generally, institutions have entered unbalanced agreements, suffered from insufficient partner due diligence and weak risk management (Ministry of Education, 2004).

Involvement in international education may also be expected to bring positive externality effects for New Zealand tertiary providers and society in general. The main impact on educational providers should be to encourage a more international outlook and to inform domestic curricula. This is analogous to the transfer of knowledge and competencies from inward investors to local firms. More generally, New Zealand's competitive position would benefit from greater exposure to knowledge of other cultures, improved cross-cultural communication and overseas linkages. Sadly, the evidence suggests that these things are not happening to any great extent (Back et al., 1998; Ward, 2001). Even the interaction between international and domestic students appears low (Ward, 2001).

Role of government
The New Zealand government through the Ministry of Education is heavily involved in the export education industry. As well as providing much of the indirect funding (the establishment and support of tertiary institutions), it has also funded international student recruitment. Its visa and immigration policies also influence the demand for export education. Recently, it has announced two major policy initiatives. The first is a Compulsory Code of Practice for the Pastoral Care of International Students, which is intended to create a safe environment for students. All educational institutions must be signatories to the Code if they are to accept international students.

A more controversial initiative was the Export Education Levy, which requires institutions to pay a percentage of international fee income to the government to be used to fund promotion and communication, industry capability building, research and quality assurance. A prime motivation behind this initiative has been the instability of English-language schools, a number of which have collapsed, badly damaging the overseas reputation of the New Zealand education industry. The government is also taking the key leadership role in the industry with a high-level inter-agency strategy group that is moulding the future direction of the industry (Ministry of Education, 2002c).

Internationally, the New Zealand government participates within organizations such as the WTO, the APEC forum, the OECD and UNESCO on educational issues. New Zealand also has Memoranda of Understanding for cooperation in education with a number of countries, including China.

Government can also be expected to play a leading role in addressing the challenges faced by educational institutions. The key issues relate to capacity (the number of international students that can be accommodated), regional concentration (some 40 per cent of all international students are in the Auckland area), problems of monitoring quality, and market risk. Compared with competitor countries, New Zealand's export education industry is highly dependent on a narrow range of markets, particularly China. Vulnerability to a downturn such as that triggered by the Asian economic crisis of 1997 means that diversification is highly desirable. Government is likely to play a role in this process simply because competitors are pursuing similar diversification strategies and, in comparison, New Zealand has very limited marketing resources (Ministry of Education, 2004).

Information communications technology (ICT)
ICT is underpinned by electronics, software and/or telecommunications, and is typically split into two industry sectors: telecommunications and IT (ICT Taskforce, 2003, p. 6). In 2004, the New Zealand ICT sector generated an estimated $5 billion or 4.7 per cent of GDP and 41 000 full-time jobs representing 2 per cent of the workforce. Exports have been growing on average 23 per cent each year for the past decade, and are forecast to rise from $1.25 billion to $16 billion by 2012 (NZTE, 2004; Software NZ, 2004).

The main advantage of the high-tech sector in New Zealand appears to be its ability to develop high-value, innovative products for niche markets such as mobile communications, software and IT services (NZTE, 2004; Sanders and Dalziel, 2003). This advantage has arisen from the technical capability of New Zealand entrepreneurs, and the ability to adapt locally developed products to the sophisticated demands of international customers. The main challenges facing the ICT industry are shortages of capital and management skills.

The ICT sector has experienced high levels of inward investment, largely in the form of subsidiaries or branch offices and acquisitions of existing high-tech firms. Of the 18 largest firms in the industry, ten are foreign owned. FDI has played an important role in continued expansion of international and development activities within the sector.

Factor endowments
New Zealand's ICT industry derives factor endowment advantages from relatively low-cost but technically skilled labour, coupled with an innovative and entrepreneurial culture. Although labour costs relative to low-cost countries preclude competitiveness in large-scale manufacturing, the cost-to-return ratio for New Zealand based engineers, technologists, scientists and computer technicians is much lower than in comparative locations (McPherson et al., 2004). Software companies such as Orion, Peace, Binary Systems (Symantec) and Tacit retain R&D centres in New Zealand at approximately one-third the cost of their US counterparts (Oram, 2002).

New Zealand's entrepreneurial culture, ranked fifth out of 40 countries in 2003, favours independent thinking and innovative cost-effective solutions (GEM, 2004). Such ingenuity is often born out of the necessity to make the best use of limited human and financial resources. Employees in small ICT companies frequently become 'jacks of all trades', encouraging flexibility and speed in the innovation process (INZ, 2004).

New Zealand's geographic isolation has also fostered an entrepreneurial and outward-looking approach to business. Companies tend to overcompensate for being based in a peripheral economy on the 'other side of the world' by developing leading-edge, high-quality products. International connectedness, via exports, travel and use of communications technology, is very high in New Zealand (A.T. Kearney/*Foreign Policy*, 2004). Unfortunately, the small size of New Zealand companies and their long distance from key customers frequently undermine their credibility as suppliers internationally (Davenport, 2004; ICT Taskforce, 2003).

Other areas of concern relating to factor endowments include managerial and technical skills, domestic capital and electricity supply. New Zealand's strength in innovation does not appear to be matched by business acumen. This is a particular concern for smaller firms owned and operated by a technological entrepreneur who is often less well equipped to deal with the commercialization, managerial and marketing aspects of the business (McGregor et al., 2000; Tantrum Ltd, 2003).

Capital constraints arise due to New Zealand's relatively underdeveloped stock market, negligible venture capital funding, and reluctance on the part of banks to lend to businesses perceived as high risk (software companies, for example, rarely turn a profit in the first two to three years).

Electricity shortages over several consecutive winters have been of particular concern to foreign investors, who cite the risks and costs associated with the uncertainty regarding electricity supply (Sanders and Dalziel, 2003). Measures have been taken recently by government and industry to alleviate these problems.

Other factor conditions that have contributed to the development of the ICT industry in New Zealand include the time zone (firms can process Northern Hemisphere requests overnight), good physical infrastructure in the form of roads, transportation, airports and ports, the cost of living, and the lifestyle relative to other countries.

Demand conditions
New Zealand is among the fastest-growing e-commerce regions of the world, and its early adoption and rapid uptake of new technologies have had a positive impact on employment and output in the ICT sector (McPherson, 2004). This is shown by New Zealand's rankings relative to the rest of the world. In 2002, spending on ICT was the highest in the OECD, at just under 15 per cent of GDP (OECD, 2002). In the year to 2003, New Zealand rose from 17th to sixth place on the Information Society Index, above the USA, the UK and Canada. In 2004, it was ranked 19th out of 64 countries in an e-readiness survey (EIU, 2004a).

However, despite widespread adoption of ICT, the New Zealand market is too small to support high growth of the sector domestically. This forces companies to internationalize well ahead of their international counterparts, who are able to grow successfully for much longer on the basis of domestic demand. Unfortunately, sales in New Zealand are typically insufficient to support the substantial entry costs of international markets (ICT Taskforce, 2003). Compounding this problem is evidence that ICT is not being fully utilized by New Zealand businesses, nor prioritized by government procurement agencies (ICT Taskforce, 2003). Therefore international activities, and exporting in particular, are considered crucial to growth. The USA, the UK, Singapore, Australia and Asia have been identified as priority markets (NZTE, 2004).

Related and supporting industries
ICT can be described as an enabler, providing technological solutions to increase efficiency and productivity in other sectors. Productivity in ICT is double the New Zealand average, and spending on ICT has important spillover benefits for the growth of other industries (OECD, 2002). This may take the form of capital deepening, increased labour productivity, or enhancing the productivity of other industries through the provision of high-tech solutions for manufacturing and service provision (Sanders and Dalziel, 2003). ICT solutions have been employed in many traditional resource-based, manufacturing and service industries in New Zealand, and ICT has also contributed to the emergence of new technology-based industries, including creative technology, agritech, health IT, outsourcing, wireless/mobile devices, security, digital games and entertainment, and marine electronics (INZ, 2004).

International investors have made an important contribution to related and supporting industries through the activities of their subsidiary branch offices. These include suppliers of equipment in computing and telecommunications; distributors and wholesalers of electronic components; providers of professional and educational IT services; and network operators (ITANZ, 2004; Tantrum Ltd, 2003).

Support for the industry is offered by central government agencies including New Zealand Trade and Enterprise (NZTE), the Ministry of Economic Development (MED) and Investment New Zealand (INZ); industry associations such as the Information Technology Association (ITANZ) and the New Zealand Software Association; and regional development organizations. The Foundation for Research, Science and Technology (FRST) funds public and private sector IT research. Currently 14 incubators around New Zealand support business start-ups, most of which are in the IT, creative or biotech sectors (NZ Silicon Valley, 2004).

Firm structure, strategy and rivalry
Of the estimated 7700 ICT companies in New Zealand, 98 per cent have revenues of less than $5 million. Eighteen have sales over $100 million and ten of these are foreign owned. Concentration in the industry is high: 78 companies (1 per cent of the total) generate approximately 80 per cent of the sector's contribution to GDP. Small firms account for half the employees in the sector, contributing to lower levels of productivity than the OECD average (ICT Taskforce, 2003).

Telecommunications contributes the most to output in New Zealand and is dominated by a single foreign-owned firm, Telecom NZ, which accounts for 2.2 per cent of GDP and 21 per cent of the value of the New Zealand stock market (other listed ICT firms account for just 1 per cent). Entry of other foreign players, such as TelstraClear and Vodafone, has contributed to the quality and variety of products, services and technology platforms while lowering prices. However, competition continues to be restricted by Telecom's continued monopoly over line access.

Although software and IT services are smaller than telecommunications, their compound annual growth rates from 2003 to 2008 are high – forecast at 7.4 per cent and 7.1 per cent respectively (McPherson et al., 2004). The software sector consists of a large number of smaller, locally owned entrepreneurial firms, while many of the larger software companies have been acquired by or invested in by MNEs (e.g. JADE Software). The June 2004 takeover of systems integrator Gen-i by Telecom NZ left a single New Zealand-owned firm (Datacom, with 7.1 per cent market share) among the top ten IT services providers. The remainder, including the top three, EDS (14 per cent), Telecom Advanced Solutions (8.5 per cent) and IBM (8.4 per cent), are all foreign owned (McPherson and Muller, 2004). Similarly, the electronics sector is dominated by foreign-owned firms.

Due to the small size of the New Zealand market, competition in the electronics and software sectors is primarily at an international, rather than a domestic, level. The principal strategy is the development and international marketing of niche products. Key players hold technological or market leadership positions in a number of niche areas. For example, Software of Excellence holds 50 per cent of the dental software market in the UK, and Rakon holds more than 50 per cent of the world market for global positioning systems (GPS) (Oram, 2002; ICT Taskforce, 2003, p. 23). Initially, international expansion is undertaken via offshore distributors or MNE alliance partners, then via outward FDI into offshore sales subsidiaries or strategic-asset-seeking investment.

Company structure is centred on the owner/entrepreneur. This structure typically endures through the initial stages of international growth, but evolves to a New Zealand-based professional management team supported by offshore sales offices as the firm grows. Firms moving beyond critical thresholds in terms of size (estimated to be above $100 million in turnover and/or 500 staff) frequently seek investment from, or partnerships with, multinational enterprises to address deficiencies in resources and experience (ICT Taskforce, 2003).

Role of foreign investment in ICT

The telecommunications sector in New Zealand was completely owned and operated by the state until 1990, when Telecom NZ was privatized and sold to an American consortium. The sale followed deregulation of the sector in 1989 (Scott-Kennel, 1998). Demand for software was initiated following the purchase of an IBM mainframe computer for the New Zealand Treasury in 1960, which required some software development in house. In the 1970s, use of minicomputers encouraged wider use of computer technology locally and import restrictions made imported hardware expensive, thus increasing demand for locally produced software.

In the 1980s, the rapid growth in IT coincided with the introduction of the IBM PC and the increasing need for services and software. However, as local markets became better developed and eventually saturated, exports increased. Local demand for sophisticated niche software products was used as a springboard to target similar niche segments internationally. Exports of New Zealand software began in 1980 and grew at almost four times the rate of all New Zealand exports, reaching $100 million in 1990. Of the 300 firms in the industry at that time, 25 per cent were involved in exporting. Outward investment by leading firms involved the establishment of offshore sales offices and research facilities (Crocombe et al., 1991).

Inward FDI in the industry in the past decade has largely been in the form of acquisition of local firms. Most of these firms are very small by world standards. As a result many lack capital and specialist business skills, and have limited offshore presence (NZTE, 2004). Ownership by MNEs has helped address these constraints (Davenport, 2004; ICT Taskforce, 2003; Sanders and Dalziel, 2003; Tantrum Ltd, 2003; Tweed and McGregor, 2003). For example, Navman, a leading developer of GPS-related products, recently sold a majority equity stake to Brunswick New Technologies in order to fund expansion and to gain access to Brunswick's extensive marine distribution channels.

Investment by MNEs has addressed deficiencies in the local venture capital and lending markets. Full, or even partial, investment by an MNE can significantly increase the capital available for funding development or international expansion. For example, Right Hemisphere (visual communication software) is funded by Sequoia Capital (USA) (Right Hemisphere, 2004). EMS-Global (managed data services) is partially funded by 3i, a global venture capital company. Jade Software funded international expansion through major investments by USA Health Investors LLC, and I-Cap Nominees (Peart, 2004).

MNEs also contribute to the development of local talent and skills by training their employees and exposing them to business strategies and international activities. Some employees even go on to establish and run their own businesses. For example, employees at Pulse Data International initially developed technology for the visually impaired as a subsidiary of MNE Wormald International Group, but then established local ownership via a management buyout. Since then, revenues have increased twenty-fold (ICT Taskforce, 2003).

In many cases, MNEs have provided the means for specialization and further advancement of innovative software to world leadership positions. For example, The National Health Index, among the first of such systems in the world, was developed through collaboration between Eagle Technology, a local systems integrator, Telecom NZ and Hewlett-Packard (USA). Other New Zealand subsidiaries act as centres of research excellence within the MNE. For example, EDS (NZ) Limited specializes in applications support, database management and technical helpdesk operation (ICT Taskforce, 2003, p. 34), and Allied Telesyn maintains a key research centre for network switches at its New Zealand subsidiary based in Christchurch (Graham, 2002).

MNEs have also improved access to international markets. This is particularly important for small firms that have reached a point in their development where further growth is reliant on overseas markets, yet lack the necessary marketing experience and distribution infrastructure (Scott-Kennel and Akoorie, 2004). For example, since being acquired two years ago, iTouch's revenues have grown exponentially as a result of access to an established logistical presence in offshore markets (Tantrum Ltd, 2003). EDS (NZ) has secured offshore contracts through existing networks of companies and clients connected to its computer giant parent, EDS (USA) (ICT Taskforce, 2003). MNE alliances also provide access to global networks. For example, Descisys, a developer of business intelligence software, has formed an alliance with IBM that provides access to the critically important US market through established networks.

Motives for foreign investment
The globalization of the ICT industry has encouraged MNEs to fuel their growth by tapping into new centres of scientific and technical excellence around the world and by acquiring innovation, research talent and skilled labour embodied in smaller, more nimble companies (EIU, 2004b). Inward FDI is attracted by New Zealand's competitive advantage and innovation in high-tech research, design and quality control, through which investors can gain significant cost advantages compared to Europe and North America. A number of multinationals have established R&D subsidiaries in New

Zealand to tap into local centres of innovation, while others use New Zealand as a test bed for new innovations. For example, Geovector (USA), a producer of mobile information devices, established its development facility in Christchurch. Ericsson (Sweden) and Telecom NZ formed a marketing arrangement to conduct trials of cellular products in the New Zealand market (INZ, 2004; MediaLab, 2003).

Strategic-asset-seeking FDI has acquired intellectual property and capabilities unique to New Zealand firms. Acquisitions of high-profile New Zealand ICT companies in the past decade have included Switchtec (acquired by DTR Power Systems/Invensys, UK), Binary Research (Symantec, USA), MAS Technology (DMC, USA), Holliday Group (iTouch, UK), Deltec Telesystems (Andrew Corp., USA), Marshall Software (NetIQ, USA), Navman (Brunswick, USA), Gen-i (Telecom NZ) and Jade (USA Health, I-Cap Partners, USA) (Davenport, 2004; Muller, 2004).

Decline in the global ICT industry since 2000 has also seen a shift towards greater convergence and consolidation of ICT worldwide. This means that post acquisition, some or all activities may be relocated offshore in line with the rationalized global structure of the MNE. New Zealand cases of acquired ICT companies suggest that activities retained locally correspond to areas of location-specific advantage. For example, many MNEs retain local R&D centres in New Zealand, but relocate less cost-effective production activities offshore (e.g. Navman). Where advantages acquired are firm specific but spatially mobile (i.e. specific technology or products), these are frequently integrated into the MNE's global operations – sometimes at the expense of the New Zealand operation (e.g. Deltec Telesystems, Marshal Software) (Davenport, 2004; Scott-Kennel and Akoorie, 2004). The need for market presence also supports retention of local operations (e.g. Telecom NZ), although the sales and marketing activities of the acquired New Zealand firm are frequently integrated with the MNE's existing New Zealand subsidiaries (e.g. PDL Electronics, Schneider Electric, Holliday Group (iTouch)).

Motives for outward FDI by New Zealand ICT companies are closely linked to the need to gain presence in important offshore markets. This is driven by a number of factors: the small size of the New Zealand market, proximity to customers, manufacturing or technological capability, and market position. Many larger companies such as Orion Systems International (New Zealand's leading health software company) establish sales offices in strategic markets such as Australia, the UK and the USA (Orion Health, 2004). Costs and information relating to market entry are the major barriers to outward FDI and a number of initiatives aim to help New Zealand companies expand internationally. For example, the Silicon Valley Beachhead intends to establish distribution channels and attract investment via collaborative partnerships with North American firms (NZ Silicon Valley, 2004).

Acquisition of related firms abroad has enabled domestic firms in the ICT sector to instantly accelerate their growth through access to innovation, brands and manufacturing capability, and to international markets via existing distribution channels. Examples of recent acquisition-driven FDI include IT companies Prolificx and Endace, which acquired US-based design company Avnet and an integrated circuit design house in Australia, respectively (Flagler, 2004).

Size and market presence internationally are important contributors to a New Zealand company's credibility. Many companies have found retaining large customers in the USA impossible from a New Zealand base due to the perception that New Zealand is simply 'too small and too far away' to ensure reliability and timeliness of supply (Scott-Kennel and Akoorie, 2004; Davenport, 2004). Some New Zealand companies have moved their head offices overseas to take advantage of a more attractive regulatory regime. This allows them to lower the costs of doing business or position themselves more conspicuously in the industry (ICT Taskforce, 2003).

The strategy of foreign subsidiaries in New Zealand reflects the global nature of the ICT sector. The majority act as team players, carrying out a specific range of production, marketing or research-related functions in line with global or regional corporate strategy. In contrast, most New Zealand-owned ICT companies remain focused on an export strategy, where foreign subsidiaries are primarily involved in sales and marketing activities, or occasionally as offshore research centres located in close proximity to key customers. These subsidiaries could be described as more detached, with a specific focus on development and marketing in the host location (Taggart, 1998).

The Canterbury software cluster
The majority of ICT activity in New Zealand is based in the three main urban centres, Auckland, Wellington and Christchurch. Specific clusters include the NZ Software Association, Auckland's Wireless Forum, Wellington's Mobile Internet and Creative Capital clusters, the health IT cluster, the security IT cluster, and the focus of this section, the Canterbury software cluster (Hi-Growth, 2004; Pamatatau, 2002).

The Canterbury region of the South Island is home to New Zealand's largest concentration of IT companies, including 98 in electronics and 107 in software. The cluster has been built on strengths in high-tech and smart manufacturing, and has attracted considerable inward FDI. Many of the larger firms are foreign owned – all but one of the six largest electronics firms are subsidiaries of foreign MNEs (Tantrum Ltd, 2003).

Direct output from the cluster was estimated at NZ$792 million in 2003 ($618 million in electronics, $174 million in software). Conservative projections expect this to rise to $1480 million in the next four years. The total contribution of the cluster to the national economy is estimated at NZ$1.6 billion ($1.25 billion in electronics and $351 million in software). Direct employment in the region by high-tech companies is 3400 employees, 2801 in electronics (including 2165 in the six largest firms) and 1235 in software, and is expected to rise to 6920 employees in the next four years. If indirect effects are taken into account, the cluster generates approximately 13300 jobs nationwide. This figure is expected to rise to 24759 in the next four years (Sanders and Dalziel, 2003). Productivity per employee within the high-tech sector is approximately $196000 ($221000 in electronics and $141000 in software) compared to the national average of $61000. Exports are crucial to company growth, and currently 57 per cent of output is exported, estimated at NZ$553 million in 2003 ($481million in electronics and $72 million software). The top six electronics firms export over 90 per cent of their output (Sanders and Dalziel, 2003, p. 15).

Key constraints to the development of the cluster are similar to those to the industry as a whole, and include international market access, distribution and market information, fostering and maintaining linkages with tertiary institutions, commercialization of new ideas, and ability to offer a wide range of complementary capabilities including managerial and marketing expertise, venture capital and funding for development.

Acquired firms have found that foreign ownership typically addresses many of these issues, but at the expense of local control and potential loss of certain local activities.

Some firms believe that foreign ownership may also reduce incentives for local employees within the firm to innovate and diversify production (Sanders and Dalziel, 2003, p. 29; Tantrum Ltd, 2003).

Foreign subsidiaries have contributed to the cluster directly through employment and by providing supplies and services, and indirectly by acting as exporting channels for intermediate goods and services supplied by other cluster members, and through networking and demonstration effects. Recent surveys of cluster participants have found support for further MNE involvement to encourage development and growth within the sector (Sanders and Dalziel, 2003, p. 17).

The cluster is also supported by a number of initiatives aimed at strengthening or supporting high-tech firms in Canterbury. These initiatives have come from both industry and tertiary sectors and include the Human Interface Technology (HIT) lab at the University of Canterbury, the Canterbury Innovation Incubator, and the Canterbury Tertiary Alliance, as well as self-help and service organizations such as the Canterbury Electronics Group, Canterbury Software Incorporated, CanTech and Electronics South. The Canterbury Development Corporation has played a key role in facilitating development of the industry and industry associations, but fragmentation still exists – there is no single organization to coordinate all these initiatives on behalf of the cluster (Sanders and Dalziel, 2003).

Role of government

The New Zealand government has implemented a number of initiatives to increase funding and growth in the ICT sector. In 2003, the ICT Taskforce identified ways to grow New Zealand's ICT sector, and these ideas are currently being implemented through the Hi-Growth programme. In addition to that provided by FRST (Foundation for Research, Science and Technology), funding initiatives include the Strategic Investment Fund, designed to supplement and facilitate investments that create new jobs or new investment, and the Venture Investment Fund, a joint partnership between the government and the private sector, providing seed and start-up investment funds (INZ, 2004).

This funding is encouraging MNE contributions to the ICT industry by attracting new investment, funding research and strengthening network synergies. For example, EDS (NZ) will establish a Global Partners Solutions Programme to help local software companies penetrate global markets as part of a government-funded grant (INZ, 2004). However, smaller firms often find high transaction and opportunity costs associated with government funding applications (ICT Taskforce, 2003). Criticism has also been directed at the lack of coordination of support programmes for new start-ups. There is also a need for a better interface between public research centres, tertiary institutes and the ICT industry (ICT Taskforce, 2003). For example, tertiary training needs to be more specific to industry needs and there needs to be more encouragement of students to take technology-related courses.

There are also concerns that compliance costs and tax regulations act as a disincentive to investment relative to other countries. In a recent study of the electronics sector, over 70 per cent of SMEs considered compliance costs to be a constraint on their businesses. Larger companies voiced concern over the current tax regime relating to both R&D and capital expenditures (Tantrum Ltd, 2003). Similar concerns were echoed in a study of the software sector (Sanders and Dalziel, 2003). An internationally recognizable tax-neutral investment vehicle in line with those available in Australia and the USA (e.g. limited liability partnerships) would make investment in ICT more attractive (ICT Taskforce, 2003).

Managers of foreign subsidiaries in New Zealand have emphasized the importance of the government being seen to be supportive of business, and avoiding policies that appear hostile or indifferent to the needs of business, citing the recent electricity crises as an example (Sanders and Dalziel, 2003, p. 31). Other issues relate to the New Zealand Labour Relations Act, which increases the risk to small firms of hiring new staff, as it is difficult to dismiss non-performing employees; immigration laws that need to be more flexible to allow rapid entry of skilled workers to fill existing positions; and the reluctance of government procurement agencies to consider New Zealand-built software solutions in the tendering process, despite their wide acceptance internationally (ICT Taskforce, 2003).

Perhaps the most pressing issue in ICT is that growth remains severely constrained by the anti-competitive environment within the telecommunications industry. This could be addressed by government legislation enabling freer access to Telecom's network infrastructure ('freeing up the local loop'). Telecom's monopoly is considered a major factor in the high cost and limited availability of services such as broadband in New Zealand relative to other developed countries.

Conclusions

This chapter has considered three internationally competitive New Zealand-based industries with a particular focus on their reliance on international business activities. The above discussion suggests a number of conclusions.

First, it is apparent that while New Zealand is accurately described as a small, open economy, it is less globalized than many other small nations. Furthermore, its openness is primarily a result of trade rather than of FDI linkages. While the country has placed great reliance on inward investment for much of its historical development, it displays very low levels of outward investment. Whether this is a result of the small average size of New Zealand business, the country's geographical isolation or its commodity-based economic structure, is widely debated.

Second, the industries highlighted here are important contributors to New Zealand's GDP but none could be described as a global leader. In forestry, New Zealand accounts for just 0.05 per cent of the world's forest resource and 1.1 per cent of world trade in forest products. In export education, New Zealand is a very small player in a market dominated by the major English-language countries – the UK, Canada, Australia and the USA. New Zealand companies in the ICT sector are small in world terms with low levels of internationalization.

Third, while these industries have shown strong growth in recent years and the potential for future growth, they face considerable challenges. Both forestry and export education lack leadership and coordination. Both need to increase value added. While both have a variety of industry bodies representing sectoral interests, they display little meaningful clustering. Interestingly, the lead role in developing a strategy for these two industries is being assumed by the government. For forest products this is evident in the Wood Processing Strategy and for export education through the role played by the Ministry of Education. Within the ICT sector weaknesses in financing, business management skills and overseas market penetration have encouraged reliance on foreign ownership and acquisition of innovative small and medium-sized firms. This reliance on government direction is a major weakness of many New Zealand industries, even those such as forestry, which is populated by large, foreign-owned MNEs. The resource base as the major locational advantage of New Zealand and industry fragmentation combine to frustrate the emergence of globally competitive New Zealand-based businesses. Action to overcome some of the current problems faced by these industries is necessary. The Resource Management Act is perhaps the key impediment to further investment in wood processing. Despite numerous calls for re-evaluation to streamline and speed up processes, little progress has been made. For educational institutions, declining government financial support has engendered an overreliance on full fee paying students and acute dependence on a narrow range of Asian markets, particularly China. Increased competition within the telecommunications sector would assist growth and diffusion of benefits from the ICT sector.

Fourth, the industries considered here do not appear to have been very successful in leveraging the externalities offered by international involvement. In export education full-fee-paying students are treated essentially as a 'cash cow', with little evidence of curriculum adaptation to reflect either their needs or the opportunity for New Zealand educational institutions to learn from discerning foreign buyers. In forestry, the lack of positive spillovers is reflected in low value adding and the recent demise of New Zealand's largest commodity conglomerate. Within ICT the most promising ideas are often snapped up by foreign buyers and may not be retained or developed within New Zealand. Similarly, we know very little about the role and aspirations of foreign-owned affiliates within these industries. Very little research has been undertaken on this topic. This is most unfortunate for an economy that has experienced declining levels of inward investment in recent years and the increasing importance which then attaches to long-established affiliates. This is an area requiring urgent investigation.

Notes

1. In recent years a major New Zealand brewery company has divested operations in China, Air New Zealand has closed its Australian operations, and Fletcher Challenge, once New Zealand's largest MNE, has substantially retrenched. New Zealand's largest MNE at present, a cooperatively owned dairy producer, enjoys a high level of government protection.
2. In 2001, for four institutions full-fee-paying students were 10 per cent or more of total enrolments.

References

Akoorie, M. (1993), 'Patterns of foreign direct investment by large New Zealand firms', *International Business Review*, **2** (2), 169–90.

Asia 2000 Foundation (2003), 'The export education industry: challenges for New Zealand', an Asia 2000 occasional paper, Wellington, New Zealand.

A.T. Kearney/*Foreign Policy* (2004), 'Measuring globalization: economic reversals, forward momentum. The 2004 A.T. Kearney/FOREIGN POLICY globalization index', *Foreign Policy*, No. 141.

Back, K., D. Davis and A. Olsen (1998), 'Internationalization and tertiary education institutions in New Zealand', report prepared for the New Zealand Ministry of Education, Wellington, New Zealand.

BCG (2001), *Building the Future: Using Foreign Direct Investment to Help Fuel New Zealand's Economic Prosperity*, Wellington: The Boston Consulting Group.

Crocombe, G., M. Enright and M. Porter (1991), *Upgrading New Zealand's Competitive Advantage*, Auckland: Oxford University Press.

Davenport, S. (2004), 'The founder is "going fishing": an exploratory study of New Zealand high-tech company sales to offshore buyers', draft paper for comment, Victoria University of Wellington.

EIU (2004a), *2004 E-readiness Rankings*, London: The Economist Intelligence Unit and IBM Corporation.

EIU (2004b), *Scattering the Seeds Of Invention: Globalization of Research and Development*, London: Economist Intelligence.

Enderwick, P. (ed.) (1998), *Foreign Investment: The New Zealand Experience*, Palmerston North: Dunmore Press.

Enderwick, P. (2005), 'Multinational service firms and global strategy', in J. Bryson and P. Daniels (eds), *The Handbook of Service Industries*, Cheltenham, UK and Northampton, MA, USA: Edward Elgar, pp. 258–74.

Flagler, B. (2004), 'Fast 50', *Unlimited*, November, 49–62.

GEM (2004), Global Entrepreneurship Monitor website, www.gemconsortium.org.

Graham, I. (2002), 'On the right road for ICT', *NZ Herald On-line*, 2 April.

Hi-Growth (2004), Hi-Growth website, at www.hi-growth.co.nz.

ICT Taskforce (2003), *Breaking through the Barriers: ICT Taskforce Report*, Wellington.

IDP Australia/Australian Education International (2002), *Comparative Costs of Higher Education Courses for International Students in Australia, New Zealand, the United Kingdom, Canada and the United States 2001*, Canberra: IDP Australia.

IMD (2004), *World Competitiveness Yearbook 2004*, Lausanne: IMD.

INZ (2004), *Information and Communications Technology in New Zealand*, Auckland: Investment New Zealand: A division of New Zealand Trade and Enterprise.

ITANZ (2004), Information Technology Association of New Zealand website, www.itanz.org.nz.

MAF (2000), *National Exotic Forest Description. National and Regional Wood Supply Forecasts 2000, Edition 3*, Wellington, New Zealand: Ministry of Agriculture and Forestry.

MAF (2001), 'The Forest Processing Investment Environment', report prepared for the Ministry of Agriculture and Forestry by Forest Research Technical, Paper No: 01/05, Wellington, New Zealand.

McCann, P. (2003), 'Geography, trade and growth: problems and possibilities for the New Zealand economy', New Zealand Treasury Working Paper 03/03 June 2003, Wellington, New Zealand.

McGregor, J., D. Kolb, D. Tweed, J. Henley-King, B. Simpson and R. Seidel (2000), *Managing for Success: A Training Kit about Innovation for New Zealand Manufacturers*, Palmerston North: Massey University.

McPherson, J. (2004), *IDC Special Study: New Zealand eCommerce Review and Forecast 2003–2007*, IDC.

McPherson, J. and G. Muller (2004), *IDC Market Analysis: New Zealand IT Services 2004–2008 Forecast and 2003 Vendor Shares*, IDC.

McPherson, J., C. Tan-Wanklyn, L. Gunson and J. Bain (2004), *IDC Market Analysis: New Zealand IT Market Review and Forecast 2003–2008*, IDC.

MediaLab (2003), 'No wires – no limits: an industry analysis of New Zealand's mobile and fixed wireless communications sector', report commissioned by Trade and Enterprise NZ, prepared by MediaLab South Pacific Inc. with Innovations and Systems Ltd.

Ministry of Education (2001), *Export Education in New Zealand. A Strategic Approach to Developing the Sector*, Wellington, New Zealand: Ministry of Education.

Ministry of Education (2002a), *New Zealand's Offshore Public Tertiary Education Programmes: Initial Stocktake*, Wellington, New Zealand: Ministry of Education.

Ministry of Education (2002b), *Education Beyond Our Shores – Defining the Way Forward: Workshop Report*, Wellington, New Zealand: Ministry of Education.

Ministry of Education (2002c), *Export Education in New Zealand: Update*, Wellington, New Zealand: Ministry of Education.

Ministry of Education (2003), *APEC Joint Venture Schools Project. Improving the Institutional Capacity of Higher Education Under Globalization*, Wellington, New Zealand: Ministry of Education.

Ministry of Education (2004), *Offshore Education: A Risk Perspective*, Wellington, New Zealand: Ministry of Education.

Muller, G. (2004), *IDC Insight: Market consolidation pressure continues to mount*, IDC.

New Zealand Forest Owners Association (2004), *New Zealand Forest Industry Facts and Figures 2003/2004*, Wellington, New Zealand: New Zealand Forest Owners Association.

NZ Silicon Valley (2004), website, www.nzsiliconvalley.com.

NZTE (2004), New Zealand Trade and Enterprise website, www.nzte.govt.nz.

OECD (2002), *Information Technology Outlook: ICTs and the Information Economy 2002*, Paris: OECD.

OECD (2003), *The Sources of Economic Growth in the OECD Countries*, Paris: OECD.

Oram, R. (2002), 'A vision of Kiwi innovation', *Sunday Star Times*, 13 May.

Orion Health (2004), Orion Health website, www.orionhealth.com.

Pamatatau, R. (2002), 'Trade NZ taking Kiwi tech firms to the world', *Stuff NZ Infotech Weekly*, 8 April.

Peart, M. (2004), 'Jade forced offshore to get back on track', *National Business Review*, 14 May.

Porter, M.E. (1998), 'Clusters and the new economics of competition', *Harvard Business Review*, **76** (6), 77–90.

Right Hemisphere (2004), Right Hemisphere website, www.righthemisphere.com.

Rosenberg, B. (1998), 'Foreign investment in New Zealand: the current position', in P. Enderwick (ed.) (1998), *Foreign Investment: The New Zealand Experience*, Palmerston North: Dunmore Press, pp. 23–66.

Sanders, C. and P. Dalziel (2003), *The High-Tech Sector in Canterbury: A Study of its Potential and Constraints: A Report prepared for New Zealand Trade and Enterprise*, Agribusiness and Economics Research Unit, Lincoln University.

Scott-Kennel, J. (1998), 'Foreign direct investment and privatization in New Zealand', in P. Enderwick (ed.), *Foreign Direct Investment: The New Zealand Experience*, Palmerston North: Dunmore Press, pp. 112–33.

Scott-Kennel, J. and M.E.M. Akoorie (2004), 'Cycling in tandem: an exploratory study of MNE and SME integration', *International Journal of Entrepreneurship and Small Business*, **1** (3/4), 339–62.

Simmons, G. (2001), 'The impact of size and distance on New Zealand firm size, behaviour and performance', New Zealand Treasury draft paper, Wellington, New Zealand.

Software NZ (2004), Software New Zealand website, www.nzsa.org.nz.

Stride, N. (2000a), 'The end of the Fletcher dynasty', *The National Business Review*, 22 September 2000, 30–31.

Stride, N. (2000b), 'The end of the Fletcher dynasty', *The National Business Review*, 29 September 2000, 29–31.

Taggart, J.H. (1998), 'Configuration and coordination at subsidiary level: foreign manufacturing affiliates in the UK', *British Journal of Management*, **9**, 327–39.

Tantrum Ltd (2003), *The Canterbury Electronics Industry: a Mapping Survey and Report*, Commissioned by The Canterbury Development Corporation and supported by New Zealand Trade and Enterprise, July, available at http://www.electronicssouth.org.nz/docs/electronics_industry_survey.pdf.

Thorpe, T. (2003), *Government Involvement in Forestry Development in New Zealand*, Wellington, New Zealand: Ministry of Economic Development.

Tweed, D. and J. McGregor (2003), *Moving Forward in the New Economy: Lessons from Software Companies*, Palmerston North: Massey University.

UNCTAD (2004), *World Investment Report 2004: The Shift Towards Services*, New York and Geneva: UNCTAD.

Ward, C (2001), 'The impact of international students on domestic students and host institutions: a literature review', Victoria University, Wellington.

11 The competitive position of a developing economy: the role of foreign direct investment in Cambodia[1]

Ludo Cuyvers, Reth Soeng and Daniel Van Den Bulcke

Firms serve markets outside the boundaries of their home country by exporting their products, licensing their technology, or engaging in international production abroad through foreign direct investment (FDI). The existing literature provides a series of reasons for such outward FDI, e.g. that the investing firms possess specific ownership advantages over the indigenous, local firms that they want to exploit, or they want to tap into local resources that are unavailable or relatively more expensive in their own countries.

This chapter reviews Cambodia's inward FDI and the role that FDI has played in its economic growth and the expansion of exports in a competitive environment. Based on previously unpublished data from the Council for the Development of Cambodia (CDC)/Cambodian Investment Board (CIB), inward FDI flows into Cambodia are categorized into two main types – approved FDI and realized or active FDI. Approved FDI consists of the investment projects that have received approval from CDC, while realized or active FDI refers to the investment projects that have become operational following approval from the CDC or CIB.[2]

The chapter is organized as follows. In the second section, a short overview will be given of the relevant economic and business environment for FDI in Cambodia. Using unique data, FDI in Cambodia is then analysed by geographic origin, by ownership categories, by industrial sectors, by provinces, and by distinguishing between approved and realized FDI. The role of FDI in Cambodia's economic development and the competitive advantages according to Michael Porter's 'diamond' are then discussed, followed by some conclusions in the final section.

Inward FDI often plays a vital role in the economic growth and development of a host country, more particularly of a small and less-developed economy that needs to be integrated more closely into the world economy. Inward FDI makes available to the recipient country not only investment capital, but also modern technology and know-how. It creates jobs, brings into the recipient country foreign exchange that can be used for the import of productive capital goods, and often contributes significantly to output growth and to the expansion of exports. In addition, inward FDI may force the local (incumbent) firms to become more efficient if they are to survive in a more competitive environment.

More and more countries, especially developing countries, have become aware of these potential benefits and have made efforts to attract FDI, e.g. by creating special investment zones and export processing zones, by providing tax holidays, by allowing duty free imports of capital goods, production materials and equipment, and by introducing fast-track approval procedures for FDI by the government administration authorities. Cambodia is no exception and has developed favourable policies towards foreign investors.[3]

Cambodia's business environment for FDI

Cambodia suffered dramatically from Pol Pot's genocidal regime (1975–79) and from the invasion of foreign powers and the ensuing civil wars (1979–89), which caused enormous destruction, not only to the country's infrastructure, educational institutions, financial and health systems, but, even more importantly, to its human capital. Following the signing of the Paris Peace Accord in 1991 and the arrival of the United Nations Transitional Authority (UNTAC), Cambodia finally held its first democratic general election in 1993 with more than 20 participating political parties. The election resulted in the formation of a legitimate coalition government.[4]

To rebuild the war-stricken country, Cambodia was in dire need of capital and lacked the foreign exchange to import essential capital goods. The need to build up the nation's capital stock was very acute and could to some extent be alleviated through inward FDI. Since the UN-sponsored election of 1993, Cambodia has engaged in the liberalization of its economy by promoting domestic investment and by adopting an extremely open policy towards foreign investment and international trade.[5] The so-called Law on Investment was enacted by the Cambodian National Assembly in 1994, leading to the creation of the Council for the Development of Cambodia (CDC). The prime minister chairs the CDC, which is the highest decision-making government agency responsible for private and public sector investment, while the Cambodian Investment Board (CIB) acts as its private investment arm. The CIB reviews investment applications and screens investment projects.

The CIB serves as a one-stop agency for the screening of investment projects, both domestic and foreign. Once they are accepted by the CIB, the investment projects are eligible for a wide range of benefits as spelled out in the Investment Law of 1994 (Kingdom of Cambodia, 1994). These incentives included a 9 per cent corporate income tax rate; an exemption from corporate tax for up to eight years; permission to carry forward losses for up to five years; non-taxation of dividends, profits or proceeds of investment; tax-free import of capital goods, intermediate goods and construction materials; tax-free exports; and the permission to hire skilled foreign employees. These benefits were available to the approved projects introduced by Cambodian investors or foreign investors on a non-discriminatory basis (Kingdom of Cambodia, 1994, 2003).

The 2003 amendment to the Investment Law of 1994 has greatly simplified the licence application procedures (Table 11.1). Although there was an increase in the corporate tax rate from 9 per cent to 20 per cent, it is still much lower than in most of the neighbouring countries.[6] However, generous tax incentives may not be the best way to woo FDI inflows. Serious foreign investors are more likely to be attracted by the long-term economic prospects than by short-term tax advantages offered by the host country's government, but evidently no firm will refuse an important tax concession (Lall, 1995).

For host countries there are pros and cons associated with offering tax holidays. Countries may become engaged in so-called 'tax tournaments' and compete with one another to attract FDI because generous tax incentives are often assumed to provide a country with a competitive advantage. Especially when the economic conditions of the competing countries are very similar, there is a danger that as a result of such 'wars of

Table 11.1   Comparison of Cambodian investment incentives, 1994 versus 2003

Investment Law of 1994	Investment Law of 2003
Corporate tax of 9%	Corporate tax of 20%
Tax holiday up to 8 years	Trigger period + 3 years + Priority Period[a]
Tax-free repatriation of profits	Repatriation of profits (subject to withholding tax)
Reinvestment of earnings (tax-free)	Reinvestment of earnings (special depreciation)
No tax on imports of capital goods and intermediate goods	No tax on imports of capital goods and intermediate goods
No export tax	No export tax
Licensing (evaluation and approval)	Licensing (simple registration)

Note: [a] The so-called 'trigger period' starts with the issuance of the final registration certificate and ends on the last day of the taxation year; the maximum trigger period is to be the first year of profit or three years after a qualified investment project earns its first revenue, whichever is sooner (CDC, 2007). The trigger period is less than or equal to three years from the start of operations (Hing, 2006, p. 103). 'Three years' starts from the taxation year immediately following the trigger period and includes the two immediately succeeding years. The 'priority period' starts immediately after the third taxation year of the three-year period (CDC/CIB, Laws and Regulations on Investment in the Kingdom of Cambodia, 2006).

Source: Adapted from Hing (2006), p. 104.

competing incentives' all involved countries may lose out to the multinational enterprises (MNEs) when those firms decide to locate where they had intended to go even before the intercountry bidding started. In an effort to encourage more inward FDI, the Cambodian prime minister in 2006 urged the Ministry of Commerce to carry out administrative reforms to facilitate investment applications as well as imports and exports.

Although relatively large amounts of foreign investment have been attracted to Cambodia, long delays in investment approvals have been repeatedly reported and are partly due to the country's bureaucratic slowness (Hing, 2003, 2006). For investment projects exceeding US$50 million it is necessary to obtain authorization from the Office of the Council of Ministers. Moreover, approval from the Council of Ministers is required for politically sensitive projects, the exploration of mineral and natural resources, projects with possible negative environmental effects and infrastructure projects (CDC, 2007). These additional approval steps tend to delay the authorization process and result in fewer projects being proposed or carried out, and are one of the reasons for the differences between approved and realized investments.

Since 1994, one year after the election, the country has increasingly tried to woo both domestic and foreign investment. Especially via its liberalization policy towards international investment and trade, Cambodia has attempted to improve its attractiveness for foreign investors as an export platform to third-country markets, such as the lucrative American and European markets. During 1994–2004, inward FDI flowed into Cambodia from more than 26 countries.[7] Based on investment data measured in fixed assets, the most prominent countries of origin were Malaysia, Taiwan, China and the USA.[8]

Table 11.2 lists the percentage shares of FDI inflows into ASEAN countries over the period 1994–2004. Cambodia was only marginally attractive to FDI in comparison to its fellow ASEAN member countries during 1994–96. FDI flows into the country

Table 11.2   FDI inflows into ASEAN member countries as a percentage of FDI inflows into developing economies, 1990–2004

Economy	1990–93	1994–96	1997–2000	2001–04
Brunei Darussalam	0.01	0.34	0.30	0.64
Cambodia	0.04	0.14	0.09	0.06
Indonesia	3.07	3.45	−0.23	−0.19
Lao PDR	0.03	0.08	0.03	0.01
Malaysia	8.49	4.83	1.94	1.35
Myanmar	0.34	0.28	0.24	0.11
Philippines	1.51	1.25	0.75	0.36
Singapore	8.40	8.13	6.28	5.98
Thailand	4.15	1.58	2.41	1.02
Vietnam	0.95	1.51	0.82	0.69
ASEAN-10	27.00	21.59	12.63	10.03

Source: UNCTAD (2005).

even declined during the two sub-periods of 1997–2000 and 2001–04. The decline in FDI inflows was probably due to the internal political tension between the Cambodian People's Party (CPP) and the FUNCINPEC Party, which resulted in an armed conflict, undoubtedly scaring away existing and potential investors.

The second major factor in the business environment responsible for the decrease in inward FDI flows into Cambodia was the Asian financial and economic crisis of 1997. Thailand, Indonesia and Malaysia were hit hardest by the crisis (Tongzon, 2001, p. 155). This crisis, which started in Thailand, first affected Malaysia and Indonesia, and then spread out further to the less-developed ASEAN economies of Cambodia, Vietnam, Lao PDR and Myanmar. Whereas the spread and contagion of the crisis in Malaysia and Indonesia were to some extent due to the psychological reaction of international investors and speculators, and the weakness of the banking and financial sector in the countries involved, for the poorer transition economies it was triggered by the existing investment and trade linkages with the aforementioned stronger economies of Southeast Asia. The Cambodian economy relies heavily on foreign capital via FDI or financial assistance in the form of development loans. As intra-ASEAN investment is the largest part of Cambodia's inward FDI flows, the country was adversely affected. Fundamental weaknesses in its banking and financial sector were also factors. Cambodia's inward FDI in fixed assets from Malaysia alone accounted for more than one-third of the total FDI in the country over the period 1994–2004. Since a major share of Cambodia's FDI comes from ASEAN members and other Asian countries, the adverse impact of the Asian crisis on Cambodia's inward FDI flows can be explained with reference to the relative costs of investment in Cambodia and those in the country of origin of the FDI. The crisis caused substantial devaluations of ASEAN home countries' currencies against the dollar, which implied that, *ceteris paribus*, payments in domestic currencies to the factors of production in FDI home countries were relatively less costly than payments to production factors in the US dollar – the currency mainly used in business transactions in Cambodia.[9]

The third factor that possibly had a negative effect on FDI in Cambodia and the other

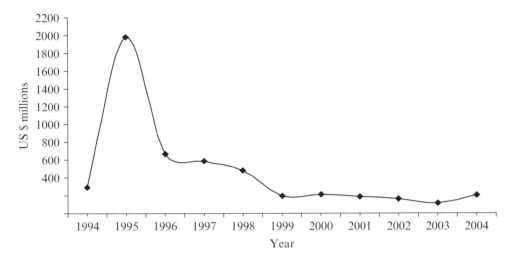

Source: Computed from unpublished data from CIB.

Figure 11.1   FDI inflows into Cambodia ($US million), 1994–2004

Southeast Asian countries might be foreign investment diversion to China. As Table 11.2 shows, the shares of FDI flows into the ten ASEAN member countries substantially declined during the two sub-periods, and this might be attributed to China's mounting attractiveness for FDI (Chantasasawat et al., 2003, 2005). Using data for eight East and Southeast Asian countries,[10] Chantasasawat et al. (2003) show that the level of the People's Republic of China's FDI is negatively related to the levels of FDI flows to East and Southeast Asian economies, suggesting that the emergence of China has crowded out FDI from Asian economies.[11]

Cambodia's foreign direct investment by geographic origin
Following the UN-sponsored election in 1993 and the opening up of policy towards foreign investment and trade, inward FDI approved by the Cambodian Investment Board increased substantially from US$288.55 million in fixed assets in 1994 to US$1979 million in 1995 and then dropped sharply to US$663 million in 1996. The sharp increase in 1995 was due to a large investment project of US$1300 million from Malaysia (CIB, 2005).[12] As shown in Figure 11.1, FDI inflows into the country declined gradually after 1995 and reached their lowest level in 2003. However, the inflows somewhat revived in 2004 and moved up to US$801 million in 2005, according to the most recent data from CIB.

As already mentioned, Cambodia has attracted FDI mainly from ASEAN member nations. With more than one-third of total inward FDI from 1994 to 2004, Malaysia was the leading source of investment in Cambodia (Table 11.3). However, in more recent years Malaysia has been surpassed by China as the dominant country of origin. Malaysia's investment in fixed assets in Cambodia went up from US$0.09 million in 2002 to US$8.42 million in 2003 and US$38.67 million in 2004 (CIB, 2005), while China's investment in fixed assets in Cambodia increased from US$24 million to US$33.05

Table 11.3   FDI in Cambodia by country of origin (1994–2004)

Economy	No. of projects	% no. of projects	Fixed assets (US$1000)	% of fixed assets
ASEAN	288	25.1	2557336	48.14
Malaysia	108	9.42	1959878	36.89
Singapore	97	8.46	284801	5.36
Thailand	59	5.14	224347	4.22
Indonesia	16	1.39	61597	1.16
Vietnam	6	0.52	25373	0.48
Philippines	2	0.17	1340	0.03
Greater China	550	47.94	1418301	26.70
Taiwan	219	19.09	655607	12.34
China	208	18.13	481600	9.07
Hong Kong	123	10.72	281094	5.29
USA	52	4.53	444638	8.37
EU	99	8.62	366608	6.90
France	35	3.05	214820	4.04
UK	49	4.27	118970	2.24
Portugal	9	0.78	15561	0.29
Netherlands	3	0.26	15166	0.29
Belgium	1	0.09	1860	0.04
Germany	2	0.17	231	--
Korea	62	5.41	318134	5.99
Canada	22	1.92	111971	2.11
Australia	34	2.96	40765	0.77
Japan	13	1.13	20308	0.38
Argentina	1	0.09	245	--
New Zealand	1	0.09	11	--
Others	25	2.18	34227	0.64
Total	1147	100.00	5312544	100.00

Source: Calculated from unpublished data of approved FDI, Cambodian Investment Board.

million and US$88.68 million during the same years. If this surge continues, cumulative FDI inflows from China will top Malaysia's in the coming years.

Concentrating on the longer period 1994–2004 might somewhat hide the most recent developments, particularly the 'China factor'. There was a sharp decrease of total inward FDI in Cambodia during 2002–03, although FDI from China increased in the same period.[13] This is surprising because, after China's admission to the World Trade Organization in 2001, China was able to export directly to the previously quota protected markets of the USA, the EU and other lucrative markets, and no longer needed Cambodia or some other Southeast Asian country as an export platform in the garment and textile sector. Companies that initially intended to invest in Cambodia may well have considered investing in China instead. That Chinese FDI continued to expand in Cambodia was therefore due to other factors.

Table 11.3 shows FDI inflows into Cambodia by regional grouping as well as

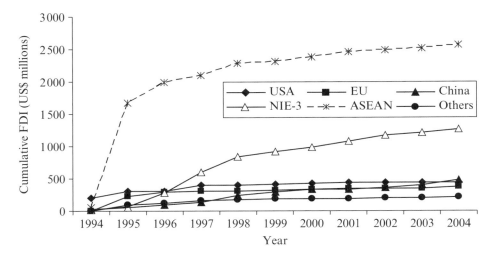

Note: *FDI stock is approximated by cumulative FDI in fixed assets; NIE-3 refers to Republic of Korea, Hong Kong and Taiwan; EU includes Belgium, France, Germany, Netherlands, Portugal and the UK as investing countries.

Source: Calculated from CIB's Cambodian Investment Statistics, 1994–2004.

Figure 11.2   FDI stock in fixed assets in Cambodia by country of origin* (1994–2004)

individual economies from 1994 to 2004. The largest share of FDI in Cambodia came from ASEAN member nations, representing almost half (48 per cent) of total inward FDI in fixed assets during this period. 'Greater China' was the second-largest source of Cambodia's inward FDI with more than a quarter (26.7 per cent) of fixed assets during the same period. Although Cambodia's inward FDI from China increased over the period under consideration (Figure 11.2), the diversion to China of Cambodia's supply of FDI from other countries was more than offset by the increase in inward FDI from China in Cambodia. This effect presents a major concern for Cambodia as it depends very heavily on foreign exchange injected by foreign investors for its economic development. FDI diversion can result from interrelations with trade/export diversion. The negative effect of FDI diversion on the Cambodian economy is especially serious if Chinese FDI in the country is export oriented. Cuyvers et al. (2008) show that China's accession to the World Trade Organization has deterred FDI flows into Cambodia.[14] In contrast to the large share of inward FDI from ASEAN member countries,[15] FDI inflows from developed countries such as the USA, the EU, Canada, and Japan were much smaller and reached 8.4 per cent, 6.9 per cent, 2.1 per cent and 0.4 per cent, respectively.

Types of FDI in Cambodia
Table 11.4 presents the modes of entry of FDI into Cambodia. Basically, FDI inflows into the country can take the form either of Cambodian–foreign joint ventures or wholly foreign-owned enterprises.[16] Cambodian–foreign joint ventures were the most popular mode of entry at the beginning of the government's liberalization policy in 1994, yet the investment amounts involved have systematically declined since then. During the period

Table 11.4   Approved FDI in fixed assets and employment in Cambodia by type of investment, 1994–2004

Year	Cambodia – foreign joint ventures		Wholly Foreign Owned Enterprises	
	Fixed assets (US$ millions)	Employment	Fixed assets (US$ millions)	Employment
1994	501.47	11611	19.96	9993
1995	481.32	20564	1669.94	33635
1996	337.55	29498	426.04	31351
1997	378.09	51418	295.57	72080
1998	338.97	26297	397.21	63380
1999	127.66	15659	131.42	41257
2000	73.98	12427	159.71	41570
2001	27.92	4172	163.34	22175
2002	30.80	2059	138.94	21108
2003	42.56	5649	91.20	30090
2004	42.99	5640	173.02	72128
Total	2383.31	184994	3666.34	438767

Source: Calculated from unpublished data, Cambodian Investment Board.

1994–97, cumulative FDI in wholly owned enterprises surpassed the Cambodian–foreign joint ventures (in terms of employment about 110000 compared to 150000) and became the preferred entry mode by foreign investors. After 1998, annual investment in wholly owned foreign businesses continued to be larger than in Cambodian–foreign joint venture projects.

The distribution of the types of foreign investment in Cambodia during 1994–2004 and the initial preference for Cambodian–foreign joint ventures is illustrated in Table 11.5. There are indeed a number of factors that might encourage MNEs to seek out local partners (Blomström et al., 2000). First, foreign investors will select local partners when they lack familiarity with the way of doing business in the host country and are afraid of being insufficiently familiar with some important local business characteristics such as the availability of reliable suppliers or the interpretation of the investment and labour laws. Foreign investors may also be interested in the firm-specific assets of the potential local partners such as knowledge of domestic marketing and production conditions. Second, MNEs may also opt for a domestic firm as business partner if they perceive, or hope for, more preferential treatment by the host country's government when they link up with domestic investors. Third, some foreign investors are risk averse, and look for a domestic partner for risk-sharing purposes, especially in developing countries, where some investment projects might be rather problematic. Moreover, MNEs may hesitate to enter large foreign markets alone if the investment project requires substantial resources for the development of local sales networks, after-sales service etc.

Cambodian–foreign joint ventures were already out of favour with foreign investors in 1995 – less than a year after the country liberalized its investment policy. In 1995, the share of wholly foreign-owned enterprises sharply increased, from 0.33 per cent in 1994 to 27.60 per cent in 1995.[17] While the share of Cambodian–foreign joint ventures further

Table 11.5 *Approved inward FDI in Cambodia in fixed assets by type of investment,*
1994–2004

Year	Cambodia – foreign joint ventures		Wholly foreign-owned enterprises	
	% no. of projects	% of total fixed assets	% no. of projects	% of total fixed assets
1994	1.91	8.29	1.31	0.33
1995	6.73	7.96	7.93	27.60
1996	8.43	5.58	7.83	7.04
1997	7.73	6.25	11.55	4.89
1998	3.82	5.60	8.43	6.57
1999	3.51	2.11	4.42	2.17
2000	2.01	1.22	6.33	2.64
2001	1.10	0.46	2.71	2.70
2002	0.60	0.51	2.81	2.30
2003	1.41	0.70	3.31	1.51
2004	1.00	0.71	5.12	2.86
Total	38.25	39.40	61.75	60.60

Source: Calculated from unpublished data, Cambodian Investment Board, 1994–2004.

declined, the wholly foreign-owned enterprises became more popular during the whole period under consideration, except in 1997.[18] This implies that, other things being equal, MNEs preferred to enter a small country such as Cambodia on their own rather than seek out a partner for a joint venture (Table 11.5), and clearly indicates that the reasons to opt for joint ventures are not applicable to Cambodia. The lack of experienced partners in a newly liberalizing and transition economy was probably the dominating factor behind this choice.

Foreign investors' preferences for wholly foreign-owned enterprises might also be linked to the lack of international arbitration and/or credibility of the Cambodian legal system in case of business disputes, which are more likely to arise in joint ventures.[19]

A recent survey carried out by the World Bank (2004) and Chap (2005) identifies corruption as the major constraint to the operations of firms in Cambodia, and finds that the fifth-highest-ranking constraint relates to the legal system and formal conflict resolution. Similarly, a more recent study, *Assessment of Corruption in Cambodia's Private Sector* by the Economic Institute of Cambodia (EIC, 2006) indicates that corruption is the most problematic factor for doing business in the country. Additionally, in a firm-level field survey of 164 garment companies operating in 2003 in Cambodia,[20] Yamagata (2006) also found that about 90 per cent of the surveyed companies admitted that 'speed money' to government officers was inevitable to allow procurement to go smoothly. This is confirmed by Transparency International (2007), which ranked Cambodia in the top quintile of countries most affected by bribery. According to the 'Global Corruption Barometer 2007', almost three-quarters (72 per cent) of the respondents declared they had paid bribes to obtain services. This is more than twice as high as the score for other ASEAN countries such as Indonesia (31 per cent) and the Philippines (32 per cent), and more than three times higher than the average for the Asia Pacific countries.

Sectoral distribution of Cambodia's FDI
The sectoral distribution of FDI in the Cambodian economy over the period 1994–2004 shows a very uneven pattern, and is probably due to the stronger competitive advantages that some sectors might enjoy. Porter (1990) has indicated that the international success of a nation's industry lies in four attributes of the national 'diamond': factor conditions, demand conditions, related and supporting industries, and local company rivalry. However, less-developed economies/developing countries are less likely to possess all of these factors.[21]

During the period under consideration, light industries, particularly the garment and textile sectors, and hotels and restaurants have been the most successful in attracting inward FDI into Cambodia. Foreign investment in the garment sector can undoubtedly be partly attributed to the most favoured nation (MFN) status that was granted to the Kingdom of Cambodia by the USA and the decision by the EU and other developed countries to accept Cambodia as a beneficiary of their generalized system of preferences (GSP).

The development of Cambodia's garment and textile industry started in the mid-1990s when garment producers from other Asian economies, such as Malaysia, China, Taiwan, Hong Kong, Singapore and South Korea, took advantage of the country's quota-free access to developed-country markets. A large reserve of unskilled labour capable of producing garments for exports and the fact that the garment exports of other more developed Asian countries, e.g. China, became quota constrained, strongly facilitated this expansion (Bargawi, 2005).[22] Consequently, Cambodia's inward FDI in the garment industry used the country as an export platform to bypass quotas and tariffs imposed by the USA and the EU. Of course, the success in attracting inward FDI into the garment and textile industries was also due to Cambodia being relatively well endowed with natural resources such as cheap land, and its low-wage workers having the necessary skills to work in labour-intensive production processes such as garments and textiles.

USAID (2005) and Yamagata (2006) found that almost all garment companies in Cambodia were owned by foreign investors, while only 5 per cent belonged to Cambodians. Most of the cloth, the raw material for the production of garments, is imported from other Asian economies – China, Hong Kong and Taiwan. Also, the garment factories in Cambodia only perform cut-make-and-trim activities, which means that value added to the finished product is relatively small (EIC, 2007). This implies that most of Cambodia's inward FDI in the garment industry can be considered as third-party market-seeking FDI that uses Cambodia as an export platform to access rich markets (Freeman, 2002).

Based on data from a field survey (Yamagata, 2006) of 164 garment companies in Cambodia in 2002, it was found that almost all garments are exported. Cambodia sold abroad no less than 98 per cent of the garments it produced in that year. Most of those exports went to markets in North America and the EU. Similarly, a study by USAID (2005) confirmed these findings by indicating that all Cambodia's garment production was indeed exported. Two-thirds of those exports ended up in the USA and most of the rest found its way to EU markets.

The second-most important sector for foreign investors in Cambodia is the service sector, which attracted almost half (45.6 per cent) of total realized inward FDI in fixed assets during 1994–2004. Within services, the subsectors hotels and restaurants (43 per

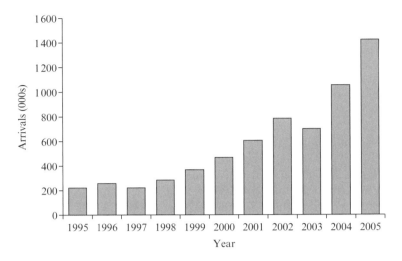

Source: Ministry of Planning (2006).

Figure 11.3   Visitor arrivals in Cambodia (in thousands), 1995–2005

cent) and the transportation sector (34 per cent) together received more than three-quarters (77 per cent). The popularity of these service sectors for foreigners is the direct result of Cambodia's exceptionally rich cultural heritage and its impressive historical sites, especially the world-famous Angkor Wat temple complex. Also the government's 'open air' policy, which allows direct international flights to the city of Siem Reap, where the Angkor Wat shrine and the other temples are located, plays an important role. According to Porter's diamond model, hotels and restaurants and the transportation sector can be considered as 'supporting sectors' for the tourism industry, which encourages other investment in these sectors.

Thanks to Cambodia's cultural heritage and the Angkor Wat temple site, as well as increasing political stability, the country has become a much-favoured destination for international tourists. Estimated total tourist arrivals in Cambodia averaged 581 000 visitors annually between 1995 and 2005, with an annual growth rate of about 22 per cent during those years (Figure 11.3). However, the growth rates of tourist arrivals for the years 1995, 1997 and 2003 were negative. The decline in visitors to Cambodia can be explained by the uncertainty surrounding the country's political situation in these specific years as a result of the factional fighting between the CPP and FUNCINPEC political parties and the election years of 1997 and 2003, respectively.

Although the government has encouraged FDI in agriculture and the agro-industry, cumulative FDI in these sectors only amounts to 5 per cent of the total (Table 11.6). The low level of FDI in agriculture is probably partly due to such adverse factors as land tenure (an unresolved problem in Cambodia), administrative barriers, security and crime, and the shortage of irrigation systems (Hing, 2003, 2006), as well as Cambodia's small domestic market for agricultural products and the protectionist measures adopted in developed countries to shield their own agricultural production.

FDI is concentrated primarily in the labour-intensive sectors rather than the relatively

Table 11.6   Sectoral distribution of realized FDI in Cambodia, 1994–2004

Sector	No. of Projects	% of no.of Projects	Realized FDI (US$ million)	% of total realized FDI
Agriculture and fisheries	11	2.32	101.87	5.13
Agriculture and related activities	10	2.11	99.41	5.01
Fishing	1	0.21	2.46	0.12
Industry	406	85.83	941.59	47.42
Food products and beverages	15	3.17	60.57	3.05
Tobacco	5	1.06	32.79	1.65
Textiles	10	2.11	72.32	3.64
Garments	298	63.00	506.53	25.51
Tanning and dressing of leather, manufacture of luggage, handbags, saddlery, harness and footwear	23	4.86	40.28	2.03
Paper and paper products	9	1.90	9.24	0.47
Coke, refined petroleum products and nuclear fuel	1	0.21	0.10	0.01
Chemicals and chemical products	1	0.21	0.47	0.02
Rubber and plastics products	7	1.48	7.79	0.39
Other non-metallic mineral products	7	1.48	18.71	0.94
Fabricated metal products, except machinery and equipment	6	1.27	7.47	0.38
Radio, television and communication equipment and apparatus	1	0.21	0.73	0.04
Medical, precision and optical instruments, watches and clocks	5	1.06	11.53	0.58
Motor vehicles, trailers and semi-trailers	4	0.85	6.64	0.33
Furniture	7	1.48	79.89	4.02
Recycling	1	0.21	2.95	0.15
Electricity, gas, steam, and hot water supply	5	1.06	77.58	3.91
Construction	1	0.21	6.00	0.30

Table 11.6   (continued)

Sector	No. of Projects	% of no.of Projects	Realized FDI (US$ million)	% of total realized FDI
Services	51	10.78	905.34	45.58
Sale, maintenance and repair of motor vehicles and motorcycles	3	0.63	3.95	0.20
Hotels and restaurants	25	5.29	388.46	19.56
Land transport	1	0.21	4.25	0.21
Transport activities, activities of travel agencies	9	1.90	307.02	15.46
Post and Telecommunication	5	1.06	46.76	2.35
Education	2	0.42	98.35	4.95
Recreational, cultural and sporting activities	6	1.27	56.55	2.85
Other business activities	5	1.06	37.10	1.87
Total	473	100.00	1985.90	100

Source: Calculated from unpublished data, Cambodian Investment Board.

more capital-intensive industries such as construction (Table 11.6). Garments and textiles, which use labour more intensively in the production process, have been particularly attractive for FDI. The combined share of realized FDI in fixed assets in garments and textiles amounted to almost 30 per cent of total inward FDI in the country. The resource-based, more capital-intensive hotel and restaurant sector attracted about 20 per cent during the same period. The share of FDI in the more capital-intensive construction and transportation sectors is negligible at 0.3 per cent and 0.2 per cent, respectively, in spite of the government's efforts to encourage FDI in infrastructure. To rebuild the country's infrastructure after its destruction during the many years of civil war and political upheaval is essential for Cambodia's further development.

Provincial distribution of FDI in Cambodia

Cambodia covers an area of 181 035 square km and consists of 22 provinces and two major cities for which the data are often published separately.[23] The distribution of FDI in the kingdom over these provinces and cities is extremely uneven (Table 11.7). Only 16 provinces succeeded in attracting foreign-invested projects.[24] Phnom Penh, the capital city of Cambodia, has been by far the most successful in persuading foreign investors to locate there as it drew about three-quarters (77 per cent) of total inward FDI measured both in fixed assets and employment. Phnom Penh City and its surrounding province of Kandal, taken together, receive 82 per cent of the country's FDI in terms of fixed assets and 92 per cent of the total employment in foreign-controlled firms. Sihanoukville comes in second position, with only about 8 per cent of total FDI measured by fixed assets

Table 11.7   Provincial distribution of approved inward FDI in Cambodia, 1994–2004

Province	No. of projects	% of no. of Projects	Fixed assets (US$ millions)	% of fixed assets	Employ-ment	% employ-ment
Banteay Meanchey	4	0.40	46.01	0.76	901	0.14
Battambang	2	0.20	9.93	0.16	484	0.08
Kampong Cham	11	1.10	47.52	0.78	4592	0.74
Kompong Speu	13	1.30	112.41	1.86	9912	1.59
Kompong Tom	1	0.10	2.58	0.04	105	0.02
Kompot	6	0.60	208.77	3.45	1437	0.23
Kandal	134	13.43	305.06	5.04	90079	14.44
Kep	1	0.10	1.03	0.02	25	–
Koh Kong	6	0.60	50.91	0.84	1144	0.18
Phnom Penh	757	75.85	4652.07	76.81	483818	77.56
Pursat	2	0.20	2.24	0.04	327	0.05
Rattanakiri	2	0.20	14.10	0.23	1805	0.29
Siem Reap	15	1.50	138.97	2.29	3003	0.48
Sihanoukville	42	4.21	463.86	7.66	24023	3.85
Svay Rieng	1	0.10	0.18	–	952	0.15
Takeo	1	0.10	1.05	0.02	1154	0.19
Total	998	100.00	6056.68	100.00	623761	100.00

Source: Computed from unpublished data, Cambodian Investment Board.

and 4 per cent by employment during 1994–2004 (Cuyvers et al., 2006). Evidently, compared to the rest of the country, Phnom Penh has more to offer foreign investors with respect to access to communication networks, transportation facilities, infrastructure, business-related services and the availability of technical and managerial personnel.

The geographical concentration of inward FDI in Cambodia also results from agglomeration effects caused by investors following others in the choices of their investment locations (Fujita et al., 1999). There are benefits for firms to be located close to each other and form industrial clusters, thus giving rise to spillover effects, specialization of factors of production and forward and backward linkages (Navaretti and Venables, 2004). The high geographical concentration of the country's inward FDI is clearly the result of location advantages. For instance, the concentration of hotel and restaurant businesses in the Siem Reap province is mainly due to the province's world-famous tourist attractions, as well as to industrial clustering in transportation and other service activities.

Although the government has promoted special promotion zones[25] in the provinces of coastal Sihanoukville, coastal Koh Kong (bordering Thailand), Banteay Meanchey (whose town of Poipet borders Thailand), and Svay Rieng and Takeo (bordering Vietnam), these provinces attracted almost no FDI, except Sihanoukville – the second city of the kingdom. Through location advantages such as proximity to an international seaport, the relatively better infrastructure, tourist attractions and basic services,

Table 11.8   Realized FDI in Cambodia by type of investment, 1994–2004

Year	Cambodian–foreign joint ventures		Wholly foreign-owned enterprises	
	Fixed assets (US$ million)	Employment	Fixed assets (US$ million)	Employment
1994	29.20	3440	3.71	7017
1995	282.58	4200	288.75	24957
1996	125.92	9775	157.13	11418
1997	30.95	13398	77.44	33765
1998	37.98	12577	129.65	35394
1999	46.59	6515	92.13	25893
2000	24.74	7831	147.11	37313
2001	22.95	2638	111.31	22043
2002	14.05	1863	46.27	20428
2003	37.56	5619	65.18	27700
2004	42.99	5640	171.72	71072
Total	695.51	73496	1290.38	317000

Source: Calculated from unpublished data, Cambodian Investment Board.

Sihanoukville managed to attract some inward FDI. However, this amounted to only 1.6 per cent of the total employment created by FDI inflows into Cambodia.

The highly uneven distribution of Cambodia's FDI is also related to the scarcity of technical and managerial personnel in the provinces, and the fact that people residing in Phnom Penh are rarely willing to work elsewhere in the country, because of the poor infrastructure, difficult transportation and shortages of basic services such as potable water in the more remote locations.[26]

This extremely uneven distribution of FDI in Cambodia and of the ensuing job creation is expected to widen the divide between the rich and the poor even more, in spite of recent impressive double-digit economic growth (Ballard, 2007; Sok, 2005). In the rural areas, the poverty rate is about four times as high as in the capital city of Phnom Penh (Sok, 2005).[27] This widening gap between the rich and the poor may cause destabilization as a result of increased migration, social pressures and rising criminality. As a consequence, poor unskilled workers (both women and men) from more remote provinces are moving to the urban areas, especially Phnom Penh, or to Thailand, to look for work because of the absence of livelihood alternatives in their villages. Migrant workers are reportedly at high risk of being confronted with cheating/exploitation, beating, rape/abuse, and security hazards (So et al., 2007).

Approved versus realized FDI: a comparison
Table 11.8 shows realized inward FDI by type of investment from 1994 to 2004, as opposed to the approved FDI figures depicted in Table 11.4. In 1994 only 5.8 per cent of the approved capital for Cambodian–foreign joint ventures was actually invested as compared to 16.5 per cent for wholly foreign-owned enterprises (see Table 11.9). Because of significant time lags between the year of project approval and the actual investment,

Table 11.9   Realized FDI as percentages of approved FDI by type of investment in Cambodia, 1994–2004

Year	Cambodian–foreign joint ventures		Wholly foreign-owned enterprises	
	Fixed assets	Employment	Fixed assets	Employment
1994	5.82	29.63	18.58	70.22
1995	58.71	20.42	17.29	74.20
1996	37.31	33.14	36.88	36.42
1997	8.19	26.06	26.20	46.84
1998	11.20	47.83	32.64	55.84
1999	36.50	41.61	70.10	62.76
2000	33.44	63.02	92.11	89.76
2001	82.20	63.23	68.14	99.40
2002	45.62	90.48	33.30	96.78
2003	88.25	99.47	71.47	92.06
2004	100.00	100.00	99.25	98.54
1994–2004	29.18	39.73	35.20	72.25

Source: Calculated from unpublished data, Cambodian Investment Board.

both measures should be compared from a longer-term perspective. On average the realized FDI in fixed assets as a percentage of approved FDI for Cambodian–foreign joint ventures and wholly foreign-owned enterprises was 29 per cent and 35 per cent, respectively, over the period 1994–2004. However, this discrepancy was mainly due to the period before 2000. More recently the differences in the ratio between approved and realized investment have strongly diminished.

The low ratio of realized FDI to approved FDI may partly be explained by investors having inflated their amount of investment as declared in the application form in order to bargain and obtain better or higher incentives. It is indeed government policy to grant larger incentives the higher the amount of investment (Chap, 2005). Chap (2005) also argued that middlemen who have close connections with (corrupt) government officials successfully obtained investment licences and concessions that were then sold to potential investors in order to make profits. If investment project 'buyers' were not found, the projects were delayed or cancelled. A number of firm-level surveys on the importance of the investment climate listed several negative factors, e.g. corruption, poor infrastructure, the high cost of electricity and weak legal and judiciary systems, which increase the cost of doing business in Cambodia (ADB, 2006; Hagemann, 2002; World Bank, 2004). However, this situation seems to be improving gradually. The proportion of realized to approved FDI, although often oscillating, shows an upward trend over the period under consideration and even reached a very high ratio in 2003 and 2004 – as much as 100 per cent – for each type of ownership.

The non-realization or delayed realization of approved projects might also be due to changes in the international environment. Factors that might have had a negative impact on the ratio of realized to approved FDI in Cambodia are the aforementioned Asian crisis of 1997 and China's accession to the World Trade Organization in 2001.

First, for both wholly owned subsidiaries and joint ventures, evidence shows a severe decrease in this ratio in terms of capital investment in 1997. This was probably due to the cancellation or delay in the planned investment, and a rapid pick-up, in particular, for wholly foreign-owned investment in 1999–2000. Second, while it might be interesting to speculate about the role of China's WTO accession in the drop in the capital investment realization ratio for wholly foreign-owned enterprises in 2001–02, and the subsequent rise of this ratio in 2003–04, this is difficult without carrying out a more detailed study.

The employment realization ratios mostly reach a higher level than the capital investment realization ratios. This means that some realized FDI projects must have used more labour-intensive production processes than initially planned. As the data include both approved and realized investment projects during 1994–2004,[28] it is likely that especially the expanded projects are relying more on Cambodia's cheap, abundant labour, while keeping the use of capital relatively constant.

The role of FDI in Cambodia's economic development
There has been an intense debate on the role of FDI in economic development in recipient countries, especially in developing economies. The entry of MNEs may produce both positive and negative impacts on the host country (Lall, 1995). For example, more competition brought about by FDI activities may induce local firms to become more efficient and may provide spillovers in skills, management techniques or technical knowledge. However, the presence of foreign firms may also drive indigenous firms out of business due to strong competition or unfair practices.

Although there are also costs associated with inward FDI, it is generally agreed that it brings into the recipient countries badly needed capital, new forms of technology, superior managerial skills and international marketing techniques, all of which are often referred to as spillover effects and externalities. In most cases, FDI transfers are not limited to the inflow of productive capital and managerial skills, but also include embodied and tacit knowledge and technology (Wei, 2003). FDI activities create job opportunities and skill upgrading of local workers, and can reinforce the export competitiveness of the host country. The impact of inward FDI on the host country ranges from economic effects (e.g. productivity increases, employment creation, trade links, poverty reduction) to more general effects (such as those on society, politics and the environment) (see, e.g., Ietto-Gillies, 2005). Here, however, the focus is on a conceptual discussion of the economic effects of FDI.

FDI and technology transfers
FDI may raise the productivity of domestically owned firms by improving resource allocation or by putting competitive pressure on local firms to imitate, to innovate or to produce at higher levels of technical efficiency (Leibenstein, 1966; Li et al., 2001; Wei, 2003). The presence of MNEs may help to speed up the process of technology transfer and lower the cost of such transfers. Imitation, demonstration and contagion effects, along with increased mobility of employees from multinational subsidiaries to domestically owned firms, may form additional routes for inducing transfers of technology. Employees trained by foreign firms may also decide to start their own businesses at a later stage in their career, thereby increasing entrepreneurship in the host country.

Studies about the technology transfer induced by FDI in Cambodia are extremely

Table 11.10   Level of technology in a sample of foreign firms in Cambodia

Technological level	Number of firms	% of total
Low	14	23
Medium	27	45
High	19	32
Total	60	100

Source: Chap (2005), p. 90.

scarce. A firm-level survey carried out by Chap (2005) and based on 60 companies indicated that the technology transfers mainly occurred as imports of technology embedded in machines and the introduction of foreign management teams. About one-quarter of the surveyed firms used only low technology, while almost half employed a medium level of technology and a third relied on a high level of technology (Table 11.10).[29] An interesting finding is that all surveyed firms provided training to their local personnel, ranging from one week to more than three months, and that a number of trained workers later found better jobs or started up their own businesses. USAID (2005) and Yamagata (2006) also stated that training is often provided to local employees in the export-oriented garment industry, which is largely owned by foreign investors. However, to better assess technology transfers or productivity spillovers from FDI in Cambodia, an in-depth analysis of firm-level data is required.

FDI and international trade
FDI is often believed to positively affect the host country's international trade patterns, and is usually considered as an engine for economic development and growth. If the FDI home country is relatively well endowed with capital while the host country is relatively labour abundant, this implies that the return on capital will be lower in the FDI home country. Therefore firms from the capital-rich country will engage in international production by exporting intermediate inputs and capital-intensive services to their foreign affiliates in the labour-rich country in return for differentiated finished products (Wei, 2003).

As was indicated above, the majority of FDI in Cambodia is foreign-market-seeking/exported-oriented FDI,[30] and the garment industry is proportionately attracting most of Cambodia's FDI inflows. Further circumstantial evidence on the impact of FDI can be found in Figure 11.4, which shows Cambodia's garment and textile exports as a percentage of total commodity exports. Following Cambodia's liberalization policy with respect to foreign investment and international trade in 1994, exports of apparel goods and textiles increased enormously, i.e. from about 12 per cent of Cambodia's total exports of commodity products in 1994 to 83 per cent in 2001.

An attempt to investigate the relationship between FDI and international trade in Cambodia was undertaken by Neak (2005). Using a gravity model with panel data on bilateral trade between Cambodia and FDI home countries, Neak established that FDI had a positive impact on the volume of trade. Another investigation into the FDI–international trade relationship at the sectoral level in Cambodia by Cuyvers et al. (2006) confirmed that FDI is positively related to international trade. Data at the level of the

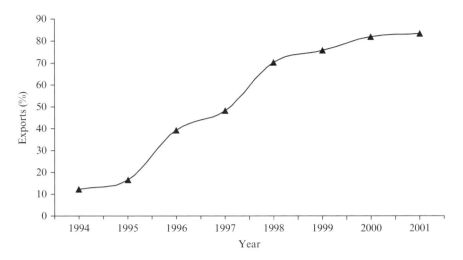

*Figure 11.4   Exports of garments and textiles as percentage of Cambodia's total
            commodity exports, 1994–2001*

firm or the product should permit an even more revealing examination of the relationship between international trade and FDI.

FDI and Cambodia's capital formation
FDI is expected to have a positive effect on a host country's capital formation. FDI
can take place either through mergers and acquisitions (M&As) of existing firms or via
greenfield establishments. Lall (1995) and Ietto-Gillies (2005, p. 26) indicate, however,
that because greenfield investments create new production units they are more likely
to lead to new productive capacity for the host country's economy. Depending on the
restructuring measures that are carried out in case of the takeover of existing firms, an
increase in capacity is less certain to occur. However, this distinction is less relevant
for Cambodia, as the large majority of foreign subsidiaries are greenfield investments,
especially in the manufacturing sector,[31] where they are encouraged by the availability of
abundant and cheap land, as well as inexpensive construction workers.

   Table 11.11 presents realized FDI in fixed assets as a percentage of Cambodia's annual
total fixed capital formation. Over the years shown, the fixed capital created by FDI
inflows ranged between 7 and 51 per cent of the country's fixed capital formation. On
average, the annual contribution of FDI to the Cambodian capital formation was about
21 per cent with a standard deviation of 13 per cent over the period 1994–2004. Thus
FDI has undoubtedly added to the available fixed capital stock of the country and in
turn improved productivity as labour had more capital to work with.

FDI, employment and poverty reduction
In 2004 the Cambodian labour force was estimated to be about 7.5 million people out of
a population of 13.5 million. While in 1994 only 0.17 per cent worked in foreign-owned
firms, this share went up to 1.74 per cent in 1997, 3.16 per cent in 2001 and reached 5.2
per cent in 2004.

Table 11.11   Realized FDI as percentage of Cambodia's total capital formation,
1994–2004

Year	Realized FDI in fixed assets (US$ millions)	Total fixed capital formation* (US$ millions)	% of FDI in total fixed capital formation
1994	24.90	323.49	7.70
1995	508.86	987.89	51.51
1996	244.76	689.10	35.52
1997	96.50	558.44	17.28
1998	152.59	539.09	28.31
1999	116.55	678.61	17.18
2000	158.89	828.10	19.19
2001	128.50	760.76	16.89
2002	59.36	862.48	6.88
2003	84.99	923.40	9.20
2004	201.89	1129.71	17.87

Note: * Total fixed capital formation is equal to realized FDI in fixed assets plus domestic fixed capital formation. Data on domestic fixed capital formation were obtained from the World Development Indicators CD-ROM (2007).

Source: Cambodian Investment Board and World Development Indicators (2007).

The relationship between FDI and employment has been debated quite extensively in the recent literature (see Lall, 1995; UNCTAD, 1994, 1999, 2000, 2004, 2006). For example, the *World Investment Report* (UNCTAD, 1994) acknowledged that MNEs account for about one-fifth of employment in non-agricultural activities in developed countries and some developing economies, implying that MNEs directly contribute to employment in manufacturing and services. MNEs also indirectly generate employment through several channels (e.g. subcontractors, suppliers and other service enterprises) in the home and host countries. Firms that are vertically linked to MNEs, including subcontractors, buyers and suppliers, will generally generate a positive effect on employment if the investors increase the demand for local inputs and services and raise their sales (Lall, 1995). Closer linkages with local suppliers can be an important vehicle for technology diffusion, skill improvement and export market penetration, all of which increase the volume of trade and generate local employment.

It is generally accepted that FDI is a powerful catalyst for economic growth in developing countries and that economic growth may in turn play an important role in poverty reduction (Zhang, 2006). FDI may have a positive impact on growth due to a number of factors, such as FDI-induced enhancement of capital formation and employment augmentation; expansion of manufacturing exports; and technology transfers and spillover effects on locally owned firms. Based on the belief that FDI helps reduce poverty both directly and indirectly, the governments of developing countries have made great efforts to attract FDI, in addition to their attempts to alleviate poverty. Cambodia is no exception. Of course, for FDI to be successful in reducing poverty, it must have trickle-down effects on the poorest sections of the population.

The growing literature on the positive impact of FDI on employment, which may in turn contribute to reducing poverty in the host country, has inspired a certain amount of research on the linkages, particularly in developing ASEAN nations. Based on their previous econometric study on the ASEAN region, Mirza and Giroud (2004) established that FDI has been poverty reducing in the region and that the effect of FDI on poverty reduction has been stronger than elsewhere. Freeman (2004) has endorsed those findings. More recently Zhang (2006) has used a growth model with Chinese cross-sectional and panel data at the provincial level and found that FDI indeed plays a crucial role in promoting the country's economic growth and therefore poverty reduction. In contrast, after a review of empirical studies, Mold (2004) was not convinced by the available evidence that FDI was an important instrument for poverty reduction.

In Cambodia, manufacturing attracted the lion's share of total inward FDI from 1994 to 2004, with the labour-intensive, export-oriented garment industry as the most attractive sector to foreign investors. While the success of the garment industry in terms of FDI attractiveness and the competitiveness of the industry has been explained as the result of the country being the beneficiary of the Multifibre Arrangement (MFA), some authors have pointed out that the garment industry in Cambodia is likely to remain internationally competitive even after the Multifibre Arrangement is phased out (Bargawi, 2005; Yamagata, 2006, 2007). Cambodia's garment exports might be considered as an example of FDI's positive contribution to poverty reduction, via exports and employment creation. The World Bank (2006) has reported that poverty in Cambodia has fallen by 10–15 per cent over the period 1994–2004, i.e. during the period that FDI started to flow into the country.

In his field survey of Cambodia's garment companies, Yamagata (2006) found evidence that the garment industry significantly contributes to poverty reduction in the country, since the industry provides employment at relatively high wages for the Cambodian poor, most of whom come from the underdeveloped rural areas. Yamagata confirmed that the garment industry does not require high levels of education from its workers and that promotion of the workers to higher skill levels is relatively easy. This means that the garment industry offers the opportunity to earn a higher income, and makes it possible to achieve a higher standard of living.

In a simple regression analysis of time-series data with nine to ten observations to investigate the extent to which FDI affected poverty reduction, Hing and Tuot (2007) found that Cambodia's inward FDI is an important source of the country's economic growth and employment generation, but indicate that the impact is limited, and not enough for rapid poverty reduction. However, their results may suffer from the limited number of observations and misspecification problems. Therefore an econometric study with a larger number of observations and more control variables is needed before more definite conclusions can be drawn.

Development of Cambodia's competitive advantages according to Porter's diamond

From Cambodia's example, it is clear that Porter's views on the determinants of the competitive advantage of industries (Porter, 1990) have either to be amended, or otherwise lead to the conclusion that Cambodia's success in attracting FDI, particularly in the garment sector, does not contribute to the building up of the country's competitive advantages. Following the typical facets of Porter's diamond analysis, the contribution to the development of Cambodia's competitive advantages will be assessed by looking at the factor conditions, the demand conditions, the local company rivalries and the supporting industries.

Evidently, many of Cambodia's factor conditions offer a solid foundation for the building up of competitive advantage. The vast pool of low-skilled workers, including female workers, has been a very attractive factor for the development of Cambodia's garment and textile sectors. Female workers are preferred in the garment factories in the country and account for a large share of total employment in the industry (Yamagata, 2006). In the case of tourism, the preponderance of a low-skilled labour force can, however, act in a negative way as international or regional tourists expect well-trained personnel and staff in the hotels. However, such negative effects can partly and gradually be offset as more Cambodians may receive on-the-job training (tourist managers, tour guides, chefs etc.) and enrol in English-language courses before being appointed in a job where contact with foreign visitors is essential. Obviously, the old Khmer temple complexes in Siem Reap and in other provinces, the unspoiled beaches at the seaside in Sihanoukville and the French colonial buildings in Phnom Penh, major provincial towns and many other historical sites, as 'historically produced' factor conditions, more than balance the likely disadvantage of Cambodia's tourism sector with respect to its low-skilled labour force. The garment and textile industry is, to a large extent, dependent on the availability of a reserve of cheap unskilled labour.

Local demand in a less-developed country can hardly be considered as a factor contributing to the development of competitive advantage. Demand in the sectors that have attracted the bulk of Cambodia's FDI does not emanate from the local market and is basically global demand. This is definitely the case for the sectors of garments and textiles, and also for the tourism and transportation sectors. Yet, in a quickly integrating region such as Southeast and East Asia, regional demand should also be taken into consideration as an important determinant, even though the regional dimension may be somewhat more relevant for tourism than for garments and textiles. However, in the latter case one should not forget the growing role of globalization and the 'slicing up' of the value chain. For Cambodia's garments the major outlet is the vast world market. Cambodia's competitive advantage, according to this factor, derives from its status as a 'less-developed country' and the special advantages it receives in the 'everything but arms scheme' and the generalized system of preferences of the industrialized countries, which make products of Cambodian origin eligible for duty and quota-free access to these markets, unlike the same products from more developed Asian countries, such as China.

In order to illustrate the role of the international market in the development of Cambodia's competitive advantage, the levels and changes over time in Balassa's revealed comparative advantage (RCA) index at the sectoral level can be used. A comparison with the RCA in other ASEAN countries, which are the natural competitors of Cambodia, reveals that Cambodia has a strong comparative advantage in the garment industry over all its ASEAN counterparts, Laos–Myanmar–Vietnam, ASEAN-9, and the rest of the world (Cuyvers et al., 2006). In contrast, Cambodia has a comparative advantage only in textile production relative to Myanmar and Lao PDR from 1992 and 1996 onwards, and it even experiences a comparative disadvantage relative to Vietnam, ASEAN-9 and the rest of the world in this sector. In tourism, Cambodia has a strong comparative advantage over some ASEAN counterparts, Laos–Myanmar–Vietnam, ASEAN-8 and the rest of the world, except Indonesia and Lao PDR. Estimation results of the impact of inward FDI on RCA, on total international trade (exports plus imports) and on exports and imports separately, of the textile, garments and tourism sectors have been reported by Cuyvers et al. (2006) for the period 1994–2001. They show that a 1 per cent increase in the FDI stock in the garment sector leads to a statistically significant increase of 1.10 per cent, 1.55 per cent, 1.15 per cent, 1.09 per cent in RCA, international trade position, relative exports and relative imports in the sector. Consequently, it can be concluded that inward FDI in the garment sector has had an important impact on overall international trade volumes, but that the net impact on the sector's external trade balance is only slightly positive. This should be kept in mind when the role of supporting industries is discussed. On the other hand, Cuyvers et al. (2006) found no statistically significant impact of changes in the FDI stock in the tourism sector on the sector's RCA, or external service trade volumes, which means that the existing international demand for tourism is not affected by FDI in the sector.

According to Porter (1990), one of the determinants of a national competitive advantage depends on the way in which firms are created and managed, and on domestic rivalry. Domestic rivalry plays an important role in the process of innovation and firms' efficiency for international success. In the case of Cambodia, firms, especially garment companies, were created by 'chance events' (Porter, 1990, pp. 124–5). The garment industry developed in Cambodia after quota restrictions were imposed by the USA and other developed countries on garment exports of some other Asian countries, particularly China. The majority of the garment and textile firms in the country are owned by investors from China, Taiwan and Hong Kong. Local rivalry is limited locally, but is fierce with other garment exporters, as Cambodia's garments are highly export oriented (see Cuyvers et al., 2006). Domestic investment in the garment sector has been relatively low, but has started to rise gradually in the form of wholly owned companies or joint ventures with foreign investors. The tourism industry shares some similarities with the garment sector, as it started to develop after the national election of 1993 when Cambodia was finally at peace. Both domestic and foreign investment is attracted to the tourist sector as demand for its services comes from both domestic and foreign markets. Local rivalry is likely to be stronger, as evidenced by the higher level of investment in the sector by Cambodians. This stimulates service improvement, which in turn creates further factor demand, and positively affects the country's 'diamond'.

A weak facet of Cambodia's 'diamond' seems to be the lack of development of supporting industries. This seems especially true for garments and textiles, where the industrial cluster is lacking important subsectors. Activities such as the production of textile machinery, the development and application of design patterns, production of basic raw materials etc. remain marginal in terms of both upstream and downstream initiatives. For instance, most of the cloth for garment production in Cambodia is usually imported from other Asian countries, in particular China, Hong Kong and Taiwan. The lack of supporting industries can also be illustrated by the estimation results of Cuyvers et al. (2006), where it was found that a 1 per cent increase in the FDI stock in the garment sector leads to increases of 1.15 per cent and 1.09 per cent in relative exports and relative imports in the sector, which implies that the net impact on the sector's external trade balance is only slightly positive. Yet inward FDI in the garment sector has had an important impact on overall international trade volumes (exports and imports) of the sector.

The lack of supporting industries for garments may be partly explained by the fact that both foreign and local investment in the textile sector has been low according to unpublished data from the Cambodian Board of Investment. Infrastructure, especially irrigation systems for agriculture and raw material production, is also underdeveloped. Investment, both local and foreign, in relatively capital-intensive infrastructure is negligible (Cuyvers et al., 2006). There is an important role to be played by the Cambodian government here in creating a sustainable, competitive advantage for the country. For example, public investment in infrastructure (paving roads, developing irrigation systems etc.) can further influence factor demand and attract more private investment. Government policies to improve the quality of education, to stimulate fair competition, to develop efficient capital markets and the like are important for shaping its 'diamond'. In the tourism cluster there are more linkages (restaurants, passenger transportation, and the government's 'open skies' policy, which allows direct international flights to Siem Reap). Moreover, as estimation results by Cuyvers et al. (2006) show, there exist significant and positive effects on RCA, international flows of trade and services and exports, meaning that local transportation services are substituting for imports of transportation services.[32]

Concluding remarks

Cambodia became an attractive destination for FDI after the kingdom's first national election of 1993, which resulted in a transformation of centrally managed socialism, first of the Khmer Rouge regime, then of the Prime Minister Hun Sen-led government, by opening up the Cambodian economy to the rest of the world and to globalization. Inward FDI increased substantially in 1995, but dropped afterwards because of the instability created by factional fighting between the ruling political parties, and also because of the indirect negative effects of the Asian economic crisis of 1997, the effect of which was confirmed by Cuyvers et al. (2008).

Although the EU, the USA and Japan are the largest direct investors in the world (Zhang, 2005), the major sources of inward FDI in Cambodia are ASEAN member nations and other Asian economies, in particular Malaysia, Taiwan and China. Cambodia got only about 8 per cent of its inward FDI in fixed assets over the period 1994–2004 from the USA, compared to 37 per cent from Malaysia, 12 per cent from Taiwan and 9 per cent from China. At the very start of the liberalization of the economy, foreign investors relied most frequently on Cambodian–foreign joint ventures as their mode of entry. However, the popularity of this mode quickly vaporized and wholly foreign-owned FDI became foreign firms' preferred mode of entry into the Cambodian economy.

The sectoral distribution of inward FDI in Cambodia is dominated on the one hand by the labour-intensive garment and textile industry with almost one-third of the total, and on the other hand by the service sector, e.g. the hotel and restaurant business, with about one-fifth of the total, and transportation (15.5 per cent). This sector's attraction is derived primarily from Cambodia's rich cultural heritage and touristic sites. FDI in manufacturing is strongly concentrated in the capital city Phnom Penh and in the surrounding Kandal province, which hosted 92 per cent of Cambodia's approved inward

FDI in terms of employment. Most of the hotels and restaurants are located in Siem Reap, because of its proximity to the country's major tourist attractions. The government's efforts to encourage FDI activities in other industries, such as agriculture and infrastructure, have not been successful. The extremely uneven geographical distribution of inward FDI coincides with the spread of the overall economic activity of the country and is related to the absence of skilled workers, and the lack of basic services such as infrastructure, security, communication and transportation in the rest of the country.

In a certain sense, the development of Cambodia's industries, in particular the garment and textile sector, happened by 'chance' (Porter, 1990). Inward FDI flows into those sectors occurred when the exports of garments by more advanced Asian countries, e.g. China, were confronted with trade barriers (quotas) in the industrial countries. In a way this resulted in the 'discovery' of the competitive advantage of Cambodia's garment and textile industries, i.e. the large reserve of low-cost, unskilled labour, by foreign companies that could no longer export directly to the markets of the EU or the USA. Because of its status as a less developed country in the 'everything but arms scheme' and the generalized system of preferences of the industrialized nations, Cambodia became a platform exporter. The competitive advantages of the tourism sector are clearly based on Cambodia's cultural heritage, which holds considerable potential for further expansion of the supporting industries of transportation, restaurants and hotels.

There are indications of technology transfers by foreign firms in Cambodia, mainly through the use of sophisticated imported machinery and on-the-job training programmes. The contribution of FDI to Cambodia's capital stock has on average been estimated to reach 21 per cent of capital formation in fixed assets during 1994–2004. Exports of the garment and textile sectors, which have attracted substantial FDI, increased steadily during the same period.

FDI is generally believed to generate employment in the host country, at least if the crowding-out effects do not surpass the crowding-in effects. Between 1994 and 2004, inward FDI in Cambodia generated 390 000 jobs. Assuming that during this period no disinvestments and job losses occurred in foreign-owned firms, employment in foreign subsidiaries represented 5 per cent of the Cambodian labour force. Two studies (Hing and Tuot, 2007; Yamagata, 2006) have confirmed the significant contribution of FDI activities to employment creation and consequently also to poverty reduction in Cambodia. The World Bank (2006) acknowledged that the poverty rate in Cambodia dropped by 10 to 15 per cent during 1994–2004. Given the creation of employment and its contribution to the country's GDP and exports, FDI has contributed significantly to the economy of this civil-war-ravaged kingdom though multiplier and spillover effects. More jobs and income might have been realized, however, if all approved FDI had materialized.

Notes

1. The authors are grateful for the detailed and unpublished data from the Project Monitoring Department, the Cambodian Investment Board (CIB) and the Council for the Development of Cambodia (CDC).
2. The distinction between approved FDI and realized FDI is based on the fact that investment projects are not necessarily realized in the same year in which they are approved. Some authorized investment projects may be postponed or may not be implemented at all.
3. See Cambodia's Law on Investment (1994) or the text below for more details about the availability of incentives for approved investment projects.
4. Yet the disagreements and sporadic disputes that arose between the two ruling parties, i.e. the Cambodian People's Party (CPP) and the FUNCINPEC, led to an armed conflict in the centre of the capital city

Phnom Penh in July 1997. The factional fighting scared away both established and potential foreign investors. FUNCINPEC is referred to as 'Front Uni National Pour un Cambodge Indépendent, Neutre, Pacifique et Coopératif' (in English, 'National United Front for an Independent, Neutral, Peaceful and Cooperative Cambodia').

5. After the Khmer Rouge regime was overthrown in January 1979 with the help of the Vietnamese, Cambodia's economy became strictly controlled. It started to liberalize its economy only in 1985, but a more far-reaching liberalization was not realized until 1989, at the time the Vietnamese troops finally left the country (Hing, 2003, p. 12). See also Gottesman (2004).

6. Lao PDR's corporate tax is 20–35 per cent, Myanmar 30 per cent, Thailand 30 per cent and Vietnam 10-20 per cent (Hing, 2003, p. 58).

7. Some countries had very small amounts of investment in fixed assets during 1994–2004.

8. Cambodian Investment Board (CIB), Cambodian Investment Statistics 1994–2004, unpublished data.

9. Dollars have become the major currency used in daily business transactions while the national currency, the riel, is used mainly for very small transactions, especially in the rural areas of Cambodia (Kang, 2005).

10. East and Southeast Asian economies include Hong Kong, Taiwan, Korea, Singapore, Malaysia, the Philippines, Indonesia and Thailand.

11. In contrast, using augmented gravity models, more recent studies do not find support for the claims that Mainland China has diverted FDI from its Asian developing countries (Eichengreen and Tong, 2007; Liu et al., 2007).

12. See note 2.

13. Some authors argue that the motivation for China's rapid and expanding investment in Southeast Asia, e.g. Cambodia, may be due to political rather than economic factors. These political factors include the establishment of formal diplomatic relations between China and Cambodia and the building up of regional alliances to counter US influences (Frost et al., 2002).

14. A number of empirical papers found evidence that the rise of China stimulated investments in its Asian neighbours (Eichengreen and Tong, 2007; Liu et al., 2007; Zhou and Lall, 2005). This may be due to the emergence of China leading to an increase in China's demand for raw materials from other countries. Therefore, a country endowed with resources may be attractive to China's investment. However, none of these studies included Cambodia in their calculations.

15. The ASEAN member countries investing in Cambodia include Malaysia, Indonesia, Singapore, the Philippines, Thailand and Vietnam.

16. Wholly foreign-owned enterprises include investment projects owned by only one foreign investor and those owned by multiple foreign investors.

17. This sharp increase was due to an approval of a big investment project from Malaysia.

18. During that year, an armed conflict between the two ruling parties – CPP and FUNCINPEC – broke out in the centre of the capital city, and most certainly scared away some potential and existing foreign investors.

19. Any dispute relating to a promoted investment established in Cambodia should be settled through consultation between the disputing parties. In case of failure to reach a settlement within two months, the dispute shall be brought by either party for consultation before the Council for opinion or referring the matter to the court of Cambodia or to any international rules (Kingdom of Cambodia, 1994).

20. This sample size represented 84 per cent of total garment firms registered with the Garment Manufacturers' Association in Cambodia – the only association of garment manufacturers in the country.

21. A more detailed discussion of the application of Porter's diamond concept to the situation in Cambodia is provided below.

22. Bargawi (2005) argues that the emergence of the garment industry in Cambodia in the mid-1990s is mainly attributable to quotas imposed by the USA on some Asian garment exporters, particularly China, who then launched their quota-jumping investment in Cambodia with no quota restriction. According to this reasoning, the low wage rate in Cambodia is a secondary factor encouraging inward FDI into the country.

23. Banteay Meanchey, Battambang, Kampong Cham, Kampong Chhnang, Kampong Speu, Kampong Thom, Kampot, Kandal, Kep, Koh Kong, Kratie, Mondolkiri, Oddar Meanchey, Pailin, Phnom Penh, Preah Vihear, Prey Veng, Pursat, Rattanakiri, Siem Reap, Sihanoukville/Kampong Som, Stung Treng, Svay Rieng, and Takeo. Kep is in Kampot province. However, FDI for Kep and for Kampot are separated by CIB/CDC.

24. Some provinces, such as Kampong Chhnang, Kratie, Mondolkiri, Oddar Meanchey, Pailin (formerly part of Battambang Province), Preah Vihear, Prey Veng and Stung Treng, did not manage to attract any FDI during 1994–2004.

25. Personal e-mail correspondence with the Deputy Director of the Project Monitoring Department, Cambodian Investment Board, Council for the Development of Cambodia.

26. In some provinces in Cambodia, people face a shortage of drinking water due to drought. For instance, cattle died because of lack of water in the remote areas of the Kompong Speu province (Radio Free Asia, 2005).
27. The Cambodian government defines the poverty line as the sum of the minimum food and non-food expenditure. The 'food poverty' line per capita per day is 2100 kcal, and the 'non-food poverty line' per person per day is 2470 riels for Phnom Penh, 2093 riels for the provincial capitals, and 1777 riels for the rural areas (the riel is the national currency in Cambodia). The population under the poverty line is defined as poor and represents 36 per cent of the population (head count index) in 1999 (Japan Bank for International Cooperation, 2001, http://www.jbic.go.jp/english/oec/environ/poverty/pdf/cambodia_e. pdf).
28. Expanded investments are included in the active investment projects, and no separate data on expanded investment projects are available (Project Evaluating Department, CDC).
29. A low level of technology is defined as the 'use of labour or work by hand', while the medium level refers to 'semi-computerized and semi-automatic' production processes, and high level is interpreted as 'high-tech, automatic and computerized operations'.
30. Data on 50 firms were obtained from the Project Monitoring Department, Cambodian Investment Board. On average, the exports of these firms represent more than 90 per cent of their total output.
31. The *World Development Report 1999/2000* (World Bank, 2000) notes that M&As are rare in both developing economies and economies in transition.
32. However, it should be mentioned that such an import substitution effect is found only when changes in the stock of FDI are considered.

References

ADB (Asian Development Bank) (2006), *The Mekong Region: Foreign Direct Investment*, Manila.
Ballard, B.M. (2007), 'Major development trends', in B.M. Ballard (ed.), *Annual Development Review 2006–2007*, Phnom Penh: Cambodian Development Resource Institute.
Bargawi, O. (2005), 'Cambodia's garment industry: origins and future prospects', ESUA Working Paper No. 13, London: Overseas Development Institute.
Blomström, M., A. Kokko and M. Zejan (2000), *Foreign Direct Investment. Firm and Host Country Strategies*, London: Macmillan.
CDC (Council for the Development of Cambodia) (2007), *Cambodia Investment Guidebook*, Phnom Penh: Japan International Cooperation Agency (JICA).
Chantasasawat, B., K.C. Fung and A. Siu (2003), 'International competition for foreign direct investment: the case of China', paper prepared for Hitotsubashi Conference on International Trade and FDI, 12–14 December, http://www.econ.hit-u.ac.jp/~trade/2003/papers/KCFung_ChinaFDIdiversion.pdf
Chantasasawat, B., K.C. Fung, H. Izawa and A. Siu (2005), 'Foreign direct investment in East Asia and Latin America: is there a People's Republic of China effect', ADB Institute Research Paper Series No. 66.
Chap, S. (2005), 'Foreign direct investment and technology transfer in Cambodia', unpublished PhD thesis, University of Sydney.
CIB (Cambodian Investment Board) (2005), 'Cambodian Investment Statistics', unpublished data, Phnom Penh.
Cuyvers, L., R. Soeng and D. Van Den Bulcke (2006), 'Foreign direct investment and the development of less developed countries: the case of Cambodia's garment, textiles, furniture, tourism and transportation sectors', CAS Discussion Paper No. 49, Centre for ASEAN Studies, Antwerp, University of Antwerp.
Cuyvers, L., J. Plasmans, R. Soeng and D. Van Den Bulcke (2008), 'Determinants of foreign direct investment in Cambodia: country-specific factor differentials', Research paper no. 2008–003, Faculty of Applied Economics, University of Antwerp.
EIC (Economic Institute of Cambodia) (2006), *Assessment of Corruption in Cambodia's Private Sector*, Phnom Penh: EIC.
EIC (Economic Institute of Cambodia) (2007), *Cambodia's Garment Industry Post Agreement on Textile and Clothing (Post-ATC): Human Development Impact Assessment*, Phnom Penh: EIC.
Eichengreen, B. and H. Tong (2007), 'Is China's FDI coming at the expense of other countries?', *Journal of the Japanese and International Economies*, **21** (2), 153–72.
Freeman, N.J. (2002), 'Foreign investment in Cambodia, Lao, and Vietnam: a regional overview', paper presented at Conference on Foreign Direct Investment: Opportunities and Challenges for Cambodia, Lao and Vietnam, 16–17 August, Hanoi.
Freeman, N.J. (2004), 'Harnessing foreign direct investment for economic development and poverty reduction: lessons from Vietnam', *Journal of the Asia Pacific Economy*, **9** (2), 209–22.
Frost, S., S. Pandita and K. Hewison (2002), 'The implications for labor of China's direct investment in Cambodia', *Asian Perspective*, **26** (4), 201–26.

Fujita, M., P. Krugman and A.J. Venables (1999), *The Spatial Economy: Cities, Regions, and International Trade*, Cambridge, MA: MIT Press.
Gottesman, E. (2004), *Cambodia after the Khmer Rouge*, Chiang Mai: Silkworm Books.
Hagemann, R.P. (2002), 'Comments', Conference on Foreign Direct Investment: Opportunities and Challenges for Cambodia, Lao and Vietnam, 16–17 August, Hanoi.
Hing, T. (2003), *Cambodia's Investment Potential: Challenges and Prospects*, Phnom Penh: Japan International Cooperation Agency (JICA).
Hing, T. (2006), *Cambodia Investment Challenges in Global Competitiveness*, Phnom Penh: Japan International Cooperation Agency (JICA).
Hing, V. and S. Tuot (2007), 'Foreign direct investment and poverty reduction in Cambodia', in B.M. Ballard (ed.), *Annual Development Review 2006–2007*, Phnom Penh: Cambodia Development Resource Institute, pp. 65–84.
Ietto-Gillies, G. (2005), *Transnational Corporations and International Production*, Cheltenham, UK and Northampton, MA, USA: Edward Elgar.
Kang, K. (2005), 'Is dollarization good for Cambodia?', *Cambodian Economic Review*, 1, 85–98.
Kingdom of Cambodia (1994), *Investment Law*, http://www.cambodiainvestment.gov.kh/cam/cambodiafiles/userfiles/file/Investment_law.pdf, retrieved March 2008.
Kingdom of Cambodia (2003), *Investment Law*, http://www.cambodiainvestment.gov.kh/cam/cambodiafiles/userfiles/file/Investment_law.pdf, retrieved March 2008.
Lall, S. (1995), 'Employment and foreign investment: policy options for developing countries', *International Labour Review*, **134** (4–5), 521–40.
Leibenstein, H. (1966), 'Allocative efficiency vs. X-efficiency', *American Economic Review*, **56**, 392–415.
Li, X., X. Liu and D. Parker (2001), 'Foreign direct investment and productivity spillovers in the Chinese manufacturing sector', *Economic Systems*, **25**, 305–21.
Liu, L., K. Chow and U. Li (2007), 'Has China crowded out foreign direct investment from its developing East Asian neighbours?', *China and World Economy*, **15** (3), 70–88.
Ministry of Planning (2006), *Statistical Yearbook 2006*, Phnom Penh: Ministry of Planning.
Mirza, H. and A. Giroud (2004), 'Regionalization, foreign direct investment and poverty reduction: lessons from Vietnam in ASEAN', *Journal of the Asia Pacific Economy*, **9** (2), 223–48.
Mold, A. (2004), 'FDI and poverty reduction: a critical reappraisal of the arguments', *Région et Développement*, **20**, 91–121.
Navaretti, G.B. and A.J. Venables (2004), *Multinational Firms in the World Economy*, Princeton NJ: Princeton University Press.
Neak, S. (2005), 'FDI and trade in Cambodia: substitutes or complements?', *Cambodian Economic Review*, 1, 99–112.
Porter, M.E. (1990), *The Competitive Advantage of Nations*, New York: The Free Press.
So, S., L. Sovannara and N. Keosothea (2007), 'Labour migration in rural livelihoods: challenges and opportunities', in B.M. Ballard (ed.), *Annual Development Review 2006–2007*, Phnom Penh: Cambodia Development Resource Institute, pp. 149–69.
Sok, H. (2005), 'Labor force, incomes and poverty', *Cambodia Economic Watch II*, Phnom Penh: Economic Institute of Cambodia.
Tongzon, J.L. (2001), *The Economics of Southeast Asia*, Cheltenham, UK and Northampton, MA, USA: Edward Elgar.
Transparency International (2007), *Report on the Transparency International Global Corruption Barometer 2007*, mimeo, 6 December, Berlin: Transparency International.
UNCTAD (1994), *World Investment Report: Transnational Corporations, Employment and Workplace*, New York and Geneva: United Nations.
UNCTAD (1999), Press Release, 'Despite disparate performance in 1998, FDI flows into the five most seriously crisis affected countries in Asia as a group remained resilient', http://www.unctad.org/Templates/webflyer.asp?docid=3104&intItemID=2021&lang=1, retrieved March 2008.
UNCTAD (2000), *World Investment Report: Cross-Border Mergers and Acquisitions and Development*, New York and Geneva: United Nations.
UNCTAD (2004), *World Investment Report: The Shift towards Services*, New York and Geneva: United Nations.
UNCTAD (2005), *Handbook of Statistics*, New York and Geneva: United Nations.
UNCTAD (2006), *World Investment Report. FDI from Developing and Transition Economies: Implications for Development*, New York and Geneva: United Nations.
USAID (US Agency for International Development) (2005), *Measuring Competitiveness and Labor Productivity in Cambodia's Garment Industry*, report prepared by Natha Associates, Inc.
Wei, Y. (2003), 'Foreign direct investment in China: a survey', LUMS Working Paper 2003/002, Lancaster University Management School.

World Bank (2000), *World Development Report 1999/2000*, http://www.worldbank.org/wdr/2000/fullreport.html, retrieved March 2008.

World Bank (2004), *Cambodia – Seizing the Global Opportunity: Investment Climate Assessment and Reform Strategy for Cambodia*, Report No. 27925-KH, Washington.

World Bank (2006), *Cambodia – Halving Poverty in 2015?: Poverty Assessment 2006*, Report No. 35213-KH, East Asia and the Pacific Region, Washington.

Yamagata, T. (2006), 'The garment industry in Cambodia: its role in poverty reduction through export-oriented development', IDE Discussion Paper No. 62, Institute of Developing Economies.

Yamagata, T. (2007), 'Prospects for development of the garment industry in developing countries: what has happened since the MFA phase-out?', Discussion Paper No. 101, Institute of Developing Economies.

Zhang, H.K. (2005), 'Why does so much FDI from Hong Kong and Taiwan go to Mainland China?', *China Economic Review*, **16** (3), 293–307.

Zhang, H.K. (2006), 'Does international investment help poverty reduction in China?', *Chinese Economy*, **39** (3), 79–90.

Zhou, Y. and S. Lall (2005), 'The impact of China's FDI surge on FDI in South-East Asia: panel data analysis for 1986–2001', *Transnational Corporations*, **14** (1), 41–65.

Index

ABN AMRO 18
Aegon 18
Agfa Gevaert 42
agriculture
  Cambodia 254
  Chile
    salmon industry 180–82, 183–4, 190–93
    wine industry 172, 177–80, 183, 184
  Ireland 52
  Mauritius sugar industry 195, 214
  Netherlands 14, 15, 25
  New Zealand forestry 222–8
Ahold 18
Aker 145
Akzo 12, 18
Amsden, A. 76
Andean Pact 185
Antwerp port 31, 44
Apple 78, 81
Austria 110, 111

banking sector, Netherlands 19
Bartlett, C.A. 156, 157
Belgium 4, 7, 30, 45
  clusters 41–2
    life sciences 42–5
  data 35–6, 48
  economy 30–35
  ownership characteristics of companies
    36–9
  Transnationality Index (TNI) 2
Bernard, A.B. 39
biotechnology, Belgium 42–3
Brazil 186

Cambodia 7, 8
  competitive advantages 264–7
  foreign direct investment (FDI) 244–5,
    267–8
    approved versus realized FDI 258–60
    business environment 245–8
    capital formation and 262
    economic development and 260–64
    employment/poverty reduction and
      262–4
    international trade and 261–2
    origins 248–50
    provincial distribution 256–8

sectoral distribution 253–6
technology transfer and 260–61
types of FDI 250–52
Canada 5–6, 154–5, 167–8
  motivations for foreign direct investment
    (FDI) 157, 160–61
  regional context 155–6
  research methodology 159
  subsidiary companies 157–8, 161–3
    comparisons 163–5
    regional integration and 159, 165–7
  survey 159–67
  Transnationality Index (TNI) 3
Cantwell, J. 138
Carlsberg 144
Casema 19
Chap, S. 252
chemicals sector
  Belgium 43–5
  Netherlands 25
  see also pharmaceuticals industry
Chile 6, 8, 170–72, 185–6
  copper industry 170–71, 173, 175–7, 183,
    184
  foreign direct investment (FDI)
    government policy and 185
    inward 172–84
    outward 184
  salmon industry 180–82, 183–4, 190–93
  wine industry 172, 177–80, 183, 184
China 248–9
Chu, W. 76
Clancy, Paula 50
clustering 3
  Belgium 41–2
    life sciences 42–5
  Chile 182–4
  Denmark 138
  Finland 138
  foreign direct investment (FDI)
    Netherlands 24–6
  Ireland 75–80
  New Zealand 226, 238–9
  Norway 138
competition, Netherlands 15–16
copper industry, Chile 170–71, 173, 175–7,
  183, 184
corporatism 26

273